FILMMAKERS SERIES

edited by
ANTHONY SLIDE

In Preparation

FRANKLIN J. SCHAFFNER

by

Erwin Kim

Filmmakers, No. 9

The Scarecrow Press, Inc.
Metuchen, N.J., & London
1985

Library of Congress Cataloging in Publication Data

Kim, Erwin.
    Franklin J. Schaffner.

    (Filmmakers ; no. 9)
    Videography: p.
    Filmography: p.
    Bibliography: p.
    Includes index.
    1. Schaffner, Franklin J. I. Title. II. Series:
Filmmakers (Scarecrow Press) ; no. 9.
PN1998.A3S33575 1985   791.43'0233'0924   85-1993
ISBN 0-8108-1799-3

CONTENTS

ACKNOWLEDGMENTS

The text of this book would not exist in its present form without the help and support of the friends and colleagues of Franklin J. Schaffner. For graciously sharing their time, reminiscences, and observations with me, I am indebted to: Mort Abrahams; Michael F. Anderson; Jacqueline Babbin; Shober Barr; Peter Bart; Philip Barry, Jr.; Robert Bendick; Alvin Boretz; Herbert Brodkin; Fielder Cook; William J. Creber; James Darlington; Robert Fryer; Jerry Goldsmith; Curtis Harrington; Charlton Heston; George Roy Hill; John Houseman; Felix Jackson; Fred J. Koenekamp; Loring Mandel; Martin Manulis; Fletcher Markle; Frank McCarthy; the late Worthington Miner; Reginald Rose; Robert Saudek; Walter Seltzer; Mayo Simon; Robert Swink; Ruth Ashton Taylor; Lawrence Turman.

For their assistance in arranging screenings of the kinescopes that pertain to this study, I would like to thank the Academy of Television Arts and Sciences-University of California at Los Angeles Television Archives; the Museum of Broadcasting in New York; the Wisconsin Center for Film and Theatre Research in Madison; and the Franklin J. Schaffner Film Library at Franklin and Marshall College, Lancaster, Pennsylvania. For the general excellence of their facilities and the helpfulness of their librarians, I extend my appreciation to the four major research resources for film studies in Los Angeles: the University of Southern California's Archives of Performing Arts; the University of California at Los Angeles' Special Collections and Theatre Arts Library; the American Film Institute's Louis B. Mayer Library; and the Academy of Motion Picture Arts and Sciences' Margaret Herrick Library.

For their various involvements in this project, I am grateful to Alana Emhardt, Ronald Gottesman, Louis Harris,

Richard B. Jewell, Arthur Knight, Sherman A. Rose, and Anthony Slide.

All photographs in the book are reproduced through the courtesy of the Franklin J. Schaffner Film Library, Franklin and Marshall College, Lancaster, Pennsylvania; Sidney Wise, curator.

Finally, I owe a special debt of gratitude to the subject of this book himself, Franklin J. Schaffner, for making himself available for a series of interviews and granting me complete access to his personal library, files, and film and television collection.

Erwin Kim
Los Angeles, 1984

EDITOR'S NOTE

Franklin Schaffner belongs to that small, elite group of filmmakers who learned their craft in television, during its so-called "golden age," when production was still both live and lively. Television required a certain directorial style, which Schaffner understood. The motion picture also requires--at its best--a certain directorial style or flair, and Schaffner has proved himself a more than capable director in a film career which began in 1963 with The Stripper.

He is a quietly aristocratic individual, a man who obviously knows what he is doing, but is also willing to take chances. One wonders why or how he could have considered accepting such a directorial assignment as the Luciano Pavarotti vehicle, Yes, Giorgio. The answer is simple; as Schaffner himself has said, it was "venturesome on my part." He has never shied away from the difficult or the unusual subject. As a television director, Franklin Schaffner was quietly confident, and that same attitude has pervaded his film work.

This is a big book about a director whose film work has been small in output. This is also a book which is large in scope, and the same can definitely be said of Schaffner's work--from the epic sweep of productions such as The War Lord, Patton, and Nicholas and Alexandra, through the adventuring of Planet of the Apes and The Boys from Brazil, to the individualism of The Best Man and Islands in the Stream.

Anthony Slide

1. INTRODUCTION

> A slender, gray-haired man with the arrow-straight carriage of a cavalry officer, Franklin Schaffner looks more like the headmaster of a boys' school or a bank president than the popular conception of a Hollywood director. [1]
>
> --Fred Robbins

> A French film critic once described Franklin J. Schaffner as a Henry James character come to life: courtly, elegant, subtle. [2]
>
> --Andrew Sarris

> [Schaffner] looks and speaks more like a college professor than a top Hollywood director. [3]
>
> --Kevin Thomas

> Mature, aristocratic and controlled, he and his hefty cigar sit heavily upon our interview. Very stiff. Very formal. [4]
>
> --Jack Hofferkamp

> Franklin Schaffner is a tall, handsome man with an almost soldierly manner.... Tough, direct, and commanding, he looks right with a long, dark cigar in his mouth. [5]
>
> --Bruce Cook

Franklin J. Schaffner's appearance is as fully distinguished as his career: cultured, well-groomed, he looks every inch the proper, sophisticated New Yorker belonging to the right club. The descriptions are accurate: he does resemble a banker, professor, or general; he also resembles a diplomat, judge, or football coach. His appearance is right for any position that demands authority, discipline, and leadership. As a director, he has all of these qualities and more. In

the tradition of Victor Fleming and William Wellman, he is
one of the few handsome film directors. Unique unto himself, he is also that rarity in contemporary Hollywood--the
gentleman director.

Directing the "Turandot" sequence for Yes, Giorgio
on Stage 27 at M-G-M, Schaffner does nothing to attract
attention to himself, but it is obvious he is in charge; he
is there. Although he no longer wears a coat and tie as
he works, he still effects a formal look in jeans and sports
shirt. Loose as the atmosphere on the set may be, he is
always reserved. When he speaks in his slow and deliberate way, considering each word before articulating it, only
a few people can hear his voice, thus earning him a reputation, as American Cinematographer once noted, as "Perhaps the quietest director in the film industry." [6] His silence is formidable.

Smoking his cigar contemplatively, he gets up from
his chair and begins to walk, moving with the grace and
confidence of an old warrior. After climbing the steps to
the proscenium stage of the Metropolitan Opera set, he goes
directly to the star, Luciano Pavarotti, who is making his
motion picture debut, looking decidedly uncomfortable dressed
in a black fur tunic and wearing heavy boots. The conference between director and star is like a meeting between a
baseball manager and his pitcher; no one else knows what is
being said. The two men talk at length, and, when both
are satisfied, Schaffner leaves the stage.

Back on the floor, the director asks all the people not
otherwise occupied to sit in the theatre seats of the opera
set. Unbeknownst to the star, Schaffner instructs the make-
shift audience to applaud extra-heartily at the end of Pavarotti's close-up. When the star finishes lip-synching to the
playback of Puccini's Nessun Dorma, Schaffner acts as a silent cheerleader to heighten the volume of the applause.
During the ensuing takes, he continues to wave and gesture
in exhortation to get the intended results. As planned, the
live audience creates an environment in which Pavarotti's
confidence has been noticeably bolstered.

What is most striking about observing Schaffner at
work is his seeming detachment from the entire process.
Although this can be distracting to the cast, crew, or

press, it can well serve Schaffner's purposes. His type of
detachment is reminiscent of Malcolm Cowley's description of
F. Scott Fitzgerald and the world of his fiction:

> It was as if all his novels described a big dance to
> which he had taken ... the prettiest girl ... and
> as if at the same time he stood outside the ballroom,
> a little Midwestern boy with his nose to the glass,
> wondering how much the tickets cost and who paid
> for the music.[7]

This seems to be a highly appropriate metaphor for a responsible film director--and Franklin J. Schaffner is a very
responsible film director. Built into this description is a
concept from symbolic interactionism: the director as simultaneous participant and observer. He interprets his material
subjectively; he judges its execution with exacting objectivity.

●   ●   ●

> I've always considered Frank one of television's and
> film's finest directors.
>
> --Reginald Rose

> I think Frank has always been at the top of the
> heap--in television, the one experience in the
> theatre, and certainly in film.
>
> --Robert Fryer

> I've always thought he was a tremendously gifted
> picture director. I can't make any criticism of him.
> I mean, there's nothing that I think he can't do....
> He's one of the best we have.
>
> --George Roy Hill

Franklin J. Schaffner has directed twelve feature
films, from The Stripper in 1963 to Yes, Giorgio in 1982.
In a survey of these dozen films, each is different in type,
genre, and style; Schaffner takes pride in the fact that he
has never repeated himself in his career as a film director.

Patton, for which he received an Academy Award for
best direction in 1970, serves as a useful model of a Schaffner

film: a big budget prestige picture that both wins awards
and makes a lot of money. His films feature excellent performances, literate writing, and impeccable craftsmanship.
Typically, his films involve strong men with heightened per-
ceptions, men with heroic visions, men who are much larger
than life.

With such films as Papillon, Planet of the Apes,
Nicholas and Alexandra, and The War Lord, Schaffner has
come to be regarded as a specialist in the big-look picture.
This refers specifically to his use of scope, be it Cinema-
Scope or Panavision; he enjoys a reputation as a master of
the wide screen. [8] It is true: Franklin J. Schaffner uses
it as well as any director who has worked with this aspect
ratio. Secondly, the big-look picture implies a lot of action;
Schaffner has an uncommon ability to marshal his resources
wisely, so that the picture explodes with action.

These observations about Schaffner and the big-look
picture, however, do not suggest the range, the richness,
and the subtlety that can be found in his body of work.
His first film, for instance, was a woman's picture, and his
most recent film is a musical comedy--two genres with which
Schaffner's name is not usually associated. Apart from being an exemplary political film, The Best Man, the film of
which Schaffner is most fond, was shot in the standard 1:33
ratio. Despite the wide screen, what is most memorable
about Islands in the Stream is how deceptively casual but
deeply touching the drama is between father and sons. He
has made a deliberate effort to stretch his directorial mus-
cles with each new project.

No matter what the size, shape, or subject matter of
his films, the intimacy of theatre and the immediacy of television course through Schaffner's body of work. There is
a simple reason for this: he worked in those media before
coming to film. He won four Emmies for his work on "Twelve
Angry Men" (Studio One), "The Caine Mutiny Court Martial"
(Ford Star Jubilee), and The Defenders. For his work on
Advise and Consent, he was named best director in the
Variety poll of New York Drama Critics. He has demonstrated excellence and versatility in a remarkably productive career.

Speaking of his friend, former partner, and fellow
director, Fielder Cook has said:

> Outside of the qualities as a human being--which is
> great compassion and grounding, I would call it,
> stability--he is a gentleman in the classic sense of
> the word. That shows up in his work, his values,
> and his stature. His pictures are beautifully man-
> aged, done, handled, and understood. There's no
> one in that area that I think is better than Frank.
> I think with all that put together, wouldn't you
> know, would make up a good man.

Not to mention, as his colleagues would hasten to add, an
uncommonly good director.

•   •   •

> Frank Schaffner is the best director in the world. [9]
>   --Jacqueline Kennedy

Franklin J. Schaffner belongs to that generation of
television directors who would exert such a strong influence
on American film in the late 1950s and 1960s. This group of
live television directors includes Delbert Mann, Robert Mulligan, Sidney Lumet, John Frankenheimer, Arthur Penn, and
George Roy Hill; for the record, Schaffner preceded all of
the aforementioned directors in television. Joining CBS Television as a staff director in 1948, the year television became a major force in everyday American life, Schaffner was
recognized within a few years as the top director at CBS--
both as a contract and free-lance director--a position he
would relinquish only when he left the network in 1962.

In his time at CBS, Franklin Schaffner was the television equivalent of a Hollywood studio system contract director. What is most conspicuous in perusing Schaffner's
television career is its sheer volume. Michael Curtiz is the
paradigm of the classical Hollywood studio system director:
in the 1930-1940 decade he directed 44 films, truly an impressive figure, one that probably will never be surpassed.
Nonetheless, that statistic pales alongside the more than 350
television shows directed by Schaffner in the 1950-1960 decade. Curtiz was the Warner Bros. house director in the
golden age of cinema; Schaffner was the CBS house director
in the golden age of television.

The director and the star who never made a movie: Franklin
Schaffner and Jacqueline Kennedy on a tour of the White
House, 1962.

In a television career that spans 16 years, Franklin
Schaffner directed over 400 shows.[10] He directed news,
public affairs programs, United Nations telecasts, Brooklyn
Dodgers baseball, the 1948 and 1952 political conventions,
and Person to Person. He directed for such dramatic anthologies as Studio One, Kaiser Aluminum Hour, Playhouse
90, and DuPont Show of the Week. The Schaffner-directed
Tour of the White House with Mrs. John F. Kennedy won
an Emmy Special Citation and a Peabody Award. Another
result of that program was that Schaffner would be asked
to direct and supervise television appearances of President
John F. Kennedy.

In their section on Franklin Schaffner in The American Vein, a standard reference book on television, Christopher Wicking and Tise Vahimagi list five series he directed
for and ten individual program titles before writing:

> While it is embarassing [sic] to have to go to press
> with such a ludicrously incomplete listing, it is im-
> portant that the research problems facing tele-
> historians be made so apparent. We are working
> miles from the source material in England. But
> even the TV museum at UCLA encounters the same
> stone walls, the same elusive information, the same
> long corridor of frustration and sheer mystery which
> seems to be the name of the game. We are merely
> trying to assemble facts and achieve sense of order
> out of the consumer industry (TV in the 1950s).
> Schaffner stayed around longer than Franken-
> heimer, Mulligan and Penn--but arguably he is the
> most successful of the generation's graduates, for
> THE WAR LORD, PLANET OF THE APES and PAT-
> TON are true fusions of cinema, style and idea.
> While it would be fun to look at a kinescope of
> Twelve Angry Men [sic] and compare it to Lumet's
> version ... and see whether Schaffner's Caine Mu-
> tiny ... works better than Kramer's movie (Schaff-
> ner won the Emmy for it), these may be impossible
> dreams (kinescopes may not exist). Certainly how-
> ever it is possible to check out The Defenders (for
> which Schaffner won the 1962 Emmy for "Outstand-
> ing Directorial Achievement"). If the iron curtain
> of apathy lifts and further research uncovers in-
> formation about the myriad of other shows for which

Schaffner was responsible we may be in for a treat. [11]

New information on Schaffner's television career has since been uncovered; there is a ray of light under that iron curtain.

Franklin Schaffner was in fact a pioneer television director, perhaps the most important director in the medium's history. The late Worthington Miner, the man who hired Schaffner to direct his first live television drama, made the following comment about his protégé:

I think Patton stays as one of the very remarkable pieces of American direction--because it is so clear. It is everything that he promised; his best moments when he was working in television were realized in that picture with the way he balanced the best of his knowledge of television shooting with the best of using the scope of motion pictures.

Within that statement is a point that cannot be stressed too strongly. It may seem paradoxical that this master of wide-screen cinema first made a name for himself directing for a five-inch television screen, but there is a definite cause and effect relationship.

From the live television experience comes a director who considers the script to be the most important factor in making a film. He will accept material conceived and initiated by someone else; although he works very carefully on the script, he has never received a screenwriting credit. All of Schaffner's films, as it turns out, have been adaptations of books or plays (even if, as will later be revealed, some of the adaptations for all intents and purposes might just as well be called originals). Rather than as the creator, Schaffner considers himself the interpreter of the work. He does not subject the material to so personal an interpretation that the meaning becomes obscured but tries to be true to the original intention of the source material.

Judging from the material he has been offered, the caliber of the casts he has assembled, and the general quality of his projects, Schaffner is a well respected film director indeed. He has directed adaptations of works by such

authors as William Inge, Gore Vidal, and Ernest Hemingway.
He has worked with some of the most notoriously difficult
actors: any man who can get Steve McQueen to eat bugs
and who can work twice with George C. Scott must have
something going for him.

In the golden age of cinema, directors were typecast
every bit as much as the stars. Some directors were con-
signed to musicals, some to westerns, some to comedies.
Michael Curtiz, the most skillful director of large-scale action in the pre-CinemaScope era, was given the biggest assignments at Warner Bros. At the same studio, William
Dieterle was known for his historical biographies. William
Wyler, with his many film adaptations of theatrical dramas,
was known as a director of important pictures. In the late
1940s, as the studio system was on the verge of collapse,
Elia Kazan and Fred Zinnemann became recognized as ex-
perts in the art of making films with ideas.

Franklin J. Schaffner's films carry on that tradition
of big but important films. In the 1977 presentation of an
honorary Doctor of Humane Letters degree at Franklin and
Marshall College, Dr. Sidney Wise made the following remark
in his introduction of the recipient:

> A generation of filmgoers has come to associate the
> Schaffner name with films that matter--films which,
> though popular, nevertheless deal with themes that
> transcend the moment, that probe the most funda-
> mental questions of the human condition. [12]

In an earlier age, Hollywood studios would wrap up a serious subject in an entertainment package; Schaffner continues
the practice--a film must be entertaining to get across important ideas.

In today's Hollywood, no major studio can afford to
produce a film more for the prestige than the commercial
return; the movie game is riskier with higher stakes involved. Schaffner's ability to keep control over his budget
would have been appreciated in any era. "He's very cost-
conscious," says Robert Fryer, "which is why he's the darling of the studios." While Schaffner does not work with
what anybody would call a low budget, he does not need a
megamillion-dollar budget to make an epic; all the money

spent on a Schaffner film can be seen on the wide screen. Franklin J. Schaffner is the modern day counterpart to the classical studio system director, working without the security and the efficiency of a studio system.

•   •   •

Franklin J. Schaffner is an exemplary director of major Hollywood films--mainstream motion pictures, the kind of commercial films that have always constituted the backbone of American cinema; he enjoys this reputation after years of work. Producer Peter Bart once said, "In choosing a director, first you look at the list of available directors and you moan and groan over the fact that there aren't more directors you'd want to hire."[13] In the 1960s, while planning a major film like Patton, Twentieth Century-Fox would have a list that included such names as John Huston, William Wyler, and Fred Zinnemann--no doubt the studio would rather have hired one of those three than Franklin J. Schaffner. How his name came to get on that particular list and other short lists of preferred directors will be detailed later in the text. What is even more remarkable is that the first four films directed by Schaffner were commercial failures. In a business where one is reputedly only as good as one's last picture, Schaffner not only was able to survive four consecutive commercial flops but still somehow managed to move his career ahead.

The Schaffner depicted in these pages is the man as seen by those closest to him at work. His career is examined in chronological order--and an investigation of it reflects a general history of the television and film media bracketed in the time period of his activity. Schaffner's television and film work are put in their proper socio-historical context; the ever changing climes of television network and motion picture studio have been observed and duly noted. Each film is taken on its own terms, from the developmental stage through production, post-production, and distribution; an attempt is made to account for the contributions of key people (producer, writer, actor, art director, cinematographer, editor, composer) and the external events or factors that shaped the final outcome of each film. This history seeks to provide a glimpse of a major director at work in the new Hollywood.

One final research note: In tracing the course of
any given film, a researcher frequently has only the trade
papers to rely on for data. Producer Lawrence Turman is
quick to point out: "The trades are notoriously unreliable.
They're totally full of bullshit all the time." Consequently,
personal interviews were conducted to supplement research;
the results yielded another, more personal, source of information. While the interviews were unquestionably helpful
for the film section, they were absolutely indispensable for
the television chapter.

The most important interviews, however, were with
Schaffner himself, a man whose memory is as accurate as
his cinematic eye and ear. So whenever a Rashomon-like
situation arose, as they always do in the investigation of a
history, when books offered conflicting information or interviews revealed differences in the testimony of eyewitnesses,
the Schaffner version was followed.

It is only proper--Franklin J. Schaffner, the director
with a historian's touch, is at the center of the text.

2. THE TELEVISION CAREER OF FRANKLIN SCHAFFNER

Background

Franklin James Schaffner was born in Tokyo, Japan on May 30, 1920, the middle child of the Reverend and Mrs. Paul Franklin Schaffner, missionaries of the Reformed Church, now the United Church of Christ.

Rev. Schaffner, a graduate of Franklin and Marshall College and The Reformed Church Theological Seminary, both in Lancaster, Pennsylvania, married the former Sarah Horting Swords of Lancaster in 1915, taking her later that year to Japan, where they would serve for over a decade. Following her husband's untimely death in 1926, Mrs. Schaffner returned home to Pennsylvania, and she and her three children settled in a small red brick house at 319 N. Lime Street.

Lancaster is basically a rural city with conservative values. A significant Amish contingent has been diffused into the population; some of America's finest tobacco is grown in the area. When America would later move into the nuclear age, the city would find itself perilously close to Three Mile Island. Missionary and teacher, Mrs. Schaffner would also work in the advertising department of the Armstrong Cork Company in Lancaster. By all accounts, she was a remarkable woman. She is most fondly remembered as a soprano soloist. Franklin Schaffner inherited his mother's artistic sensibilities and his father's patrician good looks. He delivered morning and evening newspapers, worked as a salesman in a woman's shoe store. He had a part-time job as an usher at the Hamilton Theater, earning twelve cents an hour, an experience that did not foster or further any romantic notions about movie-making; he worked on Saturdays when the program consisted of cartoons, serials, and a western double bill.

His older sister, Louise, became a foreign service officer in the State Department and would be named as an
American spy by the Czechoslovakian government in 1949.
His younger sister, Isabelle, became a medical doctor, serving many years as the Director of Geriatric Services at St.
Elizabeth Hospital in Washington, D.C. A law career was
originally envisioned for Schaffner; it seemed a logical career choice given the considerable forensic ability he evinced
in high school.

Upon graduation from McCaskey High School in 1938,
Schaffner became a third generation member of his family to
matriculate at Franklin and Marshall College. In keeping
with the plans to enroll at Columbia University Law School,
he majored in Government and English, won the Junior Ora-
torical Prize, was Senior Class Orator and president of the
John Marshall Law Club. In the meantime, he also worked
part-time as a radio announcer for station WGAL in Lancaster; this experience also failed to instill any show business
aspirations. But while he was in college, two Hollywood motion pictures that would become--and remain--his favorite
films were released in 1941: Citizen Kane, directed by Orson Welles, for its revolutionary technique, and How Green
Was My Valley, directed by John Ford, for its pure storytelling.

Schaffner was graduated in 1942. Twenty-six years
later he was inaugurated into membership in the college
chapter of Phi Beta Kappa. On December 4, 1977, Franklin
J. Schaffner returned to Franklin and Marshall College to
receive an honorary Doctor of Humane Letters degree. On
that occasion, he shared the honor with eleven faculty and
staff members who had been of help and had influenced him
in his college days. One of them was an old friend of the
Schaffner family, Dr. James Darlington, professor emeritus
of Biology, who remembers that as a student Franklin Schaffner had some problems with motivation in the sciences. Another, Shober Barr, professor emeritus of Physical Education, states that four years of P.E. helped inculcate a sense
of discipline in Schaffner; he recalled that the undergraduate Schaffner had some initial difficulty in mastering the
rope climb. Evident to all was Schaffner's abiding interest
in The Green Room Club, the college dramatic group under
the directorship of the late Darrell Larsen, who, by consen-
sus, had the greatest influence on Schaffner. Today in the

The Rev. Paul and Mrs. Sarah Schaffner and children:
Louise, Isabelle and Franklin.

Franklin Schaffner, above at age fourteen, below as an undergraduate at Franklin and Marshall.

lobby of the Green Room theatre hangs a portrait of Darrell
Larson, presented by the class of 1942, Schaffner's class.

Given his looks, speaking ability, and artistic inclina-
tions, acting provided Schaffner with something with which
he could approach with a great deal of motivation and discipline: during his four years of college, Schaffner appeared
in eleven dramatic productions and was president of The
Green Room Club. Recalling his Green Room experiences,
Schaffner says the most difficult part always was playing
his own age. His favorite playwrights were "always Shakespeare" and Sean O'Casey; in a few years his dramatic tastes
would embrace William Inge.

Schaffner's first media exposure came shortly before
graduation. In the May 25, 1942 issue of Life magazine
there is a four-page photo spread entitled "Life Goes on a
Bicycle Weekend," featuring six young ladies from Lancaster's Shippen School and six young men from Franklin and
Marshall. In one photograph, the young Schaffner can be
seen looking quite debonair, every bit a budding leading
man; the photo's caption ("Hero of the day was Frank, who
charmed not only docile garter snake but feminine audience")
is self-explanatory. [1]

The Columbia University Law School plans were aban-
doned with the advent of the Second World War. From 1942
to 1946, Schaffner served as an officer in the United States
Navy with the amphibious forces in Africa, Sicily, Italy, and
Normandy, and with the Office of Strategic Services in the
India, Burma, and China theatre.

His name and face were reintroduced to the American
public in Look magazine on December 28, 1943. Margaret
Clark, roommate of Schaffner's sister Louise, submitted a
letter and photograph of Franklin Schaffner, nominating him
as a Look "Home-Front Pin-Up." In the photograph, Schaffner, then an engineering officer on a landing craft in the
Mediterranean busy with landing operations in Sicily and
Italy, sits astride a captured German motorcycle, a dashing
grin on his face. In the letter within a letter, Schaffner
relates how the ship's crew played Santa Claus for a couple
of Italian youngsters. As for himself that Christmas, Schaffner hoped Santa Claus would bring him:

Hedy Lamarr, some good symphonic recordings, plus
Jimmie Lunceford, a taxi meter, a baked oyster,
some cokes, a million cases of beer, a ham theatrical performance, a tweed suit, a football game, and
a freshly rolled snowball. [2]

World Security Workshop

Schaffner had no film-related experience in the navy. Returning to postwar America, he realized that neither college
nor the navy had given him any practical training for the
commercial world. Inasmuch as his mother had worked in
advertising and his sister Louise had worked for ad agencies and Time/Life, he went to New York to see if he could
get a job--any job--with Time/Life or an advertising agency.
Unlucky in his search, he decided to try his hand at acting
on the New York stage, reading for a role in Charles Coburn's production of The Winter's Tale; he was never called
back.

     After several frustrating days of job-hunting, he ran
into an old friend and classmate from McCaskey High School
at Penn Station. Richard Gehman was then a speech writer
for Americans United for World Government, a peace organization, headed by Ulric Bell, of concerned scientists and
citizens advocating world law in the newly-born atomic age.
As his own beliefs were not dissimilar, Schaffner was sympathetic, and, fortunately, there was room for him in the
organization. As Gehman would later write: "We needed a
handsome, persuasive young man who could talk rich people into giving us money for hortatory newspaper adver-
tisements signed by world-government advocates." [3] Schaffner was hired as a spokesman, wrote copy, and was sent
out to such places as Westchester, New Canaan, and Stam-
ford to solicit funds.

     Schaffner moved in with Gehman, who, with his sec-
ond wife, lived in a three-story house on MacDougal Street
in Greenwich Village. Built by Louisa May Alcott's grand-
father, the Gehman house became known as a temporary
home away from home for literary figures visiting New York,
including such Nobel Prize-winning authors as Sinclair Lewis,
William Faulkner, Ernest Hemingway and John Steinbeck, and
playwrights such as George S. Kaufman and Moss Hart.

There Schaffner also met J. D. Salinger. "Salinger was not/is not, obviously, a social animal," Schaffner recalls, "but in those days he was, I think, very outgoing and had a nice sense of ebullience."

At this time Schaffner's literary tastes included Henry James, Joseph Conrad, William Faulkner, and Ernest Hemingway--he especially admired the lean and clean Hemingway style; as a Civil War buff, he would also enjoy reading Bruce Catton. On a more personal level, however, a charming young woman from Kansas named Jean Gilchrist also lived in the Greenwich Village house; she too had worked for Americans United for World Government and was then working for Look. She would soon become Mrs. Franklin James Schaffner.

Americans United for World Government later merged with a similarly minded group called the World Federalists, becoming the United World Federalists. The new organization came to the attention of Robert Saudek, then a vice-president of ABC Radio. Sharing similar beliefs, Saudek saw to it that a media offshoot of the United World Federalists was a radio series entitled World Security Workshop, to be directed by Clark Taylor, with himself personally producing it for ABC. Saudek, who would later produce such award-winning television programs as Omnibus, Leonard Bernstein and the New York Philharmonic, and Profiles in Courage, recalls that he and Clifton Fadiman developed a script contest with a $200 prize, for which Cass Canfield, publisher of Harper's, also served as a judge. Although a Ray Bradbury script and a couple of scripts by Richard Gehman were produced, the contest did not generate much useable material; in time, Saudek had to commission topics among professional writers.

Each show of this 26-week series opened with a quote from Socrates, "I am a citizen of the Universe," and announced its goal to be everlasting peace. One of the few scripts accepted from a neophyte writer was used for the final World Security Workshop broadcast on May 8, 1947: "The Cave" by Franklin Schaffner. In it, Jose (Joe de Santis), a Filipino school teacher, tells of the time during the Second World War when he and two other men were sealed in a cave after a bomb blast.

His cavemates were dialectical opposites: Reynaldo
was authoritarian, living by an "I will beat you down" philosophy, and thus identified as a fascist; Pepe was a cruci-
fier, too weak to help himself, hence an even greater enemy
than the fascists. After two years of discouragement following the end of the war, Pepe, the only survivor of the
cave, can now see some hope: what is needed is a World
Federalist government--or else there will be anarchy and
another world war. The author's point is clear--man has
the choice for peace. Following the program was a message
from Carl Van Doren, on behalf of the Ohio State Institute
for Education by Radio, presenting the "Furthering International Understanding Award" to World Security Workshop.

"The Cave" is not completely persuasive as a piece of
propaganda, but it is successful as radio drama. With effective use of sound effects, it provides the proper mood
and atmosphere, quickly taking the listener into the world
of "The Cave." The dramatic conflict is established effi-
ciently, and the script employs a multi-level time structure
that Schaffner would seldom use as a director. Although
Schaffner made his debut in show business as a writer,
"The Cave" was the first and last time one of his scripts
would be produced. Speaking on the subject of writing,
Schaffner has said:

> It's always been terribly, terribly hard for me. I
> find it the toughest thing in the world to do. I
> find it very easy to sit with a writer over a script.
> That I don't find difficult. But the act of staring
> at a piece of blank paper is torture.

After "The Cave," Schaffner decided to leave the United
World Federalists and pursue a career in broadcasting. He
had spent a year with a peace organization; he had paid his
dues. With his vast experience in network radio, Schaffner
felt certain he would be offered a job in radio.

The March of Time

Schaffner spent the next six months looking for work, managing to live courtesy of the "52/50 Club," by which veterans were able to receive $50 for 52 weeks. Finally, through
a friend who knew Richard de Rochemont, Schaffner was

introduced to a production manager of The March of Time
and was hired as an assistant director at the munificent
salary of $35 a week.[4]

An offshoot of a CBS Radio series of the same name,
The March of Time had won a 1936 Academy Award for its
significance to motion pictures and for revolutionizing the
newsreel; its distinct style and narration were parodied in
Citizen Kane. Its excellent reputation was due to the efforts of former newsreel cameraman Louis de Rochemont, a
proponent of confrontational and advocacy journalism. When
he went to Hollywood in 1943 to produce theatrical motion
pictures, applying the hardboiled March of Time documentary approach to such feature films as The House on 92nd
Street (1945) and Boomerang (1947), de Rochemont was succeeded by his younger brother Richard. But despite the
extra polish Richard de Rochemont brought to it, The March
of Time was in its declining years when Schaffner joined in
1947. Raymond Fielding has written:

> Curiously, during the last six years of the March of
> Time there was an almost complete absence of issues
> dealing with the domestic political scene.... In the
> more than seventy issues released between 1945 and
> 1951, there is not the same kind of hard-hitting,
> iconoclastic, satirical treatment that Louis de Roche-
> mont used.[5]

It is doubtful whether Louis de Rochemont or anyone else
could have prolonged the existence of The March of Time;
the times had changed too much. America had entered the
Cold War, film studios had been divorced from their theatres as a result of the Supreme Court's consent decrees;
finally, just around the corner, looming large, was the lat-
est of the mass media--television. When The March of Time
ended in 1951, its place was taken over by television news
and by such programs as CBS Reports and NBC White Paper.

The March of Time was nonetheless an excellent outfit
for a would-be filmmaker to become associated with in 1947.
There was no Directors Guild office in New York yet; The
March of Time was non-union and informal. Noted for going to the actual location of the incident and hiring people
who resembled the real newsmakers, The March of Time
would often restage an actual event, thus making it a

forerunner of the docudrama form that was to gain popularity in the 1970s. Considering the type of film career
Schaffner would have, The March of Time would seem ideal
for his apprenticeship. In fact Schaffner did not learn anything about film during his short stay. Only on rare occasions did he ever work on the set; basically his job was to
find locations. One of his assignments was going from store
to store, looking for suitable places to film interiors. Instructed to offer $50 a day for the use of a store, Schaff-
ner instead offered the store owners a subscription to Fortune magazine and pocketed the $50. With such duties as
these, it did not take too long for him to realize that he
would not become another Henry R. Luce or Louis de Rochemont if he remained with The March of Time.

A young still photographer named Robert Bendick had
been hired as a cameraman and director by CBS Television
in 1941. After serving in the air force during the Second
World War, he returned to CBS and was made Director of
Special Events in 1946. His title was soon amended to Director of TV News and Special Events; as such, his top
priority was strengthening the CBS directorial staff. Bendick wanted to hire George Black, who along with John
Glenn and William Zubiller comprised The March of Time directorial staff at the time. Black, who had no intention of
stepping down to television, wanted to remain in film and
instead recommended a promising young assistant director
at The March of Time named Franklin Schaffner.

This was the type of opportunity Schaffner was seeking. When Bendick's offer came, he accepted it with alac-
rity, even though he had yet to see a television camera.
As he had not received any practical film experience or acquired a feel for film and the documentary form in the months
he had spent with The March of Time, Schaffner had no
sense of stepping down when he moved to television. He
joined CBS in April 1948.

CBS Television

The Columbia Broadcasting System had experimented with
television as early as 1931, developing a color system that
was totally incompatible with NBC's black and white system.
In 1941, when the Federal Communications Commission adopted

NBC's standards--525 lines and 30 frames per second, which are still used today--CBS had to start all over again in black and white. Its entrance into the commercial field effectively delayed, CBS concentrated its attention on radio, ignoring the new medium. The reason was decidedly economic: in 1941, an hour of prime-time television in New York cost an advertiser $120, whereas an hour of prime-time radio cost $1200. [6]

That situation abruptly ended when the 1947 World Series, televised by NBC, turned out to be a sensation. War broke out immediately: General Electric, Dumont, Philco, Bell, and the Radio Corporation of America, parent company of NBC, wanted to control the new medium's hardware; NBC, CBS, Dumont, and ABC (formerly NBC's "blue" network) fought to win the American public.

In television, NBC, just as it was in radio, was the undisputed leader. CBS was a distant second; not until the 1950s would CBS eventually overtake NBC Television. William Paley describes the rapid growth of television in his autobiography:

> In 1946, CBS Television consisted of one station broadcasting six to ten hours a week. There were so few sets in use that we gave the air time away free and charged only for the use of our studios, sets, props and costumes. There were just 6,000 TV sets in the whole country and CBS could only reach a fraction of them. In 1947, the number of television sets out there increased to about 250,000; New York, Washington and Philadelphia were interconnected by coaxial cable, and television advertisers increased from 31 to 181. We had begun to build a network. By 1948, the coaxial cable extended north to Boston and south to Richmond and a separate microwave link connected to Indiana, Kentucky and Ohio. [7]

CBS' television programming increased from ten hours a week in 1946 to 20 hours by the end of 1947, and 38 by the end of 1948. A million television sets were in use by 1948; a typical 5" to 7" television set cost $375 to $500. Schaffner came to television at the right time: "That year, 1948," according to Paley, "was the true beginning of television as we know it today." [8]

In dramatic contrast to the size of today's audience,
at five viewers per television set, Mr. Television himself,
Milton Berle, at the peak of his popularity, could not have
reached an audience exceeding five million people. The audience was indeed small--but it was urban, literate, sophisticated, and, as they could afford to buy a television set in
the first place, affluent. Worthington Miner, a pioneer of
the golden age of television and its most able chronicler,
wrote in the 1969 Reader's Encyclopedia of World Drama:
"It would at best represent no more than 20 percent of the
audience today ... however, that 20 percent was the sole
audience whose allegiance mattered."[9]

The CBS television operations had one floor of cubicle
offices, formerly for radio operations, at 485 Madison Avenue
in New York. The main studio was above the terminal of
Grand Central Station on the Vanderbilt Avenue side; empty
drama or motion picture theatres were used when extra space
was needed. Worthington Miner, in charge of drama, and
Robert Bendick, in charge of news and public affairs, put
network programming together on a daily basis. There were
no rules; people learned as they worked. And everything,
sometimes intimidatingly so, was live. "Almost everything
we televised in those days," Robert Bendick has said, "was
a first."

The early pioneers of the television industry came
from theatrical backgrounds. Although Miner had a policy
of salvaging radio talent, almost without exception they
failed; like Franklin Schaffner, the people who built the
foundation of television were young, without any particular
experience in any one medium. Miner observed:

> Being young, they made grievous errors, took un-
> wise risks, and pressed the technical capabilities of
> the medium too far. In short, they were often out-
> rageously daring, but that very recklessness bred
> an excitement that won the allegiance of the audi-
> ences to whom they made appeal.[10]

Robert Bendick's staff at WCBS-TV included Douglas
Edwards, the first CBS network news anchorman; the other
directors were Fred Rickey and David Lowell Rich; Don
Hewitt, later to become producer of 60 Minutes, was an assistant director; cameraman Byron Paul would later become

Dick Van Dyke's producer. There was a lot of work and
everybody had to do all sorts of jobs; news directors, for
example, directed a wide variety of public affairs shows.

Schaffner's first television directorial assignment was
Brooklyn Dodgers baseball, with Red Barber as sportscaster.
Unhappily, the neophyte director experienced difficulty keep-
ing his cameras on the ball or on the action; like a pitcher
with bad stuff, Schaffner was yanked after three innings.
In addition to the news, Schaffner directed hockey, basket-
ball, beauty pageants, horse races at Hialeah, events from
Madison Square Garden, the Easter parade, and the New
York City Golden Jubilee Parade, which he made more color-
ful by utilizing frequent cutaways.

In 1948, Schaffner directed several prestigious programs produced by Robert Bendick, none more so than The
United Nations in Action, with Larry LeSueur and, on occasion, Ned Calmer as the U.N. correspondents. Covering
the sessions from the very beginning at Hunter College, at
Flushing Meadows, and finally at the present U.N. site,
these pickups were broadcast mornings and afternoons on a
daily basis, 15 hours per week. By televising plenary sessions and committee meetings as the U.N. was becoming a
reality, The United Nations in Action was important to world
and television history; the program won a Peabody Award
the following year. Schaffner also directed a supplementary
United Nations program entitled U.N. Casebook, a half-
hour discussion show with the house intellectual, Dr. Lyman
Bryson, CBS Counsellor on Public Affairs, and Quincy Howe.

The new technology made the telecasts of the 1948
Truman/Dewey political conventions from Philadelphia a reality: New York, the District of Columbia, and Philadelphia
now were linked together by coaxial cable. With Bendick
producing, Edward R. Murrow and Douglas Edwards alternated as anchorman; Schaffner, Fred Rickey, and David
Lowell Rich alternated as director. Never before had such
important national events been brought into the living room
for an American family to see as well as hear; CBS' coverage of the political conventions proved to be an enormous
boon to the fledgling television industry. "The 1948 campaign did for television acceptance what the 1928 presidential campaign had done for radio," William S. Paley asserts.[11]
Presidential politics would never be the same.

At the 1948 Philadelphia Political Conventions. Top, Robert
Bendick, center behind desk, and staff: (clockwise from
Bendick) Don Hewitt, unidentified male news writer, un-
identified female news writer, unidentified woman, Henry
Cassiere, Perry Wolff, Franklin Schaffner and Ed Chester;
below, George Herman, Douglas Edwards, Schaffner and
Edward R. Murrow.

To satisfy the FCC requirements, Bendick hired Ruth
Ashton, a young Southern Californian fresh out of Columbia
University where she had produced "Sunny Side of the
Atom," a 1947 radio program on the peaceful uses of the
atom, to produce and develop weekend public affairs programs. One of Ashton's assignments was a Sunday religious show, designed for Protestant, Catholic, and Jew
alike, which she named Lamp Unto My Feet. Beginning its
long run on November 21, 1948, the program looked into
the lifestyles and liturgies of the various faiths in panel
discussions or celebrations so that people could learn about
other religions and religious groups. Typically, Lamp Unto
My Feet put forth its message through the point of view of
children. Again, the three men who directed the show were
Rich, Rickey, and Schaffner.

"Frank was from March of Time," says Ruth Ashton,
who returned to California, got married, and today is known
as KNXT/CBS general assignment and political reporter Ruth
Ashton Taylor, "and never really let anybody forget that,
because we were pretty schlocky compared to how slick
they were." Then as now, he had an air of confidence
and made everything look easy; he had successfully created an image of himself as a director of live television.
"He was always very suave," Ashton Taylor recalls. "He
used to be called the 'Arrow Shirt Man.'"

One Sunday December afternoon, the day of the National Football League championship game in Chicago, Schaffner found himself on location at the Empire State building
for Lamp Unto My Feet. It was snowing in Chicago during
the game and, by the time Lamp Unto My Feet was about
to air, it began to snow in New York. Schaffner put a
live camera on the snow: when the show went on the air,
he superimposed the falling snow over the manger scene.
Schaffner laughs at the memory: "Marvelously corny," he
says.

Produced by Leon Levine, The People's Platform was
a forum series devoted to current national affairs; two kinescopes directed by Schaffner survive. In the December 7,
1948 telecast, Dwight Cook is the host, and J. Raymond
Walsh and Lawrence Fertig are the guests who take opposite sides on the issue of the fourth round of wage increases. The set resembles a den: the three men are seated

around a small coffee table. The director tries out various
combinations of one, two and three-shots, but the show is
still slow and heavy; instead of filmed inserts of charts, the
camera moves in to charts held rather shakily by Cook.
Seen today, when the topic is far from current, the modera-
tor looks like the program's most obvious liability: not to
cast aspersions on his undoubted intelligence or ability,
Cook is singularly unprepossessing and has distracting man-
nerisms, such as flicking his hands and wrists.

That problem was somewhat rectified in the January
24, 1949 show, moderated by Quincy Howe. Howe too is a
far cry from the more sleek and handsome types who host
such programs today, but less unprepossessing than Cook;
his guests are Norman Thomas and Major George Fielding
Elliott, who take obvious sides on the issue of the government's spending on armed forces. This show does include
filmed inserts, which greatly help, and the set is different
--two parallel couches extending to the camera. Elliott sits
alone on the couch to the top left of the screen, Howe sits
directly across from him, and, to the bottom right, Thomas
sits on the same couch; two couches and three people, however, do not make for a satisfactory visual formula--the
many camera angles confuse the geographical positions of
the three participants. Alternating with The People's
Platform in 1948 was Presidential Straws in the Wind, also
directed by Schaffner: this program featured Lyman Bryson, who would interview four studio audience members on
various issues, and Elmo Roper, who would compare those
responses with the national polls.

In March of 1949, Schaffner was given a completely
different assignment: a program produced by David Sherman entitled Preview, featuring the popular husband and
wife team of Tex McCrary and Jinx Falkenburg; apart from
being a showcase for its hosts, the purpose of the show
was to inform the New York audience what was new, what
was going on in town. Preview, which had been packaged
before it came to CBS, came with its own director. A director had to work out his shots in advance, lest his cameras get caught in a jungle of cable; the outside director
came unprepared, and the first show was a disaster.
Schaffner was immediately summoned by the network to take
over the direction. Fortunately, in addition to his technical expertise, he also had knowledge of the magazine and

interview formats; in return, Schaffner enjoyed the $100
commercial fee he received every week, even if his salary
as a CBS staff director was reduced proportionately.

Schaffner concluded his career in News and Public
Affairs at the end of his first year at CBS. Robert Bendick, his boss, would resign from CBS in 1951 to become a
vice-president of Cinerama, later returning to television to
produce The Dave Garroway Show and the pilot of The Great
American Dream Machine. To this day, Robert Bendick, who
with his wife Jeanne Bendick has co-written Electronics for
Young People, Television Works Like This, and Filming Works
Like This, follows a path consistent to his vision of how
moving images should be used in film and television with his
company Bendick Associates, Inc. Assessing the young assistant director he recruited from The March of Time, he
states:

> Franklin Schaffner learned as the industry grew.
> He understood the meaning of television as a medium
> of unique characteristics. He knew the power of
> immediacy, spontaneity and suspense that make live
> special events coverage good TV, and used his un-
> derstanding of "live" when he began directing tele-
> vision dramas.

Schaffner made his first reputation directing live public events for television; considered an expert in remote
telecasting, he would continue to direct special news and
political events for CBS for many years. By 1949, Schaffner was ready for the challenge of live drama; Worthington
Miner, CBS Director of Program Development for Television,
had his eye on him. He had first come to the producer's
attention through a parade Miner saw on television, a particularly dull parade until the director unexpectedly cut to
a man's bored reaction. Miner was impressed: it was the
right thing to do under the circumstances; the director
showed dramatic potential.

He met Franklin Schaffner at the 1948 conventions in
Philadelphia. Robert Bendick had said a minimum of six
cameras was needed to cover the events on the convention
floor adequately; CBS has only given him three. Complaining about the situation to his immediate superior at CBS,
Bendick escorted Miner to the control room. Miner sat to

the rear and soon noticed the director behind the control
panel: the young man was calm, articulate, and had a lot
of authority. Afterwards, Miner recalled, he and Bendick
had a drink:

> I said, "Bob, I will do my best to get you a budget
> so that you will have more cameras in the future
> for this type of operation. But you've lost yourself
> a director." I said, "It is a great deal harder to
> find a dramatic director than it is a news director,
> and you're going to lose Mr. Schaffner."

Worthington Miner

An alumnus of Yale and Cambridge, Worthington Miner made
his stage debut as a spear carrier in the road company of
Cyrano de Bergerac in 1924, became an assistant to theatrical producer Jed Harris, and directed 27 shows on Broadway by 1938. After dabbling in film at RKO, he joined CBS
in 1938, becoming Director of Program Development for Television in 1942. Fascinated by the new medium and convinced
that television was somewhere in between drama and film--a
live performance staged for multiple cameras--Miner spent
the next decade experimenting with his own television cameras and control room, testing everything in the American
Cinematographer Manual. Through trial and error, he became a major contributor to the code of television practice,
developing methods and procedures that are still observed
today: he saw no reason, for example, why he couldn't
cut in the middle of a pan shot--if he used more than one
television camera. "I came from over 15 years in the theatre, and I'd had ten years in television," he says, "and I
wasn't afraid to take chances." When CBS made its big
plunge into television in 1948, he was ready: "I really
knew what I was doing better than any young kid could at
that time."

    William Paley gave him orders to create four shows at
once: a variety show, a comedy, a children's show, and a
dramatic anthology. Most pressing was the variety show,
CBS' rush into television having been prompted by the runaway success of Milton Berle. Miner's answer to Berle was
a non-performing host who would display the stars of today
and tomorrow: the man who would be king was a reporter

for the New York Daily News named Ed Sullivan. This nomination was greeted with derision at CBS--until Paley endorsed the idea; Toast of the Town premiered on June 20,
1948.

Miner brought his comedy in from radio, The Gold-
bergs, a popular show about a Jewish mother and her family, starring, written, and produced by Gertrude Berg;
Miner was its original director. The children's show starred
Paul Tripp as Mr. I. Magination, and was set in Imagination
Town, where any child's wish could come true. Also helping producer-director Ralph Nelson get Mama (the television
version of I Remember Mama) on the air, Miner was instru-
mental in luring Arthur Godfrey to television, and by 1949,
Milton Berle's Texaco Star Theater, Ed Sullivan's Toast
of the Town, and Arthur Godfrey's Talent Scouts were the
three most popular shows on television.

But Miner's baby was the dramatic show, Studio One.
Westinghouse, the sole sponsor for the duration of its run,
bought Studio One for $8,100 a week; as the show cost
$12,000 a week to produce, CBS was willing to take the
loss on this prestigious dramatic show. From the start,
Miner had two significant advantages over the other dramatic anthologies: "No commercial sponsor to qualify or di-
lute its dramatic judgment and total directorial authority
over its technical personnel."[12] This was evident in the
November 7, 1948 premiere, George Washington Hill's "The
Storm," written, produced, and directed by Miner: a psychological mystery offering no solutions would have otherwise been routinely rejected by another advertising agency
or sponsor. The single greatest attraction of the show was
its star, Margaret Sullavan; this was a case of Miner lean-
ing on a friend, who just happened to be the wife of his
agent, Leland Hayward.

The CBS pecking order as Worthington Miner knew it
consisted of William S. Paley, chairman; Frank Stanton,
president; Jack Van Volkenburg, president of CBS TV;
Hubbell Robinson, vice-president and programming director
of CBS TV, to whom Miner reported; Harry Ackerman, Robinson's chief of staff; Harry Ommerle, assistant program director; and William Dozier, liaison between Miner and the
advertising agencies and sponsors. During the 1948 television season, CBS' director of program development soon

learned that the more involved he became with Studio One,
the more he would be moved down the CBS hierarchy; however, Miner's preference was clear. Beyond his executive
duties, he also discovered it was quite impossible for him to
write and direct every Studio One production. Lacking the
budget to hire both writers and directors, Miner was inevitably confronted with a major decision: he could direct and
find writers, or he could write and find directors. Miner
brought in Paul Nickell from Philadelphia to direct Studio
One.

        Producing a television drama was a two-week process;
Nickell was able to direct every Studio One production in
the first season because the show shared its 7:30 Sunday
evening time-slot with Ford Television Theater, another
dramatic anthology. For the 1949-1950 season, Studio One
would move to a new time-slot, 10:00 Monday evenings, to
present a live television drama every week; a second director was needed. Miner had specific criteria in mind: a
theatrical set of standards, and a respect for the literate
word and the provocative idea. Franklin Schaffner, despite his lack of experience in live drama, fit the bill. Although expert in live television, Schaffner knew nothing
about staging, lighting, or working with actors; these he
would learn from his producer. Worthington Miner was a
most valuable mentor.

        Miner gave Schaffner his test on a Wesley, a 1949 sum-
mer series modeled on Henry Aldrich and the Aldrich family,
created and written by Samuel Taylor, co-author of What a
Life, a play about the Aldrich family. Running from May 8
to August 30, 1949, Wesley was a show about a precocious
twelve-year-old boy, played by Donald Devlin and, in the
show's final month, Johnny Stewart; in another gimmick,
Frank and Mona Thomas, a real life couple, played Wesley's
parents. "It wasn't that funny," Miner said of the show.
"It wasn't that perceptive, and it wasn't anything very
much." Schaffner, moreover, did not get much of a chance
to work with the writer; Taylor worked at home in Maine,
and mailed in his scripts.

Studio One

Studio One was neither the first dramatic anthology on the

air (NBC's Kraft Television Theatre debuted on May 7, 1947),
nor was it the first dramatic anthology on CBS (Ford Television
Theater made its debut on October 17, 1948), but Studio
One helped set the standard for live drama.

The other notable dramatic anthology was NBC's
Philco/Goodyear Television Playhouse, produced by another
pioneer, Fred Coe. Unlike Miner, when confronted with
the choice of spending money on either writers or directors,
Coe chose writers--among them Robert Alan Aurthur, N.
Richard Nash, Horton Foote, and Paddy Chayefsky. Studio
One concentrated its major efforts on advancing visual storytelling techniques, sinking the Bismarck in the 65' by 45'
Studio 42, and staging a drama on the open decks of two
submarines for "The Lost Voyage." A few years later, NBC's
Playhouse would present a full prisoner-of-war drama on
live television based on Paul Brickhill's The Great Escape,
the same source material as used for the John Sturges/Steve
McQueen film; in the meantime, CBS would build up a stable
of writers including Reginald Rose and Rod Serling. Live
drama's two distinct styles, original material versus technical finesse, would gradually merge.

In its Monday evening time slot, Studio One was
scheduled a half-hour later, opposite another one-hour dramatic anthology, NBC's Robert Montgomery Presents, which
more often than not received the higher ratings. There
was no shortage of anthologies on the air, and the competition was beneficial to live drama. The year 1948 marked
the beginning of a shortlived era that would be later known
as "The Golden Age of Television."

The producer was in charge of a dramatic anthology;
Miner, not some committee, made all the decisions on Studio
One. In addition to writing most of the scripts, his job
also included such chores as fighting the sponsor when
Westinghouse's lamp division refused to support the adapta-
tion of Rudyard Kipling's "The Light That Failed." Miner's
efforts, however, did not go by unnoticed. Harriet Van
Horne would write of "The Living Theatre of Television":

> The first name that comes to mind ... is Worthing-
> ton Miner. His show, Studio One ... is far and
> away the best thing of its kind on television. Mr.
> Miner, like so many of his brethren, isn't afraid

of video. He dares to experiment. He dares to
defy the limitations of the medium. And he respects the intelligence of his viewers. [13]

The importance of the script was axiomatic. "Poor camera
work never made a bad play out of a good one," critic
Charles Adams once wrote. "Good camera work never made
a good play out of a bad one. The sine qua non of drama
on television is the play." [14] Schaffner learned under Miner:
"You must consider the intent of the playwright," he would
later echo, "not the presence of cameras." [15]

When he created Studio One, Miner knew he would be
producing adaptations of well-known, public domain classics
of drama and literature. To present them properly, he pro-
posed a 90-minute format: CBS resisted the proposal, and
a compromise was made to 60 minutes. The one-hour format
proved to be a blessing for the writers: it was the right
amount of time for a drama that was no bigger, no smaller
than life. Live television drama brought a measure of reality to the home screens, as Erik Barnouw has noted:

> The manipulation of "film time" offered creative
> pleasures so beguiling to film makers that they had
> virtually abolished "real time" from the screen. Its
> appearance in long stretches of television gave a
> sense of the rediscovery of reality--especially for
> people whose only drama had been film. [16]

By the mid-1950s, television writers would have their kitchen
sink school of realistic dramas produced on Broadway; in
turn, these plays would be translated to film. [17] Television,
in no small way, influenced both Broadway and Hollywood.

The nature of live television dictated the construction
of a play: "This encouraged plays of tight structure,"
Barnouw continues, "attacking a story close to its climax--
very different from the loose, multi-scene structure of
films." [18] The well-made teleplay, the late Paddy Chayefsky
noted, had a simple structure:

> A drama can have only one story. It can have only
> one leading character. All other characters are
> used in the script only as they facilitate the main
> story.... You need only one subplot, never more

> than two. Television cannot take a thick, fully
> woven fabric of drama. It can only handle simple
> lines of movement and consequently smaller moments
> of crisis. [19]

Television drama, Fielder Cook has observed, was stories of
the heart in dialogue and close-ups. The close-up became
the medium's primary shot; every director was guilty of too
many close-ups. Miner counteracted this tendency by stress-
ing the moving camera, another important lesson Schaffner
would learn from him.

Above all, a television director needed a lot of patience. In addition to the typical problems of budgets,
sponsors, advertising agencies, network restrictions, and
artistic temperaments, the director knew that on-the-air
mistakes, such as the time a moving camera caught an actress changing costumes behind a flat and exposed her
bare bottom to the nation, were inevitable. Aspirin was
known as CBS candy; directing live television was a process Schaffner likens to flying a bomber.

"He was a very, very sensitive young man who didn't
appear sensitive at all," Miner said, describing the Franklin
Schaffner who joined Studio One in the fall of 1949. "He
appeared very authoritarian and very objective and aloof
and tough." It was an appropriate attitude to take in view
of the pressures of grinding out a program every other
week; a director had to make decisions, and couldn't afford
to appear weak. Charles Adams might well have been describing Schaffner when he wrote:

> The television director appears not to be one who
> regards his players and crew as fellow artists col-
> laborating with him. Rather, as works upon whom
> he imposes his will. This is not the director's fault.
> Nor his desire. Forced to compress within six hours
> many vital decisions on mechanical matters, he finds
> himself, whether he likes it or not, acting more like
> a despot than the considerate young man he is very
> apt to be. [20]

The other Studio One director, Paul Nickell, was a
more obviously gentle person. Miner had hired him sight
unseen on the basis of the television production of Gian-

Carlo Menotti's The Medium that Nickell directed in Philadelphia; he handled the camera better than any young director Miner had seen. A technical wizard, Nickell directed
all the shows involving special effects and new techniques
that made Studio One's reputation. Paul Nickell set the
standard for technical excellence among the early television
directors.

     Though gifted with a visual and a musical sense,
Nickell had one weakness: he knew little of the theatre or
literature; Schaffner, however, did. Although Nickell and
Schaffner never did become close friends, both directors
were young, learning, and knew they could benefit from
each other. Compared with the exuberant and extroverted
Miner, the two directors were on the quiet and reserved
side. Offering them the opportunity to criticize each other's
work at meetings, Miner also cast his directors to the material: to Nickell went the more sensitive dramas; to Schaffner, the more hard-hitting melodramas. Studio One would
flourish from the working relationship among these three
men.

     Worthington Miner devised a formula of four rotating
types of shows for Studio One: (1) a drama, preferably
exciting; (2) a comedy; (3) a murder mystery; (4) an adaptation of a classic. The writer had to write a script exactly 52 minutes and 30 seconds long; Schaffner has commented
that all the Studio One scripts had the same number of
pages. In keeping with the anthology's theatrical roots,
each script observed the three-act structure; commercials
were spaced in before and after the three acts.

     Another Miner formula concerned the production pro-
cedure. After the story was chosen and, if necessary,
performance rights were cleared, the producer would begin
to make budgets and schedules, take care of the necessary
arrangements for audition dates, film locations, rehearsal
halls, and studio time. The director received the script a
couple of weeks later, about a week before rehearsal. After the producer, writer, and director had their story con-
ferences, the script was typed and mimeoed, and the show
was cast. The budget being limited, the top salary for any
actor was $750; the producer cast the stars, and the direc-
tor would cast the rest of the actors.

The director had to consult early with the scene designer. Before he received the sketches of the floor plans,
he needed to have a rough idea of the sets so that he might
know where to dolly or pan or cross-shoot without revealing
the next set. The director would also give the property
man a list of the props that were needed. If the script
called for special exteriors, the director would go on location with a film cameraman--not a television cameraman--to
get these shots; actors, if necessary, went too. This film
would later be integrated into the live performance.

Then would come the first reading with the actors.
With studio space at a premium, rehearsals were held all
over New York, usually in ballrooms. Marks would eventually be taped down on the floor, and the director would
plan camera angles. During rehearsal, the director would
decide on costumes, make-up, and music.

The sets were built in the studio carpentry shop,
then painted and fireproofed; stark whites or dead blacks
were always avoided. Sets were usually arranged in sequence, forming two semi-circular patterns around two,
three, and sometimes four walls; the center area was always kept free for camera movement; the property man
dressed the set as it was assembled. Originally lit with hot
incandescent lamps, the set required 1250 foot-candles to
illuminate it properly for the television camera; cast and
crew alike had to get used to the extreme heat. Fortunately, cooler fluorescent lamps came into use by 1949, but it
was still quite hot on the set. All the lamps were controlled
from a central lighting dock. Microphones, too, had to be
hidden--on cables or long booms.

Facilities rehearsal began two days before broadcast.
The director would meet with the technical director (T.D.),
lighting director, and audio man to go over each second of
the script so that everyone would know where the cameras
would be, what the lighting would be like, and where the
audio booms would be placed. Next, the director would
block the show from the control booth. The associate director (A.D.) would sit to his right and the production
assistant to the A.D.'s right; to the left of the director
would be the T.D. and, to the T.D.'s left, the audio man.

The customary camera set-up was two pedestals and

one dolly. The camera could be moved up and down on a
pedestal; the pedestal itself was relatively mobile. Each
television camera was four-eyed with its turret of lenses:
50mm for long shots, 75mm, 90mm, and 125mm; for even
closer shots, there was an eight-and-a-half-inch lens which,
as it involved taking the lens turret off and using a bayo-
net mount, was seldom used. Wearing headphones, the
cameramen received their instructions from the director in
the control room; the dolly cameraman used sign language
with his dolly-pusher. Mounted on each camera was a list
of the shots the cameramen would make for the show; a
light on the camera told him and everybody else when he
was on the air.

The sound effects man had his own monitor, and used
a turntable for transcribed music; on occasion, a special effects man used rear screen projection. A separate telecine
room was equipped for 16mm or 35mm film and slides. In
another recording room, kinescopes were made for the CBS
affiliates that did not have direct transmission lines to
WCBS, New York, from where Studio One originated live.
A kinescope was filmed by a single system 16mm camera and
then shipped station to station: it was called a "hot kine,"
and the shipping process was known as "bicycling." Kinescopes also accommodated the three-hour time difference between Los Angeles and New York.

On the night of the show, the control room was filled
with the director, A.D., production assistant, T.D., shader,
and audio man. Alone in a separate booth to the left of the
audio man was the announcer, wearing his headphones. The
director gave his instructions to cast and crew via the floor
manager, who carried a one-way walkie-talkie; the A.D. pre-
cued the cameras, checked timing, and cued the music and
the announcer; the shaders controlled the quality and the
brightness of the picture; the T.D. punched up the cameras' pictures and integrated films or slides into the program;
the audio man controlled the sound level.

And Worthington Miner sat back and watched it all.

Schaffner's first Studio One teleplay was "The Rival
Dummy," adapted by Worthington Miner and David Opotashu
from a Ben Hecht story. As it aired on September 19, 1949,
Schaffner thought it would be his last show:

Paul Lukas, somewhere in the third act, forgot his lines completely. And, in doing so, he first of all reverted to Hungarian and then, realizing what he had done, he just--on the air--said, "Oh, Jesus Christ!" By this time, poor Anne Francis is just standing there, shaken, and pale--she doesn't know what she's doing. But we finally got through; how I don't know.

The earliest extant kinescope of a Schaffner Studio One is "Jane Eyre," December 2, 1949. Adapted by Sumner Locke Elliott, it begins as Jane (Mary Sinclair) arrives at Thornfield. From the start of the show to its end, Miner's influence is apparent: Schaffner's camera is constantly on the move; in a few years he would be known for his long and graceful tracking shots. Oddly enough, none of the other networks used a moving camera to any extent. On television, the moving camera takes the viewer into the story, turning the spectator more into a participant; it also serves to cover the limitations of the set.

After she hears the crazed laughter of the yet unseen Bertha, Jane prepares for bed; at this point, the viewer is aware that the whole scene was shot through a mirror. The television camera itself was capable of great depth of field: in one shot, a man's feet are seen propped up on a table, followed by a cut to his hands holding a cane; Schaffner cuts back to the feet on the table, and Jane stands in full figure behind his feet--foreground and background are in clear focus. She then moves to the spinet, requiring the camera to tilt up, revealing the face of Rochester (Charlton Heston).

Schaffner makes interesting directorial choices in the show. Jane and Mrs. Fairfax are seen in the foreground of the garden as Rochester approaches from the rear; his head is meticulously arranged between two branches of a tree in a medium shot. At the end of this scene, the camera makes a shock tilt up to a turret window, where Bertha's demented face can be seen. Rochester proposes to Jane in a scene shot from an almost omniscient angle: on the rare occasions when a fourth camera was used, it would be set up in the parallels, shooting down on the cast.

The production has its share of mistakes: a careful

viewer can see folds in the backdrop; when the camera moves
in to a tight shot of the fireplace, the picture goes out of
focus, marring the first part of a move that takes the camera away from the fireplace around to Rochester, who is
asleep in his chair. The biggest trouble the cameramen had
was adjusting to Heston's height--the top of his head is
cropped in shot after shot.

Charlton Heston, although badly miscast, was the
chief beneficiary of this show. A $10 a day performer,
Heston had been brought to Studio One by Robert Fryer,
Miner's assistant and a CBS casting director. Miner hired
Heston to understudy Mark Antony for his modern-dress
production of "Julius Caesar" in 1948, and, in the best
the-show-must-go-on tradition, Heston took over when the
original actor had to leave the show. "When he was in
'Julius Caesar,'" Fryer recalls, "he was in a crowd, and
they said, 'Sit down, you stand out too much.'" He stood
out enough to attract attention from the American public.
"That kind of started his career," Fryer continues. "He
started getting all those leads and got a tremendous amount
of fan mail." Schaffner would work with Heston a half
dozen times on live television.

"We were grooming Chuck," said Miner, who also
hired him to star in Studio One productions of "Wuthering
Heights," "The Taming of the Shrew," and "Of Human Bond-
age." Although he lacked the range and experience to portray Rochester convincingly, Heston had undoubted star
quality. Hal B. Wallis happened to catch the show and was
sufficiently impressed to offer the young actor a film contract, resulting in Heston's film debut as the lead in Wallis'
1950 production of Dark City.

Towards the end of December, Schaffner prepared for
the January 1, 1950 premiere of Young and Gay for producer
Carol Irwin. Set in Greenwich Village, the show, thereafter
directed by David Lowell Rich, was a continuation of Cornelia
Otis Skinner and Emily Kimbrough's Our Hearts Were Young
and Gay, following the adventures of the two Bryn Mawr
graduates, played by Bethel Leslie and Mary Malone, after
their trip to Europe.

Returning to Studio One, Schaffner worked with Grace
Kelly, another Miner discovery, in her television debut, "The

Rockingham Tea Set," on January 23, 1950. This show also
featured, quite unbeknown to the cast, perhaps the most
hair-raising stunt ever attempted on live television: a
stagehand shot a gun to effect the climactic shattering of a
tea cup; the bullet hit its mark while the cup was held in
a character's hand. Albeit successful, it so unnerved the
cast and the creative staff that such an effect was never
again repeated on the air.

Schaffner was introduced to other new faces more
tranquilly. Two weeks later, he directed the young Jack
Lemmon in a Miner adaptation of Marc Connelly's "The Wisdom Tooth." Later in the season, he would work with an
actress who had a featured role in "The Man Who Had Influence"--Anne Marno, who became better known as Anne
Bancroft. Mary Sinclair, who had played the title role in
"Jane Eyre," starred as Hester Pryne in "The Scarlet Letter," which Schaffner directed on April 3. "She had this
wonderful white luminescent skin and very black hair and
big black eyes," Robert Fryer recalls. "She was about as
big a star as television produced as a romantic lead."

Schaffner directed Miner's adaptation of "The Ambassadors" on May 15, 1950. Today, a show based on a book
by Henry James would probably be a BBC production on
PBS, but 30 years ago adaptations of Henry James were
common on dramatic anthologies. This "Ambassadors" is an
exemplary adaptation of Henry James, a model of live television drama. Robert Markle's production design consists
of only four sets: Mrs. Newsome's drawing room in Wool-
lett, Massachusetts; Chad's residence in Paris; an opera
box at the Paris Opera; and Contessa Marie de Vionnet's
Paris apartment.

When Lambert Strether (Judson Laire) arrives in
Paris, he stands for a moment in front of a residence gate;
standing nearby for local color are a boy, a man, and a
woman. In one continuous shot, the camera follows Strether
as he enters the gate, walks through the courtyard and into
the atelier, where he meets Chad (Robert Sterling). The
former can see himself as a young man in the latter; the
latter can see what he might become in the former. Schaffner cuts frequently to a camera that peers voyeuristically
into the atelier window from the outside. Even if his mother
fears Europe is corrupting him, Chad declares, he has no
intention of returning to America and to his millions.

There is no woman involved, Strether writes Mrs.
Newsome: a cut from a close shot of Mrs. Newsome's hands
as she reads the letter to a close shot of her son's hand as
he sits in his opera box takes the viewer to Paris, where
Chad introduces the Contessa (Ilona Massey). A camera
placed on the balcony looks into the Contessa's apartment
as the drama continues: Strether now urges Chad to stay
and find his potential; besides, Strether and the Contessa
are in the process of forming a close relationship. "Evil
thoughts come to you when you're alone," she tells him in
an intimate scene, "because you're alone." A moment later
her maid walks by, disclosing another Schaffner mirror shot.

The Contessa rather coldly observes that women like
Sarah, Chad's sister who has come to Paris to rescue him,
are afraid of what's to come, afraid of life itself. In a two-
shot, the Contessa, to the left, and Strether, to the right,
are seen in medium close-up: her face is brightly lit; there
are shadows on his--he is the one who needs to be rescued.
The Contessa releases her hold on Chad, who throws a party: three couples dance in the courtyard; inside the atelier,
a man opens the shutters of a window, and, on the outside,
a couple dances by. Altogether, in a long shot of this
scene, there are a total of eight people, who, on the 5" or
7" screen, suggest a sizeable party. The theme of the show
is eventually expressed in dialogue: what moral imperative
is there for Chad or for any other to be happy? Most important is the feeling of the moment. As the party wanes,
Chad wanders outside the front gate with Mamie, his intended, with whom he plans to return to America. A lamp-
lighter snuffs the lights, which, in a technical lapse, momentarily brighten before they darken, casting the young
lovers against dramatic shadows. Strether confesses his
love to the Contessa in the last shot of the show; they toast
each other and the days to come. The camera dollies back
to reveal them framed in a mirror shot, and the program
ends with this visual cameo of Strether and the Contessa.

This is not exactly the novel that Henry James wrote,
but it is a most satisfying adaptation; omissions and simpli-
fications had to be made for even the slenderest of books to
fit the one-hour format. Miner's adaptation is particularly
lucid and coherent, Schaffner's direction extracts good performance and paces the story well, but ultimate credit for
this show's success must properly go to Henry James. If a

particular show proved to be outstanding or very popular, a common practice in the early days of television drama was to restage it, with the original cast if possible, at a later date; Schaffner restaged "The Ambassadors" with the identical cast for Studio One on February 26, 1951.

A kinescope exists of Studio One's March 13, 1950 production of "The Dusty Godmother," the story of a newspaper reporter's close relationship with his daughter, who is in her mother's custody, and his relationship with his girlfriend, who similarly was estranged from her own father. The story is far from compelling, and the show itself is none too good. In a cause and effect relationship on Studio One, the shows were good when the material was good; the material dictated the style of direction. Paul Nickell, as it happens, directed "The Dusty Godmother"; the direction might well have been Franklin Schaffner's, as far as the material is concerned. As for the technical quality and the visualization of the show, "The Dusty Godmother" does not look that much different from the shows Schaffner was directing in this period; Schaffner was quickly catching up to Nickell.

Scheduled to air on June 12, 1950 was "Zone Four," written by Fielder Cook, a producer-director for the J. Walter Thompson Agency. Then working on The Lux Video Theater, which used the same studio as Studio One, Cook had the chance to meet and become good friends with Schaffner. The show was set to air in the midst of an International Alliance of Theatrical and Stage Employees (IATSE) strike; CBS management had to man the cameras and microphones. The executives were competent enough on news and game shows, but an hour dramatic show was beyond their capabilities; the show had to be pulled. "Zone Four" was subsequently rescheduled to lead off the third season of Studio One in the fall. By that time Schaffner would be unavailable to direct it; he would be working for Ford Television Theater.

Kenyon and Eckhardt

Advertising agencies had more power than the networks at the beginning of television--they produced the shows for network airing. Broadcast over CBS from 9 to 10 on Friday

evenings, Ford Television Theater, for example, was produced by Garth Montgomery for the Kenyon and Eckhardt
advertising agency, which had the Ford account. Schaffner left Studio One for one simple reason--money. Despite
Worthington Miner and the experience, Studio One, being a
network-produced show, paid its directors the minimum
scale wages. Kenyon and Eckhardt offered him a more attractive salary to direct Ford; at $25,000 per show, Ford's
budget was also substantially higher than Studio One's.

    Ford too relied heavily on classics. Lois Jacoby, who
had been a researcher for The March of Time, was the
script editor and frequent adaptor for this anthology. On
September 8, 1950, Schaffner directed the season opener,
"The Traitor," based on the Herman Wouk play, starring
Lee Tracy as the nuclear physicist who sells bomb secrets
to Russia. On October 6, he directed Nathaniel Hawthorne's
"The Marble Faun," adapted by David Davidson. "A very
untoward thing happened on that show," Schaffner recalls.
At the end of the first act, Wesley Addy, playing Miriam's
tormentor, was supposed to be hurled off the Tarpeian Rock.
The studio facsimile was approximately five feet high, complete with mattresses on the floor. Everything went well in
rehearsal, but on the night of the broadcast, when Addy
plunged off the cliff, his body hit the mattresses, but his
head hit the floor. "I'm in the control room," Schaffner
says. "Out of the corner of my eye I see a procession coming on in front of the control room window, and it's four
guys, and they got a stretcher, and Wesley Addy's on it."
In retrospect, Schaffner can laugh. "Poor guy--he had
knocked himself out momentarily, and bled a great deal. If
he had been required to come back in later on, we would
have been in some kind of trouble."

    "Angel Street," by Patrick Hamilton, aired on October
20, 1950. The touring company of the play had just concluded its run; Ford hired them to do the show before anyone had a chance to make another commitment. "A most
amazing thing," Schaffner has commented on the rehearsal
period:

        They're off giving a performance like they did on
        stage--at the top of their voices, going lickety split.
        Finally I said, "Hey, wait a minute, folks. You're
        playing a part that's not in the script." "Oh."

> Then they'd look at the cut and say, "Okay. I
> suppose that's for time." And I'd say, "Yes, that's
> for time." And they'd see where they pick up, and
> they'd just keep going again.

The cast managed to slow down for the broadcast, and it
proved to be a satisfying show. This was the first time
Schaffner worked with Judith Evelyn, a young Canadian actress who had come down to America to do this play. Considered one of the finest actresses of her generation, Evelyn, with the stage production of Angel Street, had established herself as a star--under the softer theatre lights.
"She was a brilliant actress," Worthington Miner said, "but
she wasn't too pretty."

"Heart of Darkness" was presented on November 3,
1950 and on March 23, 1951. The repeat performance is introduced by its director, who explains the reason for the
kinescope within a kinescope: "The Touchstone," starring
Margaret Sullavan, originally scheduled for March 23, had
to be postponed. Seen on television, Schaffner looks handsome and distinguished indeed, his appearance and manner
suggesting a screen type already personified by Gregory
Peck; his tone, however, sounds distant and remote.[21]

Adapted by Joseph Liss and produced by Garth Montgomery, "Heart of Darkness," in its director's opinion,
wasn't too bad in terms of the script's approach, but the
production is embarrassing. Joseph Conrad's tale is much
too large for television; 29 years later, it would prove to
be elusive for a $30 million, 70mm, Dolby stereo film titled
Apocalypse Now. The television version features Richard
Carlson and Richard Purdy as Marlow and Kurtz respectively. The biggest set is a mock-up of a steamboat: it
is obviously fake, and the backdrop is obviously painted,
but as the camera dollies around the steamboat's paddle-
wheel and a cannibal crew, a three-dimensional effect is
created. Schaffner's moving camera brings a sense of the
journey, taking attention away from the sets' shortcomings.

Momentum is given to this show by unusual camera
angles as well. One shot of an ivory-passing slave line is
framed through the legs of the first slave. Schaffner also
stages a native dance that lasts a couple of minutes--an unusual choice, considering the wealth of material the Conrad

novella has to offer. However, more than any other scene
since Marlow left Mrs. Kurtz's drawing room in Act I, it
provides some atmosphere of the different continent. The
dance itself is well choreographed: at most, the camera reveals eight dancers; the 10" television set had now become
the new standard, but eight people still seem to be the maximum number the screen can successfully encompass.

For Schaffner, the most memorable show of the Ford
season was "The Whiteheaded Boy," on November 17, 1950.
He got the chance to meet, know, and work with Barry
Fitzgerald; the added fillip of the program was the partici-
pation of Mildred Natwick, who provided Fitzgerald's roman-
tic interest in the teleplay. But on December 15, Schaffner
directed an ill-advised musical of Lewis Carroll's "Alice in
Wonderland," adapted by Lois Jacoby, with music by Ben
Ludlow and lyrics by Garth Montgomery, choreography by
Oona White, and a cast that included Iris Mann, Richard
Waring, Jack Albertson, Biff McGuire, Jack Lemmon, and
Frances Fuller, Mrs. Worthington Miner. All the songs
were performed live by the cast--and none too well at that.
A musical production was generally more elaborate, and vir-
tually the only time a crane was ever used in live television;
ordinarily, dramas with their one story sets never required
a crane.

In the Ford Theater time slot on January 12, 1951 was
The Presentation of the Look Magazine Television Awards,
produced by Marlo Lewis and directed by Franklin Schaffner,
with Ed Sullivan as master of ceremonies. During the telecast, Worthington Miner, to no one's surprise, picked up the
best dramatic series award for his work on Studio One.

In the spring of 1951, Garth Montgomery was replaced
as producer of Ford Television Theater by Werner Michel of
the television department of Kenyon and Eckhardt. On April
6, Michel, formerly a writer-director for Voice of America,
produced "Ticket to Oblivion," a comedy Schaffner directed,
with Signe Hasso and Anthony Quinn as its stars. "He was
very funny in that," the director says of the latter. "That
guy has always had great comedic gifts that nobody's really
ever exploited."

Edith Wharton's "The Touchstone" aired on April 20,
nearly a month after its original air date. The most

A gag appearance that never materialized in "Spring Again,"
Ford Theater, 1951. (See Chapter 2 footnote no. 21.)

memorable element of the show is Margaret Sullavan, with
her distinctive voice and screen presence. It is always a
treat to see her on film, and no less so in this rare kinescope. She can misread a line and recover before anyone
notices the flub, and be all the more charming for it. Referring to the party-going habits of Barton, the villain of
the piece, she says, "He's always the first to arrive, I
mean the other way around, the last to arrive and the first
to go." In Wharton's novella the emphasis is on Stephen
Glennard, an author with a severe case of writer's block,
who, in desperation, sells the love letters he received from
Margaret Aubyn, a woman who has gained posthumous fame
as a major American author. The emphasis in the television
adaptation is on Alexa, Stephen's wife. Paul McGrath is not
especially memorable as Stephen, but perhaps that is the
way it should be: this "Touchstone" is very much a woman's
story, and McGrath in no way detracts from Margaret Sullavan.

     When someone asks Alexa how her husband is, Schaff-
ner has the camera dolly away from Sullavan to a liquor bottle on a table. The action of the teleplay is confined to
three contiguous sets: outside garden, living room, and
Stephen's study. Before purchasing the letters, Barton has
an animated discussion with Alexa in the garden; Stephen,
in the meantime, is in his study, talking to his agent on the
phone. With the help of subjective sound, one deep focus
shot delivers the drama of the situation: Stephen is to the
left of the frame in his study, the living room is in the middle, and through the living room window to the right of the
frame are Alexa and Barton in the garden set; after his
agent tells him he's finished, Stephen hangs up to the loud
laughter of Barton and Alexa.

     The letters were the touchstone of her marriage, and
Stephen failed the test. Alexa is faced with a decision:
shall she be Candida, a woman who stayed with her husband
because he was weak? Or shall she be Nora in A Doll's
House, and leave her husband? Margaret Aubyn's last letter to Stephen declared she was secure with love--the happiness of giving her love to Stephen was enough for her;
love, Alexa decides, is good enough for her too.

     "Night Over London," directed by Schaffner on June
15, 1951, was the last Ford drama on CBS: Schaffner would

would return to Studio One, and, after a year's hiatus,
Ford Theater would reappear on NBC, eventually concluding its long television run in 1957 on ABC.

The Victor Borge Show, produced by Bruce Dodge
and directed by Franklin Schaffner, began its brief NBC
run on February 3, 1951. At this juncture, Schaffner
worked neither for NBC nor for CBS; he worked for Kenyon and Eckhardt, and was given this weekly assignment
during the second half of the Ford season. Not surprisingly, Borge being an accomplished pianist and comedian,
the show featured music and comedy--Schaffner's first sustained professional exposure to the two forms. Despite the
presence of Art Carney as Borge's top banana, the show
concluded its run in five months.

Studio One, 1951-1952

Television came of age on September 4, 1951. "The nation,"
William Paley writes, "was bound into one single community
by microwave relay and coaxial cable which stretched across
the country."[22] All four networks joined to broadcast a
variety show to celebrate the link-up, television's golden
spike.

CBS had become the number one radio network in
1949, after "the Paley raids" lured NBC's biggest stars to
CBS; quite naturally, CBS Radio enjoyed its peak year in
sales in 1950. The next year, however, all radio networks
went into a gradual decline. On the other hand, ten million television sets were in use by 1951; CBS Television now
had 62 affiliate stations. Moreover, a television landmark
debuted on CBS on October 15, 1951--I Love Lucy. Shot on
film by three motion picture cameras, this series would rev-
olutionize television.

Over at Studio One, Worthington Miner knew by
Christmas 1950, when he was producing a two-part adapta-
tion of Louisa May Alcott's "Little Women," that Franklin
Schaffner would be returning to the show for the 1951-1952
season. He did not hire another permanent director for
Studio One during Schaffner's absence, using instead other
CBS staff directors, including Ralph Nelson, director of
Mama, Yul Brynner, director of Danger, and Lela Swift,
presently a director of Ryan's Hope.

Schaffner directed "Macbeth" for Studio One on November 22, 1951. Adapted by Miner, and featuring Charlton Heston ("courtesy of Hal B. Wallis") in the title role, Judith Evelyn as Lady Macbeth, and Darren McGavin as Macduff, the show opens on a tight shot of the witches' hands and ends with Macbeth's head on a pike. The sets are cunningly designed, taking full advantage of false perspectives for the television camera: a castle door opens, and the viewer can see walls, corridors, turrets, and the countryside in the distance; off-screen narration is used throughout the show to bridge gaps.

"I was afraid of Chuck in Shakespeare," Miner recalled. But Schaffner and Heston had been so eager to do "Macbeth" that he relented, only to regret his decision:

> Chuck was too heavy. Chuck needed a couple of more years while I could give him comedy. If I had had two more years to teach that boy a little bit more about what comedy is, he would have been able to temper his performances.

However, Cecil B. De Mille would cast him in The Greatest Show on Earth (1952), establishing Charlton Heston as a major motion picture star.

The Studio One production of "Macbeth" reaches its climax in a long, protracted, and surprisingly violent duel between Heston and McGavin. The viewer senses that the actors and the director were attempting a seemingly impossible task--an effective no-holds-barred fight on live television. It might have come off in rehearsal, but the televised duel brings the show to a halt: it goes on and on and on--it must last six minutes. It is an extraordinarily clumsy fight, the different camera angles only worsen the matter, and the viewer becomes embarrassed for the actors; what lingers in the mind is just how maladroit the duel was. "Frank had a good effect on Chuck, Chuck had a bad effect upon Frank," Miner commented. "Frank did not do one of his better jobs on that show."

"Mutiny on the Nicolette," with Boris Karloff, Anthony Ross, and Ralph Nelson, arrived on December 3, A lower deck and bridge of a steamer were created with three-sided housing in the studio. For one scene, Boris Karloff was

supposed to go up to the pilot house, where a camera shooting through a porthole would pick him up. As a lot of
water was needed on the set to simulate ocean waves, the
studio floor was hazardously wet. Karloff slipped and fell
to the floor as soon as he entered the room, disappearing
completely from the picture. Also in the scene was Anthony
Ross, who tried to help Karloff to his feet, but, as soon as
he did, they both slipped and fell. Being a television director himself, Ralph Nelson understood such situations,
and hurried over to assist the other two. Schaffner says:

> Tony Ross and Boris Karloff are just on their feet
> when Ralph comes through the hatch door, reaching
> for them, and all three hit the fucking deck. This
> happened three times! Three times Boris Karloff
> tried to get to his feet and each time his feet would
> go out from under him--and you'd cut away. Final-
> ly I yelled at the stage manager, "Get him over to
> the porthole, let him grab on to something, for
> Christ's sake, and hold on!" They get him there.
> It's terrible--he's holding like this onto something--
> and we're shooting a close-up through the porthole,
> and his face is just absolutely traumatized with
> fright.

"The Paris Feeling," December 31, 1951, is of personal significance to its director. George Voskovec, who
would later serve Schaffner well in "Twelve Angry Men,"
had been a member of a well-known satirical team in Czechoslovakia. When his country was overrun by the Russians
after the Second World War, Voskovec fled to America; aided
by Louise Schaffner of the American Embassy, he was able
to land at Ellis Island and enter New York. "The Paris
Feeling" was his first acting job in America.

"Waterfront Boss," January 14, 1952, was a hard-
hitting melodrama, kind of a pre-On the Waterfront, written
by Joseph Liss. A documentary-like exposé of Cockeye
Dunn, who was executed in 1949, it even included narration
by Don Hollenbeck of CBS News. In the daring tradition of
Studio One, Schaffner took cast and crew on location at
Pier 69, where the actual story had taken place, to spend a
day filming inserts. The company was not warmly received
by the dock workers; trouble was brewing until Roy Hargrave appeared on the scene. He bore such an uncanny

resemblance to the real Cockeye Dunn that the dock workers immediately began to cooperate. This location experience serves as another example of the difference between
Schaffner and Nickell: "Paul couldn't have done it," Miner
insisted. "He was gentler, he was enormously sensitive."

On February 25, Schaffner directed Miner's adaptation
of "Letter from an Unknown Woman." In one scene, Viveca
Lindfors and Melvyn Douglas walked down a small Parisian
street in a studio snowfall, entered a cafe, sat down, and,
when they suddenly became aware that it was snowing inside the cafe, broke out in simultaneous laughter. The
show came to the critical attention of Harriet Van Horne, who
wrote: "[It] had so many technical errors--snow falling indoors, doors jamming, cameras coming into view--that it became a news story solely on the merits of its defects."[23]

The Easter show for that season was Michael Dyne's
"Pontius Pilate," adapted by Miner and directed by Schaffner, and starring Cyril Ritchard and Geraldine Fitzgerald.
This April 7, 1952 telecast was the last show Miner would
ever produce for Studio One: in the second half of the
1951-1952 television season, Worthington Miner left CBS and
moved over to NBC. Making a scant $500 a week at CBS,
Miner thought, in view of his stature and accomplishments,
he was worth $750 a week; when CBS refused to give him a
raise, NBC quickly offered him more money. The other
great inducement was the opportunity to work with Sylves-
ter (Pat) Weaver, the visionary head of television at NBC;
unfortunately, soon after Miner reported to NBC, Weaver
was removed from the programming arena. Still, in the
next few years at NBC, Miner would create and produce
such shows as Curtain Call, Medic, and Frontier.

The remaining eleven shows of the 1951-1952 Studio
One season were produced by the husband and wife team of
Donald Davis and Dorothy Matthews: Davis was a writer
with Broadway and television experience; Matthews had been
an actress. Together, they leaned heavily on public domain
material for Studio One. Schaffner's first assignment for
the new producers was Paul Gallico's "Lily, the Queen of
the Movies," April 21, 1952, starring Glynis Johns, a co-
medienne admired by the director. Also featured was David
B. Greene, who would drop his middle initial and become a
most highly regarded television director with such credits
as Rich Man, Poor Man and Roots.

Schaffner's next two shows were "Treasure Island"
and "A Connecticut Yankee in King Arthur's Court." Broadcast on May 19, the latter stands as a typical Davis and
Matthews production. It begins with a guided tour of an
English castle where the camera moves in to an anomaly: a
suit of armor with a bullet hole in it. The camera moves
out to reveal Hank Morgan, who begins his tale. At the
end of the hour, after Hank's adventures in Camelot, and
13 centuries of sleep induced by Merlin, the camera moves
in again to a close shot of the armor. Thomas Mitchell is
somewhat miscast as Hank, but Boris Karloff is wonderfully
droll as King Arthur. Alvin Sapinsley's adaptation of Mark
Twain's novel is at the very least entertaining, but once the
production gets rid of all necessary exposition and begins
to build some dramatic momentum, the hour runs out. The
material cries out for the length, budget, special effects,
scope, and color of a major motion picture.

The Studio One director had what amounted to a ten-
week vacation in the summer. As a CBS staff director, he
would be reassigned to summer activity, and, as such, might
be summoned to do some work. If there were something coming up that he was particularly interested in doing, the director would ask for it. Such was the case for Schaffner
in the summer of 1952, an election year. Seeking some exercise in instant drama, real drama, Schaffner asked for the
assignment of directing the Stevenson/Eisenhower political
conventions. This time, in contrast to his convention experience in 1948, there were six pool cameras, and each network brought an additional four cameras. An NBC director,
an ABC director, and Schaffner, the CBS director, rotated,
working assigned shifts. These conventions offered Schaffner his only opportunity of working with CBS correspondent
Walter Cronkite.

Studio One, 1952-1953

Fewer adaptations of great literature were presented in the
new season of Studio One. Completely gone was Worthington Miner's formula of four rotating types of shows, and, in
Miner, the dramatic anthology had lost its most reliable adaptor. Davis and Matthews began the season as the producers; on September 22, 1952, Schaffner directed Grace Kelly,
Nina Foch, and Dick Foran in the season opener, "The Kill,"
from a script by Reginald Rose, who would play a significant

role in <u>Studio One</u>, television drama, and Schaffner's career.

After producing a half dozen shows, the Davises were
fired. John Haggott, who had worked with the Theatre
Guild and had been a film producer at Columbia, stepped in
for a month as interim producer. Barely getting his feet
wet, he produced two shows for Schaffner, the second being "The Formula" on November 24, another adaptation by
Reginald Rose.

Fletcher Markle had built a considerable reputation in
radio as a writer, producer, and director for the CBC and
the BBC before creating <u>Studio One</u> for CBS Radio in 1949,
for which he received a Peabody Award. He was in the
process of building a house in Los Angeles when Hubbell
Robinson asked him to come to New York and produce <u>Studio
One</u>. Markle agreed, but on one condition: only for the
remainder of the season. He brought in Vincent McConnor
as his associate producer; together, they selected and developed the scripts, and prepared cast lists for the director. As offices, rehearsal halls, and studio were scattered
throughout New York City, Markle estimates he spent three
and a half hours a day in a taxi. Like Miner, he cast his
directors to the material. "Paul tended to be best at rather
romantic stories," Markle says. "Frank's forte was muscular,
vivid, and fast." By now, after several years of working
together, the crew functioned smoothly as a unit under
Schaffner. "Frank's theory was that nothing was impossible," Markle recalls. "And, by God, he usually got every
member of the crew to respond to him."

"The Hospital," adapted by A. J. Russell, was Schaffner's first show for Markle. His second, on December 22,
1952, was a Christmas program entitled "The Nativity,"
written by Andrew Allan, which won a Christopher Award.
"Signal Thirty-Two," January 19, 1953, was a MacKinley
Kantor police drama, adapted by Stanley Niss, a veteran
of the genre who had written over a thousand scripts for
<u>Gangbusters</u> on radio. There was an alley to the rear of
the studio at Grand Central Station; for this show, Schaffner saw to it that a couple of police cars and a group of
extras were positioned in the alley, then opened the fire
door and brought out a camera--with all its cables--to get
the shot. Normally such a scene would have been shot on

film and inserted into the program. It wasn't an absolutely
necessary shot; it was a case of a director experimenting
with live television.

"My Beloved Husband," a clever murder-mystery written by Robert Wallsten from a novel by Philip Loraine, aired
on March 2. The title role was played by Fletcher Markle,
who, in the Forty-Second Street tradition, had to step in
at the last moment to play the lead--Michael, a sophisticated
cad. Irresistible to women, Michael casually but immediately
makes a date with Helen at the beauty shop. Bea, his very
rich and jealous wife, learns about Helen on the eve of a
party at their home. She has such a disturbing argument
with her husband that she must take her pills, which Michael
accommodatingly gets for her. When she finally joins the
party, Bea drinks some sherry and then mysteriously dies.
The next shot is a fuzzy close-up of Michael to the left
of the frame; Bea's sherry glass, in hard focus, can be
seen in the background on a table to the right of the frame.
An unidentified hand reaches out to grab the glass; Schaffner then cuts to the fireplace, where the sherry glass can
be spotted, broken.

Adria, Bea's stepdaughter, another woman in love
with Michael, confesses to breaking the glass but, in fact,
it was Helen who did it; they both wanted to protect Michael, who nonetheless is arrested and found guilty when
Bea's diary is found, disclosing how much she loved her
husband. In the meantime, Helen and Adria find proof
that Bea actually kept two diaries--Michael has been framed.
As he is scheduled to be executed at 11:00, Helen and Adria make one last desperate search to find the second diary.
There is a dizzy montage of two pairs of female hands rum-
maging through shelves and drawers, while on the soundtrack the chant of two female voices rises in crescendo:
"There isn't much time!" Schaffner cuts to the prison cell
where Michael still protests his innocence: onto a choker
close-up of Michael is superimposed a clock reading 11:00.
The final scene is set in a law office, with a package from
Bea "To be opened only at the time of my beloved husband's
death." It is the second diary containing Bea's confession--
she killed herself in order to kill her husband.

As revealed by the plot synopsis, "My Beloved Husband"'s main attraction is its story; Markle had great respect

for the script--the title he had originally considered for
the radio version of Studio One was The Play's the Thing.
Schaffner's direction displays split-second timing from cut
to cut of gesture and reaction. As for the star of the show,
Fletcher Markle is no serious threat to Charles Boyer, but
he is credible and requisitely debonair.

"At Midnight on the 31st of March," written by Robert Anderson from a novel by Josephine Young Case, aired
at 10:00 on the 30th of March. It is the most trickily directed show by Franklin Schaffner: the camera angles are
tilted to the side throughout the show; sketches are used
for locations, for establishing shots, and to denote the changing seasons. These tricks accentuate the eerie mood of
the story: a fantasy, a science fiction parable, it is also
a thoughtful show. It begins with a tilted shot of John
(director Lamont Johnson), a young poet whose poor health
has forced him to move to the country, who reads from
his diary, relating the events that transpired since midnight on the 31st of March--exactly a year ago. Schaffner
cuts to a sketch of a house. Abe and his wife Ellen are
inside; George, the milkman, is outside. Gert, the prettiest girl in town, is seen looking at herself in a mirror,
followed by a shot of May, the school teacher, who reads
a volume of John's poetry, and then a cut back to John.
These tilted introductory shots serve to set up two love
triangles.

Action begins inside a general store when it is learned
that the phone is dead; George presently dashes in from
his milk run to say that the roads have disappeared. A
couple of men rush outside (a sketch of a forest superimposed over a couple of carefully positioned actors) to discover that George is right--it is no April Fool's joke. The
lights went out, the phones went dead, and the rest of the
civilized world disappeared at midnight on the 31st of March.
In order to survive, the townsfolk must now learn to become totally self-sufficient.

The camera moves in to the church in a sketch of
the town: a dance is going on inside. John and Gert dance
together; George, who will be going to work for Abe, dances
with Ellen. In the dance scene are the customary four couples to fill up the frame; this time around, however, Schaffner adds children and bystanders to the eight dancing people

in the picture. Abe later discovers salt in his spring house:
salt can make him a rich man in this brave new world, but
it makes him eventually die of greed, enabling George and
Ellen to come together. John has been encouraged to write
again by May, who tells him he can be the new father of
American poetry; he visits her at her schoolroom and discovers he loves her. The ceiling of the schoolroom is highly visible in the scene--having saved money on the sets
by using sketches, Schaffner splurged on a ceiling.

At the end of the first new year, the townspeople
have learned that through hard work and dedication the
town can live on its own; the good have been rewarded,
the bad have been punished, and lovers have found the
right partners. The show comes full circle with a mirror
shot of John reading from his diary. Perhaps man has gotten closer to the heart of things, he concludes, but now
that a year has passed the old world just might return,
and the past year will turn out to have been a dream.

There is a plug for Meet Betty Furness in the final
credits. Furness, of the-refrigerator-door-that-wouldn't-
open fame, did all of the live commercials for the various
Westinghouse divisions on Studio One in a set known as
"The Westing House." After years of faithful service to
Westinghouse and Studio One, Furness had become a household name and, in 1953, was awarded her own show. Set
in a kitchen and living room, not unlike the Westing House,
Meet Betty Furness was a 15-minute daytime talk show that
aired on Fridays; during and after its half-year run, Furness continued to do the Westinghouse commercials live for
Studio One.

The last show of the season, "Conflict," June 8, 1953,
was written by A. J. Russell and directed by Schaffner.
As had been the arrangement, Fletcher Markle returned
to his new house in Los Angeles, and would produce such
Los Angeles-based television programs as Life with Father
and Front Row Center. Still residing in Los Angeles, Markle
offers the following anecdote. During his tenure at Studio
One, Markle produced Georges Simenon's "Black Rain," for
which Schaffner brought a couple of horses into the studio.
Shortly thereafter, William Faulkner expressed some interest
in writing for live television. Although nothing eventually
came out of it, he met with Markle to discuss the possibilities

of Faulkner scripts for Studio One. "I remember him saying
in my office one day, 'Can you use mules?'" Markle recalls.
"And I said, 'You bet you can, Bill, if Frank Schaffner's
directing it.'"

"Conflict," however, as far as Schaffner was concerned, was not an inappropriate title to describe his own
feelings at the end of the 1952-1953 season. He had been
dissatisfied with Studio One ever since Worthington Miner's
departure, and particularly displeased by the quality of
material being offered on the show. There would be a dramatic turnabout in the fall.

     After the Studio One season ended in 1953, Schaffner
began work on an educational series for CBS in June. The
pilot, alternately titled Search or In Search, was filmed
at the University of Louisville--without a script. As a result, nothing came of the show until the following year,
when the series, retitled The Search, made it to the air.
Although Schaffner would have no connection with the show,
it would follow the original premise of visiting American
colleges and universities.

Felix Jackson

CBS Television, having lost a total of $60 million in the
preceding five years, became profitable for the first time
in 1953. [24] A total of 23 million television sets were now in
use for a potential audience of 115 million people. A man
like William Paley could sense the beginning of a new trend:
it would be even more profitable for a network to produce
and control the programs it televised--the advertising agencies had previously produced and controlled the shows, had
bargaining power over the networks. By eliminating the
middle man, and producing and controlling their own shows,
the networks could reap even greater profits.

     "1984" marked the beginning of the sixth season and
a new era of Studio One on September 21, 1954. The anthology would have a new emphasis: although adaptations would
still be written, Studio One, like its chief rival The Philco/
Goodyear Playhouse on NBC, would encourage original scripts,
dramas with social conscience. Studio One became a tougher,
more hard-hitting program. This change can be directly
traced to the new producer, Felix Jackson.

A newspaperman and a playwright, Felix Jackson was
forced to leave Germany in the midst of the political up-
heaval in the 1930s, later writing about those days and
of his escape in his 1980 autobiographical novel, Secrets
of the Blood. Arriving in America in 1938, he became a
screenwriter for Universal Pictures, where he teamed with
another German emigré, producer Joe Pasternak, a collaboration which resulted in pictures starring Deanna Durbin,
such as Mad About Music (1938) and Three Smart Girls Grow
Up (1939), which made a lot of money for Universal. Jackson also had a hand in writing the scripts for Destry Rides
Again (1939) and Back Street (1941).

As a writer for television at the end of the 1940s,
Jackson soon learned that the producer was in control of
the new medium. To become a producer, he joined the Young
and Rubicam advertising agency. CBS eventually hired
Jackson away from Young and Rubicam to produce Studio
One, still riding the crest of its reputation due to the prior
efforts of Worthington Miner. Given promises that he could
be as progressive and experimental as he wanted, Jackson
also inherited Paul Nickell and Franklin Schaffner--with the
understanding that he could replace either one or both if
he so desired. Before the season began, Jackson recalls,
one of the previous producers of Studio One offered him
the following advice: "There's only one talented director--
Paul Nickell. Get rid of Schaffner." Jackson, however,
was impressed with Schaffner, finding him straightforward
and direct. He retained both directors.

Being a writer himself, Jackson was a strong proponent of a good script. To that end he brought in an
excellent story editor, Florence Britten, who brought Reginald Rose, Rod Serling, and Loring Mandel to his attention. "Felix Jackson and Florence Britten guided me through
my early career," Reginald Rose says. "Had it not been for
them I probably wouldn't have known which way I was going. I'm forever grateful to them."

"1984" was a project Jackson had long wanted to do.
The only problem was that he did not have full confidence
in his boss at CBS, Hubbell Robinson; he preferred to deal
with Harry Ommerle, the liaison man between Robinson and
Studio One. Jackson took no chances in getting "1984" on
the air: first he secured the television rights from the
widow of George Orwell for a modest sum and hired William

Templeton to write the adaptation; next he talked to McCann-Erickson, the advertising agency that had the Westinghouse account, and got its approval; then he waited for Hubbell Robinson to leave town before cabling him of his decision. Following Studio One protocol, he gave the directorial assignment to Paul Nickell: Schaffner had directed the final show of the previous season; it was Nickell's turn. Eddie Albert, Norma Crane, and, in his first television exposure in America, Lorne Greene were cast. "1984" met with great acclaim, firmly establishing the quality Jackson intended for Studio One.

Franklin Schaffner had made no secret of the fact that he wanted to direct the season premiere; Jackson was fully aware of Schaffner's disappointment over not directing the Orwell show. The inevitable clash came immediately, in Schaffner's first assignment for the new season, Fred Gipson's "Hound-Dog Man," with Jackie Cooper and E. G. Marshall. Schaffner requested a completely naturalistic set, full of brush and grass; Jackson objected. In their argument over the set, Jackson pointed out that there would be no room for all the cameras and cables; the outcome was that there would never be a completely naturalistic set on Studio One as long as Jackson was the producer. During the facilities rehearsal, the two men had another disagreement when the director asked for overtime and Jackson refused. Schaffner countered that Nickell had been given overtime for "1984" the week before; Jackson replied that Nickell had needed it, and Schaffner did not.

A couple of weeks later, Schaffner conceded that he had been wrong. Shortly thereafter, he would begin to develop a very close working relationship with Jackson. By the next season, Schaffner would find himself acclaimed as the premier director of Studio One. He had found another valuable mentor in Felix Jackson.

Every Monday, Felix Jackson had a concept meeting to discuss the show that would be aired two weeks later. Today, in Jackson's office, is a cinemascope-shaped picture of a Studio One concept meeting, painted by Willard Levitas. There are three desks. Jackson, the producer, sits behind the middle desk. Seated on top of the desk to the left are Kenneth Utt, the floor manager, and Wes Law, the set decorator. Seated on the table to the right are Willard Levitas,

the set designer, Bette Stein, the program assistant, and
Joseph Dackow, the associate director. Coming in through
the door to the far right is William Altman, the assistant to
the producer, asking how much the program will cost--it
was Jackson's job to make sure that the budget would not
exceed $25,000. Standing to the right of center, in front
of Jackson's desk, is a nude woman symbolizing the script.
Finally, to the left of Jackson's desk, there is a man with
his head buried in his hands: Franklin Schaffner, the director.

        As he had hoped, Schaffner soon came across more
challenging material and some major new writers: the first
was "Buffalo Bill Is Dead" on December 3, 1953. When
Florence Britten came across the manuscript, she found it
miraculous--it didn't need any revisions or rewriting, it was
ready to be shot--and promptly passed on her enthusiasm
to the producer. Felix Jackson remembers his first meeting
with the author: "He was small, poor; he looked like a
clean-shaven bum." The new writer showed up at the first
rehearsal a few minutes late; wearing squeaky shoes, he attracted immediate attention. According to the producer,
Schaffner looked around and shouted, "Get that sonofabitch
out of here." "He might be a sonofabitch," Jackson replied,
"but he's also the author of the show." The producer then
proceeded to introduce Schaffner to Rod Serling.

        On February 15, 1954, Schaffner directed the first
television play written by novelist Gore Vidal. Jackson had
the author rewrite the script several times, and Vidal was
eventually satisfied with the final result, saying: "It is
good melodrama without pretensions."[25] Set in Concord,
New Hampshire in 1904, "Dark Possession" concerns a de-
caying aristocratic family as might have been envisioned by
Eugene O'Neill. Emily and Charlotte, the elder daughters,
were once both in love with John; Charlotte married him,
but John was murdered shortly thereafter. Charlotte, receiving her seventh threatening letter of the year, finds
the word "murderess" written on her mirror; suspicion falls
on Emily. (Ann, the youngest daughter, is normal; her
only function in the script is to be engaged to a doctor so
that he can be around to give a scientific explanation of
what happened at the end of the show.)

        When Charlotte is attacked, she blames "her"--not

Emily, but a woman named Janet, who is revealed late in
the third act when Charlotte opens her mouth to speak and
Janet's voice comes out; having already killed John, Janet
wants to punish Charlotte, and does so by stealing poison
from the doctor's bag and killing her. Vidal based his teleplay on the Beauchamps case, the first recorded case of
schizophrenia. From a reading of the script it is obvious
that Charlotte/Janet is a tour de force role for an actress.
Geraldine Fitzgerald, playing the part with no make-up, is
good and effectively eerie; interestingly, she gives a rather
subdued instead of a bravura performance. Another strong
asset of this production is its atmosphere. "The mood of
the play, as done on Studio One by Franklin Schaffner,"
Vidal was to comment, "was beautifully dark and strange."[26]

Coming from the publishing medium, Vidal was pleased
with this experience and enchanted with television:

> The day after my debut in February of 1954, I was
> hopelessly in love with writing plays for the camera.
> I discovered that although the restrictions imposed
> by a popular medium are not always agreeable they
> do at least make creative demands upon one's euphe-
> mistic talents and, more often than not, the tension
> between what one is not allowed to say and what
> one must say creates ingenious effects which, given
> total freedom, might never have been forced from
> the imagination.[27]

Vidal's infatuation was to diminish as television became a
more powerful medium, but not before he had written other
teleplays, most notably "Visit to a Small Planet" for Goodyear Playhouse, which he later fashioned into a successful
Broadway play.

On March 15, 1954, Reginald Rose, Felix Jackson,
and Franklin Schaffner collaborated on "Thunder on Sycamore Street," a show that best typifies Studio One's new
guts. At 6:40 p.m. in a suburban neighborhood, Frank, a
hardhat type, meets Arthur, a meek type, on the way home;
Joe, the third neighbor, walks by. Act I is told from
Frank's point of view: he hates Joe and is urging everybody to join the march he is leading that evening. The
second act, also beginning at 6:40, when Frank meets Arthur, and Joe walks by, is told from Arthur's point of view.

The community is upset because Joe Blake is an ex-convict,
but Arthur is hesitant to join the march. His wife, on the
other hand, wants to join the march for fear she'll be the
next victim; she is afraid to be different.

The third act follows Joe home. Having been warned
of the mob, his wife Anna wants to flee, but Joe, whose
crime was running over an old man, will not be moved.
When rocks are thrown, Joe goes outside to confront the
mob, challenging its ringleader Frank to a fight, one on
one. Ashamed, Arthur joins Joe's side; as others follow,
Frank is embarrassed in front of all the children. The
teleplay ends with Arthur sadly telling his wife: "Well,
what are you standing there for? My neighbor's head is
bleeding."[28]

In the best 1930s Warner Bros. tradition, Reginald
Rose based his original script on a newspaper article about
the hostile reaction the tenants of a housing development in
Cicero, Illinois had toward their new Black neighbors. Joe
was originally written as a Black--a notion categorically
ruled out by Westinghouse and McCann-Erickson, the sponsor and its advertising agency; CBS went along with their
decision. The only way that Rose could get his script on
the air was to rewrite Joe as an ex-convict; even so, it is
not impossible to read Rose's meaning into the teleplay.
This compromise serves as an interesting sociological index
to its times in terms of what could and what could not be
done in the mass media. That Joe is an ex-convict seems
somewhat less than a satisfying rationale for mob action today; however, a reading of the insidiousness of a random
mob is possible in view of 1980s paranoia--a new sociological index to the times "Thunder on Sycamore Street" has
to offer.

As Joe Blake, Schaffner cast Kenneth Utt, the floor
manager for Studio One. Accustomed to listening to Schaffner over headphones, Utt listened to the director's instructions this time without headphones; the author of the teleplay found him especially memorable. The reputation of
"Thunder on Sycamore Street" indicates that Schaffner did
his customary excellent job of direction, but the real credit
for the show belongs to its author. As published, the teleplay is clear and very well written: the time structure of
the three acts is rather experimental but not difficult to

follow; the mob mentality and its potential for ugly violence
are well conveyed. Speaking of live television, Reginald
Rose once said, "In those years from 1953 to 1960 the writer
was the star of the show."[29] In his case that definitely was
so.

Schaffner's last show for the season was "The Strike,"
the third of six Rod Serling scripts he would direct for
Studio One. Set in a ruined cellar of a farm house in war-
torn Korea, January 1951, it is a very talky drama about
the psychological pressures of war. Major Gaylord (James
Daly), the commanding officer in charge of 500 exhausted
men, must order them to strike, an action that will mean
certain death for 20 men--but he cannot bring himself to do
it. The theme of the teleplay is expressed in dialogue:
"In times of sanity--it's called an attribute. Concern for
fellow man. Now it's a flaw."[30] After weighing his responsibilities to his men and to his command, he orders the
strike; the teleplay ends as Gaylord asks God for forgive-
ness. An interesting detail of "The Strike" is the radio
man who, not unlike M*A*S*H's Radar O'Reilly, talks constantly in the background. Unfortunately this detail points
out the show's weakness: everything in the script is dependent on sound; there are no battle scenes, only talk.
"The Strike" would have made a superb radio show.

In addition to the work of Reginald Rose, Rod Serling,
and Gore Vidal, Jackson's tenure at Studio One also featured
contributions from other notable authors--George Axelrod's
"Confessions of a Nervous Man" and Justice William O. Douglas' "An Almanac on Liberty," adapted by Rose. Unlike
Miner and his four-show formula, Jackson produced shows
with sharp contrasts so that the audience would never know
exactly what to expect from week to week; in general, they
received a quality product.

Franklin J. Schaffner has said that all he knows of
writing he learned under Felix Jackson.

Person to Person

Edward R. Murrow's fame and reputation stemmed from three
words, "This is London," as he reported the daily events
of the Second World War for CBS Radio. In 1951, he trans-

ferred his news analysis program Hear It Now, which he co-
produced with Fred W. Friendly, over to CBS Television,
where it became See It Now. As he had for radio, Murrow
set the standard for television journalists; Murrow and
Friendly, later to become president of CBS News, set the
standard for television journalism.

The most exciting television event of the 1953-1954
television season was Joseph McCarthy and See It Now. After two programs on the worst of McCarthy, deliberately
edited to reveal the demagogue in him, the senator accepted
Murrow's offer of equal time and appeared on See It Now on
April 6; this time around, he himself helped damage his reputation. In the same 1953-1954 season, Murrow further extended himself in television with Person to Person, for which
Schaffner served as a permanent director. Until then everything Murrow had done in the media was in the realm of news
and public affairs. Person to Person was primarily an entertainment program with Murrow as host. In his biography of
Murrow, Alexander Kendrick writes:

> Person-to-Person [sic] attracted a much larger and
> entirely different audience from the faithful follow-
> ers of See It Now and the radio commentaries, and
> the only controversy it ever aroused was the one
> among Murrow's friends of why he had ever deigned
> to undertake it. [31]

Not considering it the most effective use of Murrow, Fred W.
Friendly was not involved with Person to Person. Friendly,
however, has written pithily about the show:

> The combination of Ed's prestige and the drive and
> the talent of its producers, Jesse Zousmer and John
> Aaron, made Person to Person a Friday night ritual
> in over eight million American homes. This show
> also gave Murrow the only "keeping money" he ever
> earned. [32]

Zousmer had written copy for Murrow; Aaron was a
researcher and Murrow's idea man--indeed, Person to Person
was his idea. Murrow described the genesis of the program
in the following way:

> One night we were having a bull session about the

most common human emotion. Near the top of our
list was the sexual urge, but we had to rule that
out so far as television is concerned. Our next
vote was for curiosity in its broadest sense. Then
we narrowed that down to curiosity about how well-
known people live. One of us ... said, "No one
can walk down the street and pass a window with
the blind up and the lights on without looking in.
It's irresistible." So we concluded if we could move
our cameras inside the homes of interesting people
and show other people how they live, everybody's
natural curiosity would give us our audience. [33]

Zousmer and Aaron saw to it that the show featured mostly
show business personalities; Murrow's task was to keep the
program informal and ask the sort of questions that would
be interesting to the greatest number of people.

Person to Person depended on state-of-the-art technology. Thanks to the coast to coast cable link-up, it was
possible to broadcast this program live every week on a na-
tionwide basis. A 40' tower had to be constructed at each
location; taller towers were constructed at some of the more
inaccessible areas so that the microwave dish would be high
enough to throw a beam at the transmitter. Also crucial to
making Person to Person a reality was the new wireless
microphone, short-wave transmitter, also known as the "Murrow mike." These microphones enabled the celebrities to
move freely from room to room--where cameras had already
been set up--displaying paintings or awards, engaging in
their hobbies. The sound was carried over telephone lines.

It is important to remember that, despite the other
technical advances, the television camera then weighed in
excess of 200 pounds. Kendrick has written:

What was intended to convey the impression of a
casual call by Murrow often became, as the New
York Times called it, "a state visit." Each of the
two homes, besides receiving the cameras, the
lights and the miles of wire, was invaded by six
men of the camera crew, six more for microwave
relays, electricians, producers, directors, makeup
artists and telephone company engineers, while
twenty-six men were required at the studio to
receive the incoming pictures. [34]

Each half-hour program consisted of two interviews. The visits cost anywhere from $15,000 to $30,000; each show cost from $30,000 to $50,000 to produce.

Murrow remained at Studio 41 in New York, conducting his interviews from behind a desk, and later without a desk. To screen right of his desk was Murrow's window on the world, which functioned as a large studio monitor. Each interview began with a shot of a still photograph in Murrow's window of the exterior of the location being visited. The camera would move in on the picture, and there would be a dissolve to live action. Person to Person was a combination of an actual visit and a long distance conversation between Murrow and his guests. Murrow had an advantage as he could watch the guests on his large studio monitor; the interviewees had to be content to address themselves to Murrow's voice coming out of a loudspeaker concealed from the cameras in their homes.

Person to Person was broadcast over CBS on Friday evenings, 10:30-11:00, premiering on October 2, 1953 with visits to Leopold Stokowski and his wife Gloria Vanderbilt, and then to Brooklyn Dodgers catcher Roy Campanella. There were problems with the sound for the first interview and problems with the picture for the second. As was to be expected for any live television show, especially for an unprecedented show of this scale, Person to Person would have its share of technical difficulties: power failures, trees falling on equipment, the sound truck cutting off the audio. Nonetheless, the show quickly found its audience and was given a Sylvania Award for its technical achievements.

Time permitting, there would be a quick crawl of the credits. Murrow would simply say, "Those are some of the people who made tonight's program possible." The crawl would read: "Produced by John Aaron and Jesse Zousmer, with Charles N. Hill, John Horn, David Moore, Robert M. Sammon, Aaron Ehrlich, and Franklin Schaffner." The name Liz Schofield would later be added to the list; Schaffner's credit remained in last position. John Horn, David Moore, Aaron Ehrlich, and Liz Schofield were the researcher/writers for the show; the two field directors were Charles N. Hill and Robert M. Sammon, who had been Schaffner's technical director for the New York City Golden Jubilee Parade.[35]

Franklin Schaffner was the logical choice for the job
of studio director: he had come from The March of Time,
had a television news and public affairs background, had
worked with Murrow on the 1948 political conventions, and,
in addition to live drama, had experience with magazine and
variety shows. Person to Person was a unique amalgam of
these elements. The only problem was that Schaffner was
doing Studio One, and might not have the time.

Schaffner was delighted to be asked; he could make
time. Person to Person would take up a couple of evenings
out of Schaffner's week for four years. As Studio One rehearsals at Central Plaza always broke at 6:00 p.m., Schaffner could easily get to Grand Central Station by 6:30. During the week he would meet with the production team of
Aaron and Zousmer and field directors Hill and Sammon to
discuss what they would be doing on the upcoming show.
On Friday, Schaffner would be at the Grand Central Studios at 6:30; Studio 41 would not be available until 7:30, giving him enough time for a leisurely dinner. Although not
involved in the selection of the guests, Schaffner had experimented with the set and, in particular, Murrow's window
on the world; he was responsible for all that went in that
window. Hill and Sammon directed and edited each of their
twelve and a half- to thirteen-minute segments from the
guests' homes; Schaffner directed and edited in the studio
with Murrow.

When Studio 41 became available, everybody would
first get organized, and then the field directors would start
feeding in; Murrow's run-through served as the dress rehearsal. Schaffner would sit in the control room, wearing
two sets of headphones--one linking him to the field directors, and the other to Murrow, the floor manager, and the
cameramen. Also responsible for the live commercials,
Schaffner, during the two hours he had before broadcast,
would have to rehearse them as well. By the time the show
was ready to air, Schaffner would know every shot that
was going to come up except, of course, for a technical
emergency. Sometimes he would ask the field directors to
move in closer, or request that they not get too fancy,
considering the visual limitations of the small black and
white television screen. The studio director chose when
to cut to Murrow or to the field, and dictated the rhythm
of the program.

Fortunately, a great number of the Person to Person kinescopes survive, featuring interviews with such celebrities as Humphrey Bogart, Marlon Brando, Marilyn Monroe, and Frank Sinatra; a viewer's personal interest in a particular celebrity will determine his or her interest in the interview. Murrow is an impeccable host, and, although he is as interesting as any of the interviewees, defers attention to the guest, never asking embarrassing questions. Schaffner only cuts to Murrow two or three times during the course of an interview; occasionally there will be a wide two-shot of Murrow at his desk talking to the subject in the window on the world, thereby creating an unusual live split-screen effect.

In the beginning, as on October 30, 1953, when Person to Person visited the Boston apartment of the recently wed Mr. and Mrs. John F. Kennedy, the guests and cameras remain in the same room. What Schaffner put into Murrow's window would gradually grow more complex and sophisticated. By March 12, 1954, the cameras show General David Sarnoff of RCA walking from his study, descending a flight of stairs, and reappearing in his living room. In the April 8, 1954 visit, Groucho Marx, moving from room to room, sings with his daughter Melinda, introduces his cook and maid, shoots pool, and plays You Bet Your Life with Murrow; the framing of the peripatetic Groucho is consistently off center--not due to poor camerawork, but to Groucho's incessant pacing. [36]

By January 3, 1958, Person to Person was technically coordinated enough to visit another Marx brother: a surrealist's delight, Harpo Marx remains mute, but he doesn't stand still for a second. Move for move, the cameras follow him as he smokes, whistles, and gestures from bedroom to living room, standing on his head, reading in bed; he runs amok, in and out of his house, finally jumping into a golf cart and taking a mad spin around his Palm Springs ranch.

Perhaps Person to Person's most memorable moment came when Murrow visited Fidel Castro in Havana on February 6, 1959. Speaking in his smooth and flawless English, Castro introduces his son Fidelito, who, educated in America, is a charming and well-mannered boy; the interview with the elder Castro continues--before Fidelito's microphone

is cut off, and the younger Castro can be heard offscreen
chatting rapidly in Spanish. When Murrow casually asks
him the source of the money for his revolution, Castro
stumbles over the question, his command of English suddenly failing him. He speaks off to the side in Spanish,
and, when he recomposes himself, answers in pure American double-talk.

    Schaffner contributed to the success of Person to
Person, directing every show from its premiere in 1953 until the last show of the 1956-1957 season, when he would
find his television work coming out of Los Angeles. No
longer could he be the permanent studio director, but such
was his affection for the show that he would regularly return from his Playhouse 90 assignments in Los Angeles to
direct Person to Person in New York. "I loved that program," he says. "I got a big kick out of doing that goddamned thing."

    In a sense, such talk shows as The Tonight Show are
an outgrowth of Person to Person--but, by visiting celebrities
in their own homes, Person to Person had a more satisfying
format. The audience can watch Murrow in the studio watching the window on the world of the guests in their homes;
these different removes add to the fascination of the show.
Whereas The Tonight Show has prospered under a handful
of different hosts, it is hard to imagine Person to Person
without Edward R. Murrow--as Charles Collingwood would
discover when he replaced Murrow at the end of the show's
run. Murrow set the tone for the show: he could hobnob
with Eleanor Roosevelt, and get away with it because the
audience would want to see the rapport between the two;
the guests and the audience believed in him. Murrow and
his ethos were unique; any discussion of Person to Person
must begin and end with Edward R. Murrow.

Studio One, 1954-1956

Franklin Schaffner and Felix Jackson developed a standing
routine for the three years they worked together on Studio
One. Whenever he gave the director a new script, Jackson
recalls, Schaffner would disappear to his office, read it,
and an hour later would return to ask, "Are you serious?"

Jackson was indeed serious when he gave the director the first script for the new television year. The seventh season of <u>Studio One</u> premiered with more thunder provided by Reginald Rose on September 20, 1954. "Twelve Angry Men" was the television event of the year and the most honored show in <u>Studio One</u>'s history. The teleplay originated out of Rose's experience of serving as a juror in a manslaughter trial; Felix Jackson, himself serving jury duty at the time, urged Rose to write the script. Hubbell Robinson objected to the idea--on the not unreasonable grounds that no television drama could be successfully confined to one room. Jackson persisted, hiring Robert Cummings, an old friend from his Universal days whom he affectionately confused with Ronald Reagan, to play the lead, Juror No. 8. Still identified as a movie star, Cummings, on the basis of this show, would have his own series, <u>Love That Bob</u>, on the air by January 1955.

Well-written though it was, the script presented the director with problems beyond a one-set limitation. Ordinarily, a television drama would consist of three, possibly four characters; this show had to have twelve clearly defined characters. Rose saw to that by writing twelve different, recognizably human types--the rest was up to the actors. In executing Rose's script, Jackson and Schaffner cast it expertly: the show featured superb ensemble acting by Robert Cummings, Franchot Tone, Edward Arnold, John Beal, Walter Abel, Bart Burns, Lee Phillips, Paul Hartman, Joseph Sweeney, George Voskovec, Norman Fell, and Will West as the twelve angry men.

The show opens with the jurors entering through a door to the top left of the frame: in a foreshadowing of events to come, No. 8 (Cummings) bumps into No. 3 (Tone). The jurors proceed to sit around the long table; a boy has been tried for killing his father, and his fate is in their hands. When eleven vote guilty on the first ballot, No. 8 begins to speak out, thereafter serving, in effect, as a defense attorney for the rest of the teleplay. Robert Cummings is noticeably nervous and uncomfortable, flubbing several lines, but this does not detract from the story-- juror No. 8 alone begs to differ from the majority vote; as for Franchot Tone and Edward Arnold, they merely have to step in front of the cameras to be convincing and powerful.

Unfortunately, the second half of the show is lost:
the Museum of Broadcasting, where it is also known as "Six
Angry Men," only has the first half hour; neither producer,
director, writer, star, nor the CBS network warehouse has
a complete copy of this show. "Six Angry Men," nonetheless, captures the viewer's attention at once; Schaffner's
direction gets the viewer involved. His camera is restless,
constantly on the move; he even uses a camera crane which
periodically sweeps over the long table.

Schaffner met the technical challenge of "Twelve Angry Men" and the potentially static one-room set; he even
designed a 360-degree shot which required each of the set's
four walls to be moved in and out during the camera move.
Reginald Rose was sufficiently impressed to write:

> The production problems of Twelve Angry Men were,
> for what seemed like a reasonably simple show, in-
> credibly involved. The set, to be realistic, had to
> be small and cramped. This, of course, inhibited
> the movement and cameras and presented director
> Frank Schaffner with an endless traffic jam which
> would have had Robert Moses spinning like a ball-
> bearing top. Somehow, however, Mr. Schaffner
> managed to capture the speaker of each line on
> camera at precisely the right moment and composed
> starkly realistic, tension-filled pictures of the re-
> actions to those lines. This was perhaps the best-
> directed show I've ever seen on television and Mr.
> Schaffner won a mantel-piecefull of awards for it,
> including the Christopher Award, the Sylvania
> Award and the Academy of Television Arts and
> Sciences Award. [37]

In addition, "Twelve Angry Men" won Emmies for Mr. Jackson, Mr. Cummings, and Mr. Rose himself.

On October 18, 1954, Schaffner directed Studio One's
first color telecast, "The Boy Who Changed the World,"
commemorating the anniversary of Thomas Edison's death,
with Charles Edison, the inventor's grandson, as guest.
Since Studio 42 couldn't be dressed for color, the show had
to be televised from a rented theatre. (Actually, CBS'
first colorcast was Premiere on June 25, 1951--virtually a
meaningless gesture as only perhaps 25 out of the ten

million television sets then in use were equipped to receive
CBS color. In 1953, not unlike in 1941, when it had adopted
NBC's black and white standards over CBS' color system,
the FCC adopted NBC's color standards--RCA was obviously
larger and more powerful than CBS; for the second time,
CBS had to defer to RCA's influence, and start all over
again.) Color broadcasting had officially become a reality,
and "The Boy Who Changed the World" was televised over
CBS in NBC's "living color."

The climactic scene in "The Man Who Owned the Town,"
a western Schaffner directed on November 1, was supposed
to be when the sheriff smashed his shotgun through a bar
window to break up a fight; as televised, the actor playing
the sheriff, while getting into position, accidentally broke
the window, long before his cue. Later, the villain of the
piece lost his gun; Schaffner had to hold him in a long
close-up while the actor desperately tried to find the gun
with his feet. Eventually the stage manager found the
prop, and crawled on the floor to return it to the villain.

Schaffner directed an early instance of mass media
crossfeeding each other to mutual advantage. Jackson was
worried about what he considered a weak script until he
made a fast deal with Mitch Miller, head of CBS Records:
the show being about a disc jockey, Miller gave him a new
record, and, in return, Jackson named the show after the
record's title. "Let Me Go, Lover" aired on November 13,
and the song recorded by Joan Weber became an immediate
hit. Hanging on the wall of Felix Jackson's office today is
a gold record, autographed by Mitch Miller, of "Let Me Go,
Lover."

"A Stranger May Die" was presented on February 7,
1955 in a style now known as docudrama. Its dependent
set was the facade of a building from which a man threatened to commit suicide; Carroll Baker, in her first television exposure, was featured as a gangster moll. At the
beginning of the second act, Jack Warden, who was otherwise superb as the stranger of the title, jumped to a scene
late in the act, prompting the rest of the actors to jump
ahead and complete the later scene; there was panic in the
control room and on the floor. An eyewitness to that scene,
Felix Jackson, comments:

> This was when Frank was great. He was very or-
> ganized, and he covered it all up completely, like
> it was strategy. His alertness in these cases and
> the way he is in emergencies is fabulous. He saved
> several shows.

In this crisis, Schaffner sent a message to Warden telling
the actor to return to the beginning of the second act, and,
at its end, to ad lib a short variation of what he had already said. The show fell back in order, but when time
came to repeat the scene, Warden, instead of ad libbing,
began to babble incoherently. At the end of the telecast,
Marlene Dietrich, who only called when her daughter Maria
Riva appeared on the show, telephoned Jackson to compliment him and say how much she had enjoyed "A Stranger
May Die."

The Best of Broadway was the first color series to
air on CBS, Telecast monthly on Wednesday evenings from
10-11:00 in the 1954-1955 season, it featured adaptations of
such well-known plays as The Man Who Came to Dinner and
The Philadelphia Story. Its producer was Martin Manulis, a
stage director who had come to CBS as Worthington Miner's
assistant, and who would later become Schaffner's collaborator on Playhouse 90.

During the course of the television season, Climax, a
dramatic anthology produced in Los Angeles, ran into trouble. Manulis was reassigned to it, and moved to the west
coast, taking with him his young directorial protégé, John
Frankenheimer. Felix Jackson was called in to produce
The Best of Broadway for the remainder of the season,
while simultaneously overseeing Studio One. Not unexpectedly, he brought Schaffner over to direct the series'
final production on May 4, 1955. Based on the play by
Philip Dunning and George Abbot, "Broadway," a property
which Jackson himself had adapted for Universal's 1942
film version, it featured Joseph Cotten, Piper Laurie,
Keenan Wynn, and Gene Nelson. It offered Schaffner his
second experience with color television for the season.

For the final show of the seventh season of Studio
One on June 13, 1955, Jackson and Schaffner collaborated
on another memorable original by Reginald Rose, "The Incredible World of Horace Ford," starring Art Carney and

featuring, as Horace's friend, Jason Robards, Jr. in one of
his earliest television appearances.   The author's intention
was "to tell a simple horror story about an everyday man
with a somewhat exaggerated but everyday kind of problem,
and, in so doing, point out that the funny, tender childhood memories we cling to are often distorted and unreal."[38]

Horace (Carney), a grown-up boy who works for a
toy company, is beginning to have emotional problems.   Es-
caping to the cherished neighborhood of his youth, he finds
his old friends exactly as they were 25 years ago.   Seeing
the children, Horace is so alarmed that he flees, losing his
gold watch.   Hermy, his childhood nemesis, shows up at
Horace's house to return the gold watch at the end of the
first act, as he also does at the end of the second act.   On
his 35th birthday, the day he is fired from his job, Horace
chooses not to go home, where his wife has prepared a party, but to the old neighborhood.   Once there, Horace speaks
with a child's voice, and the other children beat him up for
not inviting them to his birthday party.   The third act ends
with Hermy once again returning Horace's watch, only this
time it is not a gold watch but a Mickey Mouse one.

The actors didn't quite understand the script as they
rehearsed.   Even though Reginald Rose, as he had with
"Thunder on Sycamore Street," volunteered to change it,
the show went on the air as originally conceived, and Art
Carney was praised for his performance.   "The Incredible
World of Horace Ford" also generated a lot of controversy--
a new dimension brought to Studio One by Felix Jackson.

CBS introduced The $64,000 Question on June 7, 1955,
and it quickly became the most popular show on television.
It was such a phenomenon that Studio One presented "Uncle
Ed and Circumstances," a story written by and starring
Jackie Gleason as a contestant on The $64,000 Question, in
the fall.   The $64,000 Question, however, would be a cas-
ualty of the quiz show scandals of 1958.   Of more lasting
television importance, Gunsmoke debuted on CBS, September 10, 1955, signalling the onslaught of the television
western.

The eighth season of Studio One proved to be the
final year for both Franklin Schaffner, after six years, and
Felix Jackson, after three years.   Until 1955, Schaffner and

Paul Nickell had rotated as the two permanent directors for
Studio One; basically, the only time another director was
ever needed was when one of the regular directors was
either ill or doing an outside assignment. Convinced that
the work load was too much of a strain on his two directors, and despite their protestations to the contrary, Jackson brought in Bill Brown to be the third regular director
for the new Studio One year.

    "Shakedown Cruise" on November 7 marked Schaff-
ner's first collaboration with Loring Mandel. Ordinarily, a
typical script for Studio One would go through three steps:
Florence Britten, the script editor, would work with the
writer until the script was ready to be submitted to the
producer; Jackson would then work with the writer until
he thought the script was in shape to be produced; at this
point, the script was turned over to the director, who, if
he felt the script needed some final touches, was free to
work with the writer. In most cases, a script was accepted
and on the air in three weeks. But "Shakedown Cruise" is
a good example of the route some scripts had to take before
they were produced.

    Mandel, a young writer with radio and television
scriptwriting experience in Chicago, came to New York with
a couple of scripts under his arm; the scripts were eventually submitted to Florence Britten who, although she rejected them, liked Mandel's writing, and asked him to come
again. Mandel returned with an idea of a documentary
based on the actual sinking of a submarine. Britten told
him a documentary was out of the question, but that Studio
One would do it as fiction. Mandel rewrote the script and
submitted it in November 1954. Jackson approved the script
and sent it to McCann-Erickson in December; agency approval came in February 1955. After screening a kinescope
of "Dry Run," the submarine show Schaffner had directed
with Walter Matthau on December 7, 1953, Mandel met with
the director to discuss the material. The script was then
submitted for Navy approval, so that Studio One could use
Navy equipment. In September, Studio One sent Mandel to
Washington to consult with the Navy and determine its ob-
jectives; Mandel then rewrote the script to get Navy approval. Finally, after some minor changes by Britten, Jackson, and Schaffner, "Shakedown Cruise" was ready to be
televised; the entire process had taken over a year. For

his extracurricular efforts, Mandel received a bonus of $200 from Studio One.

Whenever he couldn't get a big name to play the male lead, Felix Jackson likes to say, he would hire Walter Matthau or Richard Kiley. Since "Shakedown Cruise" would involve another wet floor and slippery deck, and Matthau had already done his Schaffner submarine show, it was Kiley's turn to play the lead. Half of a submarine was built for the show, to be enclosed and flooded during the telecast. Despite all the special effects, writer Mayo Simon insists the most compelling moment of the program came in a close-up of Lee Marvin: since the setting was a hot and steamy submarine, a bead of perspiration formed at the bridge of his nose and rolled down to the tip of his nose, settling there; for all of Marvin's frenzied histrionics, the drop of sweat remained affixed to the tip of his nose, just as surely as if it had been written that way.

Ford Star Jubilee was a series of monthly specials that were telecast live on Saturday nights, 9:30-11:00, from September 24, 1955 to November 3, 1956. Each program was expensively produced and broadcast in color, ranging from drama ("Blithe Spirit" with Lauren Bacall and Noel Coward) to musical ("High Tor" with Bing Crosby and Julie Andrews) to variety ("The Judy Garland Show") to film (the first telecast of M-G-M's The Wizard of Oz). But Ford Star Jubilee's most highly regarded program turned out to be "The Caine Mutiny Court Martial," produced by Paul Gregory and directed by Franklin Schaffner on November 19, 1955.

Formerly an actor and an agent, Paul Gregory began as a producer by persuading client Charles Laughton into forming Laughton Tours, for which the actor went to city after city reading from the Bible and from literary classics. Expanding on the format, Gregory next put together a reading tour of Bernard Shaw's Don Juan in Hell with Laughton, Agnes Moorehead, Cedric Hardwicke, and Charles Boyer as Don Juan. Gregory perfected his own kind of living, touring theatre with John Brown's Body, featuring Tyrone Power, Anne Baxter, and Raymond Massey; Three for Tonight, with Marge and Gower Champion, and Harry Belafonte; and most notably with The Caine Mutiny Court Martial, featuring Henry Fonda, Lloyd Nolan, and John Hodiak.

Stanley Kramer had already purchased the motion
picture rights to Herman Wouk's novel, but Gregory was
able to secure theatrical rights. Directed by co-producer
Charles Laughton, who stepped in during the last week of
rehearsal to replace original director Dick Powell, Gregory's
Wouk production was in theatres a year before Kramer's.
After producing The Night of the Hunter (1955), a film directed by Laughton, Gregory branched into television in
1955 by agreeing to produce specials for Ford Star Jubilee.
For his television production of "The Caine Mutiny Court
Martial," Gregory hired a hot young director who had recently won acclaim for "Twelve Angry Men," another strong
drama about men in a courtroom.

The program would be telecast from CBS' brand new,
state of the art facilities at Television City in Los Angeles.
Unable to bring a New York crew with him, Schaffner found
himself running training sessions for the local crews. CBS
supervisor for this program was Harry Ackerman, then Executive Director of Special Productions, who would later
produce a long string of successful series for Screen Gems,
including Gidget, The Flying Nun, and Bewitched. Although
the program was broadcast in color, only black and white
kinescopes survive: it seems more appropriate in black and
white, more realistic; some of the close-ups are as startling
as newspaper headlines. The courtroom set is sparsely
dressed and a little stylized. Source light comes through a
high window, casting dark shadows on the floor; clouds of
light bounce off the floor. The program begins and ends
with an anonymous male voice reading articles 184-187 from
the Navy Regulations; the camera slowly glides around the
courtroom.

After the opening credits, a sailor opens the doors to
the courtroom, and a subjective camera takes the spectator
into the action. After the first commercial, action begins
with a crane shot, moving left to right behind the judge's
bench. Queeg enters: the camera remains behind the judge,
Captain Blakely, facing Queeg. Schaffner cuts to a reverse
angle as Blakely swears Queeg in, and the camera booms up
accordingly; then there is a cut to a medium shot of Queeg,
already seated and ready to talk.

Originally, Schaffner had asked Loring Mandel to
write the "Caine Mutiny Court Martial" adaptation--even

before "Shakedown Cruise" was televised. Paul Gregory,
however, perhaps in hopes of winning an award, decided to
do the adaptation himself--and Schaffner ended up doing
most of the work himself. The play itself was essentially a
scissors and paste version of the novel: selected, juggled,
or abridged, all the words came from Herman Wouk, who appropriately received author's credit. In the end, the television script was essentially a scissors and paste version of
a scissors and paste job.

As its title suggests, the play concentrates solely on
the trial; the film covered more of the book. Henry Fonda
was in the play, and the emphasis was on Lieutenant Greenwald; Humphrey Bogart was in the film, and the emphasis
was on Captain Queeg. The play is concerned about Barney
Greenwald's Jewish mother; the film is not. Although Schaffner inherited an acting company with two years experience,
there had been two major changes: Henry Fonda had departed;
more shockingly, John Hodiak, who played Stephen Maryck,
had died. Like Van Johnson in the film, Frank Lovejoy is
miscast as Maryck in the telecast. Barry Sullivan is at least
adequate as Greenwald, the man of conscience who would
rather prosecute Maryck, and definitely not as supercilious
as Jose Ferrer is in the film--but he is no Fonda, and eventually becomes a little tiresome in the party scene, remind-
ing everybody that men like Queeg kept his mother from becoming a bar of soap. As a direct result, attention in the
teleplay refocuses on Philip Francis Queeg: Lloyd Nolan
would win an Emmy for his performance. A comparison with
Bogart's Queeg is inevitable: Bogart's Queeg is more arche-
typal, mythic; Nolan's Queeg more blue collar, more realistic. Both are excellent in their respective ways, the mythic
versus the real--a central difference between the film and
television media.

At the conclusion of the performance, Charles Laughton appears on camera to pay tribute to the late John Hodiak. Laughton's appearance might be perceived to raise
questions of auteurship, especially as the program contains
two direction credits: "As directed for the stage by Charles
Laughton" and "Directed for television by Franklin Schaffner"; any such discussion, however, would also have to include Dick Powell, the original stage director. In the end,
the fact remains that Schaffner worked on the material,
chose all the shots, and was in the control room the evening
"The Caine Mutiny Court Martial" was televised.

Benefiting from more money, time, and space to rehearse, the production is easily the most polished television
drama Schaffner had yet directed; he took full advantage of
the more spacious facilities he found himself in at Television City. Always graceful, his moving camera shots now
become elegant and stately; the budget also enabled him to
make effective use of a crane. With these tools, Schaffner
was able to keep a fundamentally dialogue-bound show on
the move; he richly deserved the Emmy he would receive
for his direction of "The Caine Mutiny Court Martial." Curiously, since there is no writer's credit on the teleplay,
and there is nothing in the show that isn't in the Wouk
novel, Paul Gregory and Franklin Schaffner would win Emmies for the adaptation; yet, in their respective roles as
producer and director, Paul Gregory and Franklin Schaffner
were indeed responsible for the best television adaptation of
1955-1956.

Rod Serling contributed a couple of scripts that
Schaffner directed in his final season at Studio One. "The
Man Who Caught the Ball at Coogan's Bluff," November 28,
1955, was a whimsical comedy bolstered by fine performances
by Alan Young and Giselle MacKenzie. "The Arena," April
9, 1956, was Serling's version of Mr. Smith Goes to Washington, concerning Frank Norton (Wendell Corey), an idealistic young man who has been appointed to the senate. Despite warnings from his savvy aide Feeney (Chester Morris),
Norton, himself the son of a senator, allows himself to be
baited by the press into insulting Rogers (John Cromwell),
his father's old nemesis, the senior senator of the state.
Rogers gets his revenge by humiliating Norton in the senate. The senate set is complete with gallery, where approximately 25 extras are visible--live television had begun
to go to more elaborate lengths to attract the viewer. When
Norton later watches Rogers in a live television newscast,
Schaffner, of course, shoots the interview live instead of
using film inserts. Schaffner's final Studio One assignment
on May 26, 1956 was "Family Protection," starring Joanne
Woodward, who would be the leading lady in his first film.

With the participation of a third Studio One director,
Person to Person notwithstanding, Schaffner had ample time
to go shopping around and determine his value. In addition to his Emmy-winning direction of "Twelve Angry Men,"
"The Caine Mutiny Court Martial" would win him two more

Emmies. Putting himself on the market, Schaffner received an unprecedented offer: he would produce and direct his own shows--and have absolute script control.

Felix Jackson would later become vice-president of NBC Programs, NBC-TV, West Coast in 1960, and vice-president of NBC Productions in 1963: Jackson and Schaffner would next cross professional paths at NBC. Succeeding Jackson as producer of Studio One was Herbert Brodkin. In January 1958, the show was moved to the West Coast where it would be renamed Studio One in Hollywood; its demise would come a few months later.

The Kaiser Aluminum Hour

The Kaiser Aluminum Hour was created by Worthington Miner, now a producer with the National Broadcasting Company, who went to San Francisco to meet Henry J. Kaiser and sold the show over a convivial lunch, making up the plots of 13 scripts on the spot; the next day, neither he nor Kaiser nor anyone else could remember what he had said. Miner's agent at the time was Ted Ashley of the Ashley-Steiner Agency, and, as he was a new Ashley client, Schaffner immediately became part of the package, forming Gilchrist Productions, named after his wife, Jean Gilchrist.

Schaffner recommended a friend, another new Ashley client, as part of the package: Fielder Cook had made a name for himself at the J. Walter Thompson advertising agency as a producer-director of Kraft Television Theatre, most notably for his production of Rod Serling's "Patterns." Serling having little knowledge of the real business world, Cook had helped rewrite the script and amended its title from "Pattern" to "Patterns." Televised over NBC on January 12, 1955, the program met with such an enthusiastic response that Cook not only restaged the production four weeks later for television but also directed the film version released by United Artists in 1956.

In turn, Cook recommended another friend be part of the team. A relative newcomer, George Roy Hill had sold an original script, "My Brother's Keeper," to Kraft in 1954, and quickly became a story editor, then an A.D. to Cook,

and finally a producer-director for the Thompson agency,
which produced Kraft Television Theatre. By 1956, Hill
adapted, produced, and directed Kraft's highly acclaimed
"A Night to Remember," in which he sank the Titanic on
live television.

    Under the terms of agreement Ted Ashley negotiated
with NBC and Henry J. Kaiser, The Kaiser Aluminum Hour
inherited the Tuesday 9:30-10:30 time slot vacated by Playwrights '56, Fred Coe's unsuccessful attempt to produce
another quality anthology for NBC. As executive producer,
Worthington Miner was the overseer: Unit Four would produce 20 color telecasts for Kaiser, to be broadcast on alternate weeks with Armstrong Circle Theater. Each of the
three producer-directors would direct six shows, the other
two would be decided on at a later date. Sharing the same
NBC crew at Studio 8H in New York, the three young turks
had an approximate $50,000 per show budget, out of which
they personally collected $6,000. Furthermore, Ashley had
arranged it so that they would have the contractual right to
do any type of material they wanted to do.

    Fielder Cook being a Shakespearean scholar and George
Roy Hill a music scholar, Unit Four was a company of rare
intelligence and sophistication: each was a gentleman; each
had a formidable background in the arts. The three young
producer-directors were tall, slender, and attractive; Worthington Miner was avuncular and dynamic. Schaffner, Cook,
and Hill had reached the top level of television directors, a
group that also included Delbert Mann, Arthur Penn, Sidney
Lumet, and John Frankenheimer; The Kaiser Aluminum Hour
was proof that three talented directors had made it big
enough to be given their own show.

    Since Hill had a film script commitment with Joseph L.
Mankiewicz, Schaffner and Cook agreed to do the early
shows, at the rate of one a month each. Marian Searchinger
was appointed script editor, but the material always reflected
the personality and style of the show's director. In a generalization, Worthington Miner would later say that Cook
specialized in romantic dramas, Hill in comedies, and Schaffner in action shows.

    Schaffner was set to direct the July 3, 1956 premiere,
only a few weeks after his final Studio One telecast; there

Worthington Miner and the three young turks of Unit Four, 1956: (l. to r.) Fielder Cook, Schaffner, Miner, George Roy Hill.

was then no such thing as a second season in the television
year, much less a third season, so it was not in the least
unusual for a major television show to make its debut in the
summer. Nor was Schaffner, as he would later say, especially concerned about his new responsibilities on the show:

> A producer's function is basically one of judgment
> and choice. He decides whether the script is worth
> doing. He makes his choice of the best talent but
> when the work really starts, the producer is finished.
> Then it's up to the writer and director and the ac-
> tors. They will make it come out right or wrong. [39]

In other words, the producer's role was a natural extension
of what he was already doing as a director.

Unexpectedly, Schaffner ran into immediate trouble.
For the opening show, he had chosen an original script by
Loring Mandel entitled "The Healer," about an evangelist
with extrasensory perception; Young and Rubicam, the advertising agency that had the Kaiser account, rejected the
script. The Unit Four partners found this very interesting,
as they had been under the impression that they had final
say on the script. "We had nothing but trouble on approv-
als on that show," Schaffner says. "Nothing but trouble."

Schaffner turned again to Mandel for a quick script.
Mandel had an idea for a script based on a true incident
from his army days; he would write it with Mayo Simon, a
friend since their freshman year in high school. After
"Shakedown Cruise" had finally been produced, Mandel and
Simon made a deal: whoever could next sell a script would
collaborate on it with the other; they collaborated on "The
Army Game." Making up an outline in one day, they divided
up the scenes to fit each other's strengths, and after the
first draft was completed, they rewrote each other's work.

The plot concerned a golden boy type, who, when
drafted into the army, has seizures on the rifle range.
Some of the soldiers are sympathetic; some are not. When
a friend overhears the golden boy confess to his mother that
he's faking the seizures, word of it spreads; the company
commander has him stay and lets him become the subject of
intense hazing until the golden boy really breaks down.
Paul Newman was cast as the golden boy, an anti-hero role

not unlike those that typify his film work. An up-and-
coming actor, Newman was then regarded mostly as a Marlon Brando type; although he had already been signed to
star in Somebody Up There Likes Me, Mayo Simon points
out, "It wasn't a major coup to get Paul Newman."

      For whatever reason, Worthington Miner decided to
rewrite the script. Upon learning of the original authors'
displeasure, Miner apologized to them--a producer apologiz-
ing to a writer is absolutely unheard of in today's television
--but this incident would later be used against Miner. Apparently there was a cabal of network executives who conspired to get rid of him from the very start.

      Fielder Cook and George Roy Hill were present in the
control room during the telecast of "The Army Game." Whenever possible, they would consult with each other on scripts,
and attend each other's rehearsals and dress rehearsals.
For the writers of "The Army Game," the most memorable
moment of the telecast came when Paul Newman could not
zip his pants during a scene change, and then the zipper
got stuck. This was live television, and Newman had to go
on, warts and all.

      Schaffner's big show for Kaiser was Jean Anouilh's
"Antigone," on September 11, 1956, adapted by Lewis Galantiere, and featuring Marisa Pavan as Antigone and Claude
Rains as Creon. According to the physical look of the pro-
duction, "Antigone" could take place in the past or in the
future--the limbo sets were designed by Rouben Ter-
Arutunian, who had previously worked with Schaffner on
Studio One, and, after he became a top theatrical set de-
signer, would work with Schaffner again. Joseph Dackow,
Schaffner's A.D. on Studio One, was associate producer,
the new A.D. was Dominick Dunne, and music was by Ben
Ludlow, who had provided the music on Ford Theater.

      Claude Rains is superb as always, making a dignified
and not unsympathetic Creon, saying, "Life is nothing more
than the happiness we get out of it." Dressed in a modern-
day suit, Alexander Scourby serves as on-camera narrator
and chorus, giving a very spirited performance, introducing,
commenting on, and reacting to the action. What puts a
damper on this production of "Antigone" is Marisa Pavan's
performance. She is exceptionally pretty, and her looks

have the right amount of pathos, but the demands of the
role are beyond her capabilities; not only does she speak
heavily accented English, her voice quality is also grating
--her dialogue is virtually unintelligible throughout the
show.

The show, however, is excellently directed. Although
most of the action is in dialogue--there is no on-screen vio-
lence--"Antigone" is often mentioned as an example of a
Schaffner action show, in this case meaning a large set and
a lot of involved camera moves. Even on the small television screen, Schaffner's cameras fully exploit the size of the
set; the crane shots that link Scourby to the action are impressive. The leading lady notwithstanding, the boom operators and audio man do a superlative job in keeping the
words as audible as possible, covering the wide expanse of
space on the set without intruding into camera range. Although only black and white kinescopes of Schaffner's Kaiser
shows exist, it is plainly visible that all of the special effects in "Antigone" come through the lighting. All of these
superlatives put together, unfortunately, cannot compensate
for the performance in the title role.

Unit Four achieved what it had set out to do: The
Kaiser Aluminum Hour was well received, and had higher
ratings than Playwrights '56 as well as the alternate show
Armstrong Circle Theatre--no mean feat considering that it
was up against The $64,000 Question. Trouble, however,
had been brewing from the very start. "Kaiser was the fly
in the ointment--he was more than a fly--he was an octopus,"
said Worthington Miner. "It was a disaster; there was such
bad feelings, the morale was so terrible."

Henry J. Kaiser was then living in Hawaii, and could
not receive direct transmission from the mainland. About a
half dozen shows into the season, when he was able to see
the program that bore his name, Kaiser didn't like what he
saw, specifically citing Schaffner's "Antigone" and Cook's
production of "Cracker Money." The show was too radical
for his tastes, he claimed; it was against Americana and
motherhood. Kaiser promptly demanded script control,
which had been written into his contract--NBC, in an effort to get the show on the air, had given final script approval to both Unit Four and Henry J. Kaiser. "Tony
[Miner] wanted to put on more significant social dramas,"

Hill says. "It was just a mismatching of intentions, that's all." As a result of his battles with Kaiser, Miner would be asked to leave the show--both by network and sponsor.

Perhaps as a direct consequence of this battle, the other two extant kinescopes of Kaiser shows directed by Schaffner are merely routine. "Angel's Ransom," broadcast on October 23, 1956, is set entirely on a yacht--undoubtedly the challenge to the director was to give movement to a show with a claustrophobic set. This he again accomplished with a moving camera, sometimes with a dolly on the deck of the yacht, sometimes with a crane moving around the exterior of the yacht. Although Hume Cronyn, in a shrewd piece of casting, makes a splendidly nasty villain, the script, written especially for the series by Evan Hunter from a novel by David Dodge, is entirely predictable and of no special interest.

"The Rag Jungle," written by Steven Gethers, was broadcast on November 20. Again starring Paul Newman, and featuring very intense performances by Nehemiah Persoff as a mobster named Brill and Don Gordon as his henchman Sam, it purports be an exposé of how the mob controls the $2 billion garment industry in New York. Although his business is eventually ruined, Charlie (Newman) vows to fight back against the mob. Newman is interesting to watch as a hotheaded type, but the script is muddled, unconvincing, and uninvolving. There is so much dialogue that the director can scarcely do more than photograph all the different people talking. "The Rag Jungle" was probably intended to be the On the Waterfront of the garment industry, but the story is ultimately too large for the confines of live television drama.

Kaiser had become a lost cause before the halfway point of the season. Stepping into the vacancy left by Worthington Miner was the Ashley-Steiner representative for the show, Jerome Hellman; it was the agent's first involvement in production. When Schaffner, Cook, and Hill eventually broke off from Ashley-Steiner, they signed with Jerome Hellman of the Ziegler-Hellman-Ross Agency. Later producer of Midnight Cowboy (1969) and Coming Home (1978), Hellman would produce his first film, The World of Henry Orient (1964), with direction by his Unit Four colleague, George Roy Hill.

A not inconsiderable benefit of the otherwise ill-fated
Kaiser venture was a new friendship for Schaffner. "We
played Santa Claus for each other's children for ten years,"
George Roy Hill recalls. "Finally I blew it one night by
getting drunk, and, when I left, Frank's little daughter
said, 'That was really Mr. Hill, wasn't it?'" As a Ph.D.
Candidate in Music at Yale, George Hill had gone to Dublin
to research his dissertation. "It was 'The Music and Musical Forms of James Joyce's Finnegan's Wake and Ulysses,'"
he says. "You wonder that I didn't finish?" Sidetracked
by Dublin's Abbey Theatre, he soon directed his first play,
instantly becoming theatre-crazy. Returning to New York
as an actor, he found there already was another George Hill
in Equity, and added the Roy to his name--unaware of the
late film director George Hill at the time, he would have had
to change his name anyway. Soon he discovered television,
and began trying his hand at writing.

Schaffner's final show for Kaiser was aptly titled "So
Short a Season." Hill, who did a rewrite of the Gene Roddenberry script, recalls a scene in which an extra was supposed to come through a swinging door, point his gun at
John Litel, and shoot him. Instead, as the show aired on
February 12, 1957, the gun went off as soon as the extra
got through the door. "Litel went about not realizing he
had been shot about five seconds earlier," he remembers.
Seated in the control room, Hill began laughing so hard
that he fell to the floor. "I was seated with Jean, Frank's
wife," he says, "and Jean wouldn't talk to me for a month
after that."

Unit Four steadfastly refused to give in to Henry J.
Kaiser. "We blew it," Hill says, "and Kaiser fired us, and
gave it to David Susskind." But Kaiser first had to buy
Unit Four out of the show. When Susskind took over, the
ratings decreased; The Kaiser Aluminum Hour went quietly
off the air in June.

Although The Kaiser Aluminum Hour had proved to be
a disappointing experience, Schaffner managed to salvage
the 1956-1957 season by directing "The Great Sebastians"
for Producers' Showcase on April 1, 1957.

Producers' Showcase, NBC's most prestigious and
costly live dramatic anthology, was usually broadcast once

a month on Mondays, 8:00-9:30. Offerings included "Peter Pan" with Mary Martin and Cyril Ritchard; "The Petrified Forest" with Humphrey Bogart, Henry Fonda, and Lauren Bacall; the musical version of Thornton Wilder's "Our Town" with Frank Sinatra, Eva Marie Saint, and Paul Newman. Producers' Showcase also offered major motion picture directors the opportunity to do television adaptations of their own films: Anatole Litvak directed "Mayerling" with Audrey Hepburn; William Wyler directed "The Letter" with Siobhan McKenna. NBC's redoubtable Fred Coe produced the show from 1954 to 1956. Succeeding Coe in the show's final season was Mort Abrahams, a veteran film and television executive at Columbia, the Bank of America, and MCA.

The greatest single attraction of "The Great Sebastians" was that it featured Alfred Lunt and Lynn Fontanne in their television debut. Howard Lindsay and Russel Crouse had specifically written the play for them the previous year; Mort Abrahams had seen the show on the road and had developed a cordial relationship with the Lunts. Being perfectionists by nature, intimately familiar with the play, and curious to see what they would look like on television, the Lunts asked if they could make a kinescope of a complete performance before the air date; Abrahams had to explain why this was not possible.

Schaffner was available, and Abrahams wanted him to direct the show, but first the producer had to clear the director with the Lunts. "When I suggested Schaffner," he recalls, "They wanted to know what he had done, and they wanted to meet him, and, of course, it went swimmingly because he's a very gracious, charming man, very intelligent." Although he showed the Lunts a kinescope of "The Caine Mutiny Court Martial" as an example of Schaffner's work, it wasn't necessary. "They were more interested in meeting him than seeing his work," Abrahams says. "They worked on a kind of instinct for people. They hit it off absolutely." Howard Lindsay was briefly involved in pre-production; Russel Crouse was present during rehearsal, and helpful in cutting the play down to size and writing new bridges. Once he had established a good rapport with the Lunts, Schaffner was most concerned that they not be distracted by all the technical equipment on the set. "They immediately mastered it," he says.

Set in Prague, Czechoslovakia in 1948, "The Great
Sebastians" is fluff, but entertaining fluff with a dash of
social consciousness; Lindsay and Crouse categorized it as
melodramatic comedy. Rudi and Essie, the Great Sebastians,
can perform their sham mind-reading act in five different
languages. As the play begins, Rudi teaches his wife a
new code; part of the fun is that the audience learns the
code along with Essie. "Quickly," for example, becomes
the word for "keys" in the new code, and, as keys are on
his mind, General Zandek (Akim Tamiroff) invites them to
his party: he knows one of his guests is disloyal, and
perhaps the mind-reading team can determine that guest's
identity.

Aware of the political climate, Rudi and Essie have
put all of their money into a rare postage stamp they intend to smuggle out of the country. As a precaution, Rudi
hides the stamp in a pack of American cigarettes at the
general's villa, but Sergeant Javorsky (Simon Oakland),
Zandek's aide, revealing himself to be a commissar, takes
charge and confiscates Rudi's cigarettes. Rudi's friend
Masaryk, the democratic leader, has been murdered; Javorsky wants Rudi to sign a statement damning Masaryk. Essie, on the other hand, being a British citizen, is free to
leave the country. When Javorsky, smoking the last American cigarette, throws the crumpled pack in a bowl on the
table, she steals the key to Rudi's handcuffs, and, before
she leaves, repeats the word "Quickly" and gives her husband a very long kiss. In the program's final shot, Rudi
waits until everyone leaves the room before he unlocks himself, and dashes out of the room. The camera dollies to
the right, revealing a bowl in the foreground; in a moment,
Rudi returns for the cigarette pack, but the stamp falls
out before he can make his escape. Retrieving it, the
Great Sebastian then runs to freedom; the camera booms up
to a long shot of the now deserted room in General Zandek's
villa.

The objective of any director working with the Lunts
was how best to showcase them. This was accomplished in
unhurried two-shots of the stars in "The Great Sebastians";
not a single shot or cut detracts from the Lunts. There
are stories that Alfred Lunt was sick during the broadcast
of this program, and that he lost his collar between Acts I
and II; but none of this is noticeable in the kinescope. What

is immediately obvious is that the Lunts have magic: they
have excellent voices; they have a way with throwaway
lines; they move well and are graceful down to the minutest
gesture. The teaming of the Lunts with Schaffner was fortuitous for television: "The Great Sebastians" was an exercise in elegance.

Playhouse 90

Martin Manulis, the original producer of the series, has
said:

> From the outset, there was a good aura about
> Playhouse 90. The press responded remarkably.
> In a Variety poll taken several years later on all
> shows, regardless of half hour comedy or two hour
> drama or whatever, the critics of the country voted
> Playhouse 90 number one as the all-time series.

Playhouse 90 was the most ambitious show of its kind, the
realization of an idea Worthington Miner had had in a previous decade: a live, 90-minute dramatic anthology. Hubbell Robinson, head of CBS Television, ordered a new
anthology--tentatively titled Program X, later renamed The
Gay 90s, and finally titled Playhouse 90--that would take
advantage of the new CBS Television City studios in Los
Angeles.

For the first time in television history, a dramatic
anthology would be prepared, rehearsed, and broadcast
from under the same roof: three 90-minute dramas would
be housed there at all times--one in production and two in
rehearsal under the supervision of William Dozier, west
coast head of CBS Television. Playhouse 90 was a sign of
the changing times: television was moving from New York
to Hollywood, following the allure of glamour casting. The
premiere of Playhouse 90 on October 4, 1956, Rod Serling's
"Forbidden Area," starred a television alumnus who had
made it big in the movies, Charlton Heston.

Hubbell Robinson's idea was to have three separate
units, with three separate producers; as nothing like this
had ever been attempted, he assumed that producing the
show would be more than one man could handle. His

protégé, Martin Manulis, insisted that one man could produce the show: instead of three different producers supervising the three units, the three directors could supervise
them--much the same idea as that being practiced by Unit
Four on The Kaiser Aluminum Hour for the same reason.
Robinson agreed, setting the budget at $100,000 per pro-
gram. The top price for a script would be $7,500; because
the ceiling similarly applied to adaptations--less whatever
was paid for the rights--a writer like Rod Serling always
preferred to submit original scripts. There was also a
gentleman's agreement that the top price for any star would
not exceed $10,000; as recompense, actors would be given
roles they wouldn't otherwise be able to play in films.

        Playhouse 90 aired from 9:30-11:00 p.m. on Thurs-
days, providing audiences with some of television's most
highly regarded programs, including Rod Serling's "Requiem
for a Heavyweight," William Gibson's "The Miracle Worker,"
JP Miller's "The Days of Wine and Roses," a two-part version of Ernest Hemingway's "For Whom the Bell Tolls," and
Abby Mann's "Judgment at Nuremburg." A list of directors
who worked on this anthology includes John Frankenheimer,
Robert Mulligan, Ralph Nelson, and Arthur Penn. During
the second season, 1957-1958, they were joined by Fielder
Cook, George Roy Hill, and Franklin Schaffner.

        Although Playhouse 90 retained the three-act dramatic
format, Manulis lost a crucial battle at the beginning: instead of three commercial breaks, there would be nine. Unlike Studio One, which had a single sponsor in its entire
lifetime, Playhouse 90 had magazine sponsorship, making it
difficult for a producer to grow accustomed to the policies
of a single sponsor. Each show had three sponsors; by
the end of three weeks the anthology had nine separate
sponsors and advertising agencies. This arrangement would
have its benefits at CBS--no single sponsor or agency could
become too powerful and dictate the direction of the show.
In a couple of years, producer Herbert Brodkin would perfect the practice of playing the sponsors and agencies against
each other to get the material he wanted to do on the air.

        As with all good producers of live television drama,
Manulis spent a seven-day week on the job, working with
writers and directors at home on weekends. And like all
good producers of live television drama, Manulis considered

the script to be the most important ingredient in the show:
"I was always working on about ten scripts in different
stages of decay," he quips. The second stage of script
preparation was to get the director happy going in. "The
director and I worked finally to the point where he and I
would be content with the script to go into rehearsal,"
Manulis says. "I would also discuss major casting with
him."

There was a third week of rehearsal to accommodate
the extra 30 minutes; four cameras became the new norm
for live drama on Playhouse 90. Manulis encouraged experimentation; the newly assembled crew responded enthusiastically. "The crew was willing to really kill themselves," Manulis insists. "I mean, they made moves that had never been
done on the television floor!" On his end, he was more
than willing to take risks, even bringing in blind children
for the "Miracle Worker" telecast. "There was an excitement
about it," he maintains, "and I think the audience felt that
excitement, that we were doing it now--anything could happen." And after the live performance was over, everybody
gathered at Manulis' home to watch themselves on the kinescope that was televised on the west coast three hours later.

At the end of the year, Hubbell Robinson acknowledged
the quality of the show by granting an additional $10,000 to
the show's $100,000 budget. The second season of Playhouse
90 premiered on September 12 with "The Death of Manolete"
by Barnaby Conrad and Paul Monash. Then at the peak of
their enthusiasm for series, Martin Manulis and John Frankenheimer felt they could get away with anything; the director even went so far to stage a live bullfight with a wooden
bull. "It was the classic flop of all times," Manulis comments. "We really got our comeuppance."

In 1957, Playhouse 90 also got Franklin Schaffner,
who signed to direct approximately ten dramas a year, nearly a quarter of Playhouse 90's 39-show season. Schaffner
was the type of director able to inspire confidence in everyone with whom he worked; Manulis enjoyed working with
him. Especially important was Schaffner's "clarity of thought,
clarity of what he's looking for," the producer says. "We
got the most out of the material and people."

At present, only one Schaffner-directed Playhouse 90

seems to have survived: "The Eighty-Yard Run," adapted
by David Shaw from the Irwin Shaw story and starring Paul
Newman and Joanne Woodward, January 16, 1958. The structure of the story is simple: the climax comes shortly after
the first act begins when Chris, a 19-year-old college boy,
scores the winning touchdown in a football game, becomes a
hero, and marries Louise, the girl of his dreams, whose
father likes him enough to give him a job. The rest is
downhill for Chris.

Newman and Woodward look a bit old as college stu-
dents in the early scenes; they look just fine once they
move into business and married life. Newman gives a very
sincere performance as a loser, and Joanne Woodward is
quite convincing as a woman torn between love and a career.
During a commercial break there is a voiced-over plug for
Twentieth Century-Fox's The Long Hot Summer, also starring Newman and Woodward, produced by Jerry Wald and
directed by Martin Ritt.[40] Richard Anderson, as he also
does in the aforementioned film, appears as the third corner of a triangle with Newman and Woodward, this time as
Orrin, a publisher who allows Louise to pursue a career of
her own on the editorial staff of his magazine.

Filmed inserts are quite apparent in this show. Some,
like the football sequences shot at UCLA, establish exteriors; others are used for very practical reasons--if Paul Newman is in uniform on a football field for one scene on live
television, he can't easily be dressed in casual clothes for
the next shot in a dorm without a filmed insert. While there
was definitely a difference in visual quality between a television image and a film image, filmed inserts were still a
convention of live television; cuts to inserts were noticeable, but not terribly jarring.

As evidence of his own as well as the program's penchant for testing the limits of live television, Schaffner
staged a dialogue scene between Newman and Woodward in a
moving car in front of rear screen projection. This is hardly gratuitous; it conveys information without dialogue--
Louise is driving the car, a sports car at that. Act II begins with a dolly shot past a series of photographs of Chris
and Louise's marriage, and their subsequent graduation
from college. A photographic montage providing exposition
of Chris' progress, it also serves as a visual transition tak-

ing the audience several years ahead into the story. But there is more to the shot, and the camera continues to dolly: the pictures, it is revealed, are hung on the walls of Chris' office; the camera stops before his desk. Chris' unsuccessful career as a businessman begins in media res.

Although "The Eighty-Yard Run" was based on the work of a well-known author and features incisive acting, only the director could give the last shot of the show the significance it has. Returning from his alma mater, where he is now employed as an assistant football coach, Chris visits Louise, who has been jilted by Orrin: Woodward is in darkness to the right of the frame and, to left of center, stands Newman in the light of the open door.

"Point of No Return," adapted by Frank D. Gilroy from the novel by John P. Marquand and the play by Paul Osborn, was televised on February 20, 1958, reuniting Schaffner and Charlton Heston in a live television drama. Also featured were Hope Lange and Katherine Bard, Mrs. Martin Manulis. On June 26, Schaffner directed Manulis' final production for Playhouse 90, "The Great Gatsby." Adapted by David Shaw, the program featured Robert Ryan, miscast as Jay Gatsby, and Jeanne Crain and Rod Taylor as the Buchanans. It was not an auspicious swan song for Manulis: F. Scott Fitzgerald has never translated well to a visual medium, and this was no exception. Those who worked on a live show were always the first to know if it were a bomb; "The Great Gatsby" was not well received by the public either. The opening and closing shows of Manulis' last season were critical flops.

Manulis left Playhouse 90 after two years. Money was not an issue; his seven-year CBS contract had expired, and he just didn't want to continue. Later in 1958, he was appointed head of Twentieth Century-Fox Television. Tiring of that position, Manulis moved into film production with properties influenced by Playhouse 90: JP Miller's The Days of Wine and Roses (1962) and Tad Mosel's Dear Heart (1964).[41]

After Manulis' departure, Hubbell Robinson returned to his original notion of multiple producers. In the third season of Playhouse 90 there was not one but four producers --Fred Coe, John Houseman, Peter Kortner, and Herbert Brodkin.

Like Worthington Miner, Fred Coe was one of the pioneers of television drama, developing a stable of writers in
his tenure at NBC including Paddy Chayefsky, Tad Mosel,
JP Miller, Horton Foote, Sumner Locke Elliot, and Robert
Alan Aurthur. At this stage in his career, Coe was out to
conquer Hollywood, already having made his first film, The
Left-Handed Gun (1958), directed by protégé Arthur Penn
and starring fellow Yale Drama School alumnus and sometimes television star Paul Newman; Coe kept busy in the
meantime by producing shows for Playhouse 90. Schaffner
and Coe teamed for the first time on "Word from a Sealed-
Off Box," October 30, 1958, adapted by Mayo Simon, based
on a New Yorker article by Henriette Rosenburg, detailing
her experiences with the Dutch underground, how the Nazis
had imprisoned her, and later shipped her off in a box,
destination unknown.

Looking forward to working with Schaffner, Coe negotiated for the director's services; Schaffner sent back word
that he wanted to read the script first. Coe somehow took
this as a personal affront to his name and taste, but since
he wanted Schaffner, and the director himself wanted to do
the show, the necessary arrangements were made. In general, Coe was a courtly man--and Schaffner is never less
than so--but as soon as production commenced, Coe was obviously irritated; there was tension throughout the three
weeks of the show. Cast and crew never got the chance
for a complete run-through. Schaffner knew the show would
be long and he would have to shorten it during the course
of the broadcast. Adding to the complications, this was
star Maria Schell's first live television show, and her English was a bit shaky. That the program flowed, and flowed
smoothly, can be attributed in equal measures to the cool-
headedness of the director, the skill of the technical people,
and an alert cast. Coe and Schaffner, however, would never
work together again.[42]

John Houseman's association with the Mercury Players,
his career as the film producer of Letter from an Unknown
Woman (1948) and The Bad and the Beautiful (1952), his
career as an actor (an Academy Award for his performance
in the 1973 film of The Paper Chase), and his career as an
educator (Vassar, UCLA, Juilliard, and USC) have been
well documented. The protean Houseman was also a television producer as early as 1947 with the short-lived Sorry,

Wrong Number, directed by Nicholas Ray, who would shortly make his film directorial debut in Houseman's 1948 production of They Live By Night. Coming to CBS Television
in 1957 to produce The Seven Lively Arts, a quickly cancelled program modelled along the lines of Omnibus, Houseman, having signed a two-year contract with CBS, was
moved over to Playhouse 90 to become one of the rotating
producers and an occasional director.

    On December 11, 1958, Franklin Schaffner teamed
with John Houseman on the first television revival of the
gangster genre: "Seven Against the Wall," a realistic account of the St. Valentine's Day Massacre, written by former FBI agent Howard Browne. Houseman was familiar with
Schaffner's work; Schaffner seemed to be the perfect choice
for such a major undertaking--there would be no less than
44 speaking roles. "It was a very, very big show for Playhouse 90, one of the biggest," Houseman recalls. "In fact,
we had two whole studios connected--they opened doors between them."

    This was the first time Schaffner worked with two
contiguous studios, necessitating the use of a fifth camera,
which required a third boom for the sound and another
video man at the monitors. Five cameras were used only
when an overhead shot was needed from the parallels or,
as in this case, when the program involved two studios--it
would have been impossible to move the four basic cameras
in and out of the studios in time. Despite the scale of the
show, one filmed insert had to be shot of a man being gunned
down in a telephone booth--it was just too dangerous a stunt
to try on live television.

    Always an incomparable raconteur, Houseman recalls
an incident involving language, live television, and Paul
Lambert, who played Al Capone: "Lambert--you know they
were live--blew his lines. He used a four letter word on
the air ... oh, no, I think he said 'screw' twice. Once
was the limit." Houseman was satisfied that he had produced excellent television drama in "Seven Against the
Wall"; he had enjoyed the collaboration with the director.
"What a brilliant job Frank Schaffner did on it," he says.
News reporter Eric Sevareid served as the narrator of the
show. "I'll never know just how you did it," he would
write Schaffner. "I still quiver in awe."[43] By coincidence,

an enormously popular television series dealing with the
same era, the same city, and the same characters would
debut on ABC the following year: The Untouchables also
featured a narrator, an even more high-powered reporter
than Sevareid, Walter Winchell.

Herbert Brodkin might well be the most courageous
producer in television history. A Yale alumnus and a theatrical set designer, Brodkin produced such live dramatic
anthologies for television as The Alcoa Hour and The Elgin/
Motorola Hour, moving out to Hollywood with Studio One in
1956, and remaining to produce Playhouse 90. Herbert
Brodkin was the man who created an art form in turning
sponsors and ad agencies against each other to sneak in
the material he wanted to do. Typical of Brodkin is that
he brought Abby Mann's "Judgment at Nuremburg," directed by George Roy Hill, to Playhouse 90; typical of the
battles he fought with network and ad agency, the sponsor
--the gas company--objected to the use of the word "gas."
In a technical miracle, still unknown to Brodkin, who was
in the control room as a witness, the word "gas" was said,
but mysteriously disappeared from the live broadcast of the
show.

Schaffner teamed with Herbert Brodkin on "The Velvet Alley," January 22, 1959, a show that directly mirrors
the concerns of its author, standing as the watershed script
in Rod Serling's career. Although he had written scripts
for radio, and would eventually write film scripts, Serling
was above all a television writer. "TV's the toughest medium to write for," he once said. "Maybe that's why I like
it best. It's the only art form on earth that's entirely the
slave of the clock. An art form you've got to hold to the
minute, to the second."[44] At the beginning of his career,
Serling was known as an angry young man, writing plays
about the important social issues of the day. A constant
theme in his work was the contrast between the innocence
of youth and the corruption that age brings. With "Patterns" and "Requiem for a Heavyweight" behind him, Rod
Serling was in the process of becoming a household name.

"The Velvet Alley" is semi-autobiographical, dealing
with Ernie Pandish (portrayed by Art Carney), a talented
writer who goes to Hollywood and finds himself seduced by
fame and fortune. Ernie finds it all heady stuff; now that

he has it all, he doesn't want to lose it. Max, his agent, urges caution, warning: "In forty-eight hours a man can option off his soul, a good right arm, and his sanity.... And you can get hooked just as if it was dope."[45] Pat, Ernie's wife, disapproves of Hollywood, insisting that it's all Disneyland and keeping desperately up with the Joneses, but Ernie has been discovered by the big agents, who want to turn him into a giant--starting at $250,000. "Tonight," Pat wryly comments when he signs with another agency, "you got raped."[46] Max eventually dies; Ernie is so devastated that he returns to New York in hopes of rediscovering his roots.

Rod Serling, however, stayed in Hollywood, later in 1959 creating Twilight Zone, the show that would bring him his greatest fame and fortune. Serling had always detested the commercial aspects of television. "You try to deal tragedy, and in come rabbits dragging a roll of toilet paper," he complained. "Commercial television is man-made leprosy."[47] Tired of fighting with censors, Serling moved off into fantasy; his greatest success came when he departed from the arena of social significance. The ultimate irony must have come in the last phase of his career, when Serling found that his voice could earn more in ten minutes of commercial narration than his pen could in ten weeks of writing a script. "Rod," Herbert Brodkin comments, "could never face himself as to what the meaning of having gone to Hollywood to be a TV writer was."

Schaffner would subsequently direct most of his Playhouse 90 dramas for Brodkin. Loring Mandel's "The Raider" was broadcast on February 19, 1959, starring two insecure actors: near death, Paul Douglas would sip from a concealed bottle whenever his energies would flag; Frank Lovejoy was constantly calling his psychiatrist for dramatic coaching. The cast also included the distinguished Donald Crisp, who at the age of 80 had become senile and had to rely on cue cards, prompting Fielder Cook to observe at a rehearsal: "Donald is not crisp." Mandel's script concerned a man (Douglas) who raids other companies, gets into a proxy fight, and finds his own tactics being used against him. Neither director nor actors had a third act by the end of facilities rehearsal. Typical of Playhouse 90, "The Raider" fell together on the air. "Many shows jelled at the very last moment," Loring Mandel observes. "It was a frightening and very exhilarating show to do."

Herbert Brodkin came up with the idea of "In Lonely
Expectation," concerning a home for unwed mothers. Why
do some women become unwed mothers? What do they do
with their babies? What are the psychological effects? Hiring Mayo Simon to write the script, Brodkin presented this
virtually all-woman drama as a challenge to Franklin Schaffner, who already had acquired the reputation as a man's director. During the April 2, 1959 telecast, Susan Harrison
got her heel caught, tripped on the stairs, and accidentally
dropped a baby she was holding, which then proceeded to
bounce down several steps. "We're sitting in the control
room," Simon recalls, "Frank Schaffner half out of his
chair--that's about as much emotion as he allowed himself--
and the T.D. says, 'Gee, there goes the rerun.' " There
was no rerun--the baby incident, although a doll had been
used, provoked irate letters, and the show proved to be
controversial--just as Brodkin had intended.

The fourth producer, Peter Kortner, had been a story
editor for Playhouse 90 during Martin Manulis' tenure. Later
to produce The General Electric Theatre and The Farmer's
Daughter on television, Kortner worked with Schaffner on
Merle Miller's "Dark December," a drama about American
soldiers during the Battle of the Bulge, April 30, 1959.
Historically, "Dark December" is more interesting for the
young people who worked on it: featured in the cast were
Richard Beymer, the actor who would play the male lead in
Schaffner's first film, and the actor who would first create
that part on Broadway, Warren Beatty; the show also pre-
sented Michael Landon and Ronny Howard in one of their
earliest appearances; finally, the music was written by
Jerry Goldsmith, who would prove to be a consistent collaborator of Schaffner's in film, beginning with the first,
The Stripper.

Brodkin produced and Schaffner directed "The Rank
and File" on May 28. Written by Rod Serling, it was based
on Jimmy Hoffa's career as a labor boss, with Van Heflin in
the central role. "It was a bang-up script," Brodkin says.
"Frank did a wonderful job on it." The producer also remembers, "We got a telegram after that show from Robert
Kennedy saying, 'You have done a great service to your
country.' "

Hubbell Robinson, vice-president of programs, and

ultimately everybody's boss at CBS Television, left the network at the end of the 1958-1959 season; he had not been
promoted. Even more damagingly, CBS brought in James
Aubrey from ABC to do a job that was essentially the same
as Robinson's. Trading in his executive's hat, Robinson
quickly signed with NBC, and was given $15 million to pro-
duce his own show, becoming the biggest producer in television overnight. With the blessings of the Ford Motor Company, he tried to outdo Playhouse 90 by producing a weekly
90-minute dramatic anthology in color, the quality program
of all times. Ford Startime was even given the following
slogan: "The show you dress up to stay at home to see."
Ford Startime managed to achieve that status with "The
Turn of the Screw" featuring Ingrid Bergman in her television debut, and "The Wicked Scheme of Jebal Deeks"
featuring Alec Guinness, fresh from his success in The
Bridge on the River Kwai, in his American television debut.

    "The Wicked Scheme of Jebal Deeks" was produced
and directed by Franklin Schaffner through his Gilchrist
Productions for executive producer Hubbell Robinson.
Written by John D. Hess, and broadcast from NBC's Brooklyn Studio on November 10, 1959, the program concerned a
middle-aged bank employee who defrauds his employers to
become bank president. Admittedly, with an Alec Guinness,
the director did not have to worry much about comedy or
the quality of the performances. "Rose." of Variety observed: "Schaffner concentrated on the little areas for
definition, extracted beautiful satiric touches."[48] The star
was also pleased with the director's work. "You are a fine
director," Guinness wrote Schaffner, "ideal from my point
of view."[49]

    Unfortunately, Ford Startime never managed to live
up to its advance billing, and ended its run before the
season was over; it was not one of Hubbell Robinson's finer
moments in television. However, given the success of "The
Wicked Scheme of Jebel Deeks," Schaffner again teamed with
John D. Hess to create a television series, The Two-Timers,
a comedy about the schemes and adventures of two old men:
David, an idealist; Lloyd, a cynic. It never sold.

    Schaffner next joined forces with writer Alvin Boretz
to produce--and only produce--a television series entitled
Headquarters. Based on a book by Quentin Reynolds, it

Alec Guinness and Franklin Schaffner, "The Wicked Scheme of Jebal Deeks," 1959.

was, in Boretz's description, "a realistic view of the New
York police, very much like the Hill St. Blues so in vogue
today." A deal was made with NBC in November 1959. As
co-executive producers, Schaffner and Boretz signed Walter
Grauman to direct the pilot; Tim O'Connor and Fred Scholze
were hired to portray the veteran policemen, while George
Segal and James Caan were cast as rookies. Among those
turned down for the latter roles were such actors as the
then unknown Burt Reynolds and Robert Redford. "We
worked hard," Boretz says, "but there was always time
for some laughs and [Schaffner] only took seriously that
which was serious. He had no patience for fools, igno-
rance, cant or pretense."

In a move that must have tried Schaffner's patience,
NBC cancelled the show in January 1960, the night before
the pilot was to be shot; the sets had been built, the show
was fully rehearsed. Boretz can only say:

> Their reason was that they had overextended them-
> selves with commitments and saw no way to get our
> show on the air, even if the pilot had been made.
> I didn't really understand it at the time and still
> don't except further experience has led me to un-
> derstand that I am a man in a child's business.

Playhouse 90, 1959–1960

Playhouse 90 was a tight-knit community of artists and
artisans. Despite the complications of producing such a
mammoth series, the producers had always gone out of
their way to accommodate the schedules of actors, writers,
and directors if they had other film or television commitments. As writers would be brought to Hollywood for a
month to work on a show, rooms had to be reserved for
them at the Montecito or Cavalier. Actors stayed at the
Chateau Marmont; directors stayed in the two tiny rooms
at the Bel-Air Hotel known in a foregone era as the writers' rooms.

Under Herbert Brodkin, Playhouse 90 had the feel of
a Broadway opening night in Hollywood. After the live
telecast, the producer would throw a party at the Beverly
Hills Hotel: while the participants in the show celebrated,

people would phone in their congratulations and make their
comments. Schaffner seldom attended these parties. He
was directing about ten shows a season for Playhouse 90,
effectively taking up all his television availability; however,
as old habits die hard, Schaffner was given permission to
return to New York to direct Person to Person. After the
Thursday night Playhouse 90 telecast, Schaffner would walk
across Fairfax Avenue to Kelbo's, where he would have a
few drinks and watch the kinescope of the show at 9:30
p.m. The quality of the kinescopes had vastly improved
since the days of bicycling hot kines; never before had
west coast viewers been able to see the three-hour-delayed
dramas with such clarity. When the program ended at 11,
Schaffner would be driven to Los Angeles International,
where he would take the midnight flight on a four-engine
Constellation to New York, and arrive at his 72nd Street
home by 11:00 a.m. Eastern Standard Time. After some
rest, Schaffner would be ready at the Grand Central Studio
at 7:30 Friday evening to begin directing Person to Person.

     Hubbell Robinson had been a controversial boss at
CBS, but in his administration there had always been a
Studio One or a Playhouse 90; with Robinson gone, the man
they called the smiling cobra was in charge. James T.
Aubrey had made his name at ABC with action series, most
notably the Warner Brothers western and detective shows:
Maverick, Cheyenne, Bronco, Sugarfoot, 77 Sunset Strip,
Hawaiian Eye, Surfside Six. In the 1960s, he would give
CBS a rural look with The Beverly Hillbillies, The Andy
Griffith Show, Gomer Pyle, Petticoat Junction, Green Acres,
and Mayberry, R.F.D.

     Aubrey was aware that television was no longer a mil-
lion dollar business--it had become a multi-billion dollar
business. Network television had successfully ousted the
advertising agencies from power; the networks now were
able to take a bigger piece of the show. The television
industry having relocated in Hollywood, the series were
all filmed, could be rebroadcast, and even syndicated;
profits were never higher. The live dramatic anthology
had become a dinosaur.

     Herbert Brodkin has said:

     It was no longer a regular series. The network

could not keep a good series on the air. Networks
destroy things, you know. Playhouse 90 is one
of the very most successful series of all times. It
couldn't be allowed to go unscathed. It had to be
destroyed. Too good for television. That sounds
a little cynical, but that's what happened.

The creative environment had become more efficient and im-
personal, one more interested in business than in art. In
its final year, Playhouse 90 became a series of specials,
broadcast irregularly, approximately every other week.

Schaffner directed "The Silver Whistle" by Robert
McEnroe, based on his stage play of the same name; Brodkin had been the set designer for the original Broadway
production, and wanted to do it again. The cast had no
big stars, but featured in this comedy about a tramp in an
old folks home were such reliable and gifted actors as Eddie Albert, Henry Jones, Bethel Leslie, and Margaret Hamilton. Adding to the nostalgia was that Brodkin and Schaffner were able to do the show live from New York on December 24, 1959.

Schaffner's final Playhouse 90 was "The Cruel Day"
on February 24, 1960. Fittingly, Reginald Rose wrote the
script and Herbert Brodkin produced it. Set in Algeria,
the drama concerned a moral struggle between a French
captain (Van Heflin) and a corrupt lieutenant (Cliff Robertson). The strong male cast also featured Raymond Massey,
Peter Lorre, and Charles Bronson. For his participation in
the show, Franklin Schaffner received a Directors Guild of
America award for television direction.

Videotape was an early sign of the coming times.
Schaffner got his first exposure to videotape on Playhouse
90, using it in place of film inserts. An immediate problem
of going from live to tape, and from tape to live, was getting both simultaneously up to speed. The director would
have to anticipate the five- or seven-second roll in; on-air
performances and rhythms frequently and drastically changed
as a result. Everything more or less worked out in his
case--Schaffner was never forced to go to black; by the
time the series went off the air, however, the entire program was recorded on videotape. Kinescopes were extinct.

The biggest problem with videotape was editing. "You could make an edit that you thought was right on the pulse and right in sync, and put it together," Schaffner says, "and you'd hit that splice, and everything kept flopping over thereafter." Simply, wisdom was not to edit at all. The only time the director ever edited was in case of a serious emergency; the editing limitation preserved the live tradition of Playhouse 90. Eventually, machinery and human skill became more sophisticated, facilitating editing. Until that time came, producers and directors had to go into post-production, transfer videotape to 16mm film, edit the film, and then transfer back to tape; two decades later, filmmakers go through the same process, similarly for economic reasons, only in reverse.

The final presentation of Playhouse 90 was Rod Serling's "In the Presence of Mine Enemies" on May 18, 1960, with Charles Laughton, Arthur Kennedy, Oscar Homolka, Susan Kohner, George Macready, Sam Jaffe, and Robert Redford. Its director, Fielder Cook, calls the demise of Playhouse 90 the 1066 of television.

Herbert Brodkin still mourns the passing of an art form:

> Live television was on its way to becoming a great medium. We had developed a way to do shows which was as distinctive and unique as the theatre or motion pictures ... and to have that pulled away was a terrible, terrible tragedy because it'll never come back.... It was too bad, but the minute the industry went to film, live shows were lost. Purely for financial reasons.

Worthington Miner wrote:

> Thought, imagination, and daring were relegated to the dustbin.... With the salesman again in the saddle, it took a very short time to liquidate a taste for literacy. Caution became the watchword in place of excitement. [50]

With more money at stake, the networks, and the sponsors and their advertising agencies became more conservative; their idea was to reach the widest audience

possible, and offend the fewest possible.   As early as 1956,
Reginald Rose had perceived:

> I assume it is felt that antagonizing even a small
> minority of the audience would relate immediately to
> the sale of the sponsor's product, diminishing same
> to the point where it hurts.   This kind of reasoning
> is pretty maddening and leads me to believe that
> agency men have no faith in either the product they
> try to sell or the advertising they have created for
> it. [51]

On October 15, 1958, no less an observer of American mores
than Edward R. Murrow stated:

> If there are any historians ... a hundred years
> from now and there should be preserved the kine-
> scopes for one week of all three networks they will
> find recorded, in black-and-white or color, evidence
> of decadence, escapism and insulation from the real-
> ities of the world in which we live.... If we go on
> as we are, then history will take its revenge, and
> retribution will [catch] up with us. [52]

Television programming since 1958 has hardly affected the
meaning of Murrow's message.

      Television, as Worthington Miner once observed, is at
its best in live, reportorial coverage.   In a sense, he suggested, the decline of live television drama began in 1951
when I Love Lucy arrived on the air.   As well as being a
pioneering television show, it was also a phenomenally
popular series: the shows were permanently preserved on
film and have been endlessly rerun.   Thirty years later, it
is still reaping enormous profits in syndication; indeed, the
sun never sets on Lucy.   Film, to be sure, cost a lot more.
A one-hour dramatic show that cost $10,000 in 1950, cost
$150,000 by 1960, and, in the 1980s, close to $1,000,000--a
case of spending more to make more money.   Erik Barnouw
has written:

> The anthology form survived to some extent on film,
> but was eclipsed by filmed episodic series of upbeat
> decor, preferred by most sponsors.   Identification
> with a continuing, attractive actor had merchandising

advantages.... Above all, the series formula offered security: each program was a variation of an
approved ritual. Solutions, as in commercials, could
be clear cut. [53]

In truth, filmed westerns, action shows, and comedies had
clearly proved to be more popular in the ratings than the
live dramatic anthologies. No longer were actors chosen to
fit the script, but scripts were written to fit the actors.
Hollywood and film (and videotape) were the victors.

With the pressures and parameters of live television,
it is remarkable that so many excellent shows, so many memorable original dramas, were produced. "The limitations in
those days," Schaffner once noted, "enforced a concept of
realism ... which, I am convinced, influenced for a while
the theater in this country." [54] Indeed, such television writers as Robert Alan Aurthur, Paddy Chayefsky, Horton Foote,
Tad Mosel, and N. Richard Nash easily made the transition
to Broadway in the 1950s; such well-regarded Broadway
plays as Gore Vidal's A Visit to a Small Planet and William
Gibson's The Miracle Worker were originally produced on
television. Such television directors as Arthur Penn, and
George Roy Hill, Fielder Cook, and Franklin Schaffner of
Unit Four would all direct plays on Broadway.

That influence extended as well to film. Paddy Chayefsky's "Marty," originally produced by Fred Coe and directed by Delbert Mann for Philco Television Playhouse on
May 24, 1953, had such an impact that Hecht-Lancaster Productions produced a film version for United Artists in 1955,
proving that a big budget, a big-name star, and an experienced film director were not necessarily needed to make a
commercially and critically successful motion picture. Although the television version was much the more realistic
show, concerning a less than heroic character who becomes
heroic for being so unheroic, the film proceeded to win
Academy Awards for best picture, director (Delbert Mann),
actor (Ernest Borgnine), and writer (Chayefsky).

Perhaps many of the directors of the golden age of
television might have been content to direct live dramas forever. The pay was low, and there was a lack of recognition,
but there was job security in a live anthology; a director
didn't have to worry about when his next assignment was

coming up. He was exposed to a wide variety of material, an interesting assortment of actors and personalities, and the very experience of doing live television provided a type of stimulation unmatched by any other medium.

These are moot points: the directors had already seen the handwriting on the wall. Some, like George Roy Hill, moved to the theatre. As for television, "The dramatic pendulum swung to TV series; you either worked on these or nothing," Martin Manulis said. "I chose to move into film production."[55] The sentiment was echoed by most of the generation of live television directors; they moved to film for artistic and commercial survival, to direct the type of material they wanted to do. The film industry of the late-1950s witnessed a steady invasion of television directors: Delbert Mann, Marty, 1955; Fielder Cook, Patterns, 1956; Martin Ritt, Edge of the City, 1957; John Frankenheimer, The Young Stranger, 1957; Robert Mulligan, Fear Strikes Out, 1957; Sidney Lumet, Twelve Angry Men, 1957; Arthur Penn, The Left-Handed Gun, 1958. Not until the film school graduates of the 1970s would one single kindred group have so much influence on the film medium.

Except for news and sports--which, along with films, ironically, feature the best moments found in the medium-- live television is pretty much a thing of the past. Apart from NBC's infrequent Live Theatre Presentations in the 1980s, there are no remnants left of live television drama on the air--barring an occasional rebroadcast of original kinescopes from the golden age of television on PBS. A mystique, abetted by a less than desirable number of available kinescopes, has enveloped the golden age of television. In a remark that the more than casual researcher of live television will find dear to his or her heart--and a not inaccurate assessment of the situation--George Roy Hill says: "I think the reason it's called 'The Golden Age of Television' is all the kinescopes are lost." Not all, but nearly all.

Of the extant kinescopes, it can only be said that some programs hold up very well indeed; others do not. Generally, they are primitive and primordially interesting. If the writing and the acting are good, the show is good-- but even the acting is dependent on the material. Worthington Miner urged caution lest the golden age of television be romanticized too far--there is the sobering thought of

the supply of quality material. Twenty-five hours a week
of network time had been given to dramatic anthologies; no
one expected excellence in every show of every series every
week. There are even limits, as Miner opined, to the public domain:

> In the early years the pioneers were spendthrift--
> they had the whole range of theatre and literature
> to choose from--yet the law of diminishing returns
> had begun to operate well before the Golden Age
> began to fade. The entire Elizabethan period pro-
> duced in toto less than a hundred plays of substan-
> tial worth--and that bridged a span of forty years.
> The entire range of the theatre from Aeschylus to
> Albee would have difficulty supplying the networks
> with quality programming for more than a year.[56]

That was already past history in 1960, when the golden age
of television officially ended with the death of Playhouse 90.

Franklin Schaffner would still have three years to wait
before he saw his first film in release.

CONCLUSION

The immediate consideration in Franklin Schaffner's television career is the prodigious amount of work he accomplished.
To be sure, Franklin Schaffner directed his share of material
that both he and his audiences found lacking in substance
or interest, yet, in the constant flow of material for a dramatic anthology, Schaffner was given more than a passing
familiarity with any number of subjects, periods, and genres. He has said:

> The director in those early days of television was
> dealing with every conceivable kind of material. He
> got his feet wet on almost anything. It didn't mat-
> ter whether he was right for the material. The fact
> of the matter is, his turn came up and he did it.[57]

Franklin Schaffner brought a considerable native intelligence to his work: with a background in literature and
drama, he had also acted and written; coming from The
March of Time through News and Public Affairs, he was

considered a technical expert at CBS Television. He became
the regular studio director of Person to Person, and achieved
preeminence as a director of live television drama; Studio One
could only have widened and deepened his literary and dramatic background.

   The golden age of television, in Schaffner's opinion,
reached its peak in the hour-long dramatic anthologies like
Studio One. It was in this form of television that he was
trained and recognized as one of its foremost practitioners.
It was television as he knew it best; in the 1960s, he would
continue to practice the sixty-minute format that he mastered
at Studio One.

   At this point, in a summary of his television career,
it is instructive to re-examine Schaffner's Studio One routine. The two-week Studio One process began after the
telecast on Monday evening. The director went home, slept
until noon the following day, and, Tuesday afternoon, returned to the office to read the new script, meeting with
the writer later in the afternoon. On Wednesday, he would
meet with the set designer. Normally, the director liked to
have the flats away from the control room window: if informed of a problem on the floor, the director wanted to be
able to look through the window and see what it was--a problem was always more easily analyzed and solved when he
could see as well as hear it. After discussing the sets, the
director would spend the rest of Wednesday working with
the writer.

   The producer having already cast the stars, the director participated in casting the rest of the show on Thursday; Studio One, after Robert Fryer's departure, had excellent casting directors in Jim Merrick and Alixe Gordon.
After casting was completed, the rest of Thursday was spent
on rewrites. The first reading of the script would come on
Friday afternoon; the second reading of the script rounded
out the day. The actors took the weekend off: according
to the American Federation of Television and Radio Artists
(AFTRA), actors were limited to a certain number of hours
they could rehearse, both dry and with facilities. Schaffner, however, would continue to work over the weekend at
his apartment, where he would meet with writer, set designer, and technical staff.

Beginning at 10:00 Monday morning, there were daily
rehearsals at Central Plaza in a hall run by Bernie Berns,
who also rented out the space for dances and weddings.
The director started blocking the show; the production assistant, the very capable Bette Stein, took notes of all decisions, and also timed the scenes. Rehearsals continued
from 10 to 6 until Friday, after the first run-through. Saturday at 10 a.m., there would be an additional rehearsal
based on what the director had seen in the first run-through.
In the afternoon, there were two complete run-throughs, and
then Schaffner would break early. By this time, the director would have notes written in his script of all the shots he
was going to make. The associate director would take the
director's script and copy all the notes, so he could explain
everything to the crew; a prerequisite for any Schaffner
A.D. was that he be able to read the director's eccentric
scrawl.

Sunday morning was the first time cast and crew set
foot on the set: they invariably went into a sense of shock
until they began to get used to the environment. Facilities
rehearsal would then begin, and the director spent all day
Sunday blocking the show technically. Ideally, there should
have been more rehearsal time on the set, but studio time
was prohibitively expensive; sometimes the director would
finish, sometimes he would not. Schaffner then corrected
up to 50% of his shots Sunday night and early Monday morning. The A.D. got the revisions on Monday morning, and
explained them to the crew. After another complete run-
through, the director worked on pick-up pieces. After the
dress rehearsal, the show went on the air live at 10:00 p.m.

Worthington Miner had created the ten-man crew:
the technical director, the audio man, two boom operators,
three cameramen, and three cable pullers; the T.D. was
the boss of the crew. The director had to fight hard to
get a good technical director: most of them were more interested in their time cards than in which cameraman could
do what; a good T.D. would round up a good crew. There
was no such thing as a lighting cameraman; a separate engineer was responsible for the lighting. CBS, according to
Schaffner, had two good lighting engineers, Bob Barry and
Ralph Holmes, who were worth their weight in gold; again,
a director had to fight to get a good lighting man.

Live drama could not be lit from above; sky pans had been used, but were replaced by grid-hangings. The problem with grid-hangings was the boom shadows they created; the boom operators, however, were skillful enough to avoid the shadows. After the first facilities rehearsal on Sunday morning, the lighting engineer set up lamps on the floor to illuminate eyes and faces; the problem with lamps was that they got in the way of the three cameras. As with motion picture lighting, there was a considerable amount of pre-lighting, to rough in the grid-hangings; unlike motion picture lighting, television drama was shot continuously and contiguously, and there was never a chance to change the lighting pattern or make refinements while the show was in progress. Despite the limitations, Schaffner says, "I thought some of the lighting was absolutely remarkable."

The director never could rely on certain basic hangings for mood or atmosphere because the set design was different with each show. As part of the rehearsal procedure, the lighting engineer, audio man, T.D., and three cameramen came to the last dry rehearsal run-through on Friday to see what they needed to do to accommodate the show. (On Ford Theater there had been even more preparation: the A.D. sat off to the side, following the script as he watched the run-through, and, via headsets, would tell the cameramen what shots were coming up.)

Thanks to the cooler lamps, the set was less hot than it had been in the past, but a lot of light was still needed for the show; the cameras were not that sensitive. "What would happen if you didn't have sufficient light," Schaffner remembers, "is that you would pick up dirt--what it amounts to--on the video monitors, and you'd have to add more light." Franklin Schaffner used cameras with turrets all the way through his television career--only in his last television show in 1967 would he use a zoomar lens--his dependent lens being the 50mm wide-angle lens. His cameramen were "highly competent professionals who took pride in how fast they could flip a lens turret and make the focus sharp and clear."[58]

Since the standard set piece was ten feet high, cranes were seldom used. When a crane shot was called for, the director used the Houston, on which the third camera was always mounted. The third cable puller doubled as an arm man on the crane, but an extra arm man was usually needed; use of the Houston's small crane also required the services of another boom operator. Eventually the cameramen took the crank wheels off of the crane and sandbagged it so they could lift its arms as they operated the cameras; it was far less noisy and smoother this way.

As Studio One used two booms, microphones were seldom placed on or around the set. The show never used radio microphones; they were too difficult to use as they picked up noise at the slightest movement. The Grand Central Studios had been built with a lot of steel so that radio microphones picked up a lot of interference, especially with all the traffic going under and around Grand Central Station. The "Murrow mikes" also produced an irritating noise when rubbed against clothes; although they would have been practical to use, it was technically impossible.

The boom operators took their instructions from the audio man. With proper rehearsal, they knew when wide or close shots were coming; if an actor had to move across the set, they followed, fully aware of when they would hit critical shadows, where they would have to rack back, follow, and drop in again. Occasionally, the two boom microphones were used for the same scene, if there were a large enough set involved. The second boom would have to come in to relieve the first; then the problem would be in releasing the first boom to get to the next scene without bumping into a standing lamp or a moving television camera.

A fundamental of live television is that it takes no time at all to cut from camera to camera. It takes a certain amount of time, on the other hand, to rack a boom arm in the air and drop it in place. Consequently, there was always an audio fade on a cut from a two-shot to a wide shot because the boom operator had to rack the arm in the air to avoid getting it caught in the wide shot; he would have to wait until there was a cut back to the close shot before he could drop the arm back in.

There could never be a full rehearsal for a show whenever special effects were involved; the effects were saved for the time of broadcast. The sets, for example, were painted with water paint. If water were used in dress rehearsal, the paint job would be ruined, and there wouldn't be enough time to get everything ready by the time of broadcast Monday night.

The Studio One director was not responsible for the Betty Furness Westinghouse commercials, which were directed by a McCann-Erickson agency director. The agency director used the show's cameramen and crew; on Monday, he was allotted 90 minutes of separate rehearsal for the commercials on the "Westing House" set, which would be built in along with the rest of the sets for the show. The commercial preceding Act I was shot with one camera; Act I actually began with only two cameras. The third camera caught up as soon as the cameraman and cable puller could get there. At the end of Act I, Schaffner would have to release two cameras for the commercial; the last 15 seconds of the act would be shot by the one remaining camera.

The changeover required split-second precision. Ten seconds before the act ended, Schaffner would stand up from his seat at the control room console, still talking to the cameramen, and tell the T.D. to go to black. In the meantime, the agency director would slip in, sit down at the console, and take over. Both directors used the same associate director, and, at the end of the commercial, the process reversed itself. Ten seconds before the commercial was over, the agency director would stand up and slip out, and Schaffner would slip in, sit down, put on the headphones, and check with the A.D. to see if everything was ready. The A.D. readied the cameras, and the director would go into the next act while the commercial was still on the air.

Ultimately, directing live television drama was an exercise in editing; all the shots that were going to come up had already been decided upon. "It wasn't a matter of looking at the monitor and saying, 'Oh, that looks good--take that now!'" Schaffner says. "All of it had been pre-planned. You were, in point of fact, pre-edited before you went on the air. You knew precisely what cut was coming up at what point." The director would improvise only in times of emergency.

The director's work routine having been established, it is now helpful to move in closer, and observe Schaffner at work with his colleagues in the live television drama environment.

Writing

Beginning with his days in The Green Room at Franklin and
Marshall College, Schaffner was accustomed to the three-act
dramatic structure. All the scripts he directed for live television observed the traditional beginning, middle, and end;
the same also applies when he moved to film. A quick perusal of a list of television shows directed by Franklin
Schaffner reveals a great number of prestigious titles: (in
chronological order) "Jane Eyre," "The Scarlet Letter,"
"Torrents of Spring," "The Ambassadors," "What Maisie
Knew," "Wings of the Dove," "The Marble Faun," "Heart
of Darkness," "Macbeth," "Treasure Island," "A Connecticut Yankee in King Arthur's Court," "The Great Gatsby."
Invariably, Schaffner was assigned to these properties, but
as Robert Fryer, who was there as CBS casting director,
comments, "He always had kind of first choice." The long
list of impressive titles is a sure sign of how well he was
regarded by the television industry: then as now, Schaffner was considered a director of taste and intelligence, one
who could do full justice to highbrow material.

Schaffner did not write scripts for television; he saw
his role as director primarily as that of an interpreter.
Fortunately for the dramatic anthologies originating out of
New York, most of the people working in television had
theatrical experience. Every person involved in a live drama had a lot of respect for the writer, his role in the production, and his script. When television moved to Hollywood at the end of the 1950s, writers' contracts were soon
drawn strictly according to the motion picture system; the
writers became hired hands. Today, television networks
have complete power--they cast the show, hire the producer, writer, and director; they make all the final decisions.
But in the golden age, before the age of the accountant,
television writers' contracts were drawn strictly according
to the Broadway system: the writer owned his or her material; the writer retained film rights 90 days after the
telecast.

Censors, as they were called before the days of

standards and practices, could not begin to keep up with
everything that went on and into the 25 dramatic anthologies each week. Moreover, a producer like Herbert Brodkin was able to carve out a lot of power for himself in the
wake of the rivalry among network, sponsor, and advertising agency: as a result he could afford to take a lot of
risks and try out different kinds of material. Having
earned their power the hard way, producers were protective of their writers; their first task was to create a secure niche for the writer, who, as a result, automatically
acquired a lot of power himself. With a good producer's
help, a writer could deliver a script with all of its intentions intact and stand a good chance of getting it on the
air. The golden age of television was when the writer
"worked with" not "worked for" the producer; nobody told
the writer what to do.

Given this climate of respect for the script, Franklin
Schaffner, according to Mayo Simon, was especially protective, gracious, and sensitive to his writers. He worked
with the writers to get around physical and budgetary limitations, considering the primary function of his job to find
the theme of the script and then realize it for the cameras.
The theme, Schaffner has said, had priority over any camera angle:

> It is possible in live TV that, if you stage for the
> camera, you may miss the entire meaning of the
> play. The director's obligation is to stage the play
> first. When he discovers what has been done dur-
> ing the process, he will punctuate visually. [59]

In studying the script, the director had to determine what
the author's intention was and then try to fulfill that intention visually with the actors. If he were to discover that
the relationship between a couple was distant, for example,
he would not shoot them in a tight two-shot.

Loring Mandel, who has enjoyed a long and productive
collaboration with Schaffner, says:

> If he is working specifically to make something more
> visual, the chances are that a director won't state
> his purpose in those terms. It could be a general
> comment early on, but it isn't likely to be a specific

one during the working, because it carries a possibly pejorative color.

Schaffner used a subtle and indirect method with the writer
to achieve a common goal.

In his first collaboration with Schaffner, "Shakedown
Cruise" in 1955, Mandel recalls that during dry rehearsal
he was privately approached by Richard Kiley and Don Gordon, who said they felt uncomfortable with Mandel's words,
wanted him to rewrite the dialogue, and change the climactic scene to suit their purposes as actors. Mandel was persuaded into making the changes. Schaffner overruled them
as soon as he learned what had happened. Later, Mandel
remembers, "He said, 'Don't let them push you around.
Make the actors come to me. Never let yourself get unpro-
tected in a situation like that.' He was very careful to
stand between me and them." And, as Mandel suggests,
Schaffner did as much to protect himself as well. Control
is a very important word to Schaffner: actors talking indiscriminately are a threat to his control, undermining his
authority; the director must guide the writer and the actors.

Schaffner received valuable lessons in the art of script-
writing and adaptations from Worthington Miner and Felix
Jackson. In his television career, he was also given the op-
portunity of working with the top writers of the medium:
(in chronological order) Sumner Locke Elliot ("Jane Eyre");
James Costigan ("Captain-General of the Armies"); Robert
Anderson ("At Midnight on the 31st of March"); Gore Vidal
("Dark Possession"); Loring Mandel ("Shakedown Cruise");
Tad Mosel ("The Playroom"); Frank D. Gilroy ("Point of
No Return"); Mayo Simon ("In Lonely Expectation"); Merle
Miller ("Dark December"). In addition, Schaffner also
worked regularly with two of the three greatest television
writers, Reginald Rose and Rod Serling; had he been under
contract to NBC instead, he would have worked with the
third, Paddy Chayefsky.

Acting

The writers could only contribute up to a certain point; the
rest was up to the actors. Typically, television drama was

action in dialogue: the actors gave their faces to the characters, and their voices to the dialogue. Having had acting experience himself, Schaffner fully realized the absolute importance of actors and the contributions they could make:

> Simply defined, I suppose the director's function really is just staying one jump ahead of the cast. Too often a director gets great credit for "exposing what the play is about," for "interpreting" it. But it works the other way, more often than not. Again and again at rehearsals an actor does something that opens a whole new and broad horizon about what a scene should be.[60]

Directors had different approaches to rehearsal: some would begin with a discussion of the script; sometimes the writer would first read the script. Schaffner's method was not unlike that practiced by Jean Renoir--the actors would simply begin reading, and the director would not say a word. Schaffner made no introductory remarks, said nothing at all about what he wanted or was looking for, offered no interpretations; he would only introduce everybody seated around the table, and, without further ado, begin on page one.

Schaffner was always quite adept at directing actors. "He handled his actors in a quiet and understated way," Martin Manulis says. Mayo Simon elaborates: "Visually he's very clean and neat, and, in his relationships with people, always very clean, soft-spoken--a lot of decorum. I've never seen him try to overpower anyone. He tends to say less than other people." Many actors, however, have been terrified at the first reading; Schaffner is so handsome, an actor will especially want to please him. But Schaffner does not say anything; he only looks at the actor with what seems like a cold stare.

Although he tried not to show it, Schaffner was very protective of actors, ever sympathetic to their needs. Replacing an actor was a painful task; he always tried to avoid it. At the beginning of his television career, shows were cast according to the dictates of the powerful anti-Communist publication Red Channels, so he made frequent attempts to sneak certain actors into Studio One. Once in rehearsal, Schaffner would think he was safe with the actors he wanted,

but then the CBS brass would suddenly show up, and the
actor would have to be replaced on the spot. Schaffner
never made an acting replacement because of personal chemistry or, rather, lack of personal chemistry. The only
times he made this move were when the actor just couldn't
remember the dialogue. Referring to "The Wicked Scheme
of Jebal Deeks" in 1959, Schaffner recalls:

> There was this marvelous actor named Charles
> Coburn.... Charlie arrived late at rehearsal--
> about a day--because he had just gotten married.
> We rehearsed about four days, and finally I said,
> "Charlie, you know, it's either/or." And he just
> didn't have it, so we replaced him. Not a pleas-
> ant thing to do.

Because of the importance of acting in live drama,
Schaffner worked very closely with the casting director.
Robert Fryer recalls staying on after the casting phase
was over:

> I had to be around facilities rehearsal because very
> often--because it was live television--we'd have to
> occasionally make a replacement very quickly. You
> see, a lot of actors get very tense. People dried
> up. I've seen them dry up, and Frank--he was
> always three steps ahead of them, and he'd have
> them on the monitors so he could cut away from
> them. People would forget their lines.

Actors generally behaved on the premise that bad citizens
don't get hired; they were not big movie or Broadway stars,
and couldn't afford to throw too many tantrums. Consequently, rehearsals were usually relaxed. When the time
came to talk, Schaffner would confer with the actors individually, invariably withdrawing to a private room at dry
rehearsal, or taking long walks when on the set.

Not at all interested in intellectual analyses, Schaffner had little patience with aesthetic or theoretical discussions. "It feels good this way," he would tell the actors.
Or he would say, "I like it." And then inevitably would
come his favorite expression: "Let's mush on." Felix
Jackson remembers Schaffner's skepticism of the Actors'
Studio, citing an example with John Cassavettes, who was

at a stage in his young career when he was tired of playing characters his own age. The actor had a one-line bit
in the Gore Vidal adaptation of "A Man and Two Gods" on
Studio One, May 24, 1954: he was supposed to come to a
door, open it, and give his line. After his cue was given
in the facilities rehearsal, the door remained closed. Checking with Cassavettes to find out what was wrong, Schaffner
was met with questions concerning the character's motiva-
tions. The director proceeded to give the actor a direct
order, Jackson recalls, and the next time around, the door
opened, and Cassavettes gave his line.

     Schaffner spent his formative years in Japan and lost
his father by the age of six; perhaps a sense of distance
was instilled in him at an early age. His detached personal
style, in any event, cannot be separated from his work with
actors: his cool and remote demeanor serves his purposes.
Mayo Simon recalls a time in dry rehearsal when he became
so impressed with the performance that he complimented the
actors as soon as they finished the scene. Schaffner drew
him aside and said, "Don't tell actors they're good. Don't
say anything to them. Make them want to do better."
Schaffner would only compliment an actor after the show
was over. Simultaneously, Schaffner is capable of enormous warmth and generosity--which he used to his advantage with the actors when the situation demanded it. He
also has a sly sense of humor. "He always had this great
wit," Robert Fryer says. "He would say these outrageous
things to actors because he's funny." Schaffner would
play practical jokes, do anything to encourage camaraderie
on the set.

     In the final analysis, Schaffner's greatest strength in
working with actors was, in Fletcher Markle's words, "He
has this kind of priestly air." Markle continues:

     Actors adored him because he never talked to them
     in front of the whole cast--I'm talking about prin-
     cipals. There was always a kind of walking away
     from the group, and having a moment or several
     minutes of confession. And star performers--all
     those mixed egos and difficulties that one copes
     with--Frank did it beautifully. I've heard, through
     the years, actors express their gratitude for that.

        Loring Mandel corroborates the priestly image, offer-
ing the 1959 <u>Playhouse 90</u> production of "The Raider" with
Paul Douglas and Frank Lovejoy as an example: the two
stars were at each other's throats, and finally got into a
fight that had to be broken up by Rod Taylor. "[Schaff-
ner] did as much work--if not more--as a priest to the actors than a director," he says. The first hour and a half
of rehearsal each day was spent with the two stars, Schaffner devoting 45 minutes to each, giving them equal time.
According to the billing, he would first put his arm around
Douglas' shoulders, and walk back and forth, back and
forth; 45 minutes later, he would put his arm around Lovejoy's shoulders, and walk back and forth, back and forth.

        Consider the personalities he worked with and the
quality of the performances he extracted from them. The
following list of actors may seem unduly long--it could be
much longer--but the names revealed justify its length.
Schaffner directed four of the top dramatic actors on live
television in the late 1940s and early 1950s: Charlton Heston ("As You Like It"); Mary Sinclair ("The Scarlet Letter"); Judith Evelyn ("Angel Street"); Felicia Montealegre,
then Mrs. Leonard Bernstein ("Wings of the Dove").

        Schaffner also directed, in chronological order, a
range of actors including Grace Kelly ("The Rockingham
Tea Set"); Jack Lemmon ("The Wisdom Tooth,"); Anne
Marno, who would gain fame as Anne Bancroft ("The Man
Who Had Influence"); Lee Tracy ("The Traitor"); Barry
Fitzgerald and Mildred Natwick ("The Whiteheaded Boy");
Dorothy Gish ("Spring Again"); Anthony Quinn ("Ticket to
Oblivion"); Margaret Sullavan ("The Touchstone"); Boris
Karloff ("Mutiny on the Nicolette"); Viveca Lindfors and
Melvyn Douglas ("Letter from an Unknown Woman"); Cyril
Ritchard and Geraldine Fitzgerald ("Pontius Pilate");
Thomas Mitchell ("A Connecticut Yankee in King Arthur's
Court); Walter Matthau ("Dry Run").

        Continuing on to the mid-1950s, Schaffner worked
with Robert Cummings, Franchot Tone, Edward Arnold,
George Voskovec ("Twelve Angry Men"); Charles Coburn
and Richard Kiley ("The Cuckoo in Spring"); Jack Warden
and Carroll Baker ("A Stranger May Die"); Joseph Cotton
and Piper Laurie ("Broadway"); Art Carney and Jason
Robards, Jr. ("The Incredible World of Horace Ford");

Lee Marvin ("Shakedown Cruise"); Natalie Wood ("Miracle at Potter's Farm"); Trevor Howard ("Flower of Pride"); Joanne Woodward ("Family Protection"); Lloyd Nolan and Barry Sullivan ("The Caine Mutiny Court Martial"); Paul Newman ("The Army Game"); Claude Rains and Marisa Pavan ("Antigone"); Hume Cronyn ("Angel's Ransom"); Alfred Lunt and Lynn Fontanne ("The Great Sebastians"); Patricia Neal, Tony Randall, Nina Foch ("The Playroom"); Farley Granger, Vincent Price, Judith Anderson ("The Clouded Image"); Robert Stack, Vera Miles, Lee J. Cobb ("Panic Button"); Don Murray and Hope Lange ("For I Have Loved Strangers"); Anne Baxter and Dana Andrews ("The Right-Hand Man"); Buster Keaton ("The Innocent Sleep"); Robert Ryan, Jeanne Crain, Rod Taylor ("The Great Gatsby"); Maria Schell ("Word from a Sealed-Off Box"); Paul Douglas, Frank Lovejoy, Donald Crisp ("The Raider"); Warren Beatty, Richard Beymer, Michael Landon, Ronny Howard ("Dark December"); Alec Guinness ("The Wicked Scheme of Jebal Deeks"); Eddie Albert ("The Silver Whistle"); Van Heflin, Cliff Robertson, Raymond Massey, Peter Lorre, and Charles Bronson ("The Cruel Day").

He would work with many of them again.

Schaffner's television programs consistently featured fine acting, gaining him the reputation as an actor's director. He has said:

> You have an enormous obligation to the actor or the actress in the scene and I don't think that is as often observed as it should be. I've seen many instances where actors have been forced to do things in a scene which are totally out of step with the scene for any number of reasons--mostly it's because the director's forgotten the whole continuity of the story. [61]

Always careful in dealing with the various personalities he encountered, Schaffner utilized their talents to fit the purposes and the logic of the teleplay, acquiring the reputation of being able to draw outstanding performances from some notoriously difficult actors in film. His characteristic cold/warm and strict/generous method of dealing with actors was finely tuned in his television career.

Preparation

Schaffner gets up at 4:00 a.m. on every working day,
studies the script and set design, and goes over every
single thing he will do that day. This discipline comes as
a result of directing live television, a process Fletcher
Markle has likened to sitting on the end of a branch, while,
at the same time, sawing that limb from the tree. Schaffner
had more than his share of unexpected moments in live television. Since nobody really knew what would happen, part
of his preparation then was to cover all possible contingen-
cies, to have back-up plans in case of any emergency. This
was an early habit that paid off when he went into film,
where the stakes are much higher, the risks even greater.

Filmmaking is no more predictable than television;
numerous film budgets have been known to balloon. One
of Franklin J. Schaffner's hallmarks as a director is that he
always makes pictures on time and on budget. This fact
became evident to the film world in 1968, when Schaffner
directed Planet of the Apes--a project that had first been
cancelled by Warner Bros. in 1965 because of its estimated
$10 million budget, and was subsequently turned down by
every other studio as the estimate soared to $16 million--
for $5.8 million.

The hypothesis that after a dozen continuous years
of directing live television Schaffner had the necessary
training and experience to become a film director is not
being advanced; there is a world of difference between
film and live television. A more modest hypothesis is pro-
posed: after 12 years of nonstop activity in television,
Schaffner learned how to become an excellent producer;
such intensive preparation as his is always cost-effective.
Schaffner knew how to bring in a show on time and under
budget; he knew visual shortcuts, employed false perspectives and a moving camera to cut down on his costs; he
knew the right technical people to hire, and assembled
crews that would work at maximum efficiency.

The limitations of live television helped shape this
tendency. There were the three basic cameras--four for
Playhouse 90--so there was no way he could possibly over-
shoot or do retake after retake; the show had to be good
when it was done, live. Directing meant editing; there

was no such thing as post-production a director could use
to try and save the show in the editing room.

Schaffner learned how to encourage and foster the
spirit of teamwork to keep the live television machine rolling. If he were directing, cast and crew alike would follow his plan, but, despite his extensive planning, he would
still be open to suggestion. "If you can prove that he's
wrong, he'll change," Robert Fryer points out, warning,
"but you'd better be sure of your facts." The live television experience instilled in Schaffner a set of work habits,
methods, and a knowledge of interpersonal dynamics that
he practices today. Fryer observes:

> Frank's qualities then are the same as they are
> today--he had great patience, he explained exactly
> what he wanted, and he was always prepared.
> Note: on the last film that we did, the same thing
> is true. He'd get up at four in the morning--
> truly! And the joy of Frank was that you knew
> he knew exactly what he was doing every minute,
> no surprises.

Evolution

Franklin Schaffner was a pioneer television director, coming
aboard at exactly the right time and place in 1948 and CBS
Television. Learning as the television industry grew, he
set technical standards for all television directors. He carried his technical reputation into live television drama, and
later into film as well. Under the guidance of producer
Robert Bendick, Schaffner made a name for himself in The
United Nations in Action and the telecasts of the 1948 and
1952 Political Conventions. He worked with such news and
public affairs personalities as Ruth Ashton Taylor, Douglas
Edwards, Walter Cronkite, Eric Sevareid, Don Hewitt, Quincy
Howe, Larry LeSueur, and Red Barber, and teamed with
Edward R. Murrow on the 1948 Conventions and on Person
to Person from 1953 to 1959.

Fron Worthington Miner, his first mentor at Studio
One, Schaffner learned how to stage, light, work with actors, use a moving camera, and produce a show for a television network. From Felix Jackson, his other Studio One

The neophyte CBS Television staff director, 1948.

mentor, Schaffner learned what the craft of writing entailed.
Working with script editor Florence Britten and such writers as Reginald Rose, Rod Serling, Gore Vidal, and Loring
Mandel, he became an expert in script construction and developed his skill in handling writers.

"Television depends very deeply on the word and the
face," Fielder Cook says. "All of us--even at our best--
were guilty of close-ups and close shots." With the basic
three camera set-up, one camera would usually shoot a tight
two-shot, and the other cameras would focus on close-ups
of the two principals as they talked; montage consisted of
those three basic shots. Rather than montage, Schaffner
favored mise en scène in practice: his cameras were constantly on the move, with the actors and props positioned
accordingly; he used light, music, sound effects, and special effects to enhance the scene. When his loan-out assignments in television became bigger with Ford Star Jubilee,
Producers' Showcase, and Ford Startime, Schaffner's mise
en scène took full advantage of the physical opportunities.

With his Unit Four production of "Antigone" in 1956,
Schaffner demonstrated that he could move his camera--via
dolly or crane--as gracefully as had ever been seen on live
television, his tracking shots taking on the elegance of Max
Ophuls'. It is worth mentioning that these sweeping camera moves came on color programs: most directors did not
like to use the color cameras because, like the early three-
strip Technicolor film cameras, they were too bulky and
cumbersome. Disregarding the weight of the equipment,
Schaffner used the moving camera subjectively, objectively,
omnisciently, and sometimes imperceptibly.

Schaffner never storyboarded; all of his directions
were handwritten into his script. The shots he chose for
his television shows were always neat and precise, his visual compositions always faultless--something that would become even more apparent when he later moved to the more
controlled medium of film, with its larger screen format.
To capture a script's intention, Schaffner would not hesi-
tate to select an unusual angle. Such early shows as "The
Ambassadors" and "Jane Eyre" suggest that Schaffner has
long had a penchant for mirror shots. This automatically
raises a couple of questions: Is Schaffner being reflexive?
Do they suggest a doppelganger motif? At this stage in his

career, Schaffner's mirror shots should be considered as
more ornamental than anything else.

Schaffner was accustomed to the 52-minute and 30-
second format. "It was a beautiful form to work in," Fielder
Cook insists. "It was exquisitely small, exactly deep enough
for the vignettes of human emotion that we dealt with." With
his use of the moving camera, as well as the subject matter
of his shows, Schaffner soon acquired a strong reputation
as an action director, able to accomplish difficult effects with
limited resources. As he progressed in his career, his visual touch became more subtle and refined. Nevertheless,
the fact remained, he had worked on a lot of television,
reaching the point where he had outgrown the limits of the
52-minute and 30-second format. He was growing restless;
he needed a larger canvas.

Playhouse 90 was not necessarily that larger canvas.
Although the extra 30 minutes made no real difference to
the directors, Fielder Cook has said, "The texture expanded
changes the entire texture, and multiplication will kill anything." Herbert Brodkin has spoken of the Schaffner ten-
dencies in the Playhouse 90 era:

> Frank liked to move his camera around. Frank
> liked the big picture; it was tough to get Frank to
> move in close. But he knew how to visualize, a
> lot of directors didn't. So you always were trying
> to cut Frank down a little bit--he tended to be too
> big. But that was all in preparation for his film
> career.

The Schaffner Television Show

Moving from literary adaptation to original drama, Schaffner
became associated with more realistic shows--harder hitting,
more demanding, more detailed. Particularly adept at handling shows that involved documentary or news-like techniques, Schaffner, with such programs as "A Stranger May
Die" and "Seven Against the Wall," helped pave the way
for the docudrama form.

The best of Schaffner's television shows contain the
combination of intense acting and social realism. Recalling

Loring Mandel's "The Raider," concerning a power struggle
in a corporate war, Mayo Simon exclaims: "That's not a
play. That's not a movie. That's live television--strong
action ... with men ... in rooms!" Franklin Schaffner is
automatically identified with live television drama: his
works centered on men; the men would be necessarily enclosed in space for the medium; there would be strong action, mostly in dialogue. Reduced to the proportions of
the television screen, a Schaffner show featured men talking in rooms. The courtroom would become the ideal setting for this type of drama in "Twelve Angry Men" in 1954
and "The Caine Mutiny Court Martial" in 1955. This dramatic form would reach its apotheosis in The Defenders, the
final Herbert Brodkin-Reginald Rose-Franklin Schaffner collaboration.

      In assessing Schaffner's television career, George
Roy Hill says:

> I don't think Frank is very weak on anything but I
> think his strength is in high drama, all the things
> like "Thunder on Sycamore Street"--it was just mar-
> velous, that's the kind of thing Frank does brilliantly
> --and "Twelve Angry Men."

Those are also Reginald Rose scripts. Having set the standard for television drama of social consciousness, Rose and
Schaffner's names forever will be linked. Herbert Brodkin's
1981 television production of Skokie was a fine show in the
best of the producer's tradition, based on an actual incident
of an American Nazi Party group's attempted march on Skokie, Illinois, a predominantly Jewish city with many survivors
of the holocaust; it can also boast of the offbeat casting of
Danny Kaye in a strong dramatic performance. This is the
stuff of classic Rose-Schaffner collaborations: it is all too
tempting to think of a Skokie as produced by Herbert Brodkin, written by Reginald Rose, and directed by Franklin
Schaffner. This type of show best reflects Schaffner's personal beliefs, a type of politics Richard Gehman once described in one word: "Adlaistevensonian."[62]

      Yale University produced a significant number of peo-
ple who were to prove most influential in live television in
the late 1940s and 1950s, and in film by the late 1950s. A
list must surely begin with Worthington Miner, Fred Coe,

Herbert Brodkin, and Paul Newman. Not until the USC-
UCLA-NYU film school axis beginning in the 1960s would
the academic world play as significant a role in television
or film.

The pre-film career of another New Haven product,
George Roy Hill, is similar to Franklin Schaffner's--live
television and theatre. Neither made his first film until
the 1960s; Hill's Period of Adjustment preceded Schaffner's
Stripper into motion picture theatres by eight months. "I
never really wanted to make films," Hill maintains. "I didn't
make a film until I was over forty years old." In Schaffner, he found a colleague who shared a strong theatrical
foundation; they began helping each other out on their respective scripts and shows in the 1950s. Somewhat modified, now that Schaffner no longer lives in New York, that
practice continues today. "I show him my pictures before
they're released," Hill says. "I value his comments very
much--Frank has always been very helpful with films,
scenes, helping my act."

Their relationship might be likened to a couple of
characters from one of Hill's films: Hill plays Butch Cassidy to Schaffner's Sundance Kid; Hill is immediately charming and engaging, Schaffner reserved and guarded. Moreover, George Roy Hill's film career most closely parallels
the film career of Franklin J. Schaffner: they both make
big-budget studio films with big-name actors; Hill's career
serves as a most useful cross-reference to Schaffner's career.

In an earlier generation, William Wyler began in Hollywood in 1925, directing low-budget silent westerns for Universal Pictures. Had Schaffner begun in an earlier era, he
might have learned his craft directing westerns; had Wyler
been born in a later generation, he might have started off
in live television. Leo McCarey joined Hal Roach Studios as
production chief in 1926, learning his craft making silent
comedies. Before turning Irene Dunne and Cary Grant into
a screen pair, he teamed up Stan Laurel and Oliver Hardy.
Had Hill been born in an earlier era, he might have started
off his career in a comedy factory like Hal Roach's, but at
this stage in his career he was still a long way away from
working with Paul Newman and Robert Redford.

"It was a lot of fun in those days," Hill says, recalling the golden age of television. "Really, we had a great
time." All the directors in their group--Cook, Frankenheimer, Hill, Lumet, Mulligan, Penn, and Schaffner--were
young and ambitious. "It was a young man's medium," Hill
continues. "We were too damned busy. You just worked
like a slave. You had no time to go fooling around." They
had absorbed the grinding punishment of directing live television, and time was beginning to take its toll; as the 1960s
drew near, the directors were all approaching their forties.
Describing Franklin Schaffner at the end of that era, Richard Gehman, recalling their childhood days, wrote:

> He had a habit of lounging back in his chair and
> rubbing his head against the blackboard so that
> some of Mr. Stallsmith's chemical formulae smudged
> his hair and made it seem prematurely gray. Tele-
> vision has done to Schaffner's hair permanently
> what chalk did temporarily. [63]

Film

Franklin J. Schaffner reflects on the transition period:

> It wasn't a pressing kind of "Gee, I've got to do a
> film now!" It would just lay there in your mind,
> but eventually you were going to have to make the
> transition, and the question was: "Yeah, but when?"

It had been a question in the minds of all directors of television drama ever since Delbert Mann went to Hollywood to
direct Marty in 1955. When Mann stayed in Hollywood, the
directors could foresee that their kind of television life
couldn't go on forever--five years after Marty, live television drama would be dead. If a director wanted to remain
in television, he would either have to direct filmed episodes
for series or become a television producer.

Twelve Angry Men stands as one of finest film adaptations of an original teleplay; it is a model of a motion picture
courtroom drama. The 1957 film version had two significant
advantages over the television production: (1) with 42 minutes and 30 seconds more time to work with, Reginald Rose

was able to develop and embellish the characterization of
the 12 men and delve into the trial itself in more detail;
(2) Henry Fonda--a case of the right actor in the right
film at the right time--he is ineffably right as Juror No. 8;
ultimately, Twelve Angry Men belongs to Henry Fonda.

Having missed out on working with Fonda in "The
Caine Mutiny Court Martial," Schaffner again missed out on
Twelve Angry Men. In one of those quirks of fate that be-
fall people who work in show business, Franklin Schaffner
was not chosen to direct the film; instead, Sidney Lumet
was chosen by the film's producers, Henry Fonda and Reginald Rose. "I know Frank was very disappointed not to
get it," says George Roy Hill. ("Henry Fonda, UA and I
wanted [Schaffner] to direct the film but he was contractually committed to something else, and was unavailable,"
Reginald Rose says. "Sidney Lumet was our second choice.")
("I don't remember any commitment," Schaffner says.) For
the rest, Fielder Cook's words more than suffice:

> This is not to say anything against Sidney [Lumet]
> --Sidney and I grew up together--but the absolute
> crime was that Frank did not get Twelve Angry Men.
> Twelve Angry Men, the film, was made by Frank
> Schaffner. Sidney had a road map he could've fol-
> lowed in the dark. It was really dirty pool.... It
> was just appalling that he didn't do it.

There is a scene in "My Beloved Husband," a murder-
mystery Franklin Schaffner directed for Studio One on
March 2, 1953, where the police inspector questions the
murder victim's stepdaughter in her artist's studio. The
confrontation takes place in a medium two-shot: the stepdaughter, to the left, faces the camera; the inspector's
back is seen to the right of the frame. During a tense moment, the inspector slams his right hand on a desk. At
that very instant, there is a cut to a reverse angle. As
the inspector completes the slamming motion, the camera
tilts rapidly up to his face. "It was one of the most marvelous live television kind of cuts that I recall," says
Fletcher Markle, the producer of the show. "It's so easy
to do on film, but my God...."

Markle is absolutely right. The cut is so fluid as to
be unnoticeable; it has to be seen two or three times before

it becomes apparent. Typifying Schaffner's seamless style,
a moment like this has a positive subliminal effect on the
audience. Even as early as 1953, Franklin Schaffner was
much more than just a journeyman television director: he
had good instincts and a visual flair; he was a superb technical craftsman. Given the opportunity, had Hollywood
opened its doors to him, Schaffner was entirely capable of
making good films; he had all the tools to be a film director
--yet it would be another decade before he would have that
opportunity. Perhaps he was waiting for the right property,
perhaps not; the fact remains that of his generation of directors Franklin Schaffner started the earliest--and was the
last to leave television.

    The year is 1960:   "Frank was pretty good usually at
almost everything," Herbert Brodkin says.   "He could do
comedy.... He was good at anything he wanted to do.
Frank's a good all-around director."   After a dozen continuous years in television, after four hundred television shows,
Franklin Schaffner, if nothing else, had put in a lot of time
and acquired a substantial amount of experience.   He was a
professional; long before he ever set foot in a motion picture
studio, he had seen it all.   He had worked on a lot of television, perhaps too much television.

    Schaffner had recently spent three years in Hollywood
as a director for Playhouse 90.   For a would-be film director this was a sound move, putting him in closer proximity
to motion picture studios and executives.   Ostensibly the
move paid off--Schaffner would soon have a contract to direct motion pictures--but not before a significant detour to
Broadway.

3. THE FILM CAREER OF FRANKLIN J. SCHAFFNER

Advise and Consent

"In 1960," Schaffner recalls, "everybody could see what we really had been brought up in, developed in, had an affinity for and a devotion to, and a certain skill in executing was live drama." For a confirmed New Yorker, the most logical progression would be from live television to theatre --television production had moved west, and Hollywood studios weren't breaking down his door with offers. "It was the next step," says George Roy Hill. "It was the medium that was closest to us because all the television [in the golden age] came out of New York."[1]

The Unit Four directors did not have to move to California: Hill had already directed Ketti Frings' Look Homeward Angel on Broadway in 1957; Fielder Cook would soon direct Steven Gethers' A Cook for Mr. General in 1961. Figuring prominently behind the scenes in Schaffner's 1960 Broadway debut was another Unit Four alumnus, Jerome Hellman, president of the Ziegler-Hellman-Ross Agency: also representing the play's producers, Robert Fryer and Lawrence Carr, Hellman put the package together.

Robert Fryer, of course, was an old friend from the days of Studio One. After his tour of duty in television, Fryer had left, with Worthington Miner's blessings, to work for the legendary stage producer-director George Abbott. Joining forces with Carr, he acquired a track record including such plays as Wonderful Town, Desk Set, and Auntie Mame. In the division of labor, Fryer looked after the script, casting, and direction; Carr looked after the costumes, sets, and casting. There was a third partner: Fryer and Carr, as the credits read, worked in association with John Herman; Herman looked after the finances.

In 1960, the producers took an option on Allen Drury's
Advise and Consent, a novel set in the then near future.
The Russians have already landed men on the moon: the
President of the United States of America nominates an unpopular Secretary of State who turns out to have been a
Communist in his youth; the resulting action leads to scandal, blackmail, and the suicide of an idealistic young senator. Fryer took a copy of Drury's novel to his first choice
to direct the play and asked him to read it. "I've always
been crazy in my choices of things, of getting the offbeat
person," says Fryer who, having specialized in musicals
and comedies, was himself venturing into new ground, "because Frank had never done a Broadway show."

A Broadway play would be an important credit for a
director whose career was on the rise. With such television
productions as "Twelve Angry Men," Franklin Schaffner was
known as a director of strong action with men in rooms;
such was the stuff of Advise and Consent. The director,
with his avid interest in politics, was naturally intrigued by
it, and began work on the play in June 1960. Drury had
sold the film rights separately; none of the participants of
the stage version was connected with the screen version that
was released in 1962. Political films have always been considered box office poison; it would take someone with the
flamboyance and clout of Otto Preminger to get the project
off the ground and produce a motion picture that would, as
depicted in the ads with the Capitol dome, lift the lid off
Washington.

Loring Mandel, another Hellman client (who would
write the screenplay for Hellman's 1979 film directorial debut, Promises in the Dark), was hired to adapt Drury's
sprawling political novel for the stage--as it turned out,
even as Mandel was at work on the play, Wendell Mayes
was busy writing the screenplay. Mandel and Schaffner
had spent the previous year on the road, visiting tent
shows and faith healers, researching what they hoped
would be a film version of The Healer, the script earlier
turned down by Kaiser Aluminum Hour. By now, having
worked together often enough, they were quite familiar
with each other's idiosyncrasies--a fortunate circumstance
considering the claustrophobic nature of work this collaboration would entail. "Frank was always very gracious
and respectful," Mandel recalls. "The personal situation
was, at the very minimal, pleasant."

Mandel's first draft was twice as long as it should have been; writer and director spent the summer cutting and reworking the script. As had been the custom whenever one of them started a project, the script was circulated among the Unit Four group for thoughts and suggestions, but the bulk of the work was left to the writer and director. Mandel describes what transpired in their daily script conference:

> Frank impressed me as a director who wanted to understand. We would go through the pages and he would ask a great many questions about why I made one choice or another. We would discuss the scene structure in the same way. If he had a suggestion for a different structure, or a new scene ("What if we had Orrin speak to Brig here?", "What would happen if Bill saw the letters that were coming in?", etc.), he would present it in a calm and dispassionate way. I never felt him forcing.

Afterwards, Mandel would return to his desk and spend the rest of the day rewriting the script.

There were five major male parts to be cast. On Broadway, producers generally have to go with their fifth or sixth choices: instead of a Richard Widmark as Brig Anderson, the idealistic young senator, or a Ralph Bellamy as Orrin Knox, the old and honest senator, for example, Richard Kiley and Ed Begley were hired. The three other leads were filled by Chester Morris as the majority leader, Henry Jones as the southern senator, and Richard Carlton as the right-wing senator. In the two other important roles were Staats Cotsworth as the nominee and Otto Kruger as the President.

This is not the cast that opened on Broadway a few weeks later. When the show was in Philadelphia, Otto Kruger realized he could no longer remember his lines, asked to be released, and was replaced by Judson Laire. Although a good actor, Richard Carlton was wrong for the part of Van Ackerman, and, a week before the show opened in New York, Kevin McCarthy stepped in; McCarthy's chilling charm and wit in the Joseph McCarthy-like character made a considerable difference in the play's overall effect.

The fact that Schaffner had worked with all of these

actors before in television did not turn out to be much of
an advantage. To begin with, they were a difficult bunch
to handle; secondly, they were performing in another medium, involving different stakes. Live television, on the
other hand, had provided excellent training in other areas,
as Schaffner observed, easing the transition to the stage:

> You used a theatrical scheme of rehearsal, almost a
> theatrical scheme of choreography. Certainly you
> used a theatrical scheme of lighting because lighting
> in motion pictures is totally different from lighting
> in continuous staging. [2]

Schaffner brought in another television colleague, Rouben
Ter-Arutunian, to design a set not unlike the one he had
created for "Antigone." Once the Cort Theatre was selected, the production was designed to fit its specific dimensions. "All they were," says Fryer describing the set,
"were all levels. [Schaffner] decided to take all the gela-
tins out of the spotlights, the front lights. Everything was
black and white like a newspaper report."

     Soon came the time, as Schaffner relates, unique to
the theatrical medium:

> One of the great traumatic moments is when you've
> been rehearsing in a theatre under a 1000-watt
> bulb now for three and a half weeks, and then sud-
> denly somebody throws up a set: the performances
> aren't the same, staging doesn't look correct. Every-
> thing is changed by sets and by dressing and by
> costumes.

The play opened to excellent reviews in New Haven. However, as Frank Capra learned when he took Mr. Smith Goes
to Washington to Washington, the Advise and Consent company found out just how critical Washingtonians can be
about plays or films about their city. The reviews were so
ruinous that the producers brought in the critics for a seminar; there were even rumors that the writer would be fired,
rumors that were only dispelled when the director vowed to
leave if the writer went. So extensive were the rewrites
that in Philadelphia, the next stop, the play ran too long.
Finally, a week before the play arrived in New York, most
of the rewrites were thrown away: with the exception of a

new first scene for the third act, what opened on Broadway
was basically the same play that had opened in New Haven.

Advise and Consent had its première at the Cort
Theatre on November 17, 1960. While it is quite impossible
ever to see this particular production, it is possible to envision what it might have been like based on the critical reception it received from the New York press on November
18, 1960:

> Some of the finest teamwork I have witnessed from
> a theatre chair was set in motion at 7:40 last even-
> ing. (John Chapman, New York Daily News)

> "Advise and Consent" is a big, bold, rough tough
> mean, ornery, and very exciting show about a Sen-
> ate full of bad actors, all played by good ones.
> (Walter Kerr, New York Herald Tribune)

> Loring Mandel has cut Allen Drury's Pulitzer Prize
> novel ... into a rip-roaring melodrama about poli-
> tics. (Robert Coleman, New York Mirror)

> This rousing, sardonic estimate of cloakroom tres-
> passes in the U.S. Senate has been piercingly di-
> rected by Franklin Schaffner. Mr. Mandel's drama
> is full of fury and fevers, so much so that I almost
> jumped out in the aisle to start a demonstration.
> (Frank Aston, New York World-Telegram & Sun)

> [It's] been staged, dirty blow by dirty blow, with a
> loving attention to the feel of business-as-usual by
> a master of curt and cold-blooded naturalism, Frank-
> lin Schaffner. (Kerr)

> Mr. Mandel has made his dramatization in short,
> swift scenes building up to theatrically impressive
> ones in the Senate. (Howard Taubman, New York
> Times)

> Director Franklin Schaffner has paced it expertly,
> in simple but effective Rouben Ter-Arutunian sets
> .... (Coleman)

> ... handling small and large groups with equal
> facility. (Taubman)

> Franklin Schaffner, making his bow as a director,
> had a monumental task moving all these men in and
> around sets which were changed only by the removal
> of a chair or the lowering of a flat--but I thought
> he succeeded. I didn't make a tally, but there must
> be more than 20 indicated and separate scenes in the
> three acts. (John McClain, New York Journal Amer-
> ican)
>
> I found it absorbing, exciting, and disturbing--and
> a remarkable piece of stage craftsmanship. (Chap-
> man)
>
> It's good old-fashioned theatre, and that's something
> to be grateful for nowadays. (Coleman) [3]

With the success of the show, Franklin Schaffner became a hot stage director; he was named best director in the
Variety Critics' Poll, an honor he shared that year with Gower
Champion. "Doing theatre is the hardest work in the world,"
Schaffner insists. A writer and producer have more input
but the director has less control in this medium, and, once
the curtain goes up, the actors are in charge. "It is impossible to do anything else when you're working in the theatre," he continues. "It's 24 hours a day, underpaid, hard,
and absolutely gratifying work." Schaffner had in fact developed migraine headaches during rehearsal of Advise and
Consent. After the Broadway opening, he was in a state of
exhaustion, had to leave New York, and spent two weeks in
the Caribbean to recuperate.

In 1962, he was announced to direct Touch the Sun,
a musical by Max Showalter and Peter Walker. When that
project fell through, he prepared to direct Papa Makes Music, by Charles Sherman, to be produced by Joseh Dackow,
Schaffner's erstwhile Studio One associate director. Although
devised along the lines of The Sound of Music, this musical
about Johann Sebastian Bach and his 15 children, featuring
music by Bach, was never produced. Later in 1963, Robert
Fryer and Lawrence Carr approached him about doing a
stage version of W. A. Swanberg's Citizen Hearst. This
was excellent Schaffner material: he could set up a titan,
and then cut him down in the end--it would be his Citizen
Kane, but for real. That was precisely the reason why the
play was never produced: the Hearst people blocked it.

It was a quirk of fate that Schaffner never directed another play; if, at the time, Schaffner was very interested in film, it would be fair to say he was also very interested in the theatre. "His feeling for the theatre was amazingly accurate and wonderful," says Robert Fryer, a man who has produced over 40 plays on Broadway and in Los Angeles. "He has a very good sense of construction for the theatre." Schaffner proved he had the tools for the trade but his career would move in another direction, something that Fryer bemoans:

> I think it's sad that he hasn't done more plays because there aren't that many good directors in the theatre.... I just wish he would come back to the theatre and do something.... He's been asked, God knows, enough times.[4]

Describing Schaffner's direction of Advise and Consent, Fryer gives a hint of his colleague's destination: "He did it almost like a motion picture, as it went from one scene to another." Schaffner's next career move was to Hollywood: he had signed a three-picture contract with Twentieth Century-Fox.

A Summer World

> I had a marvelous solution to my own life which was I could do television in the fall and the spring, and make a film every summer. Life would just carry me along that kind of rosy road forever, and I would never have had to move out of New York.
> —Franklin Schaffner

Schaffner took some important skills with him to Hollywood that could easily translate to the film medium: he knew how to work with a writer, production designer, actors, and he knew a thing or two about dealing with a producer. "I'm most comfortable with simple situations--four walls, with two men in confrontation, or a love story," he once said. "I am also comfortable with an adult-child relationship."[5] In that case, he must have been comfortable with his first film assignment, A Summer World.

Based on a novel by Richard Dougherty, its producer

was Henry T. Weinstein, formerly of the Theatre Guild, who
recently had worked with Jerry Wald on the Twentieth
Century-Fox lot; Schaffner was soon to discover that a
novice director might not necessarily know less about film
production than a more seasoned producer. A screenplay
had already been written by the estimable Howard Koch
before Schaffner arrived; Steven Gethers, who had written
"The Rag Jungle" for Kaiser, was brought in to do a complete rewrite.

The story concerns three triangular relationships that
eventually become encircled: 17-year-old Alex has filial
loyalties divided between his father, Peter, a cold intellectual who works for Charles Bonham's think tank, and Edward, Bonham's playboy son; loved by the sweet and simple Ellen, Alex falls in love with Kate, Bonham's sophisticated daughter visiting from England; there is also Evelyn,
an older woman, who once had an affair with Peter and will
have one with Edward. In Gethers' script, the love triangles are eventually resolved, and the generation gap somewhat bridged. "You have to stop blaming everything on
your parents," the message is, "even if they're to blame."[6]
Most unusually, considering the guidelines of the motion picture code of the time, young Alex sleeps with the 16-year-
old Ellen with no resulting tragedy; it is presented as very
much the normal and healthy thing to do, an event that en-
riches them both. All the characters in A Summer World
become wiser at no great expense to themselves.

Locations were found in Monterey and the Santa Ynez
Valley. Plans had been made to shoot the climactic Sports
Car Rally in Monterey, Carmel, Solvang, Laguna, and Peb-
ble Beach--locations scattered across California. Fabian,
Susan Hampshire, and Gig Young were cast as Alex, Kate,
and Peter respectively; Suzi Parker was tested for Evelyn.
Pre-production was virtually complete; a start date had been
assigned. Then one day, in an incident that sounds like
something out of Hollywood pulp fiction, Schaffner went to
the studio barber shop to get a haircut. As he was tipping
Sam the Barber, Schaffner recalls, Sam asked: "'You're
the director of A Summer World?' I said, 'Yep.' And he
said, 'They're not going to do that picture.'" In such
fashion was the director informed the film had been cancelled.

What is most obvious decades later is the television-
like quality of the project: the action is mainly in the dialogue and the characters' reactions; the script is about the
human heart, a very fragile piece for a motion picture.
Apparently, with impeccable logic, the studio had assumed
that a relatively small project not unlike a television drama
should be directed by a television director; perhaps this
kind of material might have been better served on Playhouse
90 than in CinemaScope.

Schaffner could have had a more pleasant stay in
Hollywood. The last straw was when William Self, head of
Twentieth Century-Fox Television, asked him to direct episodes for the Bus Stop series. In a letter to Jerome Hellman, Schaffner wrote: "Right now I feel like the aging
star whom no one will kiss." [7]

The Defenders

Simply stated, The Defenders is the finest dramatic series
ever produced for American television. Its genesis was in
"The Defender," a two-part show presented on Studio One,
February 25 and March 4, 1957, during Herbert Brodkin's
tenure as producer. Written by Reginald Rose and directed
by Robert Mulligan, it featured Ralph Bellamy as veteran
lawyer Lawrence Preston, and William Shatner as his son
and associate Kenneth Preston; Martin Balsam portrayed
the district attorney, and, in the role of the defendant
accused of murdering a psychiatrist's wife, was a young
actor then billed as Steven McQueen.

A series based on this show, given a plural title, was
sold to CBS four years later. Upon his return from Hollywood in the summer of 1961, Schaffner was asked to direct
several episodes for the first season of The Defenders. Although he was not really interested in doing a series, he
accepted the job; he could fit the work into his suddenly
less crowded schedule, and there were other good reasons.
First of all, the producer was Herbert Brodkin--Brodkin
made it attractive; he had always respected and enjoyed
working with Herbert Brodkin.

Known for giving directors an enormous amount of

freedom, Brodkin was also a strong advocate of the written
word. "The writer is essential," he has said. "Anybody
can produce shows. I can train a producer in six months."
That is an exaggeration, of course. Few producers have
Brodkin's integrity, and fewer still have fought as hard
and as persistently to get their product on the air. If
there were objections to a script that he was preparing in
the days of live television, Brodkin was renowned for going to network, sponsor, or ad agency and saying, "You'd
better have a film ready or there's not going to be anything
on the air--because this is the show we're doing this week."

     The second reason for doing the show was the materi-
al: Reginald Rose was doing an excellent job with the
scripts. As early as "The Remarkable Incident at Carsons
Corner," which preceded "Twelve Angry Men" on Studio One
by nine months, Rose had discovered how effective a trial
could be as television drama. The Defenders was the final
refinement of the form: considering the medium and its
limitations, the courtroom is perhaps the most perfect setting for a television show. Thematically, The Defenders
grappled with the most significant issues of the day, subjects new to television such as child rape, abortion, and
euthanasia--heavy subjects that can often resist dramatiza-
tion, yet the issues were carefully integrated into the
scripts, and the shows never lost their dramatic impact or
appeared too didactic. Unable to write every show, with
his investment in the series Rose could function in another
capacity: it is not difficult to understand why Brodkin
would say, "He's probably the best script editor I've ever
seen." Rose also brought something unprecedented to the
world of television law: sometimes the bad win and the
good lose.

     While simultaneously a bane to those who had estab-
lished themselves in live television drama, film was a great
attraction of The Defenders. Brodkin explains:

     There were a lot of directors who wanted to get
     some film experience who came and worked for us,
     who were fairly well known in television but were
     not known in film. Frank was one of them. The
     Defenders trained a great many film directors as
     well as film writers.

The biggest disadvantage of working with film was that, due
to the exigencies of the production schedule, the director
was given no time for rehearsal; the greatest blessing of
film turned out to be that The Defenders could be seen in
foreign countries.

Also working on the show were two Studio One alumni:
art director Willard Levitas and production manager Kenneth
Utt. Using the single camera shooting method for the first
time, the director had two new collaborators: director of
photography Morris Hartzband and film editor Sidney Katz.
Each episode had a six-day shooting schedule and a week
for post-production. Interiors were filmed at the Filmways
Studio, but, even if the heart of every show was in the
courtroom, The Defenders took visual advantage of New
York locations with film; to all those involved, it was very
important that a New York-based show succeed.

The most notable change made in the series was the
casting of the leads: E. G. Marshall and Robert Reed portrayed the father and son team of Lawrence and Kenneth
Preston, by far a much colder and more colorless team than
their predecessors. Yet their very lack of charisma only
added to the strength of The Defenders: "The Defender"
was very much about Lawrence Preston and his moral decisions; he was the character in conflict, with Ralph Bellamy
bringing great dignity and force to the role. Although
neither Bellamy nor Shatner had enough voltage to dominate
a motion picture screen, with the right roles--and the Prestons were such roles--they could exude star quality on the
television screen. Marshall and Reed were more low-keyed,
performing with an unobtrusive excellence in the manner of
the best supporting actors; in The Defenders, the Prestons
were in fact supporting characters to the defendants. Bellamy and Shatner might have easily detracted from the human drama of the defendants, but with Marshall and Reed a
perfect balance was maintained. Furthermore, Polly Rowles
as Helen Donaldson, the Prestons' secretary, and Joan
Hackett as Joan Miller, Kenneth's girlfriend, were dropped
along the way; in their absence there was less of a tempta-
tion to make the show more formulaic.

The series invariably featured excellent performances.
"We used the best actors in New York," Brodkin can right-

fully boast. "Many of them used that as a launching point."
Special credit must go to Alixe Gordin, the casting director,
another former colleague from Studio One: The Defenders
provided early jobs for such actors as Dustin Hoffman, Gene
Hackman, Martin Sheen, and Robert Redford.

Schaffner immediately tested himself in film editing in
the first of the six shows he directed for the series, John
Vlahos' "Killer Instinct," by creating a dizzy montage of
busy New York streets that opens the show. Moreover, one
can almost sense the director's delight in being able to stage
a dialogue scene at an actual Westchester County commuter
stop. The original Ken Preston, William Shatner, plays Jim,
an affluent stockbroker who accidentally kills a construction
worker; true to the pattern of the show, the Prestons are
ciphers to Jim's story. Trained to kill in the Korean War,
when it was all right to kill, Jim realizes he is lucky because
he has the money to buy a good defense; the fact remains
he did murder a man, and he must assume responsibility.
Lawrence Preston, who was winning quite handily, is proud
to lose this case.

Robert Thom's "The Boy Between" is a then ten-year-
old Richard Thomas, caught between a mother who is a
Broadway star (Norma Crane) and a mentally unstable father
(Arthur Hill). In the custody case, the Prestons represent
Belle, the mother, who is reluctant to let her lawyers be-
smirch her husband's character. When he figures out why,
Lawrence paves the way for a reconciliation between husband and wife; as a result, the Prestons are 0 for 2 in
Schaffner's shows. In one adroitly staged exterior scene
where Belle and her son are mobbed on their way to the
court by the press, the director conveys how harrowing
life can be for a celebrity in the midst of a sensational
court case, and even more so for an innocent young boy.
In a more intimate scene in the Judge's chamber, Schaffner
subtly puts the drama in its proper perspective by shooting the scene from a very high angle.

"The Attack," written by John Block, features two
kinds of attacks. When a policeman named George (Richard
Kiley) learns that his young daughter has been raped, he
kills the young man she has identified. Nobody finds George
culpable--even the D.A. admits he would have done the same
thing--but, it turns out, Arnie (Martin Sheen), the murder

victim's best friend, raped the little girl to get even with
the humorless by-the-book cop. Schaffner begins this show
with a chase, intercutting between George following Steve,
the young man he thinks is the rapist, and Arnie, who follows at a distance. The sequence is economically handled:
it is not the number of shots used but the unusual angles
that convey distance and elapsed time. At the moment
George kills Steve, the camera is in close on Arnie's face,
as he witnesses and reacts to the deed. George is photographed from a low angle when he learns he killed the
wrong person; a zoom in to a close-up only adds to the
psychological weight of his recognition--even though found
not guilty, he must live with his sense of ponderous guilt.

As its title may indicate, "Gideon's Follies," written
by Robert Crean, is a comedy. Joshua Gideon has invited
his five ex-wives to his house for a treasure hunt, during
which his dead body is discovered; the sixth and present
wife is accused of murder. Lawrence Preston gathers all
the wives back to the scene of the crime for a game of
charades, through which he learns that all five former
wives were responsible for the murder. It is typical of
Herbert Brodkin's sense of humor that he would assign
Schaffner a comedy, a black comedy at that, featuring six
women. Add a drunken butler, and the director has a
fine opportunity to work with eccentric comic types. Schaffner directs with broad strokes, getting a lot of reaction
shots from the normally unflappable Preston; the reconstruc-
tion of the murder is undercranked to look like a silent comedy, complete with player piano accompaniment. Schaffner
also uses the soundtrack to get a couple of laughs. When
Lawrence Preston visits Mrs. Maycroft (Shirl Conway), the
first wife, she is listening to a how-to-speak-Italian record.
Preston enters and begins to introduce himself, "Hello, I'm
..." "Ferdinando," the record finishes. Later, when Preston visits Mrs. Goblanski (Eva Gabor), the third wife, only
to be thrown unceremoniously out the door by her jealous
husband, he can be heard offscreen saying, "Good afternoon, Mrs. Goblanski," with full aplomb.

Reginald Rose's "The Tarnished Cross" is reminiscent
of his "Remarkable Incident at Carsons Corner," in which a
group of school children put the janitor on trial for murder.
This time around, the Boys Government League conducts a
trial, accusing Dino (Martin Sheen again) of murdering the

janitor. On the way home from a banquet honoring the
founder of the club, the Prestons are drawn into the trial
and, in effect, serve as a chorus, commenting on the action. As the mock trial is held in a gym, Schaffner has a
lot of room for his roving camera. The scene in which the
boys set up the chairs and prepare for the trial is given
special urgency with a moving camera shooting at a low
angle.

The final episode Schaffner directed, David Shaw's
"Reunion with Death," concerns six Korean War veterans
who have scheduled a reunion banquet at a hotel, where a
group of newspapermen, one of them played by a young
Gene Wilder, is on hand to get the story. Action, thereafter, is confined to the privacy of the hotel room: instead of celebrating, five of the party put the sixth surviving member of their bomber crew on trial for collaborating with the Chinese communists eleven years earlier; the
other five men were maimed and scarred, but Colonel Miller
(Lee Phillips) has since become a prominent military figure.
Brought along as a legal adviser, Lawrence Preston defends
Miller, who admits he's guilty, and, because of his coward-
ice, responsible for losing the lives of 72 men. The set is
too cramped to accommodate tracking shots, so Schaffner
relies mostly on group composition; if the camera cannot
move around the floor, it can boom up or down when a
character rises or sits. In the final shot of the show, the
camera booms down on Miller and Preston as they walk down
the hotel hallway to the elevator, and then dollies to the
left to reveal Douglas (Robert Webber), the actual traitor,
cringing against the wall.

The Defenders satisfied Schaffner's criterion for good
television--it is a two-way street, with the viewer contributing something in return to the program. The six episodes
directed by Schaffner achieved and sustained an astonishing
degree of quality: he helped establish the standard for the
series, which would run another three years. His contributions to The Defenders did not go unnoticed: he won an
Emmy for his direction. Herbert Brodkin, Reginald Rose,
and E. G. Marshall also won Emmies for best dramatic program, writing, and acting respectively in the show's first
season; it would win multiple Emmies each year it remained
on the air.

The Defenders needed Reginald Rose to create it, but
without Herbert Brodkin to do battle with the network it
never would have gotten on the air and, once on the air,
remain uncompromised. "Censorship exists only to the point
that you don't fight it," this producer has said. [8] No one
has fought harder. In the years after The Defenders, Brodkin brought the docudrama form to television with his 1973
production of Pueblo; he has also provided audiences with
such memorable television programs as The Missiles of October (1974) and Holocaust (1978). The most telling indict-
ment of television today is that there doesn't seem to be any
room left for a Brodkin-Rose-Schaffner type of show.

Leland Hayward was the original superstar agent (his
clients included Fred and Adele Astaire, Clark Gable, Greta
Garbo, Judy Garland, Dashiell Hammett, Ernest Hemingway,
and James Stewart). Later he became a powerhouse Broadway producer of such shows as South Pacific and The Sound
of Music, and produced such films as Mister Roberts as well.
Leland Hayward was involved with television as early as
1953, when he produced The Ford 50th Anniversary Show,
a $500,000 extravaganza featuring the historic teaming of
Mary Martin and Ethel Merman; with his producing associate,
Marshall Jamison, Henry Fonda's stand-in during Mister Roberts' Broadway run, Hayward produced a series of specials
for CBS in the 1960s, including The Fabulous Fifties and
The Gershwin Years.

Schaffner directed The Good Years for Hayward on
January 12, 1962; it was not one of either man's finer
achievements. Following the same basic format of Hayward's
other CBS specials, it was a loving look into the past in
song, dance, and comedy sketches. Taped in New York,
this 90-minute program was adapted by A. J. Russell from
the Walter Lord book covering the 1900-1914 period in
America, and featured Lucille Ball, Mort Sahl, and Henry
Fonda as the host. "It was neither refreshingly nostalgic
nor scintillating," 'Rose.' of Variety wrote. "It could and
should have been both." [9]

A Tour of the White House with Mrs. John F. Kennedy

Did you hear about what happened to Frank on A

Tour of the White House? An aide came to him and
said, "The President and Mrs. Kennedy are delighted
with your work but would like to make just one observation: You called the first lady, several times,
'Sweetie.' "

                                                    --Felix Jackson

Frank Schaffner's most widely viewed television program was
A Tour of the White House with Mrs. John F. Kennedy.
Originally broadcast from 10 to 11 p.m. over both CBS and
NBC, Wednesday, February 14, 1962, it was repeated on
ABC at 6:30 p.m. the following Sunday, and rebroadcast by
CBS on March 25, 1962.   The audience of this single show
surpassed over 60 years of White House tours.

    The program was written and produced by Perry Wolff,
then the executive producer of CBS News specials.   Formerly a journalist, Wolff produced over 200 documentary specials
for television, including The Italians, The Japanese, and
The Israelis.   Schaffner and Wolff had known each other
since the 1948 political conventions, which they both covered, in different capacities, for CBS Television.   For the
White House tour, Wolff was looking for a director with three
criteria: news experience, dramatic experience, and a pre-
sentable personality.   Schaffner was the obvious choice to
do the show: he was CBS' finest example of such a director.

    Being deeply immersed in White House restoration, Mrs.
Kennedy was involved in the planning of what should be
shown and discussed.   At the outset, film had to be ruled
out because it would require too much light.   Videotape
meant black and white: color cameras were still too bulky
and had no mobility; color cables were twice as thick as
black and white cables.   A live telecast, despite Schaffner's
proven expertise in directing Person to Person, was not
deemed appropriate "on the basis that the spontaneity of
the photography could not match the artistry of the objects
in the White House, nor the story Mrs. Kennedy wished to
tell." [10]

    Schaffner and a 54-man crew arrived at the White
House on Saturday, January 13, 1962, carrying five tons of
equipment and four tons of lights.   As Mr. and Mrs. Kennedy spent that weekend in Virginia, the crew was able to
set up under less pressure and to do some shooting that

did not need Mrs. Kennedy. On Monday, principal photography commenced with Mrs. Kennedy; in honor of the occasion and the place, the crew wore ties. During the taping of the show, Mr. Kennedy conducted affairs of state in the West Executive Wing, and private life went on as usual in the family quarters, but in front of the camera, as Wolff has said, "The whole history of the White House reduced itself to the almost irreducible dramatic minimum: one person on stage."[11]

Actually Mrs. Kennedy was accompanied by veteran CBS correspondent Charles Collingwood, basically in a supporting role. Providing Mrs. Kennedy with an intimate audience, he was always ready with a pleasantry or a compliment in the event Mrs. Kennedy should flub a line. As a measure of his role, Collingwood was not given a close-up until the end of the show, when the special guest of the program, Mr. Kennedy, made his appearance. Lest she become too nervous, the people surrounding Mrs. Kennedy at all times were limited to two: Collingwood and Schaffner. Radio microphones were used for the sound, but, for all the technical improvements, Schaffner points out, "It's always an interesting problem when you're fitting a radio mike to the first lady of the land." The director also had to explain some of the fundamentals of taped or filmed television to Mrs. Kennedy, who had arrived assuming that an hour show should take an hour to do.

The tour was planned and arranged in segments, each lasting five or six minutes. Schaffner rehearsed each segment with Mrs. Kennedy and Collingwood before they would be photographed. A total of five cameras was employed, shooting in two-room sequences: two cameras would be set up in the first room and two in the next room; the fifth camera was used for an emergency or as a spare or for transitions in corridors. As soon as the director finished in the first room, the crew would move ahead to the first of the next two-room location, where cables were ready and the lighting had already been set up. "The whole purpose was to do it as fast as we could to accommodate her schedule, for her convenience," Schaffner says. "What turned out to be about 45 minutes of tape that should have taken a minimum three days to shoot, I think, we did in one day." Mrs. Kennedy spent less than seven hours on the set, and everything was finished by 7 p.m. No retakes of Mrs. Kennedy were necessary.

152 Franklin J. Schaffner

The following day, Schaffner shot all the inserts that could not be covered by the cameras during the initial run; as neither Mrs. Kennedy nor Collingwood was needed for any of them, the shots had been deliberately bypassed the first time through. Having started at the bottom and finished on the top floor of the White House on Monday, the director, crew, and staff started to cover the same route on Tuesday, as planned. But President Kennedy had viewed a quick assembly of the first day's tape and was dissatisfied with his performance: his pace and rhythm had been too fast, conflicting with Mrs. Kennedy's more leisurely style; he wanted to redo his segment. Schaffner was shooting inserts on the ground floor when the president called him at 10:15 a.m. saying he wanted to start at 11:00. "He said, 'I'll be ready in three-quarters of an hour. Can you be ready?'" Schaffner recalls. "One never stops to consider in that circumstance. Ready or not you say, 'Yes, we'll be ready.'"

All the cameras and cables had already been brought down to the ground floor; they had to be taken back up to the top floor again. In the meantime, Schaffner tried to figure out how he would do the retake without Mrs. Kennedy, who was unavailable at the time; the continuity clerk was sent rushing to check if Mr. Kennedy was wearing the same suit and tie. In the end, the shots of Mrs. Kennedy from the first day's shoot were edited into the revised version of this segment. "It worked," the director admits, "but it was the fastest 45 minutes of my life."

A week later, a sound crew returned to the White House to record Mrs. Kennedy. This narration was used primarily under the animated historical sequences that were shot on film under Wolff's supervision; Schaffner was not involved with them. There is a marked difference in Mrs. Kennedy's vocal quality between the tour and the historical narration. Her voice sounds considerably more charming on the tour, most probably due to Schaffner's presence behind the cameras. There were 95 inserts in the master tape; when seen in the 1980s, the visual difference between the film image and the tape image is obvious—it is as jarring as a jump cut—but, being typical of television in the early 1960s, it made little difference to the public at the time the program aired. All in all, the show cost $130,000 to produce —even then a bargain.

Although pre-recorded, this tour is the ultimate
Person to Person. The moving camera greatly adds to the
sense of spatial continuity as it tracks with Mrs. Kennedy
and Collingwood from room to room and through corridors.
Schaffner's choice of angles is consistently interesting. The
East Room segment begins with a high-angle shot of a chan-
delier which is followed by a very low-angle shot of Mrs.
Kennedy and Collingwood entering the room; as they leave,
the camera moves in on a mirror so the viewer can catch
their reflection. When they reach the Dining Room, Schaffner cuts to an exterior view of the White House as seen
from the South Lawn while Mrs. Kennedy and Collingwood's
commentary continues offscreen. The camera pans to the
left and zooms in to establish their physical whereabouts;
when they announce they will be visiting the Blue and the
Green Rooms, the camera, still in close, pans to the respective exterior of each.

Mrs. Kennedy remains the perfect wife to the end.
Finally, when her husband is talking in the Cabinet Room,
she silently seems to recede into the furniture. She had
adopted much the same attitude when she and her husband
appeared on Person to Person on October 30, 1953: at that
time the couple had been married a month and, although a
reporter in her own right, she seemed content to play the
dutiful housewife. [12]

Calling the White House tour "a milestone in television," critic Harriet Van Horne was particularly taken by
Jacqueline Bouvier Kennedy: "It confirmed the impression
that the free world's Mrs. Kennedy is one of the most graceful ornaments of our age." [13] At times Mrs. Kennedy seems
a bit too stiff, at other times she is breathy in the manner
of Marilyn Monroe. The evidence, however, is that Schaffner was able to cut through her Stepford Wife facade and
reveal a more humorous side to her that was hidden when
she resided in the White House. When she was relaxed and
natural, the camera captured a most charming woman: this
Mrs. Kennedy is the stuff of which movie stars are made.
Indeed, Jacqueline Bouvier Kennedy Onassis is the movie
star who never made a movie. The White House tour was
the perfect showcase for her--before the tour is over she
becomes more interesting than the White House.

Accordingly, Mrs. Kennedy was awarded a Special

Trustee Emmy. The program itself also received a Special Trustee Emmy in addition to a Peabody Award. For his contributions to the program, Schaffner won a 1962 Directorial Achievement Award from the Directors Guild of America. So well had he done his job that Schaffner became typecast in a new way: CBS would ask him to guide such shows as A Tour of Monaco and The Kremlin.

John F. Kennedy's appearance in A Tour of the White House is a reminder that he was a master of the television medium. Television had become such a pervasive influence in American life that Kennedy took especial advantage of it and very conspicuously played for the camera. Mrs. Kennedy definitely had screen presence, but Mr. Kennedy had even more.

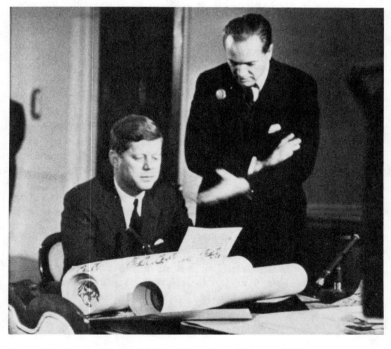

John F. Kennedy and Franklin Schaffner, 1962.

Schaffner's professionalism and personal style had
been closely observed by those who lived and worked in the
White House. "As a result of that tour of the White House,"
Schaffner says, "they simply called me and said, 'Hey, can
you do this?'" "They" included President Kennedy and his
press secretary Pierre Salinger; "this" included the State of
the Economy speech and another speech for which Salinger
suddenly called the director the night before, asking him to
come to Washington--neither the nature nor the content of
the speech was mentioned. Schaffner arrived the next day
to find more security than he had ever seen at the White
House. Nobody knew what the president would say; it was
top secret. At the last moment, before he entered the control truck, Schaffner was given a copy of the text; he was
immediately besieged by a swarm of reporters who wanted
advance word on what Kennedy would say in his Cuban Mis-
sile Crisis speech.

"The principal function was trying to make him look
effective and relaxed on camera," Schaffner recalls, "which
had to do with the way he sat, if he sat, how he was lit,
how he would move." Kennedy had an innate theatrical personality, and it was Schaffner's job to accentuate it. Because of the medicine he took for his bad back, Kennedy
had a puffy face; Schaffner chose different lenses and
lighting patterns than had been previously used, and discovered that the president looked more effective if he stood.
In addition, Schaffner always brought a make-up woman with
him. "He would never wear make-up," says the man who in
effect directed the president, "but we'd always get the make-
up on him at the last moment."

There was, however, a bit of a problem involved:
producer Fred Coe had been appointed Kennedy's official
television adviser. "Please don't be concerned," Pierre
Salinger wrote to Schaffner, "it's an occupational hazard I
suppose."[14] But Schaffner was concerned, and volunteered
to withdraw his services, but the White House would not
hear of it. "It was some source of embarrassment to me ...
but they would call me." He adds innocently, "I don't know
why that happened."

The Stripper

I happened to turn on the television the other day,

and my first film ("The Stripper") was on. I was
very struck by the fact that except for a couple of
instances, it was a television movie. I'd used television dramatic techniques—big, big close-ups, re-
sisting moving things outside, using exteriors only
as a transitional vehicle.... I had no concept at
all of how to use the screen.[15]

                                        --Franklin J. Schaffner

Schaffner worked on his first Hollywood film in 1962: John
Ford had directed The Man Who Shot Liberty Valance; William Wyler had finished The Children's Hour; Vincente Min-
nelli, Two Weeks in Another Town; Billy Wilder, One, Two,
Three; Elia Kazan, Splendor in the Grass; John Huston,
Freud; Orson Welles, The Trial. British director David
Lean had completed Lawrence of Arabia; George Stevens
was in the midst of a six-year absence from film, Fred
Zinnemann a four-year absence. The big news in interna-
tional cinema came from France, where a group of directors
and films were loosely banded together under a rubric named
the New Wave: Jean-Luc Godard, Breathless; François
Truffaut, The 400 Blows; Alain Resnais, Hiroshima, Mon
Amour; Louis Malle, Zazie in the Metro.

A new generation of American film directors had
arrived—from television studios in New York. Arthur Penn
recently had directed The Miracle Worker; Robert Mulligan,
To Kill a Mockingbird; John Frankenheimer, The Manchurian
Candidate; Sidney Lumet, Long Day's Journey into Night.
Ralph Nelson had finished his first film, based on a television play he had directed, Requiem for a Heavyweight, and
George Roy Hill was making his first film, A Period of Adjustment.

Schaffner's assignment was an adaptation of one of his
favorite dramatists, William Inge. Inge's string of Broadway
hits—Come Back, Little Sheba, Picnic, Bus Stop—had become highly successful motion pictures; in 1959, Inge wrote
a play he considered his finest, A Loss of Roses. Based on
Inge's track record, Buddy Adler (having done extremely
well with his 1956 film production of Bus Stop), head of
production at Twentieth Century-Fox, purchased the property in advance of its Broadway opening for a sum that
might have been as high as $400,000.

The play opened in December to negative reviews and
closed in three weeks, thus stripping it of any pre-sold
value it might have had as a film title. The studio had paid
a lot of money for a flop; meanwhile, Dark at the Top of the
Stairs, Inge's previous play, had been filmed and met by in-
difference at the box office in 1960. Immediate preparation
was postponed, and A Loss of Roses was put on a shelf.

Bob Goldstein, formerly head of Fox's European office,
became head of production when Buddy Adler died; in August 1960, the property was reassigned to Jerry Wald, the
one-man-mini-major within the studio. Wald began work on
it a couple of months later by hiring Alfred Hayes to write
the script; the title of the project, anything but pre-sold,
was changed to Celebration. There were the usual announcements: Jennifer Jones, Kim Novak, or even Marilyn Monroe
would play the lead; Bette Davis, Joan Crawford, or Irene
Dunne would also star.

By 1961, Goldstein was out and Peter Levathes was in
as head of production. If Goldstein had been in over his
head, so was Levathes, whose background was in advertising and television. "Levathes had two things in common
with [studio president] Skouras," Darryl F. Zanuck once
said. "He was Greek, and he didn't know anything about
making pictures."[16] Thus the stage was set for the chaos
that would ensue during the making of The Stripper.

To direct Celebration, Wald turned to a man whom he
was grooming as a major film director, Jose Ferrer, who had
recently completed Wald's Return to Peyton Place; Joanne
Woodward and Richard Beymer, both having Fox commitments, were signed to play the leads, Lila and Kenny. A
Fourth of July parade was filmed in Hutchinson, Kansas before the production was again stalled; Ferrer left the film,
and the project languished until March 1962, when Franklin
Schaffner was hired to direct the film.

In 1962, Wald was perhaps the most successful and
powerful producer in Hollywood. "In the catalogue of human wonders," Rowland Barber once wrote of him, "he might
be accurately recorded as an animated hot spring."[17] Wald
had achieved notoriety as the prototype of Sammy Glick in
Budd Schulberg's Hollywood novel What Makes Sammy Run--

a newspaper copy boy turned radio columnist turned script-
writer turned producer. Schulberg also compared Wald with
Darryl Zanuck, who similarly served his apprenticeship at
Warners, became an independent producer and studio head,
and received an Irving Thalberg Award.

> Hungry and without shame, they were eager studio
> beavers ... glib toreros who discovered in the big
> studio compound the perfect arena for their hyper-
> thyroid energies. Given the Hollywood in which I
> was raised, it was inevitable that young doers like
> Darryl and Jerry would soon graduate from novil-
> leros to full matators who cut screen credits instead
> of ears and tails and then took over the arena itself
> as front-office impresarios.[18]

Wald named his Fox unit "Company of Artists": he
had great aesthetic pretensions, but was at the same time a
very practical producer who made commercial entertainments,
not products intended for art houses. The man whose
dream was to film James Joyce's Ulysses was the producer
of Grace Metalious' Peyton Place (1957); his most ambitious
productions--D. H. Lawrence's Sons and Lovers (1960),
Tennessee Williams' The Glass Menagerie (1950), and, the
ultimate bastardization, William Faulkner's The Sound and
the Fury (1959)--were all compromised by some error in
conception, interpretation, or casting.

Despite vulgarian characteristics, Wald was a great
producer: he had tremendous clout, he got the job done--
his way; he was also responsible for fully one-fourth of
Fox's total product. Curtis Harrington, the former film
critic and experimental filmmaker who directed Games (1967)
and What's the Matter with Helen? (1971), became Wald's
assistant in 1955, and the associate producer of The Stripper. Recalling his former boss, Harrington says:

> He was in the office every morning by 6 a.m. By
> the time his staff of secretaries came in--he had
> three of them--there would be a huge stack of discs
> that he had dictated of letters and memos to be
> transcribed, and this was every single morning dur-
> ing the week. And apparently he worked on week-
> ends. I know that his wife once told me that it was
> virtually impossible to get him to take a weekend off

or to go any place or go on any kind of vacation.
He was a workaholic, and it killed him.

Wald set an impossible pace for himself trying to produce
ten films a year.

Yet no one can question his passion for film: he
lived for films, lived to make films. A voracious reader,
he kept extensive clipping files on any number of subjects.
One loose-leaf binder was marked "New People to Watch,"
filled with notes and clippings of new actors, writers, and
directors; it was this binder that Wald would open and come
up with the name of a highly respected television director,
Franklin Schaffner.

"Franklin Schaffner is an eminently reasonable and
affable man," says Curtis Harrington. "They got along very
well." Wald allowed Schaffner and screenwriter Meade Roberts to come up with a workable script on their own. On
May 28, 1962, as he prepared for his first motion picture
set-up, the neophyte film director received a letter from
his famous producer: "May this opening day be the beginning of a long 'always cheerful, never downhearted'
collaboration between us," he said. "It has been a great
pleasure working with you in preparing the script."[19]

During pre-production, Schaffner was granted a leave
of absence to do some television work. Felix Jackson, now
a vice-president of NBC, had ordered a show about the
Brinks robbery. Commissioning Loring Mandel to write the
script, he asked Schaffner to direct "The World's Greatest
Robbery," a two-part drama for DuPont Show of the Week.
To accommodate Schaffner and his film commitment, the production was moved to California and taped at the NBC Burbank Studios early in April for $170,000; featuring R. G.
Armstrong, Paul Mazursky, and Cliff Osmond, the two parts
were televised on April 29 and May 6, 1962. "DuPont Show
of the Week is at its best (and its best is often none too
good) when it deals in actualities, documentary studies and
the like," Cecil Smith wrote in his Los Angeles Times review.
"It offered perhaps the finest of these [in 'The World's
Greatest Robbery']." Smith's critique of the show also
captured something of its director's approach to his work,
describing it as "a sort of dogged determination to minutely
document each step in the massive venture."[20]

When he returned his attention to film, Schaffner
could not avoid noticing what was happening on the lot.
The situation would have seemed bizarre to even the most
seasoned Hollywood veteran, much less a television director
who was only too well aware that he was nobody's first
choice to direct Celebration. The spiraling costs of Cleopatra had the studio tottering; Twentieth Century-Fox was
on the brink of financial ruin. The economic pressures
were so severe that Spyros Skouras was forced to sell the
back lot acreage for $15 million--about one-third of Cleo-
patra's budget, for what today is known as Century City.
There were rumors, gossip, and, above all, studio politics.
There was a war going on at Twentieth Century-Fox, a
power struggle to see who would wind up in control.
Schaffner was on the fringe of all this and had little idea
of what really was going on. "I was simply a guy out of
New York who was doing his first film and hoping to do
well by it," he says, "and this was not my hunting ground
at all. I thought it was absolutely weird, absolutely weird,
but yet I had nothing to compare it to."

Wald brought in Claire Trevor, with whom he had
worked so successfully in Key Largo (1948), to play Helen,
Kenny's mother. To open up the story further, Miriam
Caswell, the nice young girl only referred to in the play,
was written into the film; the role was given to Carol Lyn-
ley, a Fox contract player Wald had been grooming in Hound
Dog Man (1959) and Return to Peyton Place (1962). Michael
J. Pollard, who had created the role on Broadway, played
Jelly Beamis, an almost one-dimensional role as Kenny's best
friend (Pollard, coincidentally, made his screen debut in
Wald's 1962 production of Hemingway's Adventures of a
Young Man, in which he played an identical role--Richard
Beymer's best friend). Pollard's eccentric screen persona
would help flesh out his character; Jelly was given addi-
tional help with a rejoinder he repeatedly uses, "Pardon me
for living." Robert Webber reprised his Broadway role as
Ricky, Lila's boyfriend, who eventually finds work for her
--in a sex act and blue movies; the versatile Webber was
properly macho and unctuous for the film. Louis Nye and
Gypsy Rose Lee were brought in to provide some backstage
color: Nye performs magic acts in the film with Joanne
Woodward and Gypsy Rose Lee, who, as Madame Olga, has
no other function in the film.

The film is set in the present, rather than the 1933 of the original. Filming the present is always cheaper than filming the past, but costs were not a determining factor; it was assumed that young audiences would not relate to anything but their own era. Instead of the dangers of the Depression, Helen talks about "the unsettled world" of today --already over 20 years ago. But then the studio was in its own depression, and "Kansas in the late 1950s," as Schaffner says of the studio attitude, "was like the Depression anyway." Schaffner is the kind of director who would have preferred the 1930s time setting: it would have created more of a nostalgic distance; Lila's lost childhood evokes a more bittersweet response when discussed in a time that is safely in the past; the same time period in William Inge's Splendor in the Grass added to the appeal of Elia Kazan's 1961 film production. Curiously, there is almost always a disjointed quality about the contemporary scene in Hollywood movies--it seldom seems, looks, or feels like the present--especially when young people are concerned. The Stripper was no exception.

The director had no say on the aspect ratio--Cinema-Scope was the Twentieth Century-Fox policy--and the choice had been made to shoot in black and white, something already frowned upon with the success of NBC's Saturday Night at the Movies. Networks were converting to full color operations in the 1960s; film studios stressed color movies accordingly. The Stripper was the last black and white film to be produced by Twentieth Century-Fox for a very long time; Wald probably had to make some concessions to get black and white.

The Stripper was made at a time when--with the exception of stars, directors, and writers--the studio system still functioned with various departments on the lot: department heads assigned people under contract to particular films. The company spent two seeks on location in Chino, California, posing as Salinson, Kansas; Schaffner had little input with the art direction. "Why you would take a so-called midwestern house in Chino and dress its exterior with lattices and growing roses on them fascinates me," he says rhetorically. "The subject was roses, right?" More beneficially, assigned to the film was cinematographer Ellsworth Fredericks, a veteran with such credits as Sayonara (1957)

and Wild River (1960), who was quite helpful, never once
taking advantage of Schaffner's inexperience. Schaffner
was lucky with cameramen from the very beginning of his
film career.

Most of the film was shot on the lot, where the director found himself somewhat bewildered by major studio
machinery. "I recall being very impatient," Schaffner says,
"having come out of television into a film form--the ponder-
ousness of the equipment, the numbers and the crew and
all." Despite the traffic on the set and the turbulence in
the front office, production continued without major incident
until Friday the 13th, July 1962: Jerry Wald died of a
heart attack. He'd had his name on 300 motion pictures; it
was hard to realize that Jerry Wald was only 50 years old
when he died.

Schaffner was working on the set when he received a
call from the studio operator asking if it were true Wald had
died; the rumor had spread across the lot. The truth was
Schaffner did not know, nor did he mention this incident to
anyone when he returned to the set. Later in the afternoon,
the production department confirmed that the producer was
dead; Schaffner was told to go back to work, finish up the
day's shooting, and only after all the scheduled work was
completed could he tell the cast and crew about Wald.

Wald's funeral was held at 11:00 a.m. Monday; Schaffner was instructed to report back to the studio at 2:00.
"They didn't dip a flag on the lot, anything else--that was
it," Schaffner recalls. When he asked about what was happening and what he should do, he was told just to keep on
shooting. "Just kept shooting," he says. "Just an absolute barbaric reaction on all parts." Jerry Wald was irre-
placeable; no new producer was assigned to the film. Producing chores fell in part to Curtis Harrington and in part
to Franklin Schaffner. Although the latter could produce
for television, he was in new territory: he knew nothing
about film budgets, and even today has no idea what The
Stripper cost to produce. Neither he nor Harrington was
in a very secure position--the Inge project was the only
film on the lot. Thanks to Cleopatra and the studio's financial woes, the commissary was closed; salaries of secre-
taries, firemen, and security guards were added to the
budget of the one remaining film.

After principal photography was completed, the front office ordered a new opening sequence that neither the leading lady nor the director wanted to film: Lila is recruited for a Hollywood party to be used for immoral purposes. Once filmed, this sequence was later discarded. The film as released starts with a Hollywood tour bus on the Sunset Strip: platinum-haired Lila, in her skin-tight pants, walks by. Is it Jayne Mansfield? the passengers ask, Kim Novak? "It's nobody," the bus driver answers emphatically, and a striptease drumbeat signals the beginning of the main credits.

Schaffner did not attempt any bravura filmmaking in his debut; his style is economical and unobtrusive. Near the beginning of the film, Kenny goes out to visit Miriam, jumping into his car and driving off. The camera follows the car down the street, and there is a cut to a closer moving camera shot; Kenny suddenly makes a U-turn and pulls up in front of Miriam's house. The visual joke is made--Miriam, for all intents and purposes, lives across the street--in a simple way, reminiscent of a 1930s Hollywood studio action scene. At an ice skating rink, Kenny becomes jealous and tries to show off for Miriam, only to crash into a refreshment stand. The scene is played for pure slapstick, with Schaffner using a four-shot sequence that goes back to silent comedies: (1) a long shot of Kenny skating out of control; (2) a medium shot of Kenny crashing into the refreshment stand; (3) a reverse angle of Kenny; (4) a close shot of Kenny's reaction.

That same evening, Kenny stumbles home drunk, taking off his clothes as he goes up to his room, jumps into bed and quickly discovers that Lila, his former babysitter, is in it; the scene is played like a boulevard farce. A crane shot follows him as he slides down the bannister--a technical feat Schaffner could not accomplish on live television because of the one-story sets. After checking on Kenny, Lila returns upstairs and stands for a moment in front of the bedroom door; the camera dollies backwards, down the hall, and pans to the left, where an open door reveals an anguished expression on Helen's face. Although the oedipal relationship was mostly removed from the film, this single shot suggests plenty.

By her mere appearance on screen, Claire Trevor

brings an appropriate amount of neuroses to the part of
Helen Baird. Still attached to her late husband, she explodes in anger when Kenny buys her a new watch; her
old watch is symbolic of her husband. At the same time,
however, she is possessive of her son, and her relationship with Lila changes accordingly when Lila moves in with
them: in a moment when Helen, on the porch, talks testily
to Lila, inside the house, an extraordinary shot of Joanne
Woodward's face as seen through the screen door explains
the entire situation.

In general, the whole approach of the film is lighter
than the play. Gone is most of the Inge hysteria and the
sense of lurking danger in any interpersonal relationship.
To broaden the film's appeal, the age gap between Lila and
Kenny was narrowed, somewhat changing the meaning of
their relationship. Also gone was the greatest--and perhaps
only--beneficiary of A Loss of Roses, Warren Beatty; Inge
also wrote Splendor in the Grass and the All Fall Down
screenplay for him. By the time The Stripper was produced,
Beatty was on his way to far greater things, and playing
Kenny in the film would have constituted a step backwards
for him. Richard Beymer played Tony in the blockbuster
film of West Side Story (1961) and was highly touted by
Jerry Wald, but he never panned out as a major star; in
The Stripper Beymer is ingratiating--no less, no more.

"Miss Woodward," James Powers wrote in The Hollywood Reporter, "is simply too bright to play with conviction
a brainless child entirely moved by the winds of random."[21]
Lila seems to be so normal in the film that it comes as a surprise to learn she has had nervous breakdowns, attempted
suicide, and undergone electric shock therapy. In that she
won an Academy Award for playing a psychologically dis-
turbed woman in The Three Faces of Eve (1957), Joanne
Woodward undoubtedly has the range to play an Inge woman,
but her Lila appears to be so practical it is hard to believe
she would be desperate enough to want to marry Kenny,
and, once rejected, attempt suicide on his account.

The actress, however, does have her share of moments. As Lila, she carries a teddy bear around with her.
When she learns that the theatrical tour has been cancelled,
she sits on a chair in front of a mirror in her hotel room,
clutching her teddy bear, looking for all the world like a

little lost girl. Woodward is especially moving when she delivers the central speech of the play, telling of the time
when Lila gave her teacher some flowers, only to get slapped
in return for talking to a boy:

> I told Teacher I wanted back my roses. But she
> wouldn't give them to me. She shook her finger
> and said, when I gave away lovely presents, I
> couldn't expect to get them back.... I guess I
> never learned that lesson very well. There's so
> many things I still want back. [22]

The loss of roses speech was moved quite effectively from
the end of Inge's play to the middle of Schaffner's film.

Joanne Woodward as Lila, sometimes distractingly so,
was deliberately made up to look like Marilyn Monroe. The
film's publicity drew attention to this fact, and reporter
Dean Gautschy reported the following exchange:

> "Are you purposely trying to be Marilyn?" I ask
> Joanne as she passes me en route to her room.
> "Why not?" she says. "Marilyn is quite a prod-
> uct of our generation and it would be an honor for
> any girl to emulate her." [23]

In other words, she plays the role as a starlet-type who
wants to be the next Marilyn Monroe. Since the film is set
in the late 1950s, this is a valid interpretation of Lila; at
times Woodward even copies Monroe's speech. The reported
exchange also reveals something else: Woodward uses the
word "girl," something that seems atypical of this actress.
The point is, Joanne Woodward was so involved in her role
that she gave interviews in character.

Marilyn Monroe herself was familiar with Inge-land.
Lila would have been a most intriguingly self-reflexive role
had Marilyn Monroe played a girl who wants to be Marilyn
Monroe. (A film version of A Loss of Roses with Marilyn
Monroe and Warren Beatty would surely have generated more
electricity than did The Stripper.) There is a final irony:
one of Lila's most prized possessions is a copy of her screen
test for the 1955 Twentieth Century-Fox production of Daddy
Long Legs for which the would-be Marilyn Monroe sang
"Something's Gotta Give"; during the shooting of The Stripper,

as coincidence would have it, Marilyn Monroe was on an adjacent stage at Fox, filming the ill-fated Something's Gotta Give.

The Stripper was poorly received. Bosley Crowther, then the dean of the New York film critics, wrote:

> Not a stitch of dramatic respectability covers its rickety bones.... It has been so deliberately denuded of the little that was worthwhile on the stage that it comes out an even duller movie, and that's about as dull as it can be.[24]

The film fared no better at the box office; the film opened in June 1963 and quickly disappeared. Neither did the director come out unscathed. "Franklin Schaffner's direction," as observed by Variety, "tends to be a bit choppy, uneven and, in spots, heavy-handed or unobservant." However, 'Tube.' goes on to make as astute comment: "There is a rather staccato tempo and a definite lack of geographic clarity about the film that indicates some editing stress and strain."[25] That is precisely what had happened. "I remember seeing The Stripper when Frank showed it to me," says a witness. "It was his version, and they took it away from him. It was a good film," George Roy Hill recalls, "he did a very good job on it."

In his first time out as a film director, Schaffner was caught in a change of administrations—something that would reoccur with such regularity in his career that it can almost be considered a common denominator of his films. In June of 1962, Spyros Skouras resigned as chief executive officer of Twentieth Century-Fox, a position he had held since 1942; the man who had championed CinemaScope became the scapegoat for Cleopatra. The victor of the power struggle was the founder of the Twentieth Century film company, Darryl F. Zanuck; backed by Skouras himself, he took over the reins of the studio on July 25, 1962. His production of The Longest Day would be the sole bright spot for Twentieth Century-Fox in 1962.

Far removed from all the internecine warfare, an obscure director named Franklin Schaffner worked with Robert Simpson, the editor assigned to the film, preparing the first cut of a motion picture now renamed A Woman in July, Inge's

original title for his play. Also beginning work was a composer named Jerry Goldsmith, who had been hired by the
film's late producer to write the score. In preparation,
Goldsmith saw the cut that Schaffner had completed. "It
was wonderful," he says. "It was so sensitive, and very
special." Had Jerry Wald still been alive, it is quite possible he could have saved the film from its eventual fate,
but only he among those involved had had that kind of
power.

"Frank, as I remember it, had eliminated Carol Lynley completely," Goldsmith says, "and cut down as much of
Richard Beymer as he could. By then it was all centered
on Joanne Woodward--it was wonderful." Miriam, as played
by Lynley, is young, pretty, and sweet; the role is completely one-dimensional. But when Darryl F. Zanuck saw
that Miriam had been removed from the picture, he complained loudly about the $30,000 salary Lynley had been
paid--she was under contract, and would not remain on the
cutting room floor. In the version according to Zanuck,
Carol Lynley went back in; Richard Beymer went back in;
Joanne Woodward, though, was trimmed and cut, trimmed
and cut.

Zanuck had the film shipped to his New York office.
Schaffner, who had already returned home, was summoned
to the Fox screening room where he finally met Zanuck--
and his entourage; also present was Robert Simpson. After viewing the film, Zanuck asked the director what the
budget was and if the sets were still standing; Schaffner
could answer neither question. Then Zanuck told Simpson
to meet him in an hour; a studio veteran, Simpson knew
that meant changes would be made. At the end of the day,
Schaffner called Simpson at his hotel room only to find the
editor had already been sent back to California. Calling
Simpson in California, the director learned about the cuts
Zanuck had ordered. So began what Schaffner refers to as
"The Longest Day Cut."

"[Zanuck] just lifted entire scenes," the director
says, "which cut out what was in many ways the most appealing part of the picture--which was non-plot line, just
color and character and that kind of thing." Zanuck, on
the other hand, was pleased with the job he had done,
writing Schaffner:

Marlene De Lamater, Joanne Woodward, Franklin Schaffner, filming A Loss of Roses/Celebration/A Woman in July/Woman of Summer/The Stripper, 1962.

> On reflection I am sure that you will find that the
> final version is, in most instances, a vast improve-
> ment over the version that was first presented to
> me. The story will always be a sort of adult soap
> opera but I am confident that we have taken out
> most of the suds.[26]

Curtis Harrington did not see it that way, and through
Richard Zanuck, fought to save the director's cut--all in
vain. "All the guts were excised from the picture," Harrington maintains.

Shortly after her arrival in town, Lila takes a walk
with Kenny, passing by a deserted bandshell--part of the
Peyton Place town square on the Fox lot. To best describe
her Hollywood dreams, Lila re-enacts a musical fantasy number, "Something's Gotta Give" from her screen test. "The
music number in the park might very well belong in 'Jumbo,'"

Zanuck complained, "but not in a serious story." Consequently, Lila and Kenny walk by the square, there is a
dissolve, and they are back at the hotel in the released
film.

The most damaging cut of all comes after the scene in
which Kenny backs out of marrying Lila: hurt and rejected,
she goes upstairs to the attic, breaks a mirror, and, with a
jagged piece of glass, attempts suicide. This was designed
as the climax of the film; the rest would be a coda. Harrington considers both Woodward and the suicide scene to
have been brilliant. "Its omission in the final cut took the
dramatic heart out of the picture," he says. Zanuck found
the scene distasteful: "The suicide attempt is really never
a genuine attempt," he maintained, "and it ends up being a
feeble piece of artificial drama." This particular cut probably lost Joanne Woodward a nomination for an Academy Award.

The Stripper was produced in an era when the production code office would not permit nudity on the screen.
In the strip scene, Woodward wore a lot of balloons (and,
under the balloons, man-made breasts). Lila's striptease is
performed to a sleazy sounding arrangement of a tune that
turns out to be none other than "Something's Gotta Give."
James Powers commented:

> The point of the play was that the girl's act was
> something much worse than a conventional strip,
> and the movie makes this point indirectly then un-
> dercuts it by the strip scene itself, which actually
> seems mild enough as a dance number. [27]

The striptease, even by the early 1960s standards, does
not justify Kenny's horrified reaction; neither is the impression given that Lila is shedding her illusions just as
surely as she is shedding the balloons.

Once again the scene was redesigned by the final
arbiter: Zanuck ordered Simpson to use as many close-ups
as he could, and, if he ran out of close-ups, to make optical enlargements of assorted parts of Joanne Woodward's
anatomy from the footage Schaffner shot for the scene; this
explains why portions of the number look so grainy. As
for the rest, Harrington explains:

> [Zanuck] wanted to make her seem more naked
> than she was, so his theory was if the audience
> didn't see very much, and he just kept cutting in
> close, they would think she was more naked than
> she was. It changed the whole feeling of her dance.
> The sequence is not designed to be beheld in close-
> ups and blow-ups.

The way that Schaffner had designed the editing of the number was to suggest that, far from being over, the striptease
was just beginning and would go on and on and on.

"The Longest Day Cut" was finished a few days before
Christmas 1962. A month later Zanuck changed the title
from Woman in July to The Stripper; the wonder is he didn't
use David Rose's song of the same name on the soundtrack
of a film already featuring Gypsy Rose Lee. As it was,
Goldsmith was instructed to deliver a jazzier score than he
would otherwise have written.

William Inge's play originally ended with Lila embarking on her sordid future with Ricky; with the involvement
of Warren Beatty, the play as briefly performed on Broadway ended with Kenny going off to Wichita to become a man.
The Stripper ends with Lila, as it rightfully should: first,
Lila throws away her beloved screen test, then walks out on
Ricky--whom she finally calls by name, instead of "Daddy"--
and walks out of the strip joint; she meets Kenny in the
parking lot, accepts Helen's new watch and his smile, and
ventures out into the night alone. The ending is optimistic:
Lila is her own person; she has made her separate peace.
She walks bravely, with new resolve, on the lonely road.
The optimism seems to be implicit in the film's final shot--
Lila is seen in a high-angle crane shot that presently booms
even higher.

Across the Atlantic ocean, Woman of Summer, as the
film was more aptly named, was a succès d'estime. Although
for the most part misguided and mistaken, Robin Bean wrote
in Films and Filming:

> [It is] notable for the unobtrusive but quietly pene-
> trating direction by Franklin Schaffner.... He gives
> as much air and movement to the story as possible,
> particularly in the exterior scenes which he handles

with an observant eye for detail and feeling rather
than treating just as linking shots as too many
directors do today. [28]

The film had all the right ingredients to be highly regarded:
it was a critical and commercial failure in America; Franklin
Schaffner was a new and unknown film director; it was based
on ambitious material by a great American playwright, a play
whose poetic title had been vulgarized by Hollywood producers; it had been tampered with and butchered by a studio
boss but still was a film of quality, featuring one of the finest
performances by its leading lady; the film ends with an at-
mospheric crane shot that reinforces the despair in its text--
seen from that omniscient viewpoint, Lila leaves the cruel
reality of Salinson, Kansas for the harsher lights of California, where she will meet her unavoidable destiny in a gutter
on Sunset Boulevard.

        Franklin Schaffner became a cult director with his
first film.

DuPont Show of the Week, 1962-1963

Broadcast over NBC Sunday evenings at 10:00, the DuPont
show was one of the last television programs with institu-
tional advertising: a different division in the company was
featured in each show's commercials. Previously a monthly
series, DuPont became a weekly series in 1961, best known
for its documentaries and dramatizations of actual events.
When DuPont decided to beef up its dramatic offerings,
Franklin Schaffner was the first person approached; "The
World's Greatest Robbery" was the result.

        Young and Rubicam, who represented DuPont, went
to Jerome Hellman, asking if they could persuade Schaffner
to stay on for the 1962-1963 season. Hellman responded by
setting up The Directors Company, consisting of Schaffner
and Fielder Cook, who had recently added the pilot for Ben
Casey to his imposing list of directing credits. "The Directors Company would not have come about without Frank
Schaffner," Cook says. Indeed, Schaffner had suggested
he be part of the team. Schaffner would be executive producer of the shows he directed through his Gilchrist Productions; Cook would serve the same dual functions through

his Eden Productions. Between the two men, The Directors
Company would be responsible for seven shows a season.

Although NBC and DuPont requested script approval,
this proved to be no major problem as it had with Kaiser.
Basically, The Directors Company could do whatever it
wanted, just as long as it provided a show every month.
Live television being a thing of the past, the shows would
be videotaped--on DuPont mylar tape, of course--using live
television methods, the type of television the directors knew
best. The Directors Company was given a $130,000 budget
for each show: according to the terms of the contract,
Cook, having been brought in by Schaffner, had to deduct
$10,000 from the budget of his shows and turn that money
over to the budget of his partner's shows. Schaffner, in
effect, had a $140,000 budget with which to pay the writer,
producer, cast, crew, and cover office and miscellaneous
expenses. The arrangement with DuPont and NBC was
flexible enough so that whenever Schaffner directed a relatively simple show, he could save the money and spend it
later when he needed to hire a larger cast or build sets
for a more elaborate production.

Jacqueline Babbin was hired away from David Susskind to produce for The Directors Company. Beginning
her career at the Liebling-Wood Agency, where she worked
with Tennessee Williams and William Inge as Audrey Wood's
assistant, she was also Irene Selznick's production assistant
before becoming a story editor for Talent Associates. More
recently, she has been an ABC vice-president, and, as an
independent producer, brought Sybil to television in 1976.
Her greatest talent has always been one for organization; as
producer for DuPont in 1962, she was the unifying factor
between Cook and Schaffner.

As always, the first step was finding and developing
scripts. The Directors Company went after the obvious
names--Rod Serling, Paddy Chayefsky, Gore Vidal, and
Robert Alan Aurthur--with no success. By now, as
Schaffner observed, Hollywood-filmed television had
brought a noticeable change:

> An east coast writer comes in, sits down and says,
> "I'm a writer. I've got an idea." Then he tells
> you his story. A west coast writer comes in, sits

down and says, "I'm a writer. What do you want
me to write?"[29]

After a script was developed, it was sent to DuPont and
NBC; casting began only after the script had been approved.
The Directors Company had the luxury of eight days rehearsal at Central Plaza, followed by two days of work at
NBC's Brooklyn Studios. The first day was spent blocking
the show; on the second day there was a run-through and
a dress rehearsal, after which the show was taped. The
producer attended the run-throughs and would later give
her notes to the director. "With somebody like Frank you
don't have that many notes," she says, echoing other
Schaffner producers. "He plans every detail; he doesn't
do last-minute changes."

The program was taped in continuity, the next best
thing to live television, the director selecting his shots
from the multiple cameras as the scenes were played. Due
to the difficulty of editing videotape, if a retake was necessary, the entire scene had to be retaped. The show would
be aired a few weeks later in color on NBC. Those familiar
with live drama would see a not unpredictable change--
videotape took the edge off the performances.

Among the programs directed by Schaffner in The Directors Company's first season was "Windfall" by Roger O.
Hirson, with Eddie Albert and Glynis Johns as an average
American couple who find that an old-fashioned commode the
husband has purchased is filled with money. The windfall
causes more trouble than anticipated; in order to return to
a normal life, the couple decides to burn the commode and
the money therein. While this teleplay is well acted and directed, and pleasantly forgettable, an hour is twice as much
time as it needs to tell the story.

"Two Faces of Treason" by Philip Reisman, Jr. has a
highly theatrical premise: a CIA-like organization, represented by Lloyd Nolan, presses a young corporal (Larry
Blyden) into impersonating his double--a double agent, no
less. The show quite properly questions government morality, but serves as proof that Pentagon drama dates very
rapidly. It also indirectly brings up an interesting critical
point about the genre: Blyden was undoubtedly cast in the
leading role because he looks like an average American guy;

the show suffers because Blyden threatens to become too anonymous. Paradoxically, this kind of drama worked better in Three Days of the Condor (1975), in which Robert Redford played an average American guy.

By far the most enjoyable of the four shows Schaffner directed for DuPont that season was "The Legend of Lylah Clare," which Fielder Cook accurately describes as "fun junk food." Written by Robert Thom, it is part Josef von Sternberg/Marlene Dietrich and part Vertigo, featuring a talented actress, Tuesday Weld, in one of the few good roles she has been given. Alfred Drake plays the megalomaniacal Zarkin, the film director who all too successfully transforms Elsie Brinkmann (Weld) into Elsa Christie into the second Lylah Clare: he teaches her to walk like Lylah, whom he taught to walk like Katherine Cornell who, in turn, was given her walk by Martha Graham; he hires Jean-Louis to dress her always in white, refitting her in Rita Hayworth and Kim Novak costumes. This is outrageous stuff--the stuff of good bad movies, as Robert Aldrich undoubtedly thought when he made his 1968 film version with Kim Novak; Schaffner's television version is lighter and wittier than Aldrich's, which mostly sinks. Despite the self-reflexive reference to Vertigo (1958), Weld is preferable to Novak: her face is expressive enough to pass from child to dying vamp; although she didn't quite make it in real life, Weld looks like a movie star. As did Lylah Clare 25 years earlier, Elsa holds a press conference in her bathtub; typically, the network chose this one element of the show to exploit-- the third bathtub scene in NBC history!

"The Legend of Lylah Clare" notwithstanding, what soon becomes apparent is that the material Schaffner directed on The DuPont Show of the Week was not as deep as that which he had directed on previous dramatic anthologies. The DuPont shows seem like light entertainments rather than the more socially significant programs his name is associated with in television. The change brought on by the new decade was more than with technique, film, and tape alone: the 1962-1963 television season also marked the debut of The Beverly Hillbillies on CBS; it would quickly become the most popular show in America.

The Best Man

In 1962 and 1963, the trade papers and some reputable
newspapers announced that Franklin Schaffner would direct
Kirk Douglas in a film entitled The Healer. This, of course,
was the project about the revival minister with ESP that
Schaffner had worked on with Loring Mandel in 1959. There
wasn't much truth to these announcements, but they did
serve the purpose of keeping the director's name alive in
the minds of motion picture people.

In May 1963, Schaffner was hired to direct The Pawnbroker for Ely Landau, a project that temporarily reunited
him with his mentor Worthington Miner, executive producer
of the film. Boris Kaufman was set as the director of photography, James Mason was being considered for the title
role, and Schaffner had several meetings with the script-
writers, David Friedkin and Morton Fine. The production
was soon stalled, eventually postponed, and during the
waiting period the director was offered a project he found
so exciting that he dropped out of The Pawnbroker.

"I have always said that out of all of my films I am
most fond of The Best Man," the director says, "because it
probably met up to about 80% of what my expectations for
the film were going in." If a director is considered very
fortunate to realize 50% of his expectations, then 80% must
involve some extraordinarily good luck. In this case the
good luck came from his actors: "It was a sublime cast,"
Schaffner says. The Best Man would give proof that its
director was good with actors; the film would solidify his
reputation as an actor's director.

Schaffner's contributions went beyond the acting. It
must have been peculiarly gratifying for him to receive
Brendan Gill's somewhat left-handed compliment in The New
Yorker:

> "The Best Man" has been directed with great verve
> and appropriate slickness by Franklin Schaffner,
> whom the Democrats and Republicans might do worse
> than hire this summer to inject into their conven-
> tions the sense of authentic hurly-burly that these
> affairs threaten to lack and that is marvellously de-
> picted here. [30]

Schaffner seems the exactly right choice to direct Gore
Vidal's political comedy-melodrama: he had directed Rod
Serling's "The Arena" as well as the 1948 and 1952 political
conventions for television; on Broadway, he had directed
Advise and Consent which, in what can only be a coincidence, was also a political melodrama with a homosexual
plot twist.

Hollywood generally steers clear of the political film,
by tradition box office poison. But with the election of
John F. Kennedy in 1960, his concept of the New Frontier,
and the style he brought to the presidency, Hollywood embarked on an unprecedented but short-lived cycle of political films: Advise and Consent and The Manchurian Candidate in 1962; The Ugly American, Kisses for My President,
and, indirectly, PT 109 in 1963; Dr. Strangelove, Fail Safe,
Seven Days in May, and, not least of all, The Best Man in
1964.

The Best Man had its genesis in a Henry Jamesian
conceit by Gore Vidal, involving two men: take "a man of
exemplary private life, yet monstrous public life, and contrast him to a man of 'immoral' private life and exemplary
public life."[31] Make these two men presidential candidates
patterned after Richard Nixon and Adlai Stevenson, and
Vidal's idea becomes a play in 1960, happily coinciding with
an election year. According to the Jamesian premise, William Russell, clearly the hero in Vidal's text, has not only
played around with too many women but, worse, has also
had a nervous breakdown; Joe Cantwell, clearly the villain,
has led a faultlessly dull private life, and plans to use the
nervous breakdown against Russell. When it is later learned
that Joe had a homosexual affair during the Second World
War, the reluctant Russell is urged to use this against him.
Between the two is the Trumanesque ex-president Art Hockstader, "The Great Hick," as he is fond of calling himself,
the kingmaker of the convention. "I tell you," Hockstader
says, "there is nothing like a dirty low-down political fight
to put the roses in your cheeks."[32] And Vidal brings it
all off.

United Artists bought the film rights for Frank Capra.
The director of State of the Union (1948) and, much more
successfully, Mr. Smith Goes to Washington (1939), Capra
was not an unreasonable choice. An expert at directing

fast-talking dialogue, he also knew a thing or two about
comedy. Pre-production began at the end of 1960 with immediate script problems. In 1959, Gore Vidal had seen his
Visit to a Small Planet turn into a movie vehicle for Jerry
Lewis and had worked on Suddenly, Last Summer, caught
between the likes of Sam Spiegel and Joseph L. Mankiewicz.
Having learned the hard way what can happen to a writer's
contribution on a film, Vidal wanted to be involved in the
production of The Best Man--all the better to protect his
work.

        The script Vidal wrote for Capra makes for fascinat-
ing reading: Vidal added even more jokes and witticisms,
strengthened the characterizations of all major participants
in the race, but the end result was a script of over 200
pages; such is its structure that Joe Cantwell, the antagonist, makes his first appearance on page 54. The Capra-
Vidal collaboration did not come to a fruitful conclusion;
their styles didn't mesh, they worked at cross-purposes.
Capra finally left the picture, and Vidal remained. United
Artists then tried to persuade one of Capra's Liberty Pictures partners into doing the film: William Wyler was interested but, in the long run, not that interested.

        United Artists turned to a young producing team in
whom they had great faith, Stuart Millar and Lawrence Turman, inviting them to do the film. Millar had been an associate producer for William Wyler in the early 1950s before
going out on his own; Turman had left the garment industry
to become an agent, and was Millar's agent before becoming
his partner. After The Young Doctors (1961) and I Could
Go On Singing (1963), The Best Man would be the third in
a four-picture contract Millar and Turman had with United
Artists.

        Millar and Turman decided on Franklin Schaffner as
the director. Turman had seen and been impressed by
Advise and Consent. "He's strong in masculine confronta-
tions," Turman says, "and he's efficient and serious."
Schaffner's background in television was of no particular
influence in the decision, but, even if they were not particularly looking for one of the new-breed directors, the
producers realized, "We had to make the picture at a modest price, and those guys would be good at that." Once
he was selected, Schaffner's television background was

indeed considered a valuable asset; he had also had the experience of working with Gore Vidal on "Dark Possession"
and "A Man and Two Gods" for Studio One.

Schaffner has always been a realistic film director.
He knew he had two producers and that he would have to
adjust to the personality of each in order to work with both.
One of them was a frustrated film director, and Schaffner
would have to dodge the weight that was thrown in his direction. [33] He would have a budget of $1.4 million, which
was small even in 1964--but then the film would have to
make almost $4 million to break even, and The Best Man
was not the type of picture that would make a lot of money
in the foreign market--it would involve a herculean effort
just to put subtitles on it; neither was a television sale
particularly meaningful to the film industry at that time.

Accompanying Millar, Schaffner went to Rome for several weeks of rewrites with Gore Vidal, who, in keeping with
his growing disenchantment with television--a Vidalian synonym for misrepresentation--had experimented with a character named "Unlucky Reporter" in his previous drafts. Serving as an incompetent chorus, Unlucky Reporter comments on
the action throughout the script, his analyses and predic-
tions invariably wrong. On paper, Unlucky is a fascinating
character; it is hard to say how he would have played on
film. As it turned out, instead of this bumbling fool, news-
man Howard K. Smith played himself, with dignity, in the
film: he provides exposition, but is in no way a chorus.
Vidal also had Judy Garland singing "I Could Go On Singing" at the party rally. "Gore Vidal making fun," the co-
producer of I Could Go On Singing comments. In the film,
a tilted close-up of Mahalia Jackson reveals her singing at
the banquet, as she had for Adlai Stevenson in 1952.

More seriously, with the recent assassination in Dal-
las fresh in everyone's memory, Vidal was obliged to delete
a few wisecracks aimed at John F. Kennedy. Since The
Best Man's run on Broadway, however, Vidal had had a
falling out with Robert F. Kennedy. The result was that
the Nixonesque Joe Cantwell became part-Bobby Kennedy;
Vidal even presents Joe as the author of a book entitled
The Enemy Around Us. As Governor T. T. Claypoole,
the southern candidate, tells him in the film, "The nice
thing about you, Joe, is that you can sound like a liberal
but at heart are an American."

The director's work with the writer is not all that apparent upon reading the various drafts of the script; indeed, the film version of The Best Man seems to be quite faithful to the play--the mark of a successful collaboration. In working with Vidal, Schaffner's object was to remove the sentimentality from the Capra script and to build up the political as well as the convention machinery which he had found made a convention so exciting. From his vantage point in the control room, Schaffner had been in a good position to observe that machinery and spot things a writer or even a politician would seldom see. Not least of all, his knowledge of the television medium, which by 1960 had become a permanent extension of the candidates and the convention itself, enabled the director to make substantial contributions to the reshaping of the script. Schaffner's attention to the details of the medium and the machinery in action would serve to open up the play even more. The results were, in the words of political scientist Sidney Wise, "The Best Man has the feel of a raucous, old fashioned suspenseful convention."[34]

Not surprisingly, the locale of the piece was moved from Philadelphia to Los Angeles. A large metropolitan city and the center of the film and television media, Los Angeles seems the logical setting for Vidal's script: the city serves Vidal's subtext that politicians are like actors, polishing their images; the notion of bikini-clad starlets at poolside clamoring for a presidential candidate's attention and autograph seems entirely appropriate. Los Angeles had also been the host city of the 1960 Democratic Convention, held in the Sports Arena; newsreel footage of the 1960 convention was available, and would be integrated into the film with new scenes filmed at the Sports Arena. The producers also obtained permission to film in and around the Ambassador Hotel, including its lobby, swimming pool, and Wilshire Renaissance ballroom. Sets of the hotel rooms were constructed at Columbia Studios.

Gore Vidal, who arrived in Los Angeles to participate in the production and make sure the actors didn't tamper with his dialogue, can in fact be spotted briefly in the film: he has a two-word walk-on role as a senator whom Mabel Cantwell encounters in the Ambassador Hotel Lobby and entreats to support her husband. For the most part, Vidal's adaptation of his play remained very much a theatrical piece, emphasizing dialogue and acting; as there were also budget

limitations, two-thirds of the script consisted of dialogue in
hotel rooms. Whatever the disadvantages from a purely
filmic standpoint, this turned out to be quite advantageous
for the cast: they would get to rehearse.

By the time Schaffner came aboard, Millar and Turman
had already secured a commitment from Henry Fonda to portray the egghead nominee, William Russell. Although Schaffner had finally had a chance to work with the actor in The
Good Years on television, this would be the first time in a
drama, and Schaffner, an admirer of the actor's performances
in The Ox-Bow Incident (1943), Young Mr. Lincoln (1939),
and the theatrical production of Mister Roberts which Fonda
reprised in the 1955 film, was looking forward to it. The
rest of the cast was soon assembled: Cliff Robertson as
Cantwell; Lee Tracy recreating his stage role as the ex-
president; Margaret Leighton as Russell's estranged wife;
Edie Adams as Mabel Cantwell; Kevin McCarthy as Russell's
Ted Sorenson-like campaign manager; Gene Raymond as
Joe's older brother and campaign manager; Ann Sothern as
the ambitious political hostess; Shelley Berman as the black-
mailer. "It was an extraordinary acting company," says its
director. "In terms of theatre it was almost like a repertory
company."

Two weeks were allotted for rehearsal, an extremely
long period of time for a medium in which no rehearsal is
the rule; by way of comparison, there are only three and a
half weeks of rehearsal in the theatre. But this rehearsal
was decidedly unusual: during the two weeks, the entire
cast rehearsed together on the sets of the hotel rooms, hall-
ways, and control room centers that had been designed by
Lyle Wheeler at Columbia; this would have been impossible
had the film been shot on location.

Even more unusual was that, according to the structure of the script, all the major characters appear continuously throughout the film. In the three-act structure of
the film, only Shelley Berman does not appear in every act.
Consequently, Schaffner put The Best Man together very
much in the way he would have a television program or
Broadway play. With the exception of the convention
scenes, everything was sufficiently rehearsed and worked
out before filming began. "The last couple of days we had
the technical crew there," Schaffner says, "much the same

Rehearsal, the Hollywood rarity, on The Best Man, 1963.
(Clockwise from top center) Schaffner, at head of table;
Lawrence Turman, Lee Tracy, Cliff Robertson, Gore Vidal,
Kevin McCarthy, Henry Fonda, Edie Adams, Gene Raymond,
Margaret Leighton, unidentified assistant, unidentified con-
tinuity clerk, and Stuart Miller.

as you would have done on old television." Everyone before and behind the camera was certain of the continuity.

The director of photography hired by Millar and Turman was Haskell (Pete) Wexler, who, despite the acclaim for
his black and white images in such films as The Savage Eye
(1959) and America, America (1963), had not been able to
join the cameramen's union. That changed with The Best
Man. "It was his first official Hollywood picture," says
Turman. With this film, the producers helped get him into
the union, Local 659. "He was chosen because his strength
was documentary--and we wanted a documentary look--and
he was also fast."

The choice of Wexler proved to be fortuitous for the
director as well. Schaffner was in no position to demand a
cameraman, and, as this was only his second film, was hardly an expert in motion picture photography. He and Pete
Wexler clicked immediately and the two men worked well together. This Best Man being a motion picture, the order
of the day was to put motion into the picture. If there are
hand-held shots in the film, they exist, not because Schaffner liked hand-held shots for their own sake or because
Haskell Wexler is a master of them, but because it is hard
to envision the jostling world of the political arena without
them.

When Russell and Cantwell descend to the hotel's bomb
shelter for their meeting with Bascomb, Shelley Berman
stands near the upper right of the frame, Cliff Robertson
is in a shadow at the lower left, and Henry Fonda is at top.
What is most arresting about the composition is the light
coming down from the ceiling onto Fonda. In many shots
throughout the film, be it a lamp or sunlight coming in
through the window, there is a bright glow of light in the
background near the center of the frame. This visual look
was chosen as an effective way to use black and white, to
balance the lean and bare look of the interiors; the sets
were designed accordingly. Some interesting compositions
and effects result, such as the time when Lee Tracy, to the
right of the frame, asks Fonda, to the left, if he believes
in God. There is no answer; as he stands in front of the
window, Fonda can only be seen darkly in silhouette.

The Best Man was edited by Robert E. Swink, a veteran known as William Wyler's editor. As such, he had
spent time with Millar during the 1950s, had edited The
Young Doctors, the first Millar-Turman production, and,
when the producers would later go their separate ways,
Swink would edit films for each. As was the case with
The Stripper, Schaffner was not heavily involved in post-
production because of his DuPont commitment; based in New
York, he found it difficult to spend as much time as was
needed for a film being edited in Los Angeles. Once again
Schaffner was the beneficiary of good luck: in the short
amount of time that he had, Schaffner developed a fine
working relationship with Swink. Several years later, when
he would finally be in a position to choose his own editor,
Schaffner would ask for Robert E. Swink.

"I like a talky movie," Gore Vidal has said to no one's great surprise. "I believe that an audience will sit still for a great deal of dialogue, if it's good."[35] However true that might be, a motion picture audience finds it difficult to sit through a photographed stage play. In describing his preparation for the task of handling the 87 pages of dialogue in the Ambassador Hotel, Schaffner says:

> It's a matter of character, it's a matter of staging, it's a matter of attitude, it's a matter of angles, finally, so that it just doesn't lie there. The first thing you do is make sure the camera position isn't the same every time they come through the door.

The pace is crucial to the drama: being a director who feels that energy is as important to a scene as its content, Schaffner tended to overpace the scenes for the purposes of the film.

The result is that The Best Man picks up a powerful head of steam as it moves along. The film crackles with energy, deriving from the rapid-fire dialogue and the performances, and from the steady stream of people coming in and out of camera range. If the people aren't on the move, the camera is on the move--panning as it dollies for even more movement; swish pans are used to good effect. Scattered unobtrusively throughout the film are interesting details like the giant posters of Russell's Life cover and Cantwell's Time cover, or the dartboard with Cantwell's picture on it in Russell's nerve center; the camera doesn't have time to dwell on any of them, and these details quickly pass by. The footage from the 1960 Sports Arena is adroitly managed: footage of people standing, applauding, or cheering is intercut with footage of 500 extras standing, applauding, or cheering. Action is cut to action; for the dialogue, cutting from shot to shot in mid-speech keeps the tempo going.

The scene best reflecting the pace begins while Russell is taking a bath in his hotel suite; T. T. Claypoole (John Henry Faulk) sits on the stool behind him, politicking away. After Claypoole leaves, Russell emerges from the bathroom already dressing himself while carrying on a conversation with Dick Jensen (Kevin McCarthy), who assists and times him: it took Russell 71 seconds to dress; the record is 58.5 seconds. To the characters in the film as well as its makers, speed was of the essence.

The film wastes no time getting started. The main
titles are presented over a rapid montage of each president
of the United States of America, from George Washington to
Lyndon B. Johnson. (Serendipitously, Schaffner's credit is
superimposed over John F. Kennedy's image.) As the film
moves to its conclusion, Schaffner throws in a semi-chase
scene: Cantwell rushes to the Sports Arena via helicopter
in hopes of securing the party nomination on the fourth ballot. Perhaps some Los Angeles residents might find it a bit
unreasonable, as the distance from the Ambassador Hotel to
the Sports Arena may arguably be traversed more quickly by
automobile, but the helicopter stunt is not atypical of Joe
Cantwell, and the aerial photography of Los Angeles is exhilarating, creating a sense of urgency to the denouement,
especially when the film crosscuts to a hospital where Russell visits the dying Hockstader.

At the beginning of the film, William Russell is nominated to a spontaneous demonstration of which, watching the
integrated convention and stock footage on the television
monitor in his nerve center, he says, "We expect 22 minutes
of spontaneity." A visual motif is established which runs
through the film: action will be compounded by the television monitors that frequently appear in the frame. The television images supplement, complement, and comment on the
action; television becomes the equivalent of another major
character in any given room.

Joe Cantwell is introduced on a television monitor in
the control room, establishing that this is a televised press
conference; presently there is a cut to the press conference
itself, where Joe stresses his humble origins. Meanwhile,
Russell and Jensen discuss campaign strategy as they walk
around the Ambassador Hotel, from the pool to the front of
the hotel into the lobby, where they are joined by the professional gossip Mrs. Gammadge (Ann Sothern). This is a
needlessly circuitous route, considering the actual geography
of the hotel, but the film picks up momentum as cameras
from different angles move with the characters while they
meet the press, supporters, and starlets. Along the way,
the moving camera underscores the placards that are seen:
"Hustle with Russell."

The introductions of the two front-runners' wives
take advantage of the visual medium, also serving to indicate

the lot of political wives. Walking briskly through a hotel corridor, Russell stops when he spots a mirror, saying, "Never pass a mirror without looking into it," only to see a tilted reflection of Alice (Margaret Leighton), his elegant but estranged wife. This irregular image hints at their relationship--harmony but disharmony--and they will have to live together if Russell wants to be president. On the other hand, Mabel Cantwell (Edie Adams) is first seen watching television in her hotel room: on the TV screen is her mother-in-law, followed by a shot of Howard K. Smith, who provides some background information on Joe and how he came to fame with his notion that the Mafia was part of the Communist conspiracy. Mabel responds enthusiastically to the commentary like an aging cheer-leader.

To Hockstader is given the saltiest of speeches, and Lee Tracy makes the most of them, as when he tells Cant-well: "It's not that I object to you being a bastard. Don't get me wrong there. It's your being such a stupid bastard that I object to." His performance is undeniably right for the film. Dying of stomach cancer, Hockstader is stricken and forced to leave the proceedings three-quarters of the way through the film; the humor and energy dissipate with his departure. In a sense, it is the climax of the film; from this point on, the film runs a more thoughtful and consid-ered course--the audience too must choose the best man.

Shelley Berman turns in a memorable cameo as Sheldon Bascomb, his performance markedly different from the rest of the cast, and rightly so. The other characters are in-volved in the campaign, sustained by their roles in party politics. Obsequious, cringing, and sweating before the household names he meets, Bascomb is a total outsider; Berman is quite believable when he says meeting Hockstader is the biggest moment in his life. Berman's interpretation of his role lends itself to Hockstader's retort, "Yes, I ex-pect this is the biggest moment in your life." Bascomb is even less than a good example of a common man.

Even though Cantwell--years before Thomas Eagleton was similarly exposed--has no scruples about using the re-ports of Russell's nervous breakdown against him, Russell ("No man with that awful wife and those ugly children could be anything but normal") is reluctant to use Bascomb's

information against Joe. Fittingly, the inevitable showdown
begins in the linen room: in a medium close two-shot,
Robertson is to the left of the frame, separated from Fonda
by a linen shelf.

The best man turns out to be the dark horse candidate, Governor Merwin, something foreshadowed at the party
rally when it is learned there will be an open convention:
after Hockstader finishes speaking, not having endorsed
anyone, there is a montage of reaction shots, the last close-
up belonging to Merwin. (The foreshadowing was far less
subtle in the Capra version: a major new character was introduced in Nancy, the dark horse candidate's wife, who
befriends Hockstader and visits him as he lies dying in the
hospital; in a Capraesque moment, Art Hockstader rises
from his deathbed to endorse the dark-horse candidate at
the convention.) In the film, Merwin is almost anonymous.
Arriving at the Sports Arena and riding the escalator up on
his way to glory, Merwin looks quizzically at Russell. Blond,
with an open and pleasant face, Merwin was portrayed by
William R. Ebersol, then the manager of the Ambassador
Hotel.

Anticipating the real political conventions in Atlantic
City and San Francisco that summer, the film was released
in April 1964 and was enthusiastically received by the critics. Arthur Schlesinger, Jr., a critic with more than casual political knowledge, praised the sharpness of the film's
conception, freshness of language, and directness of impact, while also observing:

> In a real convention Russell's objections would have
> been bypassed, because his campaign manager would
> simply have shown the Cantwell dossier to key fig-
> ures without bothering to clear with his principal.
> All this suggests that one cannot take "The Best
> Man" very seriously as political drama. But as
> political melodrama it is superb. Franklin Schaff-
> ner's brisk direction captures the convention at-
> mosphere to perfection. Vidal's dialogue is swift
> and audacious. Henry Fonda as Russell, Cliff
> Robertson as Cantwell, Lee Tracy as the ex-
> president all give strong and exact performances. [36]

Even Gore Vidal was not displeased. In his inimitable way,

discussing the films he's written, he said, "I think <u>The Best Man</u> was the least awful."[37]   The author's possessive on the title is rightfully his; Vidal is the one most responsible for the pleasure a viewer derives from the film.

The film attracted critical attention at film festivals in Cannes, Locarno, Karlovy-Vary, and Berlin.   Schaffner accompanied <u>The Best Man</u> to Moscow the following summer. As there was far too much dialogue to subtitle, a reader had to sit off to the side reading every line of every part, inevitably falling behind the film; the laughter at an end joke would come several seconds later into the next scene. The Russians, Schaffner reports, responded more to the situation jokes than the character jokes, but responded quite favorably to the film in general.   For all its critical acclaim, however, <u>The Best Man</u> failed to recoup its negative cost; Schaffner was never paid the $10,000 owed him in deferred payment.

Seen today, <u>The Best Man</u> holds up very well indeed, particularly with respect to the environment and political machinery.   With a notable assist from Franklin Schaffner, who introduced important information visually, Gore Vidal's talky script was turned into a film that is far less talky than, say, John Ford's 1958 political melodrama, <u>The Last Hurrah</u>.   Four presidents later, American politics have changed; the world has witnessed the rise and fall of Richard Nixon.   The Cantwell character was drawn in broad strokes, Cliff Robertson unmistakably played him as a heavy, and the direction further stacked the deck against him: in the scene where Hockstader changes his mind about endorsing Joe, there is a two-shot of Bob Cantwell (Gene Raymond) and Joe; Robertson lunges up very close to the camera, the wide-angle lens distorting his face to give Joe an even more menacing look.   It is doubtful if Joe Cantwell would be played or directed in such a blunt fashion today.

The intention was to load the dice against Cantwell in order to underscore the tragic waste of a man like William Russell, who is unable to win fairly.   Author of <u>The American Vision</u>, Russell is ideally embodied in Henry Fonda, an American archetype.   The Fonda manner of underplaying only adds strength to Russell's character; he refuses to blackmail not out of weakness but out of distaste for dirty politics.   Russell is hardly a perfect man, but his kind of

integrity is admirable, and apparently missing from the
contemporary political scene. The last of a dying breed--
the honest politician--and already an anachronism, he
stands near a "Hustle with Russell" sign at the end of the
film. He can only hustle with Mrs. Russell, but that's a
better deal than any other alternative he has; reunited, the
Russells climb into their limousine. The camera booms high
in the air as the car drives up the Sports Arena ramp into
the bright glare of the world outside. It is the twentieth-
century facsimile of the last cowboy hero riding off into the
sunset.

DuPont Show of the Week, 1963-1964

There was some discussion about Franklin Schaffner signing
a contract with Columbia Pictures when he was on the lot
filming The Best Man. When mutually acceptable terms were
not reached, Schaffner returned to New York, where he was
still recognized as enough of a television force for CBS to
suggest a new Playhouse 90-type of anthology with Franklin
Schaffner as its executive producer; it was a nice idea--but
already years too late. Otherwise, with two films under his
belt, Schaffner found he had no extra clout or value in the
world of television; neither did the fact that both films were
commercially unsuccessful make any real difference in his
status as a television director. Perhaps somebody might
make a comment or two, but it wasn't that important; work
went on as usual, and Schaffner returned to DuPont Show
of the Week.

At the end of the 1962-1963 season, Jacqueline Babbin
returned to David Susskind's Talent Associates. To fill
in the vacant producer's slot, The Directors Company turned
to another man with a Yale and theatre background: Philip
Barry, Jr. had come into television in 1949 and served as
associate producer to Herbert Brodkin on The Alcoa Hour
and The Elgin/Motorola Hour; more recently, he had produced such film comedies as The Mating Game (1959). After DuPont, Barry would produce such dramatic television
movies as The Autobiography of Miss Jane Pittman (1973)
and Friendly Fire (1979).

To accommodate Schaffner's Best Man schedule, Fielder
Cook directed the earlier shows in the season. Despite his

$120,000 budget, Cook was pocketing enough money from the series to purchase Sidney Carroll's "Big Deal in Laredo," one of DuPont's most highly regarded shows, which he had directed the previous year. With the money he saved, Cook was able to develop the project first before he could get his agent, Freddie Fields, to package it with Warner Bros., where it became a 1966 film entitled A Big Hand for the Little Lady, starring Henry Fonda and Joanne Woodward. [38] Schaffner began his half of the DuPont season in January 1964 with varied product. "Don't Go Upstairs" was a horror/fantasy about a young girl who imagines her father has killed her mother. "More, More, More, More" gave the director an opportunity to work with two elephants from Ringling Brothers and Patricia Barry, Mrs. Philip Barry, Jr.

"Jeremy Rabbitt, the Secret Avenger" was another black comedy written by Robert Thom, kind of a malignant Walter Mitty story, with a cast consisting of Walter Matthau, Franchot Tone, Brian Donlevy, Jim Backus, and Frank Gorshin in the title role. "You can imagine how much serious rehearsal we got," Schaffner says. "These are funny guys." A court clerk at a senate investigation of racketeers, Jeremy Rabbitt loves a woman (Jennifer West) who is only attracted to violent men, which triggers him into committing a series of murders. As the victims are all crooks under investigation and entirely deserving of their fates, good triumphs, in a way, over evil. The veteran supporting cast is fine, but not so the leads: West is pretty, but a cardboard character; without a celebrity persona to hide behind, noted impressionist Gorshin is not particularly memorable. The show gave Thom and Schaffner the opportunity to send up old movies: Brian Donlevy plays a Brian Donlevy type out of a Preston Sturges movie; Walter Matthau and Carolyn Jones play a couple straight out of Born Yesterday. Fresh from a political film, Schaffner was able to take advantage of the fact that television cameras had become an everyday reality in Senate committees. Included in one long-shot of Matthau on the stand is a televison monitor to the lower right of the frame featuring a close-up of the actor's hands.

DuPont still allowed the same production methods and schedule. Two days were spent editing--in an age before sophisticated electronic systems--when videotape editing was accomplished manually. Philip Barry, Jr. describes the process:

Editing on tape in those days was terribly tedious
and difficult. They actually spliced it. Also there
was no way to run tape slowly. You'd have to run
it at speed. It was 2" tape, so it was running very
fast. We would stand behind the tape editor, watching the monitor, and you'd get to a point where
you'd want to make an edit and you'd clap your
hands, and the editor would slash at the tape with
a grease pencil and hope he hit it somewhere close
to where you clapped your hands. It was a crazy
system.

The most ambitious program of that season was "Ambassador at Large," with Arthur Kennedy in the title role.
Loring Mandel had written a script about assassination, but,
after the death of John F. Kennedy, Schaffner lost all interest in it. Later, when news correspondent John Scali
came up with the idea of using an ambassador at large,
modeled on Ambassador Emeritus Robert Murphy, Mandel
merged the idea with his assassination script. The results
were so encouraging that the show would serve as a pilot
for a projected television series, a quality series along the
lines of The Defenders.

It would have made a fine series; it would still make
a fine series. The title character was not tied down to any
particular country and could roam the world conducting affairs of state, grappling with topical matters, encountering
human interest stories. Mandel sketched three or four script
ideas; however, such were the demands on the director's
time that he didn't have the chance to collaborate with
Schaffner as much as was their custom. Most damagingly,
a technical problem occurred during the taping of the climactic scene: the signal from a Mitch Miller show was
picked up on the tape. The Directors Company was at the
end of its studio time and could not afford to pay overtime
expenses, especially with such an unusually large cast;
NBC accepted the blame, but was unwilling to pick up the
tab. "Ambassador at Large" went on, mixed signals and
all, and that was the end of it; nothing more was said about
a series. "It was a serious endeavor," Barry says and
shrugs. "Too highbrow for television."

As had happened to Unit Four on Kaiser Aluminum
Hour, The Directors Company was replaced by David

Susskind's Talent Associates on DuPont Show of the Week.
The handwriting was on the wall: The Defenders was
nearing the end of its run, but Petticoat Junction had
joined The Beverly Hillbillies on CBS. Franklin Schaffner
would soon fire a parting salvo at network programming:
"Television has failed miserably to keep pace with the modern complexities of our 20th century and will, if it does not
soon recognize this problem, eventually be as passé as the
nickelodeon." [39]

John F. Kennedy, May 29, 1964

John F. Kennedy would have been 47 years old on May 29,
1964. This was one television show that Schaffner, along
with everybody else who worked on the production, would
rather not have done. One of the early satellite telecasts,
broadcast to the world via Telstar, this 30-minute show was
presented by CBS News as a tribute to the late president.
Airing live, Friday afternoon at 4:30, it reunited Schaffner
with three key participants in A Tour of the White House:

John F. Kennedy, May 29, 1964: Schaffner, Robert Kennedy, Jacqueline Kennedy and Charles Collingwood.

producer Perry Wolff, correspondent Charles Collingwood,
and Mrs. John F. Kennedy. They were joined in Hyannisport by Robert F. Kennedy, who shared on-camera reminiscences with the latter two.

    Some of the Hyannisport segment was shot outdoors;
when it grew dark, the participants went indoors, where
lights and cameras awaited them. The program featured
three European segments as well: Great Britain, with
Prime Minister Harold MacMillan; West Berlin, with Mayor
Willy Brandt; Ireland, with Prime Minister Sean LeMass.
These leaders paid their respects live on worldwide television. From his base in Hyannisport, the feed going from
the truck to New York, Schaffner supervised the switching
to locations and the cutaways. It was not unlike his Person
to Person procedure, only this time the program was on a
global level. "Horo." in Variety placed the program in its
proper perspective, writing: "The engineering aspect of
the telecast, feat though it may be, was minor compared to
the personalities seen and the personality honored."[40]

                        The War Lord

By August 1964, when he accepted his third film assignment, Schaffner had directed two black and white film
adaptations of stage plays, both best remembered for the
performances they contain. The War Lord, although very
loosely based on a stage play, would lead Schaffner into
new territory: Technicolor and Panavision, a large budget,
and battle scenes. Bosley Crowther would write in The
New York Times:

        The martial phase of the picture is really the major
        part of it, and for good old-fashioned castle-storming,
        it offers a lively show.... This production, directed
        by Franklin Schaffner, would warm the cockles of
        Errol Flynn's heart.[41]

High praise indeed. The combination of a distant historical
time period and large-scale action sequences making it the
type of motion picture that Hollywood calls an epic, The
War Lord would begin to move its director's reputation in
a direction closer to how he is known today.

Set in St. Omer (between Flandre and Artois) in the
mid-twelfth century, Leslie Stevens' The Lovers, the basis
of the film, focuses on the spiritual conundrum of Grigoris,
a writing monk--should he or should he not bless the bodies of three people who died in mortal sin. The play unfolds not unlike Rashomon as the monk learns of what happened through subjective viewpoints manifested in flashbacks: Chrysagon, the Warlord Knight, invoked le droit
de seigneur, took Douane on her wedding night, but failed
to return her to her husband/foster brother Marc the next
morning as was the bargain; all three died as a result.
Chrysagon surely loved Douane, as she did him, but she
also loved Marc, who surely loved her. Going against the
wishes of the church, Grigoris decides to bless the bodies
of all three lovers.

Most striking is the strong Japanese feel to the play:
in addition to its similarity to Akira Kurosawa's Rashomon
(1950), Douane's noble suicide in the face of an insoluble
situation is reminiscent of a young woman's reaction to a
scene of similar insolubility in Kenji Mizoguchi's 1942 film
version of The Forty-Seven Ronin. Placing much emphasis
on honor and observing customs, Stevens further tipped
his hand in a production note calling for "an almost 'Japanese' formality."[42]

The role of Chrysagon was originally submitted to
Charlton Heston, who turned it down; Darren McGavin,
joined by Hurd Hatfield and Joanne Woodward as Grigoris
and Douane, starred in the 1956 Broadway production of
the play, which closed after two nights. Yet there was
something about The Lovers that haunted Heston: six
years later he would join forces with producer Walter Seltzer with the express intention of turning it into a film;
the process would take three years to complete.

Walter Seltzer, as Hal Wallis' chief of publicity, was
sent to the airport to greet Charlton Heston when the
young actor first came to Hollywood in 1949 to star in
Dark City. Never having met him before, Seltzer had
only an 8" × 10" glossy taken from a hot kinescope of
"Jane Eyre" to identify him. "You can imagine the quality wasn't all that great," Seltzer recalls. "He was the
third guy I went up to and said, 'Would you by chance be
....'" This was the start of a close friendship that

resulted in Seltzer producing and Heston starring in eight
films together, beginning when they formed Court Productions to make The War Lord.

The first priority on The War Lord was to come up
with an excellent script before trying to raise the money
for the film. Deciding that the further they got away
from the play the better their chances would be at making
a deal, they entrusted the writing of the script to John
Collier, best known for his tales of the macabre and black
humor. Quickly eliminated was the Japanese mood, replaced
by the medieval; le droit de seigneur would be virtually the
only element remaining from The Lovers.

The writer of such diverse screenplays as Sylvia Scarlett (1935) and I Am a Camera (1955), Collier was known as
a classicist, and the idea of working on the twelfth-century
period appealed to him. Removing the character of Grigoris
and the theme of absolution--leaving Chrysagon alone at the
center--Collier retained Stevens' concept of Chrysagon as a
man driven beyond his understanding by the power of love,
but made the War Lord's stakes higher: Heston's Chrysagon
would be a pauper knight; he did not inherit his lot, but
earned his title the hard way--after his father had lost his
lands. In a Freudian touch, Chrysagon, who carries his
father's sword, says: "I've been married 20 years with that
cold wife." A psychologically complex relationship was also
created for the War Lord and his younger brother Draco.

For all his gifts, Collier was an obstinate and difficult
man to work with; most problematic was the speed with which
he wrote. In his December 11, 1962 entry in The Actor's
Life, Heston complained:

> [Collier's] incredibly slow, but the material is
> worth waiting for, at least for as long as we can
> wait. We're rapidly using all our script time getting
> a first draft screenplay, which should be well behind
> us by now.... The financial burden of developing
> this property personally is tough to carry.[43]

The script Collier delivered had the basic story line, but at
400 pages was overlong, overwritten, and overblown. Despite moments of brilliance, it was frequently incoherent and
impractical; it would have been unreasonably expensive to
produce.

The year of the War Lord 1963 was spent trying to
make a production deal. Mike Frankovich, head of production at Columbia, liked the idea and had a budget estimate
prepared; the plan was to shoot the film on the east coast
of England. "It would've been about a third less expensive
to do it in England," Seltzer explains, "because that was
the differential in scale." Frankovich, however, had second
thoughts about the commercial viability of the project, deciding The War Lord was not for Columbia Pictures. More encouraging news came from Jay Kantor, an old friend of
Seltzer's (Seltzer was a producer for Marlon Brando's Pen-
nebaker company when Kantor was Brando's agent), inviting
Court Productions to Universal City. But before finalizing
the deal, Universal asked for a final screenplay, a not unreasonable request as Collier had refused to condense his
script. "As a matter of fact," Seltzer adds, "he never did
come in with a complete script."

The task of rewriting and completing the script was
given to Millard Kaufman, who had written the screenplays
for such large and thoughtful films as Bad Day at Black
Rock (1954) and Raintree County (1957). Kaufman immediately went to Mexico to consult with Heston, who was filming Major Dundee at the time, before he went to work cutting the script down to size, emphasizing the main themes,
balancing it. Kaufman's screenplay was finished at the end
of March 1964, nearly two years after Collier had begun
work on it.

After the script was submitted, Universal gave the
go-ahead, but with one stipulation: in order to keep the
studio departments busy and justify the overhead, the film
would not be shot in England but on the back lot. In return, Court Productions had complete control of the film,
just as long as its costs did not exceed the budget, at this
point a very generous $4.5 million.

On the basis of the sensitivity and intimacy of his
work on such film adaptations of theatrical pieces as Come
Back, Little Sheba (1952) and The Rose Tattoo (1955),
Daniel Mann was brought in to direct the film; he left soon
afterwards. "This was very much Chuck's project," Seltzer
explains. "He was intimately involved. He after all came
up with the play and wanted to do it." What Heston and
Seltzer had insisted on from the inception of the project
was that the film should be an intimate epic--with "A Cast

of Dozens!!"[44] More to Heston's taste was a director like
Franklin Schaffner.

Seltzer went to the Bel-Air Hotel for his first meeting
with the director and found that Schaffner had similar feelings about the intimate nature of the project. Although he
was hardly an expert in the medieval period, Schaffner had
an interest in history that convinced Seltzer he had found
a director who not only had a feel for the period but also
had the ability to capture tender and internal moments on
film. Furthermore, the producer considered Schaffner's
professional background to be a definite advantage--anyone
who could direct live television drama that skillfully could
certainly handle the pressures and demands of the film.
The director's long friendship with the star was also a not
inconsiderable advantage.

In short order, Richard Boone was signed to enact
the role of Chrysagon's faithful retainer Bors, based on the
minuscule role of Blaise in the original play. Coming in
with his own idea of how his character should look and act,
down to the earring in his right ear--not at all in keeping
with the creative team's conception of Bors--Boone stubborn-
ly remained faithful to his own conception, looking disheveled
and grunting a lot. Other leads were cast from the ranks
of Universal contract players: Guy Stockwell as Draco,
Chrysagon's treacherous brother; James Farentino as Marc,
the bitter cuckolded husband; Rosemary Forsyth as the female lead, now renamed Bronwyn. The priest's role, accepted by Maurice Evans, was drastically reshaped into an
elderly but minor voice of reason and conscience.

Vittorio Nino Novarese, a medieval specialist with
whom Heston had worked on El Cid (1961) and The Agony
and the Ecstasy (1965), was brought in to design the costumes, select the right props, and attend to the furniture
and weapons. Himself an art director, Novarese would be
working in an American studio where his role in the production was somewhat limited by union regulations; he managed to work quite well with Henry Bumstead, the art director assigned to the film.[45] The War Lord was the first
time Schaffner worked with matte paintings, bringing him
into contact with Albert Whitlock, the master of his craft.
Near the beginning of the film, Chrysagon and his men
wend their way on horseback to the village: they move

left to right, the camera moving right to left, while passing
the North Sea--a matte painting that blends in well with the
location.

    Schaffner's good luck with cameramen continued with
The War Lord in the person of Russell Metty, who had been
under contract to Universal since the 1940s, winning an
Academy Award in 1960 for his work on Spartacus; his
highly stylized photography for the Douglas Sirk melodramas of the 1950s has since been rediscovered by a younger
generation of filmgoers. Charlton Heston, who had worked
with him on Touch of Evil (1958), insisted on Metty for
The War Lord. "Russ Metty is unquestionably one of the
great cameramen," Heston wrote of the 1958 experience.
"He is nearly the only one of them who is also fast."[46] In
testimony to Metty's skill and speed, Seltzer describes the
cameraman and his crew at work:

> They had a series of hand signals. You never
> heard them talk or yell or scream. It was like a
> third base coach giving directions to the batter.
> Frequently they would be ready while the actors
> were still walking off the set to go to their dress-
> ing rooms to sit down.

    Characteristically, all of Universal's color pictures of
the 1960s were very brightly lit; even a serious drama had
a musical-comedy look, which definitely was not what Schaffner, Seltzer, and Heston wanted for The War Lord. Grateful for the opportunity and challenge, Metty, who had long
worked in the Universal flat lighting style, used gels on the
lights to add to the medieval orange look of the period, providing a low-key, darker but richer, ominous visual quality
to the film. Consequently, The War Lord does not look like
a Universal picture--there are shadows in the film. "It was
exquisitely photographed," states another Metty admirer,
Franklin Schaffner. This did not delight Universal; Metty's
lighting would be sharply criticized.

    Universal was pleased to have The War Lord, prin-
cipally because of Charlton Heston: he was the most successful star of film spectaculars; he would look good wearing Universal armor. So, from the beginning, Universal
(the very Catholic Edward Muhl, head of production, and
Melville Tucker, the film's studio supervisor) saw it on a

larger canvas. In an extremely rare Hollywood occurrence,
the studio decided to increase the budget of the film: half
a million dollars was given for stunts, men on fire, and
elaborate falls. Ordinarily, a production company would be
overjoyed by such a windfall; such was not the case on
The War Lord.

The film had a twelve-week shooting schedule. In
October 1964, production commenced with three weeks of
location shooting in Marysville, California, where the countryside offered marsh land, flat land, and a river--scenery
that could pass for a Druid village in twelfth-century Normandy. Producer and director were by now friends. After
spending time with him, working and relaxing, watching him
in action with cast, crew, and studio executives, Walter
Seltzer was in a position to say:

> Frank is an unusually gifted and sensitive director.
> He is along with it practical. He is also very strong.
> Frank is not easily buffeted or pushed around. He
> has very definite concepts of what he wants to do.

Schaffner and Charlton Heston, filming The War Lord, 1964.

By no means an established director yet, Schaffner showed
strength and stubbornness when needed, traits that would
remain consistent when times were good and times were bad.
On The War Lord, they would be mostly bad.

The trouble that had been brewing over what kind of
film The War Lord should be came out in the open as soon
as the first footage was seen at the studio. In question
was a wide shot that would be used under the opening
credits: Chrysagon leads his men across the water to the
village the Duke of Normandy has given him.[47] As the men
on horseback stretch out in one continuous vertical that
bends horizontally across the wide screen, it is apparent
that The War Lord literally has Heston's cast of dozens.
This is not the way Universal saw its Charlton Heston epic;
it looked like a Universal pinch-penny, bargain basement
Charlton Heston epic. Fighting between studio and production company commenced via long distance.

With no cover set in Marysville, the company revised
the schedule to make adjustments to the weather. "If you're
on an all-location picture, you can maybe sit for two or
three days, but then you've got to move," Schaffner says.
"When you're on location a limited amount of time, you
shoot, and you try to accommodate the weather in terms
of dialogue or in terms of staging." The company experienced some rain, but nothing serious resulted from it.

Schaffner shot his first film battle scene in Marysville: on the way to the village, Chrysagon and his raggle-
taggle bunch of men encounter a small band of Frisians,
led by its Prince (former Cecil B. De Mille associate Henry
Wilcoxon, another actor who looked good in armor). Actually a minor battle, considering the number of men involved,
it is filled with energy from sword action and editing, the
assorted angles of flying arrows, and men jumping at the
camera--all very vigorous, hard masculine stuff, not make-
believe Technicolor violence.

In preparing an action sequence, Schaffner first
thinks of character--character reaction to the action--and
then the audience before determining how much action is
necessary, and how it can be executed to make it believable and realistic. "The battle scenes must have their own
surge," he asserts, "much as character development has its

own surge." A battle scene is not unlike the rest of the
action in Schaffner's films: it is based on, and flows from,
character.

Using Panavision for the first time, Schaffner deployed
three cameras for the battle scenes. Although he could see
little difference between Panavision and CinemaScope, he
could clearly see a greater need to shoot wide-open spaces
in The War Lord than he had in The Stripper. More frus-
tratingly, he knew the bulk of the picture had to be filmed
on the Universal back lot: the angles chosen for the battle
scenes in Marysville had to be carefully composed because
they would have to match footage shot at Universal City.
The Norman tower had been built, and was a pleasant surprise when the company returned to the studio; otherwise,
the director's fears were justified. "We wound up so that
we could only shoot one way--straight up," Seltzer recalls.
"Everything else was preempted by new buildings, new
roads, new tours." In order to get around these Universal
developments, not to mention the all too real houses and
telephone lines in the background, cameras were positioned
on cranes and platforms. The care and attention to angles
paid off; the extent of the back lot photography is not that
apparent in the film.

The interior tower scenes were shot on a soundstage,
as was an exterior forest set for Marc and Bronwyn's wedding ceremony, a complete Druid ritual with cakes, dolls,
and sacred ring of fire. Elsewhere, the studio assigned a
second unit to the film, purely for economic reasons--to
collapse the budget. Whenever a principal was available
for a day, the second unit would film the actor in action;
Schaffner had no real control over it. The second unit's
work would become a crucial issue in the fate of the film.

The major source of conflict was a nude scene--
actually two. Ernest Nims, whose job was pre-editing
scripts before they were filmed, did not want the nude
scenes; more importantly, neither did the boss, Edward
Muhl; neither, for that matter, did Rosemary Forsyth--
to appease her, the actress was offered a body double and/
or a false bottom to wear over her own. Schaffner chose a
lot of wide shots when he filmed the scenes. In one of the
few remaining elements of the play, Chrysagon first meets
Douane/Bronwyn as she emerges from a pond; as filmed,

this scene ended with a wide reverse shot of Bronwyn. In the second scene, after awaking from the night willingly spent with Chrysagon, Bronwyn goes out to the top of the tower where, in a wide establishing shot, she greets the new morning before the War Lord arrives to wrap a discreet cloak around her. All this would look rather innocuous two decades later, even by television standards, but in 1965 these wide shots were found offensive, caused an uproar at Universal, and were eventually cut out of the film.

A young Frisian boy is found after the first battle. When Volc, the diminutive falconer who carries the boy around on a leash, discovers the young Frisian is the son of the Prince, he betrays Chrysagon to become a Frisian Lord, thus setting the stage for the return of the Frisians and the climactic battle scene. The attack begins at night and goes on for several days. Since the night scenes were filmed at night, Walter Seltzer reported an unusual problem: when the dailies were seen, the arrows weren't seen; bow and arrow being the major weapon in the attack, this was a relatively serious matter. Proving that filmmaking is a group effort, the problem was solved by a prop man named Bill Nunley. "[He] said he would paint the arrows white, assuring us that when we reshot the scene, they would not look like white arrows, just arrows," Seltzer says. "It worked extremely well."

Most of the battle's action is centered on top of the tower, where the two stars perform individual heroics: Heston, in loincloth, goes down to the drawbridge to fight the coalition of Frisians and village people led by Marc; the following day, Boone descends into the moat, retrieving an anchor to be used as a grappling hook. Describing the realities of filming an action sequence, Heston wrote: "The script said simply, 'Chrysagon and his men defend the door.' It took us the better part of a week to shoot."[48] The Frisians bring their wooden war machine with which they can reach the top of the tower; men perish by sword, arrows, boiling oil; a good number of them have long falls. All seems to be hopelessly lost for the War Lord until Draco arrives with reinforcements from the Duke, including a catapult that flings fire balls through the air and, on a couple of occasions, directly at the camera.

Without the director's knowledge, the top of the tower

was moved to the crest of a hill on the rapidly changing
face of the studio back lot. As this gave him only a 90-
degree angle of undeveloped background to shoot, the top
of the tower had to be moved to Palos Verdes, where the
final attack was filmed; the well-traveled top of the tower
was filmed on the back lot, inside a soundstage, and finally at the beach for three more nights of shooting. A rough
assembly of the battle scene revealed that the second unit
work did not match well with the first unit footage; even
the studio agreed the second unit work left something to be
desired. Reshooting by the first unit was necessary, and
accomplished.

The late Folmar Blangsted, editor of The War Lord,
wrote of the star, director, and producer's dedication during post-production:

> Sometimes, when the phone would ring in the cut-
> ting room, Chuck would answer it with a grin:
> "War Lord Repair." At other times when energies
> might temporarily flag, Frank, that wonderful guy,
> would burst out into song (song???), improvising
> lyrics to fit the occasion, or Walter might release
> all of us into gales of laughter with his inimitable
> stories. [49]

"It was a very good company," the producer admits. "That
Frank engendered." The fellowship and good spirits lasted
until the director's cut was delivered.

"Frank Schaffner did a sensational cut," Seltzer avers.
"It really sparkled." But Universal had had other ideas
about the film all along; the subject of the second unit work
was brought up again. "We had been naïve enough to believe that if Universal agreed that the second unit work was
unacceptable they would take that into consideration in
terms of the budget," Schaffner recalls. "Well, not so."
Another week's work of night shooting on the lot had been
required to rectify the second unit's battle scene footage;
Court Productions had gone over budget, the studio claimed,
choosing to exercise its rights. Universal took control of
the film and gave it to William Hornbeck to re-edit.

Universal's version basically followed what, several
months earlier, Ernest Nims had said were scenes that should

not be filmed; 12 minutes from Schaffner's cut were eliminated
to move the action forward. Most damaging was the exci-
sion of those small and subtle details relating to character,
motivation, and reactions that had been so carefully assembled
--moments Schaffner had spent as much time constructing as
he would a battle scene. Effectively diminishing the feel for
the times, the color and atmosphere of the Druid village,
and the characterization, the cuts infuriated Heston so much
that he sent a five-page letter to his former agent, Lew
Wasserman, chairman of MCA, parent company of Universal
--but to no avail.

        Walter Seltzer had been considered an expert in pub-
licity after his 1955 campaign for Marty, revolving around
the Virgil Partch cartoon figure of the tubby man in a phone
booth; the promotion and advertising for The War Lord
would be the largest in Universal's history. In pre-production,
he had scripts mailed to the 300 key circuits; during the
production, there were weekly mailings to 250 newspapers
and semi-weekly mailings to 94 other papers; the campaign
for the ten major magazines focused on love and action;
people were constantly toured on the set. None of this
was original, but all of it was done on a grander scale than
usual--more ads, bigger ads. As it turned out, in spite of
the objections the front office had had, the Universal publicity department latched onto Rosemary Forsyth's nude scene
at the pond, using it as the focus of promotion. However,
nothing seemed to pay off for The War Lord's critical and
commercial reception when it was released at Thanksgiving
in 1965.

        Taken lightly, the film was dismissed with sarcasm,
as when Newsweek's anonymous reviewer noted:

        This is no workaday epic with cowboy knights,
        Indian Goths and a relief column of cavalry gallop-
        ing from Ghent. It is a tender and meaningful
        love story ... that dares to ask the question that
        philanderers have pondered over the centuries:
        what would happen if the seigneur, with all the
        droit in the world on his side, actually fell in
        love? [50]

Perhaps Universal's worries about the kind of film Court
Productions wanted to make were justified; The War Lord

was the kind of Charlton Heston epic the public did not
want to see. It was Schaffner's third consecutive film to
lose money; unlike the other two, this was a big-budget
flop.

The film's reception was quite different overseas,
where the critics seemed to understand the filmmakers' intentions. The War Lord was hailed by Schaffner's ever-
growing cult following. Fortunately, enough of the plas-
tique remained in the film so that Sight and Sound's David
Wilson could write:

> Schaffner punctuates the film with details ... in
> what seems an almost Frazeresque passion for the
> minutiae of heathen rites and superstitions; but
> far from being arbitrary pieces of set decoration,
> the details are always heavy with ominous sugges-
> tion.[51]

This is best illustrated in the scene where the War Lord
first enters the warden's room in the tower. After hearing
a bird's shriek, Chyrsagon discovers the dead bodies of
the warden and a woman--in a compromising position--on
the bed. Suddenly, in a close shot, a bee flies out from
the dead flowers of the woman's garland. There is a shock
cut to the shrieking bird--an eagle, played by an American
eagle named S. P. Eagle (in honor of producer Sam Spiegel),
who also serves as the bridge in the wedding night procession from the village to the tower. In each of its appearances, S. P. Eagle is used as a sign that something bad
will be revealed.

The War Lord is set in a time of fear and uncertainty,
when people were neither totally pagan nor totally Christian
but a strange mixture of both. Ostensibly a Christian service, the wedding ceremony is also a Druid totemic feast and
semi-orgy with representations of the Jack-of-the-Green, the
Corn King, the Rooster, the Fishman, and other fertility
figures and phallic symbols. Presiding over the wedding
itself is Odins, Bronwyn's foster-father and father-in-law-
to-be. Near the end of the film, during a lull in the final
battle, Chrysagon, in a medium close-up to the left of the
frame, pauses to contemplate his situation: the top portion
of his face is lit, the lower half of his face hangs in darkness; to his right is the shadow of a crucifix--he brought

on the trouble himself, and there is no clean escape, pagan or Christian.

The situation with Richard Boone worked out successfully. Bors does not have a lot of dialogue--when he does speak he nags at Chrysagon like a mother or wife--but he is always there. One wonders why Boone isn't playing the Frisian Prince, which is more an antagonist's role than the supporting role Bors so obviously is; Boone has such a sinister-looking face that the viewer begins to speculate if Bors will betray Chrysagon. Only at the end, not before some interesting tension has been created, does Bors reveal his motives: he was faithful to the War Lord's father, raised Chrysagon, and will always be loyal to him.

The casting of the female lead was, however, damaging to the film. James Powers correctly pointed out in The Hollywood Reporter:

> Miss Forsyth, a very pretty young actress, does not display much versatility.... Her passion is timidly displayed. She does not seem a woman for whom a man, a war lord, would risk and wreck his world. [52]

Touted as Universal's "Eight Million Dollar Baby" with her appearances in Shenandoah and The War Lord in 1965, Rosemary Forsyth was the best of the three contract players who had been tested for the role of Bronwyn--and the studio was grooming her. Yet she was not as successful as Heston, Boone, Stockwell, and Evans in making the transition eight centuries back in time. The same problem holds true for James Farentino as Marc--his looks and speech seem too contemporary--but Forsyth had the more pivotal role, making her discomfort and deficiency all the more apparent. No magic happened when she went on screen.

Ironically, Heston wrote about seeing Billy Liar in 1964 and being impressed by an unknown actress in it. "We tried very hard to get her, and could have, for 35,000 dollars," he commented, "but the studio balked at what they felt was an excessive price." [53] The producer concurs--the actress was quite excited by the idea of doing The War Lord. "I spoke to her agent, and he said, 'She'd give anything to do an American picture,'" Seltzer says. "I think if I had've

said, 'Fifteen,' they would've taken that too." It is evident
that Universal thought an extra $500,000 on stunts would be
more beneficial to the film than spending a tiny fraction of
that amount on an obscure actress named Julie Christie.

    In the end, the War Lord is as he was in the beginning
--alone. He no longer has family ties; he has relinquished
love and freedom. Remaining loyal to his duty, he will see
the Duke "to set right the things I put wrong here." ("You
talk like a ballad singer," Bors retorts.) Accompanied by
his faithful retainer, Chrysagon rides off to see the Duke
in a high-angle shot. The sight of the weary War Lord
favoring his wound as he rides off into the horizon is reminiscent of the ending of Shane (1953); the discussions of
honor, duty, loyalty, responsibility, doing what's right
sound similar to the cowboy code. It is here, in the ending,
that Heston's contribution is most keenly felt. Still looking
physically invincible, he plays a middle-aged man who has
been a loner in life, and who, despite his rigorous attention
to his duty, feels he has missed something meaningful in
his life and is desperately trying to find it. This personal
theme has influenced Heston's choice of material: it was explored in other films the actor made with Seltzer, most notably Will Penny (1968), in which he played an aging cowboy,
and Number One (1969), in which he played an aging quar-
terback.

    The War Lord also contains thematic material Schaffner
is fond of exploring. The core ingredients of a Schaffner
film and hero are made manifest: Chrysagon is a gifted but
obsessive man who is trapped in the wrong time; his obses-
sion reveals flaws that have been otherwise concealed by his
talent and skills. William Russell was a similar hero in The
Best Man. Discussion of his other films will show, as his
body of work enlarges, that Schaffner's heroes can escape
neither their flaws nor their times.

    Such, however, are more the thoughts of a film critic,
the type of thoughts quite absent in the mind of a practicing film director. Although it did not meet a happy critical
or commercial end, The War Lord provided Schaffner with a
theretofore unique experience--there had never been a comparable situation in television--from which he learned a very
practical and valuable lesson about studio filmmaking: one
should save as much money as possible during pre-production

and production; there should be some money left over for
post-production--in case of an emergency.

The Double Man

Television in the mid-1960s was totally unconcerned with the
drama or the techniques of live television. After his first
season with DuPont, Schaffner was eager to do something
stronger, something more realistic. In The Whistle Blows
for Victory by John Starr, a McGraw-Hill senior editor, he
had a script in development that would satisfy his desires.
Based on the 1948 dock strike in Nova Scotia, the script
was about how the Communist element of the longshoreman's
union conspired to defeat the Marshall Plan. A study in
ambiguity, it showed how social and political matters become
so complicated that a point is reached where it is impossible
to judge who's right and who's wrong.

The subject matter was too controversial for television:
DuPont would have nothing to do with it; for all his influence in the medium, Schaffner could not get it produced.
The next step was to see if he could do it as a film--
something he pursued while filming The War Lord. Schaffner tried to place the project with Universal as something
he could do following the Charlton Heston epic (the trade
papers had the customary plants announcing that Sean Con-
nery would star in The Whistle Blows for Victory after he
finished Thunderball), but the studio would not buy. "They
are not given to underwriting examinations," Schaffner says
of the media. "They're given to underwriting conclusions
in terms of storytelling."

Schaffner found himself represented by a new agent,
Robert Coryell. The Ziegler-Hellman-Ross Agency had been
purchased by Marvin Josephson, who also bought the
Rosenberg-Coryell Agency; the organization was restruc-
tured and renamed Artists Agency. It was Robert Coryell
of Artists Agency who had negotiated the contract with
Universal when the studio would only let Schaffner direct
The War Lord if he signed a seven-year option contract.
What this meant was that, apart from an occasional feature,
Schaffner would end up directing episodes of Universal's
television series; as it hardly constituted a move up, Coryell had advised Schaffner to direct the film and not sign
the contract, a gambit that worked.

Completing his duties on The War Lord, Schaffner
returned to New York with the realization that a film career
engendered long absences from his family. Now that he no
longer had any television commitments and was concentrating
on film, he felt it might be more advantageous to live closer
to the action. None of the Schaffners was particularly enthusiastic about the prospect of living in Los Angeles, but
it seemed at the time to be the only way to avoid the family's being constantly separated.

Schaffner made the move to California in September
1965. Although closer to the action, he gradually realized
that none of it was coming his way. Even if his cult following might have grown larger with the release of The
War Lord, those were not the people who offered jobs; the
reality was that none of his first three films had made money.
And so he found himself in Southern California, like one of
those stranded in Casablanca, with nothing to do but sit
and wait, and wait, and wait.

Eventually Herbert Brodkin called, asking him to direct a television pilot for ABC entitled One-Eyed Jacks Are
Wild. In an omen of things to come, for his first assignment since moving to California, Schaffner was separated
from his family once again, spending Christmas and the
New Year's in Southern France shooting a romantic comedy
set in a mythical kingdom. The title of this Plautus production referred to a suave gambler (George Grizzard) who,
when he was not in the casinos, was constantly saving a
princess (Ann Bell), heiress to the throne, from either
physical danger or political and court intrigue. It was
through the latter that writer Albert Ruben managed to
inject the Brodkin social significance--in a lighthearted and
offbeat way. Schaffner found both One-Eyed Jacks Are
Wild and Edward Woodward, featured in the role of an especially arch prime minister, civilized and amusing. "It
was a good pilot," Brodkin has commented, "but the network never understood it, and consequently it was never
picked up for a series." Schaffner is even more succinct
about the show's fate: "I never saw that pilot."

No job offers awaited him on his return to Los Angeles. During the long waiting period he would have in
store, Schaffner, dissatisfied with the rhythm of his two
two-syllable names, "carelessly meandering with nothing to

do but think about important things like that," decided to
add his middle initial to his screen credit. Over a full
year had passed since he finished work on The War Lord.
Artists Agency had been of little help; he joined Richard
Shepherd at Creative Management Associates.

Through Shepherd came an offer to direct a spy picture for Warner Brothers that would later be retitled The
Double Man. Although Schaffner is fond of the genre, the
script he received needed a lot of work; it was material he
would have ordinarily rejected, but he could afford no such
luxury. The matter was clear-cut, a matter of survival as
a film director: either do this picture or continue to wait;
at the very least, it would be a change of pace from the
more serious films he had so far directed. Franklin J.
Schaffner came aboard the project in March 1966.

The script was based on Legacy of a Spy, a 1958
novel by Henry S. Maxfield concerning an American named
Slater--known in the trade as Montague, a loner, a master
of make-up, disguises, and voices. After ten years, he
has been in the business too long; he is becoming paranoid.
Accepting the mission on condition that it be his last assignment, he goes to Kitzbühel, Austria to determine how
much information an American vice-consul has given to the
Russians and what has happened to another vice-consul,
now missing. The trip leads to some skiing adventures and
an introduction to love in the person of Ilse Wieland, a West
German agent. While Maxfield's novel is hardly the most
distinguished example in its field, it ventures lightly into
what would become Le Carré country, and constitutes a
pleasant read.

This sort of material has always been best served by
the British, so not surprisingly Legacy of a Spy was purchased by Victor Saville's Parklane Pictures, Ltd. the year
it was published. Nothing was done with it until four years
later, when I. V. Randle and Brian Clemens wrote a script
closely following the book; the year after, the duo wrote
another draft for Saville, who had made a deal with British
Lion Films to produce the film. Although Saville had some
black and white footage shot for it, Legacy of a Spy was
never made.

The property was acquired by Hal E. Chester, an

expatriate American operating out of London. As a child
actor, Hally Chester had appeared on stage in Sidney Kings-
ley's Dead End before moving out to Hollywood in 1938 to
appear in the Dead End Kids movies. After the Second
World War, Chester turned to producing with such low-
budget pictures as Joe Palooka, Champ (1946) and The
Beast from Twenty Thousand Fathoms (1953). Moving to
London, he formed Albion Film Corporation, both to produce films and serve as a small distribution company. A
short man with a bulldog face and a bulldog character,
Hal E. Chester had embarked on a campaign to make major
big-budget films. This necessitated joining forces with
major American studios and major American stars.

His first effort, Father Goose, was subsequently taken
away from him by Universal, but it served to unite him with
a formerly blacklisted writer, Frank Tarloff, who would
write scripts for Chester's two American co-productions:
The Double Man and The Secret War of Harry Frigg. [54]
Tarloff's 1965 screenplay for Legacy of a Spy departed considerably from Maxfield's book, introducing the notion of
plastic surgery and a double man; the script opens with
the double man's cosmetic surgery. CIA Deputy Director
Slater is brought to Austria upon the news of his son's
death in a skiing accident; Slater II follows to take care of
Slater I.

With Tarloff's script, Chester was able to make a
deal with Warner Brothers: if the studio could get Kirk
Douglas or, better yet, Tony Curtis, then on the lot making The Big Brass (released as Not With My Wife, You
Don't), Warners would put up $2.6 million. But when Cur-
tis turned down the script, the studio decided on a smaller
picture, shaving a million dollars off its end of the budget.
Chester, in the meantime, separately employed Larry Marcus and Clive Exton to rewrite the script and relieve it of
its grimness, and managed to supplement the budget in England with Eady funds, receiving a completion guarantee
from the National Film Finance Corporation.

Not only offering thoughts about casting stars,
Warners was also actively casting about for a director.
Since big name directors were immediately bypassed for
budgetary reasons, studio executive Robert Solo devised
a list of less expensive directors that Warner Bros. would

accept. It provides a good barometer of what Schaffner's
status among American directors at the studios was at the
time: Solo's list included Jack Smight, Stuart Rosenberg,
Desmond Davis, Michael Gordon, Gordon Douglas, Guy
Hamilton, Arthur Hill, Hy Averback, Eliot Silverstein, Clive
Donner, and John Schlesinger. [55]

When Schaffner was offered Legacy of a Spy, he flew
to London to meet Chester; they got along well, even if
their personalities and story senses clashed. "He had an
ability to push things through," the director says, not
without admiration. "I would say more often than not a lot
of china got broken." The stay in England also afforded
Schaffner an opportunity to sit down with Clive Exton and
try to reorganize the script, but the big news was that,
through all his pushing and shoving to hire a name actor,
Chester had managed to secure a star to play Slater and
Slater II--Yul Brynner. This represented a reunion of
sorts for Schaffner.

Yul Brynner had preceded Franklin Schaffner at CBS
Television. In 1946, when Arthur Godfrey was reluctant to
try out the new medium, Worthington Miner had hired Brynner as a performer for CBS' hour-long variety show At
Home; a Brynner specialty was obscene gypsy songs. Miner
then groomed Brynner to be a director, with enough success
that the actor in turn would himself train a novice television
director, Sidney Lumet. "Yul had a real instinct as a director, a good visual sense, a lot of excellent stuff," Miner
said. "While he was on Danger [CBS' suspense anthology],
he was on his way to becoming one of the best directors in
television."

In a way, Worthington Miner was also responsible for
cutting short Brynner's promising directorial career. "Yul
and Tony had a great rapport," says a witness, the director of The Double Man. "Tony was the guy who when Rod-
gers and Hammerstein were looking for a King--right?--sent
Brynner over. And Brynner got the job, when Yul still
had hair ... some hair." Robert Fryer, then Miner's assistant, recalls that Miner reassured Brynner he could return to CBS if the play were a flop. The play, which opened
in 1951, was The King and I. "Of course," Fryer says, "he
never came back." Nor did Brynner ever return to directing. Worthington Miner offered the most reasonable explanation:

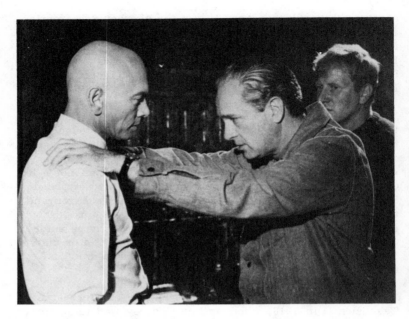

Reunion of two alumni of the CBS Television directorial
staff: Yul Brynner and Schaffner, filming The Double Man,
1966. Clive Revill looks on.

"He could do a great many other things, except I think Yul
has settled for the fact he is a bit of a sybarite. He does
love riches and luxury. He's got enough money to live that
way for the rest of his life." With success, Brynner had
discovered the obvious: the lifestyle to which he aspired
could best be realized through acting. The most logical
reason Yul Brynner would accept Legacy of a Spy would be
as a further means to support that lifestyle.

    Generally speaking, a motion picture production pro-
ceeds at a more leisurely pace than a television production;
there are fewer time constraints. Such would not be the
case with The Double Man which, if anything, was far more
chaotic than live television. Filming had to begin immediately or the services of Yul Brynner would be lost. Secondly,
as all the Alps scenes required snow, it was either start
shooting right away, before the snow melted, or wait until
winter.

There wasn't too much time to polish the script. Exton had added an elderly Duchess to be hostess of the climactic party; the Deputy Director of the CIA would not be Slater but a man named Edwards, the authority figure in the script. No actor had been cast in the role, but it wasn't that urgent--all of Edwards' scenes took place in his office, and could be done on one soundstage. More pressing was the female lead, Gina, the Duchess' secretary: as a witness to Bobby Slater's death, she was involved in the exterior Alps scenes; Legacy of a Spy had to go into production without a leading lady.

The schedule was arranged in the only way possible under the circumstances: Schaffner would shoot all the exterior sequences in the Alps during the month of April; the production would shut down completely for six weeks so that the script could be rewritten; production would resume in June at the Associated British Studios in Elstree. During the first phase of production, the company was headquartered in St. Anton, Austria, where the director worked with what was primarily a British cast and crew. Jeremy Kemp had been signed for the pivotal role of Berthold, the major villain in the piece, but was absent for the first two days of his scenes; he hadn't even arrived in Austria. Schaffner recalls the moment Kemp joined the company:

> He was loaded to the gills. I thought, "Oh boy, here comes trouble." I went up to him, and he said to the effect, "Just thought I'd come and say hello, I'm late, and I don't want to do the picture." And he turned and walked away.

German character actor Anton Diffring was summoned with dispatch to enact the role. Schaffner would make good use of Diffring--Berthold can be seen skulking around in the background of many shots where he has no dialogue.

The prospect of melting snow had been anticipated because of the season; the actual situation turned out to be more disquieting than had been expected. The director comments:

> We had to move every single day. We found ourselves unable to go back to a location the next day because the snow was melting. We would gradually

move further and further up the damn mountain
slopes day by day in order to keep up with the
snow.

The leading lady dilemma was temporarily resolved by simply
putting a hooded anorak on a double. Given Technicolor, a
1:85 aspect ratio, and the task of shooting a lot of footage
for process work, Schaffner was well assisted in his chores
by cinematographer Dennys Coop, who had won acclaim for
his realistic black and white camerawork on Billy Liar (1963)
and King and Country (1965); it is fair to say that the photography of the Alps is the highlight of the film. The location work was finished by the end of April, but the director can only say, "We got out of there by the skin of
our teeth."

The first phase of production completed, Schaffner
prepared to embark on the second. Alfred Hayes, who had
worked on The Stripper screenplay before Schaffner arrived,
was hired for the final rewrite. Instead of flying Hayes
across the Atlantic and giving him a per diem, Chester sent
Schaffner to Los Angeles, where the producer would not
have to pay for either the writer's or the director's expenses; Chester, on per diem, would also be there.

Before returning home, Schaffner made a stopover in
London to direct the television pilot of Women of the World,
more or less as a favor to John Aaron, the last surviving
producer of Person to Person. Intended as a distaff Person
to Person, only with both guests in the studio with host
John Daly, Women of the World, in keeping with the times,
would not be broadcast live. Its premise was that the program would travel all over the world to interview the most
interesting women; London had been chosen for the pilot
because the two celebrities, Lee Radziwill and Leslie Caron,
happened to be in town at the time. The first show was
obviously meant as a best foot forward: John Daly's schedule would not permit him to work on the show on a continuing basis; neither could Franklin Schaffner be expected
to show up on a different location each week.

Schaffner's schedule allowed him one full day to direct the pilot, which seemed fair enough as he was accustomed to directing Person to Person in a single evening.
The date that was chosen, however, came too soon by a

day; Schaffner had to leave helicopter shots of the Alps
for the second unit to film. Arriving in London on the day
of the shoot, Schaffner found a British crew awaiting him;
working with an unfamiliar crew on this kind of show turned
out to be a nightmarish experience. As it turned out, the
Women of the World pilot never sold, and it also represents
the only instance in Schaffner's career when he was never
paid for his services.

Working with Alfred Hayes on the Legacy of a Spy
script was a more pleasant experience. As the script had
to be rewritten anyway, Hayes carefully studied the footage
Schaffner had shot and made his changes accordingly, writing scenes that would fit what had already been filmed on
location. A good example of the Hayes patchwork is in the
scene, two-thirds of the way into the released film, where
Slater follows Max and Grigori, the men Gina saw at the
site of Bobby's death, to the Baumer Farm. Originally,
Slater went inside for a shoot-out with Max and Grigori,
and tumbled out to safety. In the film, Slater enters the
farmhouse and is forced at gunpoint to undress; he does
as he is told but, when the opportune moment arises,
fights back. During the struggle, the camera moves in on
a gun: before Slater can grab it, the gun is kicked away;
a loud gunshot is heard, followed by a medium shot of Max.
In a Volkswagen bus outside the farmhouse, Wheatly, Slater's now retired partner, reacts to the noise with fear and
drives off, returning when he regains his composure. In
the Hayes version, Slater II makes his move, and it is he
who climbs into Wheatly's van.

Hayes' handiwork represented last-minute changes
during the month and a half hiatus--there was a feeling
about The Double Man akin to treading furiously to keep
one's head above water. Typically, a new problem arose
when the second phase of production was about to begin:
the start had to be delayed a week because Yul Brynner
was now acting in Triple Cross (1967) with Christopher
Plummer. Although Chester was able to make Terence
Young, the director of the other film, pay a five thousand
pound penalty, Brynner continued flying to Paris on weekends to complete his part in the rival espionage movie.
The producer might have made a fuss, mainly about the
matter of Brynner's insurance, but it wasn't taken very
seriously; Warner Bros. was distributing both films.

Production resumed on June 20 at the Associated
British Studios where, in addition to the interiors, Schaffner had to shoot exteriors on soundstages to match the
Alps footage. Communication with his all-British crew
proved to be virtually impossible; at Associated British,
Schaffner found the strongest union control he has ever
encountered in his career, a factor that might have contributed to the eventual demise of the studios.

The CIA office awaited an actor to play Edwards. A
Henry Fonda or Fredric March being unfeasible, Lloyd Nolan,
with whom Schaffner had worked so successfully on the television production of "The Caine Mutiny Court Martial," was
signed. Even the veteran Nolan was in for a bit of surprise: as soon as his plane from Los Angeles arrived in
London, he was taken directly to the studio where, before
he knew it, he was on a set, made-up, and in front of the
camera. As usual for such a role, Nolan didn't have much
to do but provide plot explanations, give orders, and com-
plain, which he does in a properly salty fashion in the film.

Finally, two weeks after production was resumed,
Britt Ekland was hired for the role of Gina. Requisitely
blonde and pretty, she automatically fulfilled the dimensions
of the part; Gina, despite the delay in casting, is a far cry
from Scarlett O'Hara. Her big moment is a fight scene with
Slater II in which she scratches his face, so the audience
will know he is not the real Slater. Warner Bros. would
choose to exploit this scene, heralding the fight as being
in the tradition of The Spoilers, which only underscores
the stereotypical role of women in spy movies: in this case
Gina gets hit, and gets to go off with Slater at the end.

Now that the film would have a happy ending, Warner
Bros. took care of the usual details in California, changing
the title to The Double Man. After six writers' work on
the script, it scarcely bore any resemblance to the Maxfield
book; except for Slater's name, the Alps, the farmhouse,
and the mountain-top party--all of which can be construed
as mere coincidence--this might as well have been an original script. After arbitration, the Writers Guild of America
ruled that Frank Tarloff and Alfred Hayes should get screen
credit. As for the Production Code Office, in other indica-
tors of the time, the word merde was found unacceptable
and, in regards to the violence, Geoffrey M. Shurlock wrote:

"The kick in the head seems too cruel. It should not actually be photographed but only suggested."[56]

       Post-production on The Double Man was housed at
Associated British Studios; front and rear projection work
was handled at Shepperton Studios. In a pictorial trip up
a mountain, after eight shots of a red cable car, which
makes a stop at a landing where passengers switch cars,
three shots of a silver car take the audience the rest of
the way to the top--which a discerning viewer can see was
recreated on a soundstage, with front projection providing
the real mountains seen in the background. Similarly, the
close shots of the principals on skis were filmed on a soundstage and married to the action on the slopes by rear projection, the process also used for the exterior backgrounds
in train or automobile interiors; Slater's confrontation with
Slater II was accomplished with the blue screen process.
This was Schaffner's first experience shooting projection,
one of the least appealing and most maddening parts of filmmaking; always more effective in black and white, it is
rarely satisfactory in color. But aesthetics was a minor
consideration; the object was to get it done. "Happily,"
Schaffner says, summing up, "we were able to again Mickey
Mouse all this location shooting into the new approach to
the script."

       Once he completed a serviceable cut of the film with
editor Richard Best, Schaffner returned to Los Angeles.
Without informing the director, Chester hired an American
composer, Ernie Freeman, to write the music for the film.
Best known for his rock and roll classic "Raunchy," Freeman would provide a score for The Double Man which sound-
ed more like music one would expect to hear in a British
television spy series. Except for one futile effort over the
telephone, this most musically knowledgeable of directors
never had the chance to discuss the score with its composer.

       A memo from Jack Warner, while also revealing that
there was trouble between Chester and Rudi Fehr, head of
the editorial department, indicates the status of a certain
director and offers insight into the modus operandi of a
legendary movie mogul:

       For Director [sic] Guild requirements has Schaffner

> shown the picture to Chester? If not we could
> have serious kickbacks from the SDG. Be sure
> and check this with Chester. From here on let
> Schaffner out of this and straighten out the pic-
> ture with Chester. [57]

Considering the above message, the following incident points
out the maneuvers Warner had to execute, the faces he had
to wear, as the boss of a studio he succeeded in running
for 40 years.

Schaffner soon received a telephone call informing him
that Mr. Warner would be screening The Double Man and
had requested his presence. Showing up at Warner Bros.
at the appointed hour, Schaffner had to wait for Warner
and his staff to arrive. When they did, it was apparent
that they had returned from dinner--to which the director
had obviously not been invited--where fine drinks had accompanied a fine meal; everybody was in a festive mood.
Ever cordial, Warner invited the director to sit next to him.
Then, Schaffner recalls:

> He turned to me and he says, "Is this a one, two,
> or three piss picture?" I said, "Mr. Warner, I
> don't know what you mean." He said, "Well, if I
> get up and piss once, it's okay. If I go to piss
> twice, I'm losing interest." And he said, "If you
> see me piss three times, the picture's no good."

The screening commenced, and Warner remained in his seat
until the end of the film. When the lights went up, he suddenly dashed out of the room; the rest of the executives
remained silent, most likely wondering why the boss had
not gotten up earlier during the film. When Warner returned to the screening room, Schaffner remembers: "He
says to me, 'See? Didn't piss once. Pretty good picture.'
And he turns around to the other fellows and says, 'It's
okay with me. You guys do what you want with it.'"

The guys did what they wanted to do with it: the
film was turned over to editor William Ziegler, effectively
removing Schaffner from the project. After several days
of work at the moviola, Ziegler called the director to tell
him that his orders were to make the film better but that
any changes he made would in fact make the film worse.

Schaffner, like the seasoned pro he had become during this
production, offered the following advice: "Tell them that
you transposed a few things, moved up a few things, eliminated a few things, and you think it plays much better--
because they'll never remember."

Ziegler did precisely that; they didn't remember--not
that it much mattered. In the final twist to The Double
Man, Seven Arts purchased Warner Bros., and the studio
became Warner Bros.-Seven Arts. The film got lost in the
administrative shuffle and remained on the shelf for over
a year.

In his April 26, 1967 Variety review of a motion picture that would not be released in America for another 13
months, "Rich." wrote perhaps more accurately than he
realized: "Atmosphere of mystery and menace is slowly but
skillfully built up.... Franklin J. Schaffner has directed
this Hal Chester production without frills and has paced out
his dramatic highlights usefully."[58] Although The Double
Man was not the fairest test of his skills in the spy genre,
Schaffner, under the circumstances, had done his best. A
subtle effort had been made to alter Yul Brynner's voice
for Slater II: tape recording technology coupled with the
actor's efforts produced a higher-pitched Brynner voice,
speaking in a simultaneous whine and snarl, somewhat akin
to Jack Palance. To fuel Slater's already existing paranoia,
the director places him in a cafe, looking out the window at
the people walking by--he doesn't see the people themselves
but their images moving by in the window; the villains are
frequently revealed in reflections off vending machine mirrors. Berthold's two henchmen, Max and Grigori, wear a
white and a red hat respectively; thanks to this almost subliminal touch--one seldom indicated in a script--the audience
can anticipate the menace stalking the hero.

Franklin J. Schaffner even made his only film appearance, in an effort that saved The Double Man some money.
In an uncredited, wordless, almost Hitchcockian walk-on,
Schaffner can be seen in the St. Anton train station to the
bottom right of the frame; a black hat he wears somewhat
obscures his face. He is meant to be an eastern bloc spy,
which is revealed economically in a shot of a hand making a
telephone call, followed by a cut to Berthold's office where
the verbal exposition is then given.

The moment Slater first meets Slater II contains the following dialogue:

> Slater: "You're a bastard."
> Slater II: "I am you."

The exchange is amusing and reinforces something that has long since been established--Dan Slater is a bastard--and that is all that should be read into the exchange. Despite all the mirror images and the title of the film, the doppelganger theme is far beyond the parameters of the production; the intent was more melodramatic. At the conclusion of the chase scene, Wheatly, who runs a private school where he had been watching over Bobby Slater, knows he must kill one of the two Slaters. When one claims to have loved his son, Wheatly shoots him; the real Dan Slater never loved anybody in his life. The director strings the audience along to the end, getting the spectator to participate in the denouement, by not revealing the full face of the remaining Slater until the last possible moment: there are no scratches on his face; it is the real Dan Slater.

Discussing The Double Man and its genre in The New York Times, Renata Adler observed: "The whole form may eventually dissolve with a double agent chasing himself about in place, into stories of suicide from ambivalent paranoia."[59] Although the form never degenerated into that, the double agent chasing himself was also evident in A Dandy in Aspic, the last film directed by Anthony Mann, also released in 1968. In the six years following James Bond's debut in Dr. No, agents and spies had been all over theatre and television screens, over-saturating the market, increasingly featuring more sex and violence, areas in which The Double Man was relatively restrained. Casino Royale and The Spy with the Cold Nose were released in London at the same time as Schaffner's film: the genre was burlesquing itself. The spy cycle had pretty much come to a close by 1968, and The Double Man was not a commercial success. With the addition of elaborate special effects, the only survivor of the genre would be James Bond.

Warner Bros.-Seven Arts released The Double Man in Los Angeles as the top half of a double-bill with Kona Coast, directed by Lamont Johnson. Although unaware of the particulars, Kevin Thomas of the Los Angeles Times was quick to spot the sow's ear: "What is the greatest interest about The Double Man is how its talented director has created suspense and excitement from a fairly formula situation."[60] The Double Man is proof of the Hollywood adage about what can happen when a director tackles material that does not measure up to him. "It's easier to be a good director with a good script," Schaffner once said. "It is something else to turn out a workmanlike job with a script which doesn't work."[61] Such was the case with this film. But in an industry in which every motion picture production is unique, surely The Double Man was a bit more unique.

Kevin Thomas had ample reason to be as generous in his review of the film: something had happened in the meantime to influence his judgment. During the long period The Double Man remained on the shelf, Schaffner had directed another film that had been released three months earlier. Not only was it Schaffner's first commercial breakthrough, Planet of the Apes was what is known as a blockbuster.

ABC Stage 67

ABC Stage 67 was the television networks' last attempt at a quality weekly dramatic anthology; once again the man to get this kind of show on the air was Hubbell Robinson who, by placing Stage 67 with ABC, had accomplished the feat of putting a dramatic anthology on all three networks. As to the relative worth of the $9 million he received from ABC, Robinson had received $6 million more from NBC six years earlier for the short-lived Ford Startime.

Considering the fate of dramatic anthologies since the death of Playhouse 90, it was quite an achievement to get even $9 million. If the top ten television shows serve as any measure of the times, the season in which Stage 67 debuted was dominated by a western (Bonanza), variety shows with the accent on comedy (Red Skelton, Jackie Gleason), and the networks' staple, the long-running comedy series (The Andy Griffith Show, The Lucy Show, Green Acres, Bewitched, The Beverly Hillbillies, Gomer Pyle, U.S.M.C.).

Serving as executive producer of Stage 67, Robinson selected material and hired production companies to make

the shows. Shot at various studios, some shows were
filmed, some taped; generally, $250,000 was allotted for
each production, probably the most memorable being an
adaptation of Katherine Anne Porter's "Noon Wine," produced by Daniel Melnick, who hired Sam Peckinpah to write
and direct it.

Airing on April 20, 1967, "The Wide Open Door" was
produced and directed by Franklin Schaffner for his Gilchrist Productions. Taped at the NBC Burbank Studios, it
was shot an act at a time, as had been Schaffner's method
on DuPont, with pick-up shots taped only after the third
act had been completed. But there were discernible changes
in production since Schaffner had last directed a television
drama three years earlier, most conspicuously the new television camera: camera turrets were a thing of the past,
having been replaced by a zoomar lenses; a corollary of the
new lens was a propensity to overuse it. Even at the beginning of the golden age, NBC crews, compared with CBS
crews, had never been especially noted for their skill or
finesse; the old sense of trust between crew and director
had deteriorated. Schaffner had to be at his most eloquent
to persuade the crew into doing a dolly shot. "I think NBC
crews were the first ones to sit on stools," he says. "Un-
believable--something I'd never seen before."

"The Wide Open Door," written by Ealing Studio comedy specialist T. E. B. Clarke, of Lavendar Hill Mob (1951)
fame, had a sophisticated British quality not totally unlike
"The Wicked Scheme of Jebal Deeks" (featuring former Ealing
comedy star Alec Guinness), another comedy about larceny
that Schaffner had previously produced and directed for
Hubbell Robinson. Concerning two sets of twins, portrayed
by Tony Randall and Honor Blackman, and the subsequent
confusion the mistaken identities add to the heist, the show
also featured such mid-Atlantic types as Reginald Gardiner,
Leon Ames, Richard Haydn, and Bernard Fox; in keeping
with the mid-Atlantic motif, the show begins with a ship-
board romance on an ocean liner. Randall and Blackman
are fine--they and the material make for a fine television
show--but with more agile and higher voltage actors, the
material might have made for something more.

"The Wide Open Door" is noteworthy for one last
reason: Stage 67 had a 60 minute time slot; this show was

90 minutes long, a forerunner of a new television trend. A
large audience had grown for movies on television: by the
1966-1967 season, there were already five prime time slots--
ten hours a week--devoted to movies; at the rate television
was consuming movies, the demand would soon exceed the
supply. Two years later, ABC would launch a new equivalent of the dramatic anthology in its Tuesday Movie of the
Week--90-minute movies made directly for television.

   Suffering from dismal ratings, ABC Stage 67 was
promptly canceled at the end of the season. All in all, considering the shows that were selling, the virtual absence of
quality programs, the new methods, and the attitude of the
crews, there was little to hold Schaffner to television. "The
Wide Open Door" represented his last directorial effort for
the medium.

Planet of the Apes

With four films' worth of experience behind him, Schaffner
finally felt at home with the motion picture medium. Not
only was he comfortable with the big screen, in his fifth
film he found he was at last confident in his use of the
wide screen; Planet of the Apes fully reflects that assur-
ance. Kevin Thomas would write:

> "Planet of the Apes" is that rarity, a Hollywood
> blockbuster that not only attempts much but actual-
> ly accomplishes all that it set out to do. A triumph
> of artistry and imagination, it is at once a timely
> parable and a grand adventure on an epic scale.
> Provocative as it is entertaining, it is a true screen
> odyssey. [62]

   For all its success, the four subsequent sequels and
two television series it spawned, Planet of the Apes would
seem a hot property that every studio would be anxious to
underwrite. Such was not the case; the subject matter was
entirely resistable to the studios. Only through the persis-
tence of producer Arthur P. Jacobs was the film made, but
not without a five-year struggle. Known as a good idea man,
Jacobs was the only one who had the idea that Apes would
make a good movie.

The late Arthur P. Jacobs was formerly a Warner
Bros. publicity man, who began his own public relations
firm representing the likes of Gary Cooper, Marlene Dietrich, James Stewart, and Gregory Peck; he had handled
Franklin Schaffner's publicity on The Stripper. Forming
APJAC Productions, he moved into film production with
What a Way to Go (1964), which originally was to have
starred his client Marilyn Monroe; his aim was to make
films that were, while entertainments, different from the
standard Hollywood fare. In 1963, he came across a very
different kind of project when Pierre Boulle's Planet of the
Apes was published in its English-language version.

Rather than science fiction, the book is more an extended allegory, with the fantastic elements allowing Boulle
to comment on contemporary human behavior and morality.
The novel begins with a young couple named Jinn and Phyllis, on an outer space holiday, who spot and retrieve a
bottle containing a message which, like the letter in Mary
Shelley's Frankenstein, comprises most of the book. A plea
for help from Ulysse Merou, a journalist who accompanied a
scientific mission in the year 2500, the letter tells how he
landed on an earth-like planet where people are savage and
mute, where human sounds are made by gorillas, who presently captured him. This space-age Ulysse describes a sophisticated ape civilization in which humans are treated like
wild animals, changing his perception of apes and men: "I
soon succeeded in convincing myself that well-trained animals might well have been able to ... become expert in all
the human arts, including the art of cinematography."[63]
He becomes involved with two women: Nova, the savage
whom he physically desires and impregnates, and Zira, the
chimpanzee scientist whom he grows to love intellectually.
When Zira and her friend and fellow scientist Cornelius learn
that Dr. Zaius, head of the Institute, plans to assassinate
the human being, they send Ulysse, together with Nova and
their infant son, back to earth in a satellite. When he lands
in Paris, Ulysse writes, he and his family are met at the
airport by a gorilla. Being chimpanzees, Jinn and Phyllis
shrug off this crackpot letter.

Jacobs acquired the property at once. "That tenacity," says Mort Abrahams, the associate producer of the
film, "that dogged refusal to be turned off, plus his own
originality of thinking were his main attributes." Jacobs

would need all of those attributes to get the film off the
ground. His first move was to hire Rod Serling, the best
choice he could have made; apart from his undoubted skill
at writing, Serling had the highest profile in the media for
this type of material. Serling would eventually share script
credit with Michael Wilson. It would seem most likely that
Serling was responsible for the monkeyshines ("I never met
an ape I didn't like," "Human see, human do") and Michael
Wilson, who won an Academy Award for his work on the
script of A Place in the Sun (1951) and, while blacklisted,
contributed to the film script of Boulle's Bridge on the
River Kwai (1957), was responsible for the social and political elements in the film. Not so.

   Serling's is much the more thoughtful script--more of
an examination of human society as revealed by the apes,
more concerned with moral issues, and going into detail to
describe the simian society and its architecture. On Serling's planet, the apes, dressed like British hunters, descend in helicopters to capture Thomas, the main character,
who eventually becomes a media superstar--as the talking
and reasoning human being. Most importantly, Serling
came up with a new ending: in the wake of the film's success, many people have either been credited or taken credit
for the idea of the Statue of Liberty; Mort Abrahams simply
says, "The concept was Rod's."

   Selling the project was Jacobs' job. As befitting his
reputation as a great salesman and an exceptional talker,
Jacobs did things in an elaborate way, going so far as to
hire a team of artists to sketch an entire film, thus giving
him a visual aid as he made his pitch; typically, the Planet
of the Apes presentation was a thick collection of handsome
water colors. When the producer managed to interest Blake
Edwards, then directing The Great Race for the studio,
Warner Bros. finally showed some interest in the project.
With Serling's script as a reference, a conservative budget
was estimated: $10,325,625.[64] In 1965, a $10 million budget was astronomical; Apes would be a very expensive picture by a very expensive director whose films had a tendency to run over budget, as indeed The Great Race had.

   Edwards eventually dropped out of the picture and
moved to the Mirisch Brothers and United Artists to make
What Did You Do in the War, Daddy?[65] Jacbos remained

at the studio, making a pitch for Sidney Pollack to direct
at half the estimated budget, but Warners had misgivings
about the commercial prospects of the project. A memo
written by studio executive Walter MacEwen indicates that
management had other plans in mind: "I intend to tell
Jacobs thereafter that we are definitely shelving the picture at this time--inasmuch as we only took it on in the
first instance in the hope it could be done with Blake Edwards."[66]

   Moving on to M-G-M, where he tried to get a First
World War Air Corps drama off the ground, Jacobs met an
old acquaintance, Mort Abrahams, then producing The Man
from U.N.C.L.E. for M-G-M Television; in the 1950s, Abrahams had produced General Electric Theater with Ronald
Reagan, a show for which Jacobs had handled publicity.
At Jacobs' invitation, Abrahams joined APJAC Productions,
becoming an active participant in the selling of Planet of
the Apes:

      I gave up several times but [Jacobs] never gave
      up. I had as much confidence in the project as he
      did but he had more confidence that we could get it
      going because we were turned down by every studio
      in town at least twice.

After a rejection, Jacobs' procedure was to wait until a new
administration took over at a studio, whereupon he would
make his pitch anew.

   In a production considered as risky as this, the producer would need a major star to attract financing. Jacobs
was fortunate that Charlton Heston was himself looking for
something different and, upon reading Serling's script,
shared his enthusiasm for the project. Yet even with a
star of Heston's magnitude, Jacobs was still unable to get
a definite commitment from a studio; for his part, Heston
remained loyal to the project for the years it took to get
the film made. At this point, Franklin J. Schaffner's name,
suggested by Heston, first came up as a possible director
for the film.

   Shrewdly juggling projects, Jacobs made a deal to
produce a musical version of Doctor Dolittle at Twentieth
Century-Fox, the studio responsible for The Sound of Music

(1965). As no expense was spared, which gave him ample opportunity to meet with production head Richard Zanuck, Jacobs invariably found a way to work Planet of the Apes into the conversation. Although he soon grew tired of hearing about the project, Zanuck was not completely discouraging, only expressing reservations about the make-up.

Making a trip to England in the summer of 1966, ostensibly to check out the make-up Stanley Kubrick was using for his apes in 2001 and to scout possible locations for his Apes, Jacobs wanted primarily to meet the director Charlton Heston had recommended. Schaffner, then filming The Double Man in London, was given a copy of the script. "I read it," he says, "and I said, 'Sure,' on the basis that I never really thought it would be made."

Fondly remembering his association with Schaffner on "The Great Sebastians," Mort Abrahams, who would supervise the production, was pleased with this development:

> Frank had a vision of [Planet of the Apes] which, in our meetings, was obviously exactly what the picture should have been and exactly what I had in mind visually for the picture. So there was an immediate community on the vision of the picture.

Although aware of the producer's limitations, Schaffner found himself attracted to the bundle of energy that was Arthur P. Jacobs:

> He had this quality that still to this day impresses me--I never heard him say a harsh word about anybody. Arthur knew that he was not equipped to deal with the nuts-and-bolts of putting a picture together.... An oversimplification is Arthur's attitude was: "Well, you make a picture. Make it! Right?"

The rest was left to Schaffner and Abrahams, who not only was very helpful to the director but was a stabilizing influence on the producer. With their complementary skills, Jacobs and Abrahams functioned as a good team on a film that needed teamwork to get it made right: Jacobs was imaginative in casting and exploitation; Abrahams provided strength in areas where Jacobs was weak, notably production and script.

Edward G. Robinson came aboard as Zaius, the antagonist further strengthening the package. But, feeling he
had written himself out on the project and had nothing left
to give, Rod Serling was unavailable for rewrites; Schaffner
was denied the opportunity of again working with his frequent collaborator from the days of live television. Michael
Wilson was recruited to rewrite the script with an eye to
lowering the budget: gone would be the modern civilization,
its architecture and hardware; instead of fancy flying machines, the apes would ride horses. The writer reorganized
the hierarchy of the ape society: the orangutans would be
the lawgivers; chimpanzees would be the scientists; the
gorillas would be the ones to employ brute force. Determining that all other animals, including the native humans,
would be mute, Wilson emphasized the inherent overtones in
the plot of the Bible, Will Rogers, George Orwell, Jonathan
Swift, John Milton, Edgar Rice Burroughs, and King Kong.
When Wilson later grew too ill to work, John T. Kelley, who
had written the 1965 film adaptation of John O'Hara's A Rage
to Live, came in to polish the script.

Richard Zanuck provided money for experimentation
on what he still considered the weakest link--the make-up.
That task was given to Fox make-up artist John Chambers,
creator of Lee Marvin's nose in Cat Ballou (1965), Leonard
Nimoy's ears for Star Trek (1966), and Richard Harris'
chest for A Man Called Horse (1970). Chambers eagerly
accepted the assignment and, assisted by Paul Malcolm,
spent over half a year coming up with the right look, meeting the challenge without resorting to immobile ape masks.
Art director William J. Creber pitched in with sketches of
primitive men, even briging in a live chimpanzee for research purposes.

The Apes' progress eventually reached a standstill:
either go ahead with production or cancel development.
The studio was unsure whether the film would really work
or not; and specifically, whether an audience would laugh
at a talking ape or actually listen to what it was saying.
There was only one way to find out: Zanuck ordered a
test. Heston had misgivings--no actor of his stature did a
test for a film that hadn't even been approved--but it was
necessary if the film were going to be made.[67] Originally
chosen was a scene in which Heston lies unconscious on an
operating table while three ape surgeons discuss his condi-

tion. Schaffner thought the scene missed the point of the
show: it wouldn't be a fair test unless there was a showdown between the man from earth and the Chief Minister of
Science. The director was allowed to prepare a climactic
scene in which a talking human doll is found at the excava-
tion site, enabling the man to point out that an ape would
not have made a talking human doll.

Schaffner was given a mere $5000 to film the test.
Set inside a tent, the scene introduces Robinson as Zaius,
dressed in vest and tie, covered by a smock. He wears
simplified make-up from the initial stages of Chambers' experimentation; his hands are bare. Robinson and Heston
discuss the relative merits of apes and humans, while two
Fox contract players--James Brolin and Linda Harrison,
who would eventually play Nova--stand around in the background, unrecognizable in their make-up as Cornelius and
Zira. [68]

The test was taken to New York and screened for the
Twentieth Century-Fox board of directors. No one laughed;
no one questioned that man and ape both spoke English.
What must have been of some importance was that Zaius'
lines were delivered by a superb screen actor--and that an
actor of Edward G. Robinson's caliber was willing to don
the make-up for a test. Nonetheless, despite the test and
the New York reaction, no green light awaited the film at
the studio.

Help came with the release of Fantastic Voyage (1966),
another Twentieth Century-Fox science fiction gimmick picture, about a team of doctors who are miniaturized to perform brain surgery within a stricken scientist--a premise
Jacobs found no more far-fetched than the one he was pitch-
ing. He went to work immediately, assembling a scrapbook
of Fantastic Voyage ads, reviews, and grosses for a presentation he would make to Richard Zanuck, demonstrating
that Planet of the Apes could also be successful. He was
asked to wait, to see if Fantastic Voyage would still be making money after its first few weeks in release. When Fantastic Voyage proved to have "legs," Zanuck said the film
could be made on one condition: the budget must not exceed $5 million. By this time, APJAC had pared the bud-
get down to a bare minimum of $5.8 million; Abrahams knew
that Apes could not possibly be made at Zanuck's price.

There were two options: (1) make the picture, go over
budget, and get into trouble; (2) not make the picture.
The choice was obvious.

In his preparation, Schaffner busied himself with details about the film's apes, how they would walk, how they
would sit, what they would eat, how they would live, and
how their dwellings would be furnished. Chambers' work
on the make-up had progressed well, complemented by the
costumes designed by Mort Haack; at the suggestion of the
art department, the clothes would match the color of the
apes--orangutans would dress in reddish-gold, chimpanzees
in green, and gorillas in dark brown-black. Although not
readily apparent in the film, a special rifle, Rea Voom 88,
was made, designed to accommodate an ape's paw.

Nearly 20% of the budget had been allocated to the
make-up. It was imperative that the actor's eyes be visible
and that, under the various layers of make-up, the actor
could move his nose and mouth. Four basic pieces of foam
rubber were used for the brow, nose, chin, and ear; blue-
eyed actors had to wear contact lenses. Eventually a bevy
of make-up people were hired for the hundreds of actors
who played orangutans, chimpanzees, and gorillas. As the
make-up required three hours to apply, the actors had to
show up for work at 4:30 a.m. During the day, they could
only eat small chunks of food and drink liquids through a
straw. An hour and a half at the end of the day was required to remove the layers of foam rubber appliances, carefully saved for use the next day. Perspiration often proved
to be a problem; the company would have to carry portable
air conditioning units.

Edward G. Robinson was a casualty of the make-up:
although he wanted to make the film, he bowed out due to
ill health; the make-up only exacerbated his condition.
Maurice Evans stepped in to play Zaius and would make a
formidable looking and sounding Minister of Science and
Chief Defender of the Faith. James Whitmore and James
Daly were added to the cast, almost anonymous under their
orangutan make-up as President of the Assembly and Deputy
Minister of Justice respectively. Not least of all, Roddy
McDowall and Kim Hunter were signed to play the chimpan-
zee scientists and lovers, Cornelius and Zira.

In a not unpolitical move, a special friend of Richard
Zanuck's, the former Miss Maryland, Linda Harrison, who
for similar reasons had appeared in the test, was cast as
Nova. "Her hair is long and black, her skin nut brown,"
Nova is described in Wilson's script, "her face hauntingly
lovely and hauntingly stupid."[69] Schaffner would properly
keep her as still as possible and add another expression to
her part--worry. In post-production, Schaffner and editor
Hugh Fowler would have to eliminate the scene establishing
Nova's pregnancy; the screenplay had departed far enough
from Boulle's novel that such a revelation would detract
from the direction the film was headed in, and, besides, as
Michael Wilson speculated, it might have suggested that
Taylor had committed sodomy.[70]

Art director William J. Creber had worked seven
months on George Stevens' The Greatest Story Ever Told
(1965), becoming so familiar with the Page, Arizona and
Lake Powell, Utah areas that he even knew the right times
of day to shoot at the best locations--locations more convincing, more suitable for science fiction than the New
Testament. Being department head, Jack Martin Smith was
also given art director's credit, but, in fairness, it was he,
recalling Creber's experience on the earlier film, who suggested the locations to Creber, who then handed over his
maps to the location manager.

Principal photography began in May 1967 with the
most difficult sequence: a week was allocated to film the
ten pages of script detailing the astronauts' trek across the
desert to the greenbelt. Certain locations were so inaccessible a helicopter had to take cast and crew there; the
cameras and equipment were often pulled up to locations by
ropes. The heat was so intense that Jeff Burton, who
played Dodge, fainted on the first day of filming during a
tracking shot of epic length in which Landon (Robert Gunner) accuses Taylor (Heston) of being a cynic and misan-
thrope; the actor would not be the last to faint in the des-
olate terrain.

Schaffner shot so much footage of the trek that
Abrahams soon heard from Zanuck, who complained about
the endless footage that was arriving at the studio, and
that the company was already behind schedule. When he

brought the matter up, Abrahams recalls, Schaffner replied in characteristic fashion: "This is really the most important sequence in the picture. If we don't get the mood and the atmosphere now we're finished, the picture's dead. It's got to be set up properly." Truly the forbidden zone, the empty expanse of space and the ominous rock formations would provide the proper introduction to the rest of the film. Jerry Goldsmith, whose music underscores the vastness of the lifeless landscape, says, "I don't think I've ever seen anything staged or directed as well as that whole trek across the desert." However, at the end of the first week of production, the APJAC company was already two days behind in a tight 45-day shooting schedule.

Assigned as director of photography was an old Twentieth Century-Fox veteran, Leon Shamroy, winner of Academy Awards for The Black Swan (1942), Wilson (1944), Leave Her to Heaven (1946), and Cleopatra (1963). Charlton Heston was dismayed to learn this. "Shamroy takes too long," the actor wrote about The Agony and the Ecstasy experience. "On this picture, Carol [Reed] and the actors are getting the set about 15 per cent of the time; Shamroy has it the rest of the day."[71] Schaffner too had heard the stories about Shamroy, who was supposed to have struck the fear into younger hearts: "I've never found a more helpful fellow in my life," he says. Returning the compliment, Shamroy would say, "We enjoyed an especially close rapport because [Schaffner] is very pictorially minded and has a fine feel for the camera." Apes was the type of physical assignment that appealed to Shamroy—he had worked with Robert Flaherty—so he could later say with some satisfaction, "It was the roughest filming experience I've ever had."[72]

In their discussions, Shamroy told Schaffner to go as fast as he wanted, he'd keep up—in spite of the fact he was then in his late sixties. To the star's surprise, Shamroy showed he could work as fast as anyone. Such was the trust between cinematographer and director that Schaffner recalls, "Some days on location he would say, 'Hey, I am too old to go down there for a full day and walk through those canyons.' He says, 'That guy's got a light meter. Shoot what you want to shoot.'" Through the exhausting location work, Schaffner was a familiar sight climbing mountains and rocks, looking for shots, staging dialogue scenes

with characters positioned on opposing cliffs. Despite the
heat and inconvenience, the location shooting worked out
well for the film: as Shamroy pointed out, "God is a helluva
designer."[73]

In preparation for the end of the trek sequence, the
company took a dozen oak trees to Utah and planted them
in the sand of a mesa. In the film, the astronauts see the
scarecrows, then hear the sound of water, and turn in that
direction; there is a cut to a pool of water, and the astronauts are in the greenbelt. That cut bridged the distance
from Utah to the Fox Ranch in California, where movie magic
and 35 hoses created a waterfall. It had been made the
year before, Creber recalls, for Jacobs' Doctor Dolittle:

> They had the waterfall in the same area but we took
> ours up higher and made more water and made it
> bigger because Frank wanted it bigger, and just
> created that whole transition to the greenbelt, and
> somehow everybody believed it. We did a few matte
> shots in to help sell it.

Fast-growing corn was planted at the ranch for the scene in
which the gorillas capture the astronauts.

Boulle and Serling's concept of the modern ape city
being no longer possible, Creber had to design a more primitive looking village. His inspiration included troglodyte
cave dwellings, sites in Turkey and Tunisia, and the un-
dulating forms of Spanish architect Antonio Gaudi; somewhat
resembling vines and tree trunks, the village structures
were made out of polyurethane foam at the Fox Ranch. Ce-
ment was used in areas where weight was needed; the village was designed so that certain buildings could also serve
as modified camera platforms for the chase scenes. Rushed
for time on the interiors, Creber designed rooms with odd-
shaped windows that produced unwieldy shadows when the
set was lit. Posing even more lighting problems were the
cages and cells whose bars cast unwanted shadows, especially since Schaffner, as is his wont, would frequently
dolly across the floor, executing 360-degree patterns; flat
lighting was the only practical solution.

The ape make-up also demanded technical adjustments.
John Gregory Dunne has written:

Filming Planet of the Apes, 1967:   Schaffner, Rod Serling,
Arthur P. Jacobs, Charlton Heston.

> The dark furry makeup offered nothing other than
> eyes that could be effectively highlighted. And
> since the actors wore false protruding jaws fitted
> with ape-like incisors, care had to be taken in
> lighting and the selection of camera angles so that
> both the actors' real and ape teeth were not visible
> on film. [74]

The actors had their work cut out for them. "Franklin
Schaffner," Kim Hunter commented, "found that, unless we
kept the [makeup] appliances moving, they looked like
masks." [75]   When dialogue scenes involving apes were filmed,
it was discovered that the make-up affected the sound of
the voices: the dialogue recorded better in the medium
microphone position than in a close position; even when
shooting close-ups of the apes, the microphone would be
three feet higher than usual.

The final beach sequence was filmed at Point Dume,

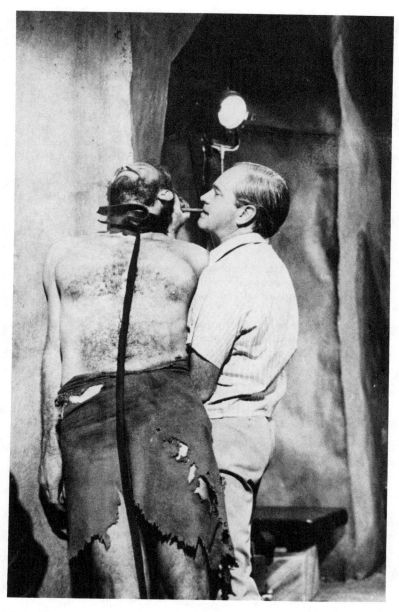

Schaffner staging an action shot with Charlton Heston for
Planet of the Apes, 1967.

between Malibu and Oxnard on the California coastline. According to Serling's script, Thomas returns to the excava-
tion site, sees something, and stands immobile, refusing to
escape when apes descend on him; saying there's nowhere
to go, he is shot and killed, and presently the Statue of
Liberty is revealed. A new ending was prepared in which
Taylor survives--not for the purposes of a sequel but more
to stress the futility of his plight. In the destiny which
Zaius has predicted, Taylor is seen in a high-angle shot, a
tiny figure in the surf, framed between two metal protuber-
ances. "We finally did it," he rages. The recent breaking
of the language barrier in American film adds to the final
punch: "You maniacs," he screams. "Damn you. Goddamn
you all to hell." In a reverse angle, the camera zooms out
to reveal the Statue of Liberty. Visually, the ending is as
effective a statement as Percy Bysshe Shelley's verse in
"Ozymandias":

> Nothing beside remains. Round the decay
> Of that colossal wreck, boundless and bare
> The lone and level sands stretch far away.

In the pre-credits sequence, Taylor, seated near the
console of the spaceship, dictates a report, verbalizing his
thoughts. The many-colored gas clouds, courtesy of special
effects man L. B. Abbott and the blue screen process, are
visible through a large window. Taylor straps himself into
his sleep chamber, and the credits begin. As intended, the
crash scene zooms out of the credits, creating a dramatic
bridge between the time the four astronauts go to sleep in
the spaceship and when they wake up on the planet of the
apes. [76]

The crash scene was literally saved in the editing
room. Schaffner and editor Hugh Fowler could not get the
footage of the Utah and Arizona terrain (shot from a B-25
with a camera in its nose) to work; it wasn't exciting
enough. Schaffner reached the point where he thought he
would have to go back and reshoot footage for the crash,
and then he remembered that Frank Tallman, using a 500 to
1 zoom, had shot a roll of film, forgetting that the zoom
was all the way in; although not processed, the roll of film
had been saved. "The majority of the stuff on the crash,"
says Schaffner, "is from that roll that [Tallman] said was
not going to be any good." It made all the difference:

wide shots were mixed with close shots, some footage was reversed, and the crash scene finally took shape.

What is remarkable about the scene is that the exterior of the spaceship is never shown; the montage mostly features a subjective camera view of the crash. Not only did this approach save a lot of money, it proves that an effective crash can be accomplished without complicated special effects, without building a spaceship. For the rest of the sequence, a mock-up of the spaceship's tail was put into Lake Powell for the breathtaking helicopter shot that arcs around the tail, gathering momentum as it leaves the spaceship behind. A five-foot model was later used in a studio tank for the final sinking of the ship.

Curiously, there is no music in the film until after the crash; when it comes, the music sounds more primitive than futuristic. As a composer who writes his music based on character, Jerry Goldsmith found himself on a picture that didn't really contain a character study; as a result he wrote what he considers an impressionistic score. "I said to myself," Goldsmith has remarked, "'this picture is so far out and so absurd in many respects, let me do the music in an old-fashioned way. I will use an old-fashioned orchestra with strings, woodwind, and percussion.'"[77] Although it is not electronic, the music is appropriately eerie, evocative of an alien culture.

John Gregory Dunne has reported that during post-production, after Jacobs and Abrahams had already succumbed, Schaffner resisted suggestions from the front office about a new credit sequence that he felt would tip off the surprise ending.[78] The original credit sequence was retained, demonstrating Schaffner's perseverance. Moreover, the director's skill points out how a motion picture's impetus can carry it through some potentially thorny areas: the astronaut's mission is never established; the apes conveniently speak in English; Taylor never wonders if it's possible for him to be on earth. The film is so well crafted, moves so quickly, that these points don't matter. The care invested in the beginning scenes--crash and trek--provides the necessary basis for a willing suspension of disbelief. Planet of the Apes is a movie-movie. Even such ape epigrams as "The only good human is a dead human" and the tableau of three apes seeing, hearing, and speaking no evil

serve to break up the tension and provide a measure of
comedy relief. If the story doesn't stay a step ahead of
the audience, the direction does. That the Statue of Liberty comes as a surprise makes the ending particularly satisfying.

Roddy McDowall, as Cornelius the archeologist, and
Kim Hunter, as Zira the animal psychologist, turned out to
be the scene-stealers and the crowd-pleasers of the film.
This was emphasized in the direction: despite being rational apes of science, they give each other furtive and
soulful glances whenever they are together; when Zira
speaks out on Taylor's behalf during the monkey trial,
Cornelius clandestinely covers her paw with his. Ultimately, they are the most sympathetic characters in the film,
a counterpoint to Taylor's pronouncement about leaving a
world without love. McDowall is very droll when delivering
such lines as, when Taylor shaves his beard, "Somehow it
makes you look less intelligent." Hunter makes the most of
one of the film's best lines after Taylor, saying goodbye,
asks if he may kiss her: Zira reacts with some embarrassment and gently says, "But you're so damned ugly."
Schaffner follows the kiss with a shot of Cornelius hissing.
Zira and Cornelius are so appealing that they add to Joseph
Morgenstern's contention in Newsweek: "The film catches
us at a particularly wretched moment in the course of human events, when we are perfectly willing to believe that
man is despicable and a great deal lower than the lower
animals." [79]

The film, above all, remains a star vehicle for Charlton Heston. Pauline Kael wrote:

> I don't think the movie could have been so forceful
> or so funny with anyone else ... he's an archetype
> of what makes Americans win ... he represents
> American power ... [he] is so absurdly a movie
> star myth. He is the perfect American Adam to
> work off some American guilt feelings or self hatred
> on. [80]

Heston is most shrewdly used in the film, and is effective
both for those who like him and those who do not. Physically, he looks exactly right as astronaut or captive.
Hardly a sympathetic character, Taylor, in his capacity as

an astronaut, literally starts at the top of the world, quite
happy to be leaving earth. Taylor is arrogant, overbear-
ing, just begging for a fall; it comes immediately. When he
is caught, an ape photographer takes a picture of the human
trophy; at best, Taylor is considered a mutant. In his humiliation, he is caged, put on a leash, stoned by angry and
frightened apes, and, when put on trial, he is stripped bare.
With such a drastic reversal, the audience becomes sympathetic if not to Heston then to Taylor's plight: if it can
happen to Charlton Heston, it can happen to anyone.

     Taylor is another obsessive Schaffner character, lit-
erally out of his depth and time. "Of all the roles I've
played," Charlton Heston says, perhaps because of its built-
in ambivalence, "this is the closest to my own personality."
It is quite possibly his finest screen performance. Something else is intriguing about the actor's interpretation of
the role: while in the spaceship, Taylor states he is confident there must be something better than mankind: "Has
to be," Heston recapitulates in a manner duplicating Franklin J. Schaffner's speech. Normally a non-smoker, Heston
carries and smokes a long cigar like Schaffner's in the film;
although Taylor's cigar was in Wilson's script, the actor
allows for the possibility that he was subliminally influenced
by the director and subconsciously copied him.

     Planet of the Apes was completed and ready for re-
lease in November 1967. As for the studio, "They were of
the same nature as myself," says Schaffner. "They didn't
know what they had, nor did I." Release was postponed
until February 1968, so as not to interfere with Jacobs'
Doctor Dolittle, the film the studio had enthusiastically supported all along and was now pushing for Academy Award
consideration. As it turned out, of the two APJAC productions, the riskier one, Planet of the Apes, was the one to
receive critical accolades and amass a fortune.

     Accompanying the release of the film was a deluge of
Apes-related products on the market, thanks to Jacobs; he
had come up with the ideas for merchandising before the
film went into production. Although studios had been reluctant to take on a film about apes, Mort Abrahams points
out, "The merchandising people saw the advantage of it very
early on--it was very unique--and grabbed on to it." They
had to take the risk if the film flopped, but, as it turned

out, the toys, dolls, and games proved to be more profitable
than the motion picture itself. Not until Star Wars (1977),
also released by Twentieth Century-Fox, would the likes of
this type of merchandising be seen again.

The film came in for exactly $5.8 million, the original
pared-down budget estimate--$800,000 over the budget to
which Fox had given the green light. There was a basic
lesson about motion pictures to be learned from this experience: "It doesn't matter if you're over budget when you're
doing a picture for a studio if it's successful," Abrahams
observes. "If it's not successful, your ass is in a sling."

It is a great tribute to the filmmakers that the picture looked more expensive than its actual cost. Pauline
Kael commented:

> "Planet of the Apes" is one of the best science-
> fiction fantasies to come out of Hollywood.... When
> expensive Hollywood engineering works, as it rarely
> does anymore, the results can be impressive. Schaff-
> ner has thought out the action in terms of the wide
> screen, and he uses space and distance dramatical-
> ly. [81]

Having grasped command of film techniques and the Panavision screen, Schaffner made a motion picture that looked as
if it could have cost $15 million, as it once was estimated;
he was able to make a dozen ape horsemen look like the
Seventh Cavalry. "Planet is the best American movie I have
seen so far this year," Richard Shickel wrote in Life. "It
is alive to--and delighted with its own possibilities." [82] The
possibilities were achieved by a collaboration of artists who
provided a sociology of simian society, successfully creating
its own world on film. For his contribution, John Chambers
would be honored with a special Academy Award for his
make-up design.

First and foremost a rousing entertainment, Planet
of the Apes is a film that has elements of many genres:
it is as exciting as an adventure story, similar to a western when Taylor shoots it out with apes on a cliff; it has
moments of humor and satire, both Horatian and Juvenalian;
it boasts a strong star performance from its leading man.
"Schaffner deserves a great deal of credit for his work on

this film," Leon Shamroy said. "He was indefatigable on
the set and his energy was so contagious that everyone in
the cast and crew became dedicated--determined to make it
a good picture."[83] The man who in effect was the line producer agrees. "Nothing threw Frank," says Mort Abrahams.
"And when nothing throws your director, your crew is under control." That had been evident even under the most
adverse conditions. One key contributor, although he had
departed early and wasn't around the production, was well-
acquainted with what this director could do: "Schaffner
did a corker of a job directing it," Rod Serling announced
after seeing the film.[84]

The film has multiple levels above and beyond sheer
entertainment: it is thought-provoking as well. "If man
was superior, why didn't he survive?" Zaius asks rhetorically, before reading the 23rd scroll, 9th verse from the
Lawgiver:

> Beware the beast man, for he is the devil's pawn.
> Alone among God's primates, he kills for sport, or
> lust or greed. Yes, he will murder his brother to
> possess his brother's land. Let him not breed in
> great numbers, for he will make a desert of his home
> and yours. Shun him. Drive him back into his
> jungle lair: For he is the harbinger of death.

In the penultimate scene, Taylor and Nova ride a horse,
moving right to left along the beach, heading north on the
east coast if they are to find the Statue of Liberty; it could
well be that the ape civilization they have left is located in
the vicinity of Washington, D.C. In the years that have
passed since the initial release of the film, more has been
learned about nuclear war and genetic change; if mankind
can be made to revert to a simian state, then a Planet of
the Apes is not impossible. For better or for worse, the
film has held up very well indeed. From a director known
for more than a passing familiarity with mirror shots, Planet
of the Apes is a work in which the entire film itself is a
mirror shot.

Patton

After the success of Planet of the Apes, Schaffner was

asked to direct the sequel, Beneath the Planet of the Apes.
Even if he could have, he wouldn't have; neither did he
profit from the four Apes sequels.[85] On the other hand,
the sequels profited from the original picture: the make-
up appliances and costumes were saved and did not require
a major outlay of money. Schaffner, however, having a
percentage of the profits of the first Apes, would be ran-
kled to learn that over three minutes of footage he had shot
was used in the prologue for Beneath the Planet of the Apes;
he was not reimbursed.

In the meantime, Charlton Heston wanted Schaffner to
direct him in Pro, a football drama about an aging quarter-
back which he and Walter Seltzer were trying to place with
United Artists. There were a few meetings regarding the
film that would become Number One, but nothing resulted
from them. Mort Abrahams tried to get the director for
another APJAC production he was producing for Twentieth
Century-Fox, The Chairman, a spy melodrama set in the
People's Republic of China; there were a few meetings, but
again nothing materialized. Something else had materialized:
on the strength of his most recent performance, Franklin
J. Schaffner had become the fair-haired boy at Twentieth
Century-Fox; in June 1968, Schaffner was offered a studio
plum--Patton.

This was not to be the first time fate had brought him
near General George S. Patton, Jr.: during the Second
World War, while serving in the Navy, Schaffner had had a
chance to see him in person. In Palermo, on his end run
to beat Field Marshal Montgomery to Messina, Patton had
requested a detachment of three landing crafts; Schaffner,
on one of the three chosen, had watched the general standing on the docks as the soldiers boarded the landing craft.
Although Patton meant little to him at the time, the man
would posthumously play as significant a role as anyone in
Schaffner's career.

In George S. Patton, Jr., Schaffner found a real-life
figure who fit in his gallery of men out of their times: a
16th-century warrior trapped in the 20th century and to
whom a war was a holy crusade, Patton was unable to cope
with the peacetime world. As the film would show, he was
a man of extreme contradictions: although a strict Calvinist
who believed in reincarnation, he was also profane, as shown

in the film when a chaplain asks if he prays and Patton replies, "Every goddamn day"; the richest officer in the
United States Army, he was ruthless on the battlefield and
yet a man easily moved to tears; Patton was a soldier who
wanted the classic military death--to be killed by the last
bullet in the last battle of his last war.

The film would be a new kind of venture for Schaffner, a physically demanding job on a much more spectacular scale than anything he had so far attempted. But, as
Gerald Pratley observed in Focus on Film, it would pay off
handsomely:

> PATTON is Franklin Schaffner's film and in this
> respect it is a masterpiece.... It seemed likely
> that Schaffner, a film-maker of great distinction
> and sensitivity, would in spite of his experience
> with large scale production for THE WAR LORD,
> be lost entirely in the immensity of this film....
> That PATTON remains personal, beautifully sty-
> lized, strikingly photographed, poignant and pene-
> trating in its dramatic and psychological truths, is
> a tribute to his skill and concern. [86]

In Patton, Schaffner found the vehicle that would take him
to the top echelon of film directors.

The source books for the film, Ladislas Farago's
Patton: Ordeal and Triumph and Omar N. Bradley's A
Soldier's Story, present George S. Patton, Jr. as a man--
for all his frailties, accomplishments, inconsistencies, and
contradictions. Unbeknown to the authors, the books also
provided clues regarding a future motion picture biography.
According to Farago, Colonel Darryl F. Zanuck of the Signal
Corps was with General Dwight D. Eisenhower at Gibraltar
on November 8, 1942, when it was learned that Patton had
forced the German surrender in Casablanca. [87] General
Bradley wrote admiringly of a man with whom he had frequent dealings, "General Marshall's youthful Secretary of
the General Staff, the brilliant Colonel Frank McCarthy." [88]
These two Colonels would join forces after the war.

In his Los Angeles Times review of Patton, Charles
Champlin would write, with unerring accuracy:

> I suspect that to an unusual degree the producer
> deserves credit not only for the fact that "Patton"
> exists but for its touch. As a study of a military
> mind, it is at once judicious, unsparing, and in-
> sightful, free of derived attitudes. [89]

After duty under George C. Marshall during the war, Frank
McCarthy served as Assistant Secretary of State under
James F. Byrne and became a brigadier general of the Army
Reserve.   Due to his friendship with Darryl F. Zanuck,
McCarthy, who had been bitten by the show business bug
and had handled public relations for George Abbott before
the Second World War, was invited to Twentieth Century-Fox
as an executive. So that he could learn the motion picture
business, Zanuck gave McCarthy permission to sit in on any
story conference and visit any set or department on the lot
for a year. At the end of that year, McCarthy produced a
military drama directed by Anatole Litvak entitled Decision
Before Dawn (1951). In October of that year, McCarthy
sent a memo to Zanuck suggesting a film biography of
George S. Patton, Jr. So began Frank McCarthy's 19-year
effort to see the project reach the screen. [90]

During the Second World War, McCarthy had had the
opportunity of seeing for himself just how theatrical Patton
was--a complete showman, at that--and had become attracted
to him because they were opposite types: "He was a warrior," General McCarthy quips, "and I'm a lover." Most
importantly, unlike the other famous generals whose careers
steadily ascended during the war, Patton's story was re-
plete with hills and valleys, the essence of good drama; it
would make a good film. Zanuck was equally enthusiastic
about the idea: "He had a macho complex in a way,"
McCarthy says, "and he liked the idea of the military."
This is evident in the numerous war films that were produced at Fox during his regime, culminating in his own
production of The Longest Day. Furthermore, Zanuck was
a fervent admirer of Patton: "Personally, I look upon him
as a great man," he wrote his son Richard. "I think he
was right in kicking the soldier in the ass." [91]

In contrast to Planet of the Apes in its long road to
being filmed, Patton's even longer journey was never the
result of studio resistance. Even in the early 1950s, the
energetic producer discovered, the right package was

necessary to get a film off the ground. The first actor approached, Spencer Tracy, refused to play the part; another
idea was Burt Lancaster as star and Richard Brooks as director, both being strong masculine types, but neither one
wanted to be part of the film. "Really," McCarthy insists,
"most of the rest of the years was spent trying to put together a team of people that Zanuck would feel could bring
it off."

A production of Patton involved another formidable
obstacle--the Patton family. Most outspoken was Colonel
George Patton III: "Young George went about the countryside saying he would shoot any sonofabitch that made a
movie about his father," McCarthy recalls. Not very appealing to the family either was the fact that McCarthy had
had a treatment written by Robert S. Allen--author of Patton: A Profile and Lucky Forward, partner of Drew Pear-
son, the man who had sensationalized the slapping incident.
When Warner Bros. acquired the Allen property as a possible John Wayne vehicle in 1953, that studio ran into the
same problems as well. [92] Zealously protecting the late general's image, the Patton family had only approved or cooperated with books written by such authors as Fred Ayer,
Jr., Patton's son-in-law, and Charles Codman, Patton's
faithful aide. On the eve of publishing his 1964 biography,
Ladislas Farago would find the Patton family had not mel-
lowed at all; in fact the family sued him.

Throughout the years, Zanuck would continue to give
McCarthy seed money to develop a script. Although there
were constant rumors of other Patton pictures (Frank H.
Ricketson, Jr.'s production of Blood and Guts in 1960 and
Al Zimbalist's production of Two-Gun Patton in 1965), Zanuck and McCarthy were not particularly concerned; theirs
from its inception had been envisioned as a major, big-
budget picture. Nonetheless, it still had been no easier to
put the right package together: John Huston, of whom
McCarthy has said, "I should've thought would be perfect
for it," didn't want to do it; Fred Zinnemann simply refused; as for the stars, he says, "The usual answer was,
'I don't want to play any goddamned general.'"

McCarthy left Fox for Universal in 1963, leaving
Patton behind until the following year, when the Farago
book, the most comprehensive work on the subject, was

published--it had everything needed for the film. Darryl
Zanuck, based in Paris, had it purchased, instructing Fox
production boss Richard Zanuck to bring McCarthy back to
the fold. Upon his return, McCarthy hired Calder Willing-
ham, author of End As a Man, to work on the script; this
proved to be an unproductive and unpleasant experience.

The producer's next move was to call the UCLA film
department and ask for its brightest graduate. Sent over
was a young man by the name of Francis Ford Coppola, who
had already written a couple of produced screenplays, most
recently Is Paris Burning? (1965), another war film. As
McCarthy had hoped, the young writer had no pre-conceived
notions, no bias one way or another about Patton; Coppola
provided the fresh point of view he was seeking. As Coppola was basically unfamiliar with Patton, the producer supplied him with the right books to study, gave pointers on
military operations, and instructed him to confine the script
to the Second World War years so that no Patton family members would be involved. "He really knew the drama of it,
he really knew the scenes, and he really knew how to get
the character into it," McCarthy recalls. There was only
one problem: "It was like a handful of wonderful pecans
but no pie to put them into."

Coppola's contributions cannot be underestimated: he
was the one to come up with the prologue, Patton's hortatory speech in front of the American flag; and taking a cue
from Farago--"Patton was, like Miguel de Cervantes' Don
Quixote, part product of his readings and part of his own
imagination"[93]--Coppola imagined the final scene in the film
to be Patton, reading his "All glory is fleeting" speech offscreen, while walking his bull terrier Willy towards a wind-
mill. Making a concerted effort to use Patton's own words,
Coppola also thought up the black-and-white newsreel device to provide exposition on the war's progress, and the
character of Captain Steiger at the Reischschancellery Map
Room to provide background on Patton. Not uncharacter-
istically, at over 200 pages, the script is too long and undisciplined: Coppola soon uses the newsreels not only to
comment on the war but the film medium as well; Steiger
becomes more than a means of providing exposition, turning into Patton's double, receiving his own command, and
eventually dying in battle against his American counterpart.

        Darryl Zanuck rightfully found the Coppola script "a
remarkable first draft."[94] It was enough to give him the
idea, which McCarthy had been subtly cultivating, of involving Omar N. Bradley in the production; he also thought
the script might be enough to interest William Wyler, then
completing How to Steal a Million (1966) for Fox. Wyler,
however, was more interested in Patton than he was in the
script. When Coppola departed to direct You're a Big Boy
Now (1967), McCarthy hired the veteran James R. Webb,
winner of an Academy Award for his script of the 1963
Cinerama epic How the West Was Won. Webb's version was
more in the nature of an old-fashioned biography, beginning
when Patton was aide-de-camp to General Pershing, in pur-
suit of Pancho Villa, and including flashbacks to scenes of
his earlier years; one of its main themes was how Patton had
championed tanks for military use.

        Screening a 1966 film Fox was releasing, modestly ti-
tled The Bible, Darryl Zanuck was seized by the notion that
the actor playing Abraham was the ideal choice to play Patton. At the time, George C. Scott was a powerful and well-
respected actor without any particular screen image. In
earlier films, though, he had threatened to upstage such
strong leading men as Gary Cooper (The Hanging Tree,
1958), James Stewart (Anatomy of a Murder, 1959), and
Paul Newman (The Hustler, 1962), and Patton would establish him as a most unconventional leading man. Scott found
the role quite intriguing, especially in the Coppola script,
but did not care for the revised script. When Wyler insisted on the Webb screenplay, Scott, never being one to
back away from a fight, quarreled with him. There were
two immediate results: Scott withdrew, and without an actor the Patton project was again stalled. William Wyler himself departed to direct his first musical, Funny Girl (1968).
As for the producer, instead of sitting around and waiting,
Frank McCarthy proceeded to produce A Guide for the Married Man, a 1967 comedy far removed from Patton.

        Richard Zanuck--"the spur behind finally making the
movie," according to McCarthy--had been highly impressed
with Planet of the Apes and its direction. Even if Franklin
J. Schaffner had no experience with a project this broad,
Zanuck thought he might be the man to direct Patton; if
nothing else, he was less expensive than John Huston or

William Wyler. McCarthy liked the idea; he and Schaffner
knew each other socially and "on the campus," as the director refers to the studio where his film career began.
Final approval came from Paris: Schaffner was more than
satisfactory to all involved.

    "Nor Frank nor I had much enthusiasm for the Webb
version," Schaffner says, "because the other seemed so
much more appropriate conceptually." Coppola, however,
having launched his own directorial career, was embarking
on The Rain People (1969) and thus was unavailable for
further rewrites. Edmund H. North, who had written
scripts for the Signal Corps during the Second World War
and, later, a couple of war films (Sink the Bismarck!,
1960; The Battle of Leyte Gulf, 1961) and a science fiction
movie (The Day the Earth Stood Still, 1951) for Fox, was
hired to bring narrative strength to the Coppola script and
cut it down to a reasonable size. Since screenwriters who
rewrite scripts often have a tendency to make drastic changes in order to receive solo credit, some of Coppola's scenes
had to be protected; overall, McCarthy and Schaffner were
able to maintain the proper script balance between Coppola's
imagination and North's craftsmanship.

    That much resolved, the most pressing matter re-
mained finding a leading man. John Wayne had already
turned down the role. (When McCarthy would later prepare his 1977 production of MacArthur, he recalls hearing
from Wayne who said, "Keep me in mind, because I don't
want to make the same mistake I made before.") While the
John Wayne persona might have obscured the Patton image,
it is undeniably true that Wayne had an overwhelming presence on screen and people reacted to that image in much
the same way people had reacted to Patton. Schaffner
would have been more than willing to do the film with
Wayne: "I had an unshaken belief that John Wayne was
never forced to stretch in anything he did," he says, "and
it would've been enormously interesting to see him stretch
because I believe he could've made the stretch." Also considered, Robert Mitchum, Rod Steiger, and Lee Marvin were
found to be lacking in enthusiasm for the role. But as soon
as he learned that the production would be moving back in
the direction of the Coppola script, George C. Scott returned.

    A package finally had been put together that appealed

to Darryl Zanuck. McCarthy, North, and Schaffner were called to Cap d'Antibes, France for a three-day script conference. "I suspect that Darryl Zanuck never even remembered me," Schaffner says, referring to the unpleasant memory of The Stripper. Wanting to be closely involved in the film, Zanuck intended to spend time with the company on location; a broken ankle in a skiing accident would prevent that. The three men from California kept quiet as Zanuck pored over the script, exhaustively making corrections, until he announced the script was ready and ordered McCarthy to stamp it final. The production was given a $12.8 million budget and a 90-day shooting schedule. Rewrites, of course, continued.

As McCarthy was very anxious to have Bradley's name on the credits as "Senior Military Adviser, General of the Army," an important task for North was to beef up the Bradley role; to that end, Bradley's book was purchased. In his military career, McCarthy was quite familiar with the Pentagon; as Fox's Director of Public Relations, which meant primarily government relations, he had secured Army, Air Force, or Navy assistance for many films. If Omar N. Bradley, the most beloved military man in America, were involved in Patton, the Pentagon could scarcely refuse to cooperate. Ironically, as it turned out, the Defense Department would only participate in one scene, the nighttime landing and invasion of Sicily that was to be filmed in one day on Crete. The live ammunition and Navy were ready, but rain made the shoot impossible; the amphibious portions of the scene had to be cancelled and were later covered by the newsreel device. Thus, no footage in the final film represents the efforts of the Defense Department.

Bradley, assisted by his wife Kitty Buhler, herself a screenwriter, spent days going through the script, checking for inaccuracies. "His contribution to the script itself was minimal," McCarthy says of the man he had known when they were both colonels on General Marshall's staff. "His contribution to the execution of the script was much more than minimal." In October 1968, Bradley accompanied McCarthy and Schaffner to Belgium, France, and Tunisia, visiting the actual battlefields on which Patton had fought. "I wanted to be educated on the terrain if I had to pick the locations," Schaffner says. "Having him along to make sure that we didn't do anything which was outrageous or silly was a

source of strength for me and also in particular for Franklin," McCarthy adds. Producer and director were relieved
to learn that Bradley understood dramatic license and the
need for it in a major motion picture such as this. Karl
Malden, whose performance would please the general, was
cast as Omar N. Bradley, thereby providing a saner and
more rational point of view that allowed the screen Patton
to be controversial, and rant and rave about the British,
his fellow Americans, and the Russians as the real Patton
had.

The other military adviser was Paul Harkins, the
four-star general who preceded General Westmoreland in
commanding the American troops in Vietnam. As a colonel,
Harkins had served as Patton's chief of staff and was considered to be like kin; on Patton, he would serve as the
day to day adviser. With the involvement of Bradley and
Harkins, the Patton family was somewhat relieved, assuming that the generals, especially Harkins, would protect
its interest.

Leon Shamroy, with whom Schaffner had worked so
successfully on his previous picture, was assigned to Patton, but, under contract to Fox, was reassigned to Justine
(1969), a production with more than its fair share of problems. This momentary setback resulted in a new partnership. Now that Schaffner was finally in a position to
choose his own cameraman, he selected a man who would
be cinematographer on many of his films thereafter: Fred
J. Koenekamp--son of Hans F. Koenekamp, the noted
Warner Bros. special effects cameraman--a second generation member of the American Society of Cinematographers.
Starting as a television cameraman in 1963, Koenekamp had
become used to doing things the hard way and doing them
fast, without the best equipment; the four years he spent
in television turned out to be an asset. Breaking into
feature films with Doctor, You've Got to Be Kidding (1967),
he was then at Warner Bros., filming The Great Bank Robbery
(1969), which had gone into night shooting, enabling him
to show up for a daytime interview at Twentieth Century-Fox
in December 1968. The meeting with the director of Patton
was typically formal: "I thought the man was English,"
Koenekamp says. "He had that air about him."

Schaffner was more concerned about his potential

director of photography's attitude and character than his credits:

> I knew it'd be a hard picture. I wanted someone
> durable and alert, and fast but good, because I
> had great qualms about the adequacy of the shoot-
> ing schedule. He had an enormous amount of work
> to do in the amount of time we were being given.

Illustrating Schaffner's statement, Patton's entrance into Djebel Kouif, his visit to the graveyard, march into Palermo, and tour of Malta would all be filmed in a single day while on location. Sympathetic to the director's ideas, Koenekamp in return described how he worked on the set, how he liked hand-held shots. Even though he didn't know how big and important the film would turn out to be, the cinematographer was quite eager to do Patton. Schaffner had a good feeling about him; Koenekamp was hired on the basis of a strong hunch. "I think it was a wise selection," Schaffner says.

The film would be shot in Dimension 150, a non-anamorphic camera lens and projection system that had been developed ten years earlier by UCLA professors Richard Vetter and Carl Williams. In his deal with Fox, Vetter could choose one of three films for Dimension 150: Doctor Dolittle, Hello, Dolly, or Patton; he chose the war movie. The picture would be shot with lenses adapted to a Todd-AO-Mitchell camera, printed on 70mm film, and projected on a larger and more deeply curved screen that approached the size and shape of the Cinerama screen. Most valuable and useful was the 19mm lens with its 150-degree angle of view. A natural for battle scenes, this lens would be the workhorse of the film: having great depth of field, sharpness, and resolution, it was relatively free of distortion compared with the 23mm Panavision lens frequently used today. A striking use of the lens is in the scene that begins with a shot of a detailed ceiling fresco in the chapel of the palazzo Patton is using as headquarters in Messina: the camera pans down from the ceiling to the altar, where Patton quietly prays; as the prayer continues offscreen, Patton walks around the exterior of the palazzo to face his troops and apologize for slapping the soldier--and captured by the lens in all its clarity is what appears to be the entire Seventh Army.

Patton was easily Koenekamp's biggest assignment to
date--it made an excellent Christmas present. His next opportunity to discuss the film with Schaffner didn't come until he arrived in Spain on January 2, 1969. Once they
started visiting locations, they began to talk about what
they were going to do and to plan around a problem with
the camera equipment: the first unit carried four cameras,
but Dimension 150 had only supplied two different lenses;
more lenses arrived as shooting progressed, until eventually there was a full complement. Removed from union regulations, Koenekamp would be able to do his own hand-held
shooting.

Although Patton would be filmed on 71 locations in
six countries on three continents, the majority of it was
shot in Spain, a logical choice not only for the variety of
its terrain but also for the Second World War equipment the
United States had given it. Tanks, which had played such
a vital role in Patton's career, were found to be in mint
condition; McCarthy also discovered that if the American
tanks were driven backwards they then resembled German
tanks. The Spanish government promised its army and full
cooperation if McCarthy would pay for the transportation,
gas, and the soldiers' salaries. The government also asked
for spare parts, something beyond McCarthy's jurisdiction;
it was a matter for the Defense Department, which turned
down the request. The production was headquartered in
Almeria, in Southern Spain. There it was arbitrarily decided that--facing the Mediterranean--the terrain to the
left would be North Africa and the terrain to the right
would be Sicily. Filming began in February.

Schaffner made an unlikely choice for art director--
Urie McCleary of M-G-M. Since William J. Creber was
working on Justine, Fox art department head Jack Martin
Smith had recommended McCleary, perhaps best known for
his work on National Velvet (1944). Considered a specialist in interiors rather than exteriors, he had had some experience with a military picture in Command Decision (1948),
but that was very much a theatrical piece. McCleary's
work on Patton, however, would turn out to be the crown-
ing achievement of his career; after it, he retired. Also
working as an art director was Gil Parrondo, who would
later work on every Schaffner film made in Europe. So
effective was their work that, for the first and only time

in his career, Schaffner never had less than two and up to
five possible locations for any given scene. Also deserving
credit was Jose (Pepe) Lopez Rodero, the Spanish assistant
director, who would become a fixture on future Schaffner
productions.

Battle scenes are mandatory for any film with a
Second World War background--even for what primarily is
a character study. One of Patton's strengths is that it
does not skimp on the action; a viewer tends to recall a lot
of battle scenes in the film. In point of fact, Patton only
has one real battle scene, the Battle of El Guettar; there
are a mere eleven minutes of battle footage in the entire
film. At Schaffner's command were 200 tanks and 300
soldiers, but rather than carry the equipment and personnel throughout the production, the schedule had been arranged so that El Guettar would be shot at the beginning;
excess baggage would gradually be shed until there were
only six tanks and 300 men by the end of filming. The
second unit--equipped with three or sometimes four cameras
and its own military adviser--was directed by Mickey Moore.
In contrast to, and perhaps because of, his experience on
The War Lord, Schaffner supervised the second unit with a
vengeance. "He planned that out more carefully and knew
more about what was to be done and required more to be
done to meet his standards than any other director I've
known," McCarthy comments. Not unpredictably, considering the new D-150 equipment, there were problems dividing
up the available lenses with the first unit.

The Battle of El Guettar had been planned for two
months: first the German infantry would approach, followed by the tanks--a model of Field Marshal Rommel's
strategy. Two days before the scene was to be shot,
General Harkins checked the official publication on battles, the Army Green Book, and found that Rommel had
moved the tanks in a box formation with the infantry sand-
wiched in between. The battle had to be changed and re-
planned in 48 hours.

As it plays on film, the Battle of El Guettar opens
with a shot of camels spying something in the distance; a
mule brays, and animals gradually begin to flee. Schaffner cross-cuts to Patton as he dresses for combat. [95] The
last animal, a homeless goat, runs off before the German

tanks of Rommel's Tenth Panzer approach, with the infantry
marching between the tanks, clearly visible at battalion
strength. In the long wide shots, the Germans are located
in the background near the top of the frame; the camou-
flaged American soldiers are in the foreground at the bottom of the frame; Heinkels, Messerschmitts, Nords, and
T-6s fly through the middle portion of the screen. Patton
is merely a spectator, watching his Second Corps in action
through binoculars. This modern form of combat, as the
film shows, is decidedly impersonal--a general fights at long
distance--giving credence to Patton's statement about how
he would have preferred a duel with Rommel himself.

      The rest of the film contains moments of filmed war-
fare but no elaborately staged battles. The need for snow
for the Battle of the Bulge scenes was a reason for starting
production early in the year; Segovia had been chosen because the terrain looked "European" with its mountains and
stone cottages. The schedule had been arranged so that
the company could get the snow scenes out of the way as
soon as possible, but it had enough flexibility so that
filming could go on in and around Almeria in case weather
conditions were not right. Schaffner was fortunate for that
bit of planning: nature was not cooperative; there was no
snow. Located in Almeria, the director went back and forth
to his left and right, shooting Tunisia and Sicily respectively, hoping for snow. The company didn't have many
cover sets; Schaffner had shot everything he needed in
Almeria--and even in Madrid--before it finally snowed.

      It turned out to be a blizzard. Coming at 5:00 a.m.
on the first day of the scheduled shoot in Segovia, the
storm prohibited any filming. By 8:00, Schaffner, improvis-
ing, decided to move the company to a castle in Rio Frio,
eleven miles away, and film an interior. The scene chosen
comes near the end of the film: Patton is in Bad Tolz, posing for a painting; the war in Europe is over. Patton looks
very weary, as if he's lost all his vitality, but when a phone
call comes from General Bedell Smith, he rises to the occasion, speaking his mind on what he thinks about Russia and
how he would finish the war by invading Russia. It is a
complex moment as Patton must appear to be old and tired
yet still ferocious and bloodthirsty, on the brink of a nervous breakdown but still coldly rational. Not surprisingly,
filming the scene unexpectedly early was quite hard on

George C. Scott, who suddenly became indisposed and, in protest, did not show up on the set until 2:30 p.m.

Thereafter, the company made several more trips to and from Segovia, moving briefly to Marrakech, Morocco for the scene in which Patton is decorated by the Sultan while a 10,000-man honor guard--provided by the real Sultan of Morocco--passes by in review, prompting the general to remark with some accuracy that Morocco is a cross between the Bible and Hollywood. While on the other side of the Mediterranean, Schaffner found the location of the ruins which serve as the backdrop to the story Patton tells Bradley: he was there 2000 years ago when three Roman legions attacked the Carthaginians. Returning to Spain, the company used the terrain around Pamplona for the scenes near the end of the film in which Patton's Third Army steamrolls through France, across the Rhine River, and into Germany. These sequences were filmed in the spring; the events had actually taken place in the summer, and, accordingly, some of the trees had to be dressed with leaves. The company then moved to Knutsford, England, where Patton had given his notorious speech to the women's group, neglecting to mention the Russians.

As producer, McCarthy spent his time in the office, lining up the material needed for the next day, handling personnel problems, communicating with the home office, and adjudicating disputes; as a rule, he was not on the set, going only out of curiosity to see such scenes as the slapping incident and the killing of the mules. In the latter scene, Patton's column, the easy prey of a German air attack, is stalled on a bridge in central Sicily, blocked by two mules; after Patton personally shoots them, the mules are seen in a long shot being dumped off the bridge. Chosen for the purposes of this scene were the oldest mules that could be found; they were given injections and death was instantaneous. "You know," the producer comments on the outcry that would come from the American Humane Association, "it's more humane when it's animals than when it's people."

Patton returned to California in May 1969 for filming of the black and white newsreel sequences and the beginning of post-production; Hugh S. Fowler, who had functioned in the same capacity on Planet of the Apes, was the

editor. Stock footage was incorporated into the newsreel--
nothing from The Longest Day was used--and, as none of
the writers had been able to write the newsreel narration
because nobody knew exactly what the footage would be
until post-production, Schaffner himself wrote the narration and sent the copy to Africa, where Lowell Thomas
could record it.

Under contract to Fox in 1969, Jerry Goldsmith recalls how Schaffner would collar him, bring him to the
editing room, and show him footage as an enticement to
compose the score for Patton. Even though he wanted the
job and Schaffner kept after him, Goldsmith was committed
to Beneath the Planet of the Apes. Arrangements were
finally made to free Goldsmith to do Patton, "which," he
says, "was the luckiest thing that ever happened to me."
He responded by writing one of his finest scores. In
George S. Patton, Jr., Goldsmith found a classic three-
dimensional character study:

> He was a complex man. I approached him on a
> three-tier level with a theme for each facet of his
> personality: the warrior (a march), the strong
> Protestant (a chorale), and the archaic man who
> believed in reincarnation (a trumpet fanfare). [96]

The different musical themes defining Patton's character can
be heard separately, ironically, in counterpoint, or in concert.

Patton begins with a long shot of a gigantic American
flag; stereophonic crowd noise is heard offscreen. In an
effort to get right into the meat of the film, the Twentieth
Century-Fox logo and fanfare were eschewed; there is no
"Star-Spangled Banner." An offscreen voice calls attention:
General George S. Patton, Jr. strides out on the platform,
standing five stripes high against the flag, and salutes. A
bugle is heard on the soundtrack as close shots reveal Patton's four stars, decorations, ivory-handled pistols, and
West Point ring. Dressed in riding pants and carrying a
crop, he is reminiscent of an old-time movie director; with
the performance he is about to give, there can be no doubt
that Patton is a master actor in the theatre of drama and
the theatre of war. "I want you to remember that no bastard ever won a war by dying for his country," he growls.

"He won it by making the other poor dumb bastard die for
his country." The language is rough but authentically Patton's, deliberately used for shock value. The general talks
about how real Americans love to fight, have never lost a
war and never will, and paces restlessly on the platform,
saying how a soldier should never have to say to his son,
when asked what he did during the war, that he shoveled
shit in Louisiana. Snarling, "That's all," in his gravelly
voice, he begins to leave the platform before making a sudden stop. In a close shot, he turns his head and glares
at the camera.

Designed as a limbo speech to provide the ground
rules for its audience, the prologue is cunningly theatrical
and outrageous, meant to show Patton at his most colorful
and flamboyant. "Before Patton had finished his address,"
Stanley Kauffmann would observe, "before the picture had
really begun, it was a solid hit."[97] As the filmmakers had
intended, the six-minute prologue captured the quintessence
of Patton, establishing the tone for the rest of the film.
The boldness of its conception and the simplicity of its
presentation--a soldier and his flag--created a mythic dimension to the man and the moment: it has become an en-
during symbol of the Second World War.

George C. Scott was so eager to do the speech that
he wanted to film it right away; Schaffner, however, was
of the opinion the actor should acquire more experience
with the role in other scenes before attempting it. Neither
did the actor see the speech as a prologue; fearing he
wouldn't be able to top it, Scott was convinced the scene
should come a bit later in the film--before the Battle of El
Guettar--and that it should be filmed realistically, with the
soldiers looking on instead of an audience becoming the
troops. As the speech had always been envisioned as a
prologue, and a highly stylized one at that, Scott's ideas,
in spite of his continual protestations, were never seriously entertained. As might be expected, the actor was in an
angry mood when the time came to film it at Madrid's Sevilla
Studios on the final day of location shooting. The huge
American flag was painted on a flat backing; it was easier
than making a real flag of that size and facing the herculean task of lighting it. Three camera positions were employed, the cameras locked down so that the flag's stripes
would not cause a strobe effect. Double covered, the speech

was filmed three times, resulting in six takes; afterwards a
camera was moved in to pick up the details. In the end,
Scott's anger only enhanced his performance.

     The film proper begins with the opening credits over
a shot of a vulture (strapped down to remain stationary)
which looks down on the Kasserine Pass in the smoky aftermath of the German victory over the undisciplined and ill-
prepared Americans. Arriving in Djebel Kouif to rectify the
American shortcomings, Patton establishes his leadership
and authority in a sequence ending with a surprise air attack: as the Heinkel fighter-bombers roar overhead and
the other officers dive for cover under the conference room
table, Patton, wearing his ivory-handled pistols, climbs out
of the second-story window and descends to the ground,
where he takes on the bombers single-handedly. With his
two guns, Patton is like a legendary cowboy--reminiscent of
the Wyatt Earp who establishes himself in Tombstone, albeit
in a much more low-keyed way in John Ford's My Darling
Clementine (1946); if Patton is not already mythic at this
point, he certainly is heroic. Schaffner's visual and aural
topper is the frightened chickens who intermittently fly in
and out of the frame, their squawking mixed in loudly on
the soundtrack with the noise of the gunfire and the bombers.

     Scott had painstakingly researched his role, reading
books and studying films of Patton. To help him get deep-
er into the part, John Chambers provided him with a new
nose; he wore false teeth so that his upper teeth would jut
out, added moles, and shaved his head. As the film bears
out, Scott buried himself in the role to such an extent that
it is not unfair to say he became like the actor playing Na-
poleon who comes to believe he is Napoleon--or like the Patton who awarded himself three stars before the Battle of El
Guettar. [98] The scene of the traffic jam on the way to the
Seine serves as a good example: tanks stretch vertically to
the top of the frame, blocked by another column moving
horizontally across the screen; Patton steps out of his jeep
to direct traffic--like a maestro. When one tank almost runs
into another accidentally, Scott checks it out, gives his approval, and resumes conducting: this was not planned;
Scott was so immersed in his part that he ad-libbed in character.

George C. Scott and Schaffner, filming the prologue of
Patton, 1969.

"I really honestly cannot envision another American actor," Schaffner says, "who would have as fully developed all the sides of that character as Scott." On view is the Patton who appropriately holds a press conference in a riding rink, fielding questions while mounted on a white stallion; the urbane man who speaks fluent French to Codman as they, accompanied by the camera in a long dolly shot, discuss the guest list and the wine for an upcoming party in a moment with all the civility of a scene from Grand Illusion (1937); the general who explosively slaps the soldier in Sicily and tenderly kisses a soldier on the devastated battlefield in France. He is the pure warrior, as Steiger describes him, the magnificent anachronism.

None of this made Scott any easier to deal with; filming was frequently tempestuous. "When Scott was ornery," says the film's civilized producer, "Franklin and I had a tacit agreement that I would try to handle him. And Franklin would pass on his ornery moments to me because I can be an S.O.B., and it wouldn't hurt Franklin's relationship with him." Adding that the actor continually rewrote the script, General McCarthy continues: "He has his own opinion about everything, he's inflexible, he's difficult--I don't know how Schaffner got along with him. I think that's one of the marvels; I was constantly at odds with him."

Part of the problem stemmed from Scott's inability to accept the relationship between Patton and Bradley; feeling that Patton would have reacted more strongly to some of the situations, Scott could not change the fact that General Bradley was involved in the film. In preparing for the role, he had only Farago's, Hawkins', and Bradley's words to accept; Karl Malden had Bradley to consult with and, thus, more security in his role. Schaffner continues:

> I think it's fair to say that George was unhappy
> playing the part, not because he by any means
> made the assumption that the script was unfair to
> the character--he may have made that assumption
> from time to time--but I have always analyzed his
> attitude as having been generated out of self-
> criticism. I knew that he felt that he perhaps was
> not doing as good a job as he might, for whatever
> reasons I don't know. I certainly never felt that.

Director Schaffner viewing star Scott through Dimension 150
camera during filming of Patton, 1969.

Neither does an audience. Scott provides no easy answers
or insights into the character, opting to be him in his
glory and humiliation, a historical personage but a real human being, and, in his complexity, a tragic hero of Shake-
spearian dimensions. Patton will always be associated with
George C. Scott's towering performance.

In an earlier age, Hollywood dealt with less than complete accuracy when handling a controversial military figure;
an Errol Flynn would portray a George Armstrong Custer as
an impetuous but romantic character. In The War Film,
Ivan Butler perceived:

> The appalling egotism, narrowness, conceit and ar-
> rogance of the military type of which Patton was no
> more than an outstanding example, are presented
> with a frankness that in earlier years would only
> have been accorded to the enemy. [99]

In the old-fashioned military biography, Errol Flynn's

recklessness and excesses would be tempered by the patience
and reason of Olivia de Havilland, who would show admiration, have a steadying influence, and gently nag at the
swashbuckler. Women have no real place in the world of
Patton; the calming functions are performed by men. The
very lack of another character who performs with any degree of star quality only adds substance to the heroic
stance Scott assumes as Patton. "Give George a headline
and he's good for another 30 miles," Bradley says with
irony and less than grudging admiration. One of the purposes of the Bradley role is to supply caution and conscience, and gently nag at the wayward Patton. But if Bradley sometimes sounds like the better half, Paul Stevens as
the obsequious Colonel Charles Codman is positively uxori-
ous.

Schaffner's first cut of the film was four and a half
hours long, giving him a worthy idea: since it would inevitably be sold to television, why shouldn't he prepare a
TV version of the film to be seen over four consecutive
nights? This suggestion went unheeded; the concept,
however, was later used in NBC's presentation of The God-
father saga. As was his custom, Schaffner again brought
the film in on time and under budget: the final cost was
$12.5 million. Patton was ready to be released in the fall
but, as had happened with Planet of the Apes, was postponed until the next February: this time around, Twentieth Century-Fox was counting on Hello, Dolly! to generate
good business and attract Academy Award consideration. [100]

In order to woo a young audience, the studio added
a colon and a subtitle to Patton: A Salute to a Rebel. [101]
Schaffner objected; the film was not a salute, nor was the
late general exactly a rebel. There had been no apprehen-
sion about the young audience during the making of the
film, but now there was. Schaffner went to a meeting with
the marketing division in New York where the following bargain was made: the colon and subtitle would be removed if
Schaffner would make an extensive tour of college campuses,
in effect promoting the film. As due his background with
the United World Federalists and because he considered Patton to be an anti-war picture, Schaffner had no qualms
about making the trip. As it turned out, there were only
a few discussions in which the subject of Vietnam was introduced; the film proved to be very popular with young

people, despite a general who says of war, "I love it.   God
help me I do love it so.   I love it more than my life."

       An interesting critical response greeted Patton when
it was released in February 1970.   Vincent Canby's New
York Times review was most representative, calling Patton
"the epic American war movie that the Hollywood establish-
ment has always wanted to make but never had the guts to
do before."   On the other hand, Canby also found the film
appalling, concluding: "If I sound ambivalent about 'Patton,' it's because the movie itself is almost ambivalent about
its hero."[102]   Pauline Kael added, "The Patton shown here
appears to be deliberately planned as a Rorschach test."[103]
Some found Patton a hero, some a villain; some found Patton
a pro-war film, some an anti-war film.   McCarthy was soon
to receive a letter from an ex-actor who praised the film,
saying it was high time somebody made a pro-military movie.
"I once told you," Ronald Reagan went on to say, "I would
hate anyone who ever played that role other than myself."[104]

       Kael also commented on the film's imperial look:
"[There's] more compositional use of the sky than I've ever
seen before in a movie.   There's so much land and air--and
it's so clear--that we seem to be looking at 'Patton' from
God's point of view."[105]   This also holds true for the interiors, namely the foyer of his Knutsford residence in
which an extreme long-shot from a high angle captures
Patton as an insignificant figure raging loudly against God
over his destiny to be left out of the rest of the war.

       The Schaffner-Koenekamp collaboration on this war
film gave it a look that is decidedly modern, including the
use of a tool mostly unavailable to the makers of old-
fashioned war films--the zoom lens.   Some of the landscapes
look so unusual as to be unreal: before revealing the
graveyard, a slowly panning long-shot shows Dick Jensen
and Patton in Tunisia, standing on the desert sand; an expanse of sky behind them fills up the top third of the
screen.   The motion of the pan only adds to the feeling of
disorientation; this real locale looks like the work of a sur-
realistic art director gone berserk on a soundstage, particularly when Patton grumbles about hating the 20th century.
A discussion of landscape inevitably leads to a comparison
with Planet of the Apes, as Andrew Sarris wrote: "Schaffner has worked in both instances on a planetary scale with

vast, empty landscapes dwarfing the physical scale of the
characterizations, while at the same time enlarging their
metaphysical concerns."[106]

The boss was elated. "One of the greatest films I
have ever seen," Darryl Zanuck wrote to his associate
Elmo Williams:

> Scott's performance has never been surpassed in
> film history.... McCarthy's production and
> Schaffner's direction were basically responsible for
> the strange and ironic poetry and beauty that even
> continues to prevail throughout the grim battle se-
> quences.[107]

Perhaps the film's greatest accomplishment was that peace
was finally made with the Patton family. After the film
opened, the general's daughter, Ruth Ellen Totten, was
scheduled to meet with her attorneys to discuss how best
to proceed in a suit against Twentieth Century-Fox. When
she did not arrive for the 9:00 a.m. meeting, the lawyers
called her. "I saw the film last night," she is reputed to
have said, "and in the words of my father, 'Call off the
dogs, piss on the fire, and everybody go home.'" Moreover, "I think it is the best movie I have ever seen since
'Gone With the Wind,'" she wrote to the producer of the
film she had been dragged so unwillingly to see. "My
brother George and his wife saw it in New York ... and
he was thrilled."[108] A few days later, she was coaxed into
writing what must have been the most gratifying review the
makers of Patton received; it stated candidly:

> We could not imagine a media [sic] as vulgar as the
> movies giving him any kind of break at all.... We
> were wrong to this extent; they were more sensitive,
> more just, and more realistic in their portrayal than
> any of the contemporary people who portrayed him
> and judged him. We were right in this respect; if
> we had not fought so long and so hard to block the
> motion picture, they might have made it sooner and
> not have had George Scott for the title role.[109]

Soon the man who had so successfully captured the
"mirthless smile" of Mrs. Totten's father ran into some more
controversy by openly criticizing the Academy Awards. In

spite of its February release, <u>Patton</u> had made a strong im-
pression on the members of the Academy of Motion Picture
Arts and Sciences; Frank McCarthy's fears that Scott's re-
marks might have hurt the chances of the film's other nomi-
nees proved to be ungrounded. <u>Patton</u> garnered seven
Academy Awards: Best Picture (McCarthy); Best Director
(Schaffner); Best Actor (Scott, refused); Best Screenplay
(Francis Ford Coppola, Edmund H. North); Art Direction/
Set Decoration (Urie McCleary, Gil Parrondo/Antonio Mateos,
Pierre-Louis Thevenet); Sound (Douglas Williams, Don Bass-
man); Film Editing (Hugh S. Fowler). Schaffner was on lo-
cation in Spain the night <u>Patton</u> swept the 43rd Annual
Academy Awards; accepting the award for best direction
from Janet Gaynor, Karl Malden succinctly but aptly stated,
"You couldn't have given it to a better fellow. He deserves
it. I was there."[110]

   Throughout it all, from pre-production to post-
production, one man had been the judge of everything that
went into the film. "I regard you as the great hero of this
battle so nobly won," Ladislas Farago wrote. "I see and
feel you behind every scene--the Schaffner touch that <u>made</u>
this picture."[111] <u>Patton</u> was almost a textbook example of
all the right elements coming together and jelling for a film;
the names of the Academy Award winners of the film and
some of the names that did not win awards indicate that
many people made contributions to the whole. "It was
Schaffner who put all of those things together," comes the
generous statement from a man who realized a 19-year-old
dream with the film, "and got what I think was the nearly
perfect if not perfect portrait of the general." With due
consideration of their respective duties as producer and director, <u>Patton</u>, as listed in the credits, is properly styled
"A Frank McCarthy-Franklin J. Schaffner Production."

Nicholas and Alexandra

Perhaps the greatest pleasure a director can derive from
establishing his name in films is that producers and executives start coming to him, respectfully submitting offers.
In July 1968, during post-production of <u>Patton</u>, Schaffner
was asked to direct the Dino de Laurentiis-Columbia Pictures co-production of <u>The Captain</u>, based on the Jan de
Hartog novel of the same name, a story of the sea and the

making of a captain during the Second World War. Although
the script was by Daniel Taradash, who had written the
exemplary screenplay for From Here to Eternity (1953),
this potentially interesting project was never realized; de
Laurentiis and Columbia had fundamental differences about
the budget.

Before embarking on Patton, Schaffner had signed a
multiple-picture contract with the Mirisch Brothers: discussed as a possible film was a loose remake of the 1932
romantic classic One Way Passage, to be written by Barbara Turner, an idea soon abandoned. While filming the
Patton sequences in Knutsford, Schaffner was visited by
Walter Mirisch, carrying a project that had previously been
developed by Roman Polanski, The Day of the Dolphin.
Based on the book by Robert Merle, the plot concerned a
scientist who teaches dolphins to speak, only to have bureaucracy come in and take over; it would have made an
interesting change of pace after Patton. Schaffner worked
on the script with Roger O. Hirson, with whom he had
worked on DuPont, and who would later write the book for
Pippin, but Schaffner's involvement turned out to be a
stop on The Day of the Dolphin's way to being realized as
a 1973 Mike Nichols film starring George C. Scott. During
a lull in the work, Schaffner briefly explored the possibilities of filming Flannery O'Connor's Wise Blood; he was still
laboring on The Day of the Dolphin when an offer came
through from Sam Spiegel to direct Nicholas and Alexandra,
based on Robert K. Massie's 1967 best-selling biography.

Massie's interest in Nicholas and Alexandra was in-
spired by his son's affliction with hemophilia, which eventually led to some research on the only son of Russia's last
monarchs, Alexis, the world's most famous hemophiliac.
This disease accounts for one of Massie's major premises:

> Had it not been for the agony of Alexis' hemophilia,
> had it not been for the desperation which made his
> mother turn to Rasputin, first to save her son,
> then to save the pure autocracy, might not Nicholas
> II have continued retreating into the role of consti-
> tutional monarch so happily filled by his cousin King
> George V?[112]

In the midst of the fall of the Romanovs and the Russian

Revolution, the opulence and the squalor, the chaos and the
confusion, is this royal couple; the book, as the film would
be, is more of a character study than a historical study.
In Nicholas and Alexandra, Sam Spiegel had found tormented
characters caught in a world not of their choosing or making
--material that lent itself to an intimate epic, a type of film
synonymous with his name.

Sam Spiegel was the prototype of the maverick super-
producer who rose to power at the end of the 1940s with
the fall of the studio system. Famed for his New Year's
Eve parties, his big tips, and the 300' Malhane, the $500,000
yacht which The Bridge on the River Kwai had bought,
Spiegel lived in a glamorous lifestyle more appropriate to
the golden age of American cinema; he was and is a man to
whom style is everything. Considered by some to be the
greatest producer of them all, he also had the reputation--
enhanced with ominous looking cigar in hand--of being a
ruthless, double-talking, two-faced tyrant. Yet, whichever
reputation one subscribes to, Sam Spiegel, as Schaffner
says, "certainly is an entrepreneur in the best and the
classic sense."

Spiegel drained swamps in Palestine and lectured in
drama at Berkeley, breaking into the film industry as a
scout of European plays. In 1930, he moved to Universal
to supervise the European-language versions of the company's pictures, eventually being sent to Berlin to help ped-
dle All Quiet on the Western Front. Ever the showman, he
returned to America in 1939 as S. P. Eagle, which created
a Hollywood parlor game: M. A. Yer, Z. A. Nuck; and the
1946 film he produced, directed by Orson Welles, was
dubbed The S. T. Ranger.

Always partial to offbeat characters and unusual story
material, he formed Horizon Productions in 1947 with John
Huston, who shared his propensity for filming on real lo-
cales; Huston left the partnership after The African Queen
(1951), and Spiegel retained Horizon. In Peter Viertel's
White Hunter, Black Heart, a thinly disguised roman à clef
about Huston and the making of The African Queen, Paul
Landau, the Sam Spiegel character, is given the following
description:

[He] always ate in the best restaurants, rhumbaed

in the most fashionable night clubs, and never allowed anyone else to pick up the check. However,
it was quite commonly known that he usually had
trouble paying the grocer and the butcher bills at
the end of each month.... He had a truly charming manner, a sad continental grace and polish. He
had the elaborate manners of a Hungarian cavalry
officer.... Headwaiters, hotel managers, and but-
lers immediately recognized him as a king. [113]

S. P. Eagle died in 1954 with On the Waterfront, which Sam
Spiegel produced for Columbia. Thereafter, he would produce nine more films for the studio, most notably The Bridge
on the River Kwai (1957) and Lawrence of Arabia (1962), in
which he helped introduce literacy and taste to the screen
epic form.

    Spiegel's close relationship with Columbia Pictures
would continue through Nicholas and Alexandra. Board chairman Leo Jaffe, who in his many years at the studio had been
an eyewitness to the wonders wrought by Spiegel and the
fortunes his films had earned, wholeheartedly endorsed the
project in January 1968. A month later, Columbia had further cause for celebration when George Stevens agreed to
direct the film. Though very likely an odd couple, on paper
Spiegel and Stevens made a powerhouse team; the two Irving
Thalberg Award winners were given the royal treatment and
carte blanche. Even though Stevens had increasingly shown
a tendency to work slowly and expensively on his film spectaculars, especially with his most recent production, The
Greatest Story Ever Told (1965), Leo Jaffe felt the studio
had its best safeguard in Sam Spiegel: " 'No one guards
money like Sam does,' Jaffe said, 'and this is one of the
elements of insurance that we will have a picture that will
qualify as a blockbuster.' " [114]

    Stevens was only to work a few months on the project
before pulling up roots and moving over to Twentieth Century-
Fox to begin pre-production on The Only Game in Town
in May 1968. George Stevens was unquestionably a great
director, one of the finest pictorialists who ever worked on
film, but one can only wonder about the type of film he
would have made of Nicholas and Alexandra when one considers his statement that the material was an "account of a
wonderful family living in a wonderful time and place in
history." [115]

Despite his successful collaboration with Spiegel on Lawrence of Arabia, British playwright Robert Bolt was not particularly interested in writing the script; he had covered the same ground in his screenplay for Doctor Zhivago (1965). Spiegel instead hired an American playwright, James Goldman, primarily on the strength of his historical play The Lion in Winter, featuring another royal couple--Henry II and Eleanor of Aquitaine. Not surprisingly, Anthony Harvey, the director of the 1968 film version of Goldman's play, was recruited in October 1968. This arrangement was not to work out; in February 1969, Harvey withdrew because of the customary but vague prior commitments he had.

Although promised a bonus for a quality script, Goldman could not find a way around the difficulties in adapting Massie's book; because of the ever-present script problems there were rumors that the film would be cancelled. Those rumors were belied when Charles Jarrott, who had recently completed Anne of a Thousand Days (1969), was brought in as the new director in November 1969. Time went on, but no forward progress was made; Jarrott left after half a year's work on the project.

After Patton, the rare combination of film epic and prestige picture, Franklin J. Schaffner would seem the ideal director to work with a producer of Spiegel's stature--it would seem like a match made in heaven--collaborating on a historical film intended to entertain and instruct. Schaffner was signed to direct Nicholas and Alexandra in July 1970. His interest in the material is evident:

> I always was casting around to find a mature love story. Elements of this satisfied that wish. I've always been interested in history. Also, it was a costume piece, which I feel comfortable with. What's more, there isn't any question that what happened in 1917-1918 has radically changed history. [116]

Signing in July, Schaffner had much too short a time in pre-production for a picture of this size--it would begin production in November. Exhaustive research had been completed; there was a library of 8" by 10" stills. Already chosen were such key participants as Freddie Young, the director of photography, Yvonne Blake, the costume designer, and John Box, the production designer; there would be an English crew. Much to the director's disad-

Sam Spiegel, Janet Suzman and Schaffner, filming Nicholas and Alexandra, 1971.

vantage, most of the major decisions for the film had already been made by Spiegel, the previous directors, and Box.

The winner of Academy Awards for his work on Lawrence of Arabia, Doctor Zhivago, and Oliver, John Box, who would later win another Oscar for his work on this film, is unquestionably a master of his craft. Regarding his influence on Nicholas and Alexandra, Schaffner has said:

> John Box had a very definite idea of what kind of colors he wanted to use in this, and he had a very definite idea of what the relationship between the costumes and his sets was to be--not only in terms of color but in terms of the reaction of the set on the costume and the costume on the set and indeed of the costume of a character--so that his input into this was enormous.

Some evidence is in the following message Box sent to costumer Antonio Castillo:

The dress to be gold and not silver, with particular reference to jewelry. The furlined cloak to be
apricot, in which case sash should be blue and not
red.... Alexandra may need a shawl for this scene.
For colour please refer to the sample of wall fabric
in bedroom. [117]

Being a man who stakes out a lot of ground whenever he
works on a film, Box, at one point, probably had strong
notions of directing this film--as it stands, he also receives
credit as second unit director. In effect, the visual look of
the film had been determined before Schaffner's arrival.

Although Hollywood studios had clamped down on big-
budget motion pictures (1971 was the year of The French
Connection, The Last Picture Show, Klute, The Hospital),
Spiegel received a $9 million budget from Columbia and a
20-week shooting schedule--the longest in Schaffner's career
--for what would be the biggest picture of the year. When
he had first bought the book, Spiegel wanted to shoot in
Russia but was unable to get the necessary permission;
Spain, as it had for Doctor Zhivago and later would for
Reds (1981), would have to substitute for Russia.

At this point, as it had been from the start, the
most troubling issue was the script: James Goldman had
spent a year and a half working on it, and was already
gone before Schaffner began his two years of work on the
project; Edward Bond's rewrite was still too talky, too confusing, and, at 213 pages, too long. Working feverishly
with Bond in the little time he had, Schaffner knew the
script was far from ready to be shot, but ran into a brick
wall named Sam Spiegel. An immediate source of disagreement was the prevalence of interior scenes that Schaffner
found more than a little suffocating. In hopes of opening
up the script drastically, the director argued he could always pick up time on location as opposed to the costly and
time-consuming problems he would encounter on a soundstage; he was, however, overruled. "It was one of those
unfortunate tussles," he says, "because I was not happy
about the script and Sam was happy about the script."

It must be granted that an adaptation of Massie's book
is an almost insurmountable task. The script begins in 1904
with the birth of Alexis (ten years after the book begins),

and has 14 years to cover, including such items as the
Romanov court, the Russo-Japanese War, the rise of the
Bolsheviks, the First World War, and the Russian Revolution. These are all exceedingly complicated subjects, each
requiring a modicum of exposition for a film primarily intended for an American audience whose knowledge of its
own Revolutionary War might be more than a little shaky.
There are a multitude of characters with a host of names
not easily remembered: subtitles for each major character
as he/she enters the frame would be self-defeating--Schaffner
had ruled that out in Patton; nor does the device of introducing important characters through dialogue (Lenin: "You've
been avoiding me, Trotsky") seem very satisfactory. As it
is, the script focuses on a family that included four daughters, who are given little to do to distinguish themselves as
Olga, Tatiana, Marie, or Anastasia. This is the type of
material that is better read and digested at the reader's individual pace than seen on a theatre screen by a mass audience.

     Still, it is not difficult to see why Schaffner was drawn
to Nicholas. "He was one of those marvelous victims caught
in the wrong place at the wrong time," he says. "If he had
had a little more of the eastern barbaric muscle to him he
would have survived." The script fully underscores the
historical Nicholas as a weak and passive character who said
of himself, as quoted by Massie: "I am not prepared to be
a Tsar. I never wanted to become one. I know nothing of
the business of ruling. I have no idea of even how to talk
to the ministers." [118] Alexandra, the German granddaughter
of Queen Victoria, from whom the hemophilia was inherited,
was not the family choice to be Tsarina; unpopular with the
court, extremely shy by nature, she, like the Tsar, was
essentially a passive character. Consequently, the script
was stuck with two historical characters who, despite their
titles and fate, were basically mediocre people and dramatically unexciting. When the script cuts from Nicholas and
Alexandra's imperial lifestyle, complete with two Ethiopian
doormen, to the squalid and slimy environs of a hemp factory in St. Petersburg where entire families live in the tiny
areas by each machine, it seems hard to generate much
sympathy for Nicky and Alix: they seem to be frivolous,
like Tom and Daisy Buchanan in The Great Gatsby, care-
less people. This was only part of the challenge facing
Schaffner.

Considering the script ready to shoot, Spiegel began
working on the next phase--finding the right people for the
roles. Nicholas and Alexandra would be a far cry from Irving Thalberg's 1932 production of Rasputin and the Empress,
which starred John, Ethel, and Lionel Barrymore, and two
films directed by Russian-born Anatole Litvak--with whom
Spiegel had worked in his previous production, The Night
of the Generals (1967)--dealing with Russian royalty:
Tovarich (1937) with Claudette Colbert and Charles Boyer
and Anastasia with Ingrid Bergman. There would be no
major stars playing Spiegel's Nicholas and Alexandra; although Charles Jarrott had once tested Liv Ullmann, that
casting idea had been discarded. From the inception of
the project, Spiegel's plan was to hire unknowns for the
leads and surround them with star character actors, not
unlike what he had done so successfully for Lawrence of
Arabia.

Shortly after he joined the film, Schaffner made a
test of Janet Suzman, an actress he remembered seeing
when she had toured America with the Royal Shakespeare
Company; as he had not yet adjusted to the concept of the
production or to London, the results were less than felicitous. On the other hand, in a test he made of Michael
Jayston, Schaffner found his Nicholas immediately. Something about Janet Suzman, however, stuck in the director's
mind: a second test proved to be successful enough to
land her the role of Alexandra. [119] Whether or not everyone agrees with the policy of using unknowns, no one can
deny that Jayston and Suzman bear uncanny resemblances
to the characters they portray in the film.

As far as the Russian characters were concerned, it
was decided to keep the accents uniformly British. Casting
director Maude Spector had a monumental task in finding
actors to fill out hundreds of speaking roles in the film.
Ultimately, a veritable Who's Who of British Theatre was
hired for the supporting roles, including such luminaries
as Laurence Olivier, Michael Redgrave, Harry Andrews,
Irene Worth and Eric Porter, with Curt Jurgens and Alexander Knox joining in as well. They would strengthen the
characterizations of the two actors in the leading roles and
help solve the problem of an audience's identification of the
characters: if, for example, a viewer neither knows the
name of Count Fredericks nor who he is, he/she will quickly

recognize the familiar face of Jack Hawkins. In this large
and august cast, special praise must go to the less recog-
nizable Alan Webb as Yurovsky, the seemingly saintly phi-
losopher who turns out to be the royal family's executioner.

Principal photography commenced at the end of November on Spanish land familiar to Schaffner from his previous film. The company was headquartered in Madrid,
where interiors would be shot on 30 sets that had been
built at the Sevilla Studios. Some locations would be shot
in Madrid, such as the Teatro Espanol for the Kiev Opera
House where Stolypin (Eric Porter) is assassinated in the
midst of loud applause, and the Estacion Delicias for the
Finland Station where Nicholas blesses the soldiers departing to fight the Japanese; the Siberian scenes were shot in
Soria, three hours away from Madrid, and the Bloody Sunday riots were filmed in Yugoslavia.

Even though it had a cast of thousands, Patton only
had a few speaking roles; one of the reasons for Nicholas
and Alexandra's long shooting schedule was to accommodate
the availability of the British actors. Accordingly, the sets
at the Sevilla Studios had to be converted, reconverted,
and even duplicated, depending on which actors were on
hand; the principal set was put together on three separate
occasions. The company, for example, had to be flexible
enough to adjust to the health and schedule of Laurence
Olivier, who, recovering from thrombosis, had accepted the
part of Prime Minister Witte on the assumption that a small
film role would be the best means of therapy and exercise
to get him back into artistic shape; the sets were recon-
structed to fit the times he could do his scenes. Neither
large nor glamorous, the role of Count Witte gave Olivier
the most important speech in the film when, as the Russians prepare to enter the First World War, he predicts:
"Everything we fought for will be lost, everything we
loved will be broken. The victors will be as cursed as
the defeated. The world will become old and man will
wander about lost in the ruins and go mad."

In the short time he was connected with the film,
Olivier provided a solution to the nagging problem of the
third lead in the film, Rasputin. Originally, Spiegel had
wanted Peter O'Toole in the part; having introduced him
to the international public in Lawrence of Arabia, he still

had an option on his services. After <u>Lawrence</u>, O'Toole
had specialized in portraying a wide variety of madmen, but
did not want to play the notorious Russian madman. By
the time Spiegel decided to force the issue and exercise his
option, it was too late--the option period had expired. Max
von Sydow had been tested before Schaffner arrived but,
as with his colleague Liv Ullmann, that idea had not worked
out; Marlon Brando, who would have been acceptable to
Spiegel, was reluctant to play the role. Shooting moved
into 1971: scenes requiring Rasputin would inevitably be
coming up and could not be postponed indefinitely. Aware
of this dilemma, Olivier recommended Tom Baker, an actor
with the National Theatre. Word was sent to the National
Theatre to have one of its directors shoot a test of Baker.
The results were a bit too theatrical and bravura; however,
this was not inappropriate to the part. In February 1971,
Tom Baker, in his motion picture debut, joined the company
to take on the film's most dynamic role.

Not unnaturally, Baker figures prominently in the
film's most striking sequence--the death of Rasputin. The
infamous priest joins Prince Yussoupov (Martin Potter) and
Grand Duke Dimitri (Richard Warwick), two exceptionally
fey and hedonistic youths, in the cellar of the former's
palace. Action--suitably decadent and insane--begins with
an establishing pan shot that moves from the silverware to
the left, to Rasputin, and then on to the right, where Dr.
Lazovert carries his tray of specially prepared cakes and
vodka; Yussoupov, in a toga, and Dimitri, in a Russian
Oriental outfit, smoke from Turkish water pipes and giggle
senselessly. Yussoupov suddenly runs upstairs, grabs a
flautist from a full orchestra which is playing to no one,
and returns to put a record of "Yankee Doodle" on the
gramophone. An exotic dancer materializes, doing a modified can-can and Russian dance to the tune, thoroughly de-
lighting Rasputin--who is further delighted when the dancer's wig falls off to reveal the male flautist. When Lazovert
finally steps out of the shadows, Rasputin realizes he has
been poisoned--Yussoupov and Dimitri's giggling becomes
hysterical--and deliberately drinks more poison to demonstrate his masculinity. Yussoupov shoots him in the back
and, noticing that "Yankee Doodle" has wound down and
come to a halt, rises to turn the record over. Rasputin,
in the meantime, has run to the corridor, something this
royal couple finds especially hilarious; tittering still, they

pursue him. Yussoupov shoots him three more times; giggling demoniacally, Dimitri lashes the fallen body with a
chain in an overtly sexual fashion. Yussoupov stops him
and then, suddenly sober, says, "God bless the Tsar."

On the morning of April 16, 1971, three men working
on Nicholas and Alexandra were informed they had won Os-
cars: Schaffner and Gil Parrondo, now working as an art
director under John Box, had won for their work on Patton;
the third man had won for his cinematography of Ryan's
Daughter. In Freddie Young (aka: F. A. Young and
Frederick Young), Schaffner's luck with cameramen continued. Like Russell Metty and Leon Shamroy when they
worked with Schaffner, Freddie Young was in his late sixties; like Metty and Shamroy, Young moved at Schaffner's
tempo. Some of the Schaffner-Young teamwork is evident
in a scene at the birthday party of the Dowager Empress
(Irene Worth): during a waltz, the camera dollies past a
row of faces in a diagonal move towards the right center of
the frame before moving at a 90-degree angle down to the
bottom; Nicholas and Alexandra suddenly sweep into the
picture in the space freed by the second camera move; the
camera sweeps along with the couple as they waltz, moving
in a line parallel to the first diagonal.

Another film unit was on the set: as befitting his
status among film buffs in Great Britain, Schaffner became
the subject of a BBC documentary entitled Portrait of a
Director. Separate units making short films or featurettes
have become so commonplace in the contemporary filmmaking
scene that Schaffner does not remember the BBC crew:

> They usually have these film crews around on the
> set, and you pay no attention to them. You try to
> find out, "Are you comfortable?" You know, "If
> you get in my way, I'll tell you, but please stay
> out of my way." Then you pay no more attention
> to it.

What was apparent to anyone on the set was the director's
way with the performers. The actors portraying the Romanov
family had come a long way together during the course of
production; by the time the final execution scene was filmed,
they had become as a family. Michael Jayston gave due
credit to Schaffner: "He is the most tolerant human being

Schaffner and cameraman Freddie Young, filming <u>Nicholas and Alexandra</u>, 1971.

I've ever met. I never once heard him raise his voice to
anybody.... It was incredible."[120]

Schaffner devised the title sequences: the opening
credits are presented over a background of flickering red
balls of light which, as the camera rack focuses to a tight
shot of Alexandra giving birth to Alexis, are finally revealed to be the flames of candles. In the final scene of
the film, the family is led to the basement of the Ipatiev
House where Nicholas and Alexandra sit on chairs as if posing for a photograph: Alexis sits on his father's lap and
the four daughters stand behind their parents. When Yurovsky and the Cheka men burst in, Nicholas covers his
son's face with his hand; a closer shot discloses that the
first bullet goes through the former Tsar's hand into Alexis' head. After the executioners have completed their job,
the camera moves in on the wall in the aftermath of the
carnage. Schaffner then returns to the image of the
blurred red balls of candle lights for the final credits.

As is his custom when filming overseas, Schaffner
spent 16 hours a day, six days a week at work; on Sun-
days, he spent an additional six hours planning the next
week's work and looking at locations. By the end of April
1971, Schaffner had had 20 weeks of such a schedule; it
had been a grueling shoot. With tongue slightly in cheek,
Schaffner has called Patton his 16-pound picture and
Nicholas and Alexandra his 26-pound picture-referring to
the amount of weight he lost on each production. Fortunately, a director has a chance to recuperate during the
post-production period. Schaffner moved to London for
five months, enabling him to rest up, bring his family over
from California, and work with Ernest Walter, the editor,
and Richard Rodney Bennett, the composer.

It was at this point that the circle of war montage
that precedes the intermission was put together: as the
Romanov family waves to the soldiers marching off to the
First World War, there is a freeze frame and all the color
bleeds out of the picture, turning it into a black and white
still; there is a cut to a still image of the Hohenzollerns in
Germany, followed by a still image of Raymond Poincaré in
France; the circle is completed in Russia as the color returns to the picture and the soldiers continue to march,
their footsteps thundering ominously on the soundtrack.

Somewhat similarly, making effective use of color and the
absence of color, when Lenin arrives at the Duma and announces to the cheering throngs that the government has
fallen, there is a freeze frame of a close shot of his left
profile: the background gradually turns black and then
the color fades from his face; he has become a statue--
from this point in time he no longer is a man but a symbol. There is great balance to the structure of the film:
the Romanovs and the peasants, the aristocracy and the
revolutionaries, the suffering of the Russian people and
the suffering of Nicholas and Alexandra; one side rises
and the other side falls. In that respect, this is probably
Schaffner's most formal film.

While the director was completing post-production,
Queen Elizabeth made a commitment to attend the November
Royal Premiere in London; in America, the National Association of Theatre Owners, in anticipation of the film's December release, honored Spiegel as Producer of the Year
and Schaffner as Director of the Year. Nicholas and Alexandra
would be exhibited on a reserved-seat basis, complete with
intermission. Although it was eventually nominated for five
Academy Awards (best picture, actress, music, art direction, and cinematography) and did respectable business,
Nicholas and Alexandra was not the critical or commercial
blockbuster that Columbia and Spiegel had predicted it
would be.

Richard Schickel offered one reason why, commenting
on the adaptation process:

> The book was fascinating for precisely what no
> movie can show--the historian's careful tracing of
> the events, great and small, that shaped, from birth
> onward, the characters of Nicholas and Alexandra,
> determined the quality of their court and govern-
> ment. [121]

The filmmakers had been determined to show the times,
present the political situations and structures of both sides,
but, as was pointed out in The Hollywood Reporter, "It's
next to impossible to keep all the statesmen and ambassadors
and generals and revolutionaries in the movie straight."[122]
In the first half of the picture, Nicholas and Alexandra's
drama, intercut as it is with the external events and figures

leading to the fall of the 300-year-old Romanov dynasty,
never builds up much momentum. The film requires all
this exposition, but it weighs heavily on the human drama;
the cross-cutting brings on a not necessarily desired alien-
ation effect.

In the world of history on film, the couple whose
character, rank, and fate most resembles Nicholas and
Alexandra is Maximilian and Carlotta, the main characters
in a 1939 production directed by William Dieterle. If that
film was more successful overall than the Spiegel-Schaffner
film, the reason might be revealed in its title--Juarez.
Like Nicholas, Maximilian recognizes both himself and his
situation, but, with the addition of Benito Juarez, it is the
stuff of Hegelian tragedy in that both sides are quite sympathetic. Nicholas and Alexandra does not have this advantage, and certainly not in America where Juarez's name
has greater currency than Lenin's.

After his abdication, Nicholas returns home feeling
compelled to apologize to his wife. In an unexpectedly
powerful moment, he drops to his knees, repeating, "I'm so
ashamed," as if expecting--or begging--Alexandra to hit
him. This is Jayston's strongest scene, one that is later
recapitulated when Alexis (Roderic Noble) cries, "I'm so
ashamed of you." Alexandra, however, seems to disappear
thereafter, leading one to think the film might be more aptly titled Nicholas--and adding fuel to the argument that
Schaffner has difficulty with women characters. Yet a
second viewing of the film reveals an Alexandra who is demanding, bitchy, hysterical, and scared in the first half;
as a reaction to her fate, she is totally withdrawn in the
second half--involving a more difficult and less rewarding
type of acting by Janet Suzman. Considering what they
had in the beginning and how they ended up, Nicholas and
Alexandra, with the able assistance of Jayston and Suzman,
certainly emerge as tragic figures, but--unfortunately for
the film in its initial release--usually only after a second
viewing.

In the years since its release, Schaffner has noticed
another interesting pattern concerning an audience's reaction to the film. As a general rule, the section before the
intermission of a roadshow picture is usually the more interesting. "Not so Nicholas and Alexandra," he says.

"Somehow or another the second part happens to be better than the first." It is because the film finally begins to concentrate on the family drama. As the locations move from the colorful opulence of the Tsarskoe Selo Palace to the dingy gray of Siberia, there are fewer and fewer distractions. The drama grows more intense, more powerful, and truly moving.

Even though Nicholas and Alexandra separately take personal responsibility for the family's fate, they are not alone: Alexis has the ponderous awareness of his role in their destiny. At Tobolsk, Siberia, Alexis, seeing no hope, takes a sled, closes the door, and climbs the stairs. What follows is not unexpected; what is unexpected is how economically yet effectively Schaffner, in only three shots, stages this particularly painful suicide attempt: (1) the camera zooms in on Alexis' face; (2) a subjective camera hurtles down the steps; (3) there is a shot of the other side of the door as the wood splinters and breaks on the sled's impact.

With the family drama now rolling, Schaffner satisfies his intention of keeping the characters in sharp focus against the broad canvas of history, and can move in even closer. When Nicholas sees his son sleeping at the Ipatiev house, the audience sees dozens of flies crawling around Alexis' pillow; in the same house, the Romanovs' final destination, Nicholas casually looks out a window, and, in the reverse angle, his face is seen for a fleeting moment before the glass is covered over with a coat of white paint. A few moments later, Nicholas is slapped by a soldier, a type of man to whom a few years earlier the Tsar was as remote and almighty as God. "I have learned," the former Tsar says when he makes his separate peace, "that a strong man has no need of power ... and a weak man is destroyed by it." Indeed, as the film progresses, Jayston's Nicholas seems to possess what Alexandra has described as the gentlest eyes on earth.

Generally speaking, Schaffner got along well with his powerhouse producer, Sam Spiegel. "There is no question that Sam can make a claim to being the finest producer of all time." But he adds, "I don't know that that claim is supported by everybody who has worked with him closely." The director can testify to the producer's business acumen,

taste, imagination, casting ability, and tenacity, but Schaffner's working experience with him did not bear out Spiegel's
reputation for dexterity with the script or the editing. A
clue to the producer-director relationship is provided in a
letter from a man who also had close dealings with Spiegel
on the film. "I know from many of the actors and others
around the set," wrote Robert K. Massie, "that your relations with Sam also have not been easy."[123]

The last dispute came over the final cut of the film.
As its running length was well over three hours, Schaffner
wanted to cut out 18 minutes, feeling the picture would play
better that way; Spiegel was, at the least, equally adamant
about retaining those 18 minutes. Even though Spiegel
might have had final cut, written into Schaffner's Nicholas
and Alexandra contract was a clause stating that if an insoluble difference arose with the producer, the director
could appeal to Leo Jaffe, Columbia's chairman of the board,
who would then be final arbiter; fortunately, the matter did
not have to reach that stage. When the film was screened
for the executives in New York, Stanley Schneider, studio
president, and John Van Eysen, head of the European office, thought the film too long--thus supporting Schaffner's
position--and went to battle with Spiegel. In a lopsided
compromise, 12 of the 18 minutes were finally removed.

The fate of Nicholas and Alexandra was especially be-
wildering to its producer. Like its protagonists who watched
their world die to be replaced by a new order, Sam Spiegel,
a king in his own way, saw the end of the motion picture
world as he knew it:

> During the years 1952 to 1962, when I had five
> classic successes, I was convinced that I would al-
> ways be able to sense the pulse of the public. Sud-
> denly, I found I couldn't. "Nicholas and Alexandra"
> had proved a disappointment at the box office, though
> I still think it was a fine film.... I was making
> films aimed at the highest level of taste, and sud-
> denly I realized I was out of touch.[124]

When Bridge on the River Kwai set television rating records
in April 1966, landmark films were gobbled up and broadcast with increasing frequency over a medium for which they
were never intended; material he might have considered for

a film was soon produced directly for television. Paradoxically enough, the new breed of stars was smaller than life,
and yet a movie could make more money in one summer than
Gone with the Wind had in four decades. His was not the
taste of the new cinema; fittingly, the producer's next film
would be an 1976 adaptation of F. Scott Fitzgerald's The
Last Tycoon.

        Nevertheless, Sam Spiegel must have taken pride in
Arthur Knight's Saturday Review critique:

> By a miracle ... the film unfolds its complex drama,
> swiftly, economically, and engrossingly.... History
> seems to come alive in this movie, in a manner once
> envisaged by D. W. Griffith as an ideal for the
> then-new medium.... Nicholas and Alexandra has
> an immediacy that makes one feel that, while it may
> be magnificent entertainment today, it might well
> replace a classroom text tomorrow. [125]

As for the director, the film consolidated Franklin J.
Schaffner's reputation as a man who could work with a
cast of thousands and multi-million dollars without ever being overwhelmed, or neglecting small details and personal
touches. "I can't think of another director who could do
what you've done," wrote James Goldman, who knew the
particulars well. "It's not only an impeccable performance,
it's a triumph over the most resistant and unyielding material." [126]   The one-time master of the small television
screen was now acknowledged as a master of something
much larger: with this film, Craig Fisher of The Hollywood Reporter noted, "Schaffner has attained a command
of the wide screen that is surely unique." [127]

        The word was out: whenever an American director
was needed to handle a large-scale production involving
truly fearsome logistics and an uncanny use of the wide
screen, the name to call was Franklin J. Schaffner.

The French Lieutenant's Woman

Schaffner was first approached to direct Papillon during
the making of Nicholas and Alexandra. There were no
particulars as to how or when; everything was very vague

and up in the air--no package, no deal, nothing but a
question asking him if he would be interested in doing the
film. All he could do was reply, yes, he was very interested, and then that was the end of the subject. His attention moved on to another promising project, Joseph Lash's
Pulitzer Prize-winning biography of the Roosevelts, Eleanor
and Franklin; it was never realized as a theatrical film.

However, while working on Nicholas and Alexandra,
Schaffner had chanced upon a book that seized his imagination and artistic passion. So completely captivated was he
by John Fowles' The French Lieutenant's Woman that Schaffner immediately began asking around about the rights; it
would be something different, a smaller picture, an intimate
exploration of a woman's psyche. The novel turned out to
be the property of Lester Goldsmith, who had recently produced Kurt Vonnegut, Jr.'s Happy Birthday, Wanda June
(1971) for Columbia. The two men joined forces at once,
and, having missed the opportunity of working with him on a
day-to-day basis on Nicholas and Alexandra, Schaffner
brought James Goldman in to write the screenplay.[128] As
was to be expected, various press releases stated that the
film would star Julie Christie, Glenda Jackson, Janet Suzman, Vanessa Redgrave, Sarah Miles, Faye Dunaway, Jane
Fonda, or even Ali McGraw.

In preparation, Goldman, Goldsmith, and Schaffner
went to Lyme Regis to visit John Fowles and discuss the
property with him. "We spent the night in his house,"
Schaffner says, "we wandered all over those areas that are
referred to in the book, including the walk that she took
daily." Work resumed in California as Goldman tried to
come up with a suitable approach to the novel. These efforts resulted in a "very slim development deal" from M-G-M.
Their end of the bargain was to deliver a first draft of the
screenplay in six months, and then Schaffner would have,
in all likelihood, a $3 million budget to direct the film.
Things, however, did not work out that way. Schaffner
recalls:

> After about two months, James Goldman called Gold-
> smith and said he was unable to lick the project. I
> went back to London, talked to Pinter. Pinter said,
> yes, he knew how to lick the project but he was not
> about to tackle it at this point because he was going
> to do a Proust piece.

It is entirely possible that the approach Harold Pinter had in mind was the one he subsequently used for the 1981 Karel Reisz film version of The French Lieutenant's Woman, but in 1972 Schaffner was frantically racing around to meet a deadline; four of the six months given to him by M-G-M had elapsed. Returning to London, Schaffner met with another of Great Britain's finest contemporary playwrights, John Osborne:

> [He] said, yes, he'd love to do it and said, "Within ten days I'll have about twenty-five pages which will illustrate the terms of our discussion and how I think this whole project should be done." Unhappily, Osborne had an automobile accident thereafter.

Also unhappily, James T. Aubrey, the smiling cobra who had made such drastic changes as head of CBS Television, had come to M-G-M as head of production and would wreak similar havoc in his short tenure at the studio. The new boss wanted to put his stamp and use his scissors on every studio project; one of the first cuts he made was The French Lieutenant's Woman. Schaffner and Goldsmith took the property over to Columbia--and fared no better.

Papillon

> I was astounded when I got back to this happy town to hear of the rumors circulated about PAPILLON. The financial difficulties, the artistic differences, and the production problems. Some day perhaps I will have a forum from which to put the rumors to rest by declaring all of them to have been true. [129]
> --Franklin J. Schaffner

The inspiration for Papillon was Albertine Sarrazin, who wrote of her prison life and escapes in L'Astragale. Following her example, and hoping to duplicate her success, Henri Charrière sat down in Venezuela and wrote about his adventures and nine cavales (escape attempts)--as he knew and remembered them--titling the book after his ethereal nickname, butterfly, from his days in the French underground when he was known as a young man with a light touch with the hearts of women and the locks of safes. After Papillon was published in 1969, the expatriate and

ex-convict Charrière found himself the biggest celebrity in
France: at one million copies, Papillon was the all-time
best-selling book in France; the next year, he even wrote
and starred in a movie, Popsy Pop. So phenomenally successful was Charrière's "true" life story that in short order
Georges Menager and Gerard de Villiers, riding the wave of
his popularity, each wrote books indignantly protesting the
inaccuracies and untruths in Papillon. Charrière was
prompted to hedge a bit and reply, "Let's say I lived
through only 75% of what I wrote. So help me, the rest
is purely a question of errors of memory."[130]

   The book sold 2.5 million copies in America and 10
million throughout the world. With its elements of Alexan-
dre Dumas, Victor Hugo, and Daniel Defoe, it is a surefire
crowd-pleaser, with a first-person narrative and a hardboiled style not unlike Mickey Spillane's. Establishing his
character and how he adapted to his new lifestyle, Charrière writes:

> I got my plan. It was a highly polished aluminum
> tube, that unscrewed right in the middle. It had
> a male half and a female half. It contained 5600
> francs in new bills. When I got it, I kissed it.
> Yes, I kissed that little tube, two and a half inches
> long and as thick as your thumb, before shoving it
> into my anus. I took a deep breath so that it
> would lodge in the colon. It was my strongbox.
> They could make me take off all my clothes, spread
> my legs apart, make me cough or bend over double,
> for all the good it would do them. The plan was
> high up in the large intestine. It was part of me.
> Inside me I carried by life, my freedom ... my road
> to revenge. For that's what was on my mind. Re-
> venge. That's all there was, in fact.[131]

In short, at no time does the reader ever expect Papillon to
sit on his plan and discuss weighty or philosophical issues.
Papillon, as Charrière presents himself, is cool and courageous, loyal and fair. The book is a lark of an adventure
and, in the Guajira Indian idyll, includes every boy and
man's fantasy: not only is the hero rescued and taken in
by the tribe, he is also given the two most beautiful girls
in the village as wives. Papillon then goes on to describe
his living arrangement:

> I was caressing Zoraima's breasts and belly and she
> was biting my ears. Lali arrived, took her sister
> by the arm, passed her hand over her sister's
> swollen belly, then over her own slender flat one.
> Zoraima got up as if to say, "You're right," and
> gave her place to her sister. [132]

Whether or not any of it is true, preposterous or not, the
book is a highly interesting and entertaining read.

If a film were to be faithful to Charrière's book, it
would probably have all the elements to make a guaranteed
fortune. In a curious reversal of the usual book to film
adaptation, the film took a lighthearted and light-headed
book and transformed the material into something serious
and thoughtful; instead of aiming at the lowest common denominator, a filmmaker took a sure thing and made something commercially risky out of it. This was due to a personal vision that reshaped the material into as naturalistic
an interpretation as can be found in American film: Papillon, in Franklin J. Schaffner's hands, became a statement
about a man with a moral rage to be free.

First to recognize Papillon's tremendous pre-sold value
as a film was Robert Laffont, publisher of the book, who,
knowing a good thing when he saw it, zealously guarded its
rights; anticipating a film bonanza, Laffont included his own
involvement in the production as part of the price tag.
Richard Davis of the Walter Reade Organization said the
right things to get the rights, but, when Reade passed on
it, Davis sold the property to Robert Dorfmann for $600,000.
Even though he would have nothing to do with the production, Laffont was still involved as associate producer, eventually settling for publishing credit on the finished film.

While making Mayerling (1968), Robert Dorfmann,
chief of Corona Films and producer of Forbidden Games
(1952) and The Confession (1970), became convinced that
the French film business should think in terms of the international market--specifically America. With that in mind,
he joined forces with a veteran American producer who had
relocated in Paris, Ted Richmond, whose Copa Productions
was founded in the early 1950s with Tyrone Power. Best
known for such westerns as Return of the Seven (1966)
and Villa Rides (1968), Richmond would be working on his

75th film in Papillon. Before all the details on Papillon
were finalized, Dorfmann and Richmond were respectively
producer and executive producer of Red Sun (1971), a
paradigm of an international picture--a western featuring
an American leading man (Charles Bronson), a French villain (Alain Delon), a Swiss leading lady (Ursula Andress),
a British director (Terence Young), and Toshiro Mifune as
the lone samurai out in the west.[126] A most intriguing idea
that never really came off, Red Sun would have been far
better served had it enlisted the services of the eventual
star and director of Papillon.

A film starring Jean-Paul Belmondo as Papillon could
be excellent and do fine business throughout Europe, but
chances are it would not attract a very large American audience; an American superstar, on the other hand, like
Steve McQueen, could attract audiences in America as well
as Europe and Asia. The price Dorfmann had paid for the
film rights was the indicator of the route Papillon would take:
the biggest star in France and reputedly Henri Charrière's
choice, Steve McQueen was hired to play the title role in
this international prison picture; Dorfmann and Richmond
could now raise money on their star's name. "The only
people who make international pictures are the Americans,"
Schaffner has said. "That is why, obviously, they came
first to McQueen and then they came to me."[133]

In ten years, McQueen had moved from The Blob
(1958) to Bullitt (1968). He was the "ballsy young actor
who threw seismic hints of erupting into a luminary," whom
Frank Capra wanted to cast as the male lead in his 1961
production of A Pocketful of Miracles.[134] As Josh Randall,
the bounty hunter in television's Wanted: Dead or Alive
(CBS, 1958-1961), he had established a cool anti-hero's
image which he carried into films with him. Howard Koch,
author of screenplays for Errol Flynn (Sea Hawk, 1940),
Bette Davis (The Letter, 1940) and Humphrey Bogart (Casablanca, 1942), was no stranger to superstars, but, when
asked to write a profile about one, chose McQueen, whose
early maneuvers to stardom he had observed while working
on The War Lover (1962). Koch best captures the actor's
appeal in an article aptly titled "Power Drive":

> He doesn't need a stunt man--he isn't afraid to do
> his own stunts. It appears that these "real" quali-

ties in his make-up are sensed by audiences. And
the arrogance which motivates some of his actions
is mitigated by the charm of that quick half-smile
which assures us that, at bottom he is a "good
guy."[135]

As the years went by, the actor's style was more clearly
defined--never less than macho, he was a man at work, absorbed in his work, defined by his work; his acting style
became more minimal. He had a unique screen persona,
knew how to act for the camera, and, not least of all, he
moved well, a rather essential quality for moving pictures.
In Europe or Asia, he was the embodiment of what an American was or should be. Perhaps the greatest tribute is that
no less than John Wayne would star in a modern-day detective movie named McQ (1974), directed by John Sturges, the
man who had made The Great Escape (1963), the film that
made McQueen a star.

In 1972, McQueen was at a crossroad in his career:
he could continue, most profitably, to make strong action
movies, repeating himself over and over, or he could take a
risk and try something different; in Papillon he chose the
latter. This decision, however, would not mean too much
without the right director--the material could easily get out
of hand or be turned into a pulp movie--and a bankable director is not always a good director, a good director is not
always a strong director. In Franklin J. Schaffner, a man
with all the requisite qualities was found to direct Papillon;
he would be the right taskmaster for Steve McQueen.

Now that Dorfmann and Richmond had finally come
around to talk business, Schaffner made one demand before
he would commit to a project that would take the next 33
months of his life--he asked for a producer's credit on the
film:

> I guess I insisted upon that title or that position
> because I didn't have any kind of confidence in the
> man who was supposed to produce it and equally
> lacked confidence in the man who was going to ex-
> ecutive produce it. And it seemed to be wise in
> order to protect myself and protect the project as
> best I could just to insist on co-producing it. I'm
> not at all sure it would have made any difference.

It, I guess, just lent more authority to the office I
was occupying.

Contractually, Franklin J. Schaffner would get first billing
over Robert Dorfmann in the eastern hemisphere; in the
western hemisphere, their positions would be reversed.

In keeping with the scale of the production, Dorfmann
spent $500,000 getting a screenplay out of the book, begin-
ning with a treatment by Robert Benton and David Newman
that was discarded before Schaffner came aboard. Having
had a good working relationship with James, the elder of
the writing Goldman brothers, Schaffner turned to William
to write the script. William Goldman established the essential structure that would be used in the film: as it would
be impractical to dramatize all nine, three escape attempts
were chosen; also, Goldman's idea was to end the script
with the first part of the book, before Papillon arrives in
Venezuela to settle down, get married, and lead an honest
life. The Goldman script is closer to the spirit of the book
than the final film--the revenge motif, absent in the film,
is prominent in his script. The writer worked from October
1971 to April 1972, submitting three drafts of the script, but
the final result of his labor was: "There's only one line of
mine in the movie--the last line of the movie."[136] In view
of the film that was to come, Goldman's work stands at the
halfway point--it has the elements of a romp but it also contains the base of the more sober film realized by Schaffner.

Before leaving to begin The Great Waldo Pepper
(1975) for George Roy Hill and Robert Redford, Goldman
recollects: "I was present at the meeting at which some
guys said, 'Dustin Hoffman is getting hot. If we only had
a part for Dustin Hoffman, that would be terrific.' And we
scoffed because there was no part."[137] The only way to
create a part was to combine all the secondary roles. When
asked how he felt about the idea, Schaffner replied that it
was fine by him, if Hoffman could be had, but that the actor probably wouldn't like the script. While Hoffman was
pursued, and pursued relentlessly, Lorenzo Semple, Jr.
came in to spend six weeks writing three quick drafts of
the script.

The Hoffman idea seems to run against the grain of
Papillon: the protagonist is a loner; he alone is the unify-

ing character in the book, having no real continuing relationship with anyone that lasts over a handful of pages.
But now, according to the script, he would--in the person
of Louis Dega. The addition of Dustin Hoffman was sure
to increase the film's box office appeal; if things went well,
Dega could give Papillon someone to play against, showing
his humanity--and to rescue repeatedly. For the co-star,
there would surely be the challenge of working with Mc-
Queen, but, more pertinently, as Schaffner stated: "Dustin was bought--not brought--into the film."[138] The immediate implication was that there should be something akin to
a buddy-buddy script for McQueen and Hoffman; ironically,
William Goldman, who had single-handedly created the sub-
genre with Butch Cassidy and the Sundance Kid (1969),
had already completed his stint on the film and was gone.
Meanwhile, having completed a workable script to the point
where Papillon comes out of his first term in solitary, Semple had finished his term of duty. It would be up to the
estimable Dalton Trumbo, the next screenwriter on the
project, to rework the Dega character, restructure and rewrite the rest of the script.

As usual, Schaffner researched the subject extensive-
ly, finding, in the widely disparate sources that were
checked, many of the adventures Charrière had claimed for
himself. Most evident to him was that a truly unhappy existence seemed to be the common thread among these books
and stories told by prisoners and non-prisoners of colonial
garrisons. The penal system created an administrative society that bred frustration and despair; it was precisely
this type of atmosphere Schaffner wanted to infuse in his
film. That Paul D. Zimmerman would somewhat glibly write
in Newsweek, "'Papillon' offers torture as entertainment but
winds up making entertainment a form of torture," suggests
that the director successfully captured the intended milieu.[139]
It is strong stuff indeed: along with numerous knifings, an
attempted homosexual rape, disembowelment, throat slashing,
and a visit to a leper colony, a crocodile's belly is slit, a
man is impaled on stakes, bullets go into men's heads, and
when a man is guillotined his blood splatters on the camera.[140] None of this is treated in a gratuitous way, but
these events only add to the already somber mood of the
film. As "Murf." astutely observed in Daily Variety: "The
very underplaying of degradation actually makes it psychologically more powerful, and herein far more depressing."[141]

As was becoming a custom with Schaffner's films,
Papillon had an unusual production history. Although co-
producer, he had no idea what Dorfmann and Richmond
were doing, what was going on with the financing of the
film, or what type of arrangements had been made with the
stars; on his end, just getting the script ready was adventure enough. At this stage, most of the money for this
multi-national co-production had come from advances and
guarantees, involving all kinds of currency; Twentieth
Century-Fox France, for instance, then quite autonomous
from its American parent, contributed francs. Filming
would commence without either a distributor or most of the
money needed to cover the budget.

The film was picked up by Allied Artists, which in
1973 was virtually out of the production and distribution
business; its last film had been Cabaret (1972). At an
estimated $13 million, Papillon's budget was more than six
times Allied Artists' net worth. In a complicated deal involving Corona, Allied Artists, and Walter E. Heller Factors,
Inc. of Chicago, Heller provided Allied Artists with $7 mil-
lion, plus $2.5 million to cover budget overruns, with a
then staggering 20% interest rate. The film would have to
gross $14 million before Allied Artists was off the hook for
its $7 million. These dealings, of course, were conditional:
McQueen, for example, very definitely had to be part of
the package, and, as Schaffner says, "Steve had many misgivings about it. He was in and out, in and out, in and
out; or, if he wasn't in and out, he was threatening." In
order to appease McQueen, his salary was upped to $2 mil-
lion; with Hoffman's $1.25 million and the director's salary,
this highly publicized two stars-director combination doubled
the previously widely publicized high when John Wayne and
William Holden each received $750,000 and John Ford $500,000
to make The Horse Soldiers (1959). Adding the costs of
the property and script, plus two clever Paris-based producers, Papillon's above-the-line figures represented quite
a sizable amount of money.[142] It was a hazardous situation;
things could all too easily get out of control once principal
photography began.

There was one final condition: Papillon had to be
delivered to the theatres for a Christmas 1973 release, meaning that filming had to begin immediately, whether the script
was ready or not. Schaffner has described the circumstances:

> We started shooting late February of 1973 with about
> 60 pages of script. That, on the surface of it,
> would appear to be madness, but either we pro-
> ceeded, or the financing would be jeopardized,
> morale among the crew was hitting a questionable
> plateau, and after all the months I had been on
> the project, it seemed the wisest course of action
> was to sink or swim.[143]

What resulted were a couple of unlikely events in motion
picture production: first, the writer, in this case Dalton
Trumbo, accompanied the production on location to keep the
script ahead of the filming; second, the picture, perforce,
would virtually be shot in sequence.

Finding locations for the film was a difficult task.
The actual French Guiana locations had gone to ruin and
could not be used; Guatemala, Honduras, the Grand Cayman Islands, and Barbados were all scouted and considered.
Needed were a jungle and surface area to house the crew;
more importantly, the company had to be situated in a politically and economically stable country. Jamaica was finally selected because the company could get what was
needed and get out without becoming embroiled in any
socio-political problems. Devil's Island being off-limits,
Schaffner shot the footage of the nearby St. Joseph and
Royale, which Albert Whitlock later matted with Jamaican
locations.

The crew was a combination of American, British,
and Spanish. Fred J. Koenekamp had been so anxious to
work with Schaffner again that he took a cut in salary to
do the film. As the plot covered an eleven-year time span,
the proper creation of the make-up design for the two
stars was crucial to the film's success; although William
Tuttle, Allan Snyder, Robert N. Norin, and Monte West-
more also worked on make-up, Charles H. Schram received
sole screen credit and the praise of the critics. Schaffner
unsuccessfully sought John Box to be the production designer; he was lucky to get Anthony Masters, the talented
designer of 2001 (1968), who not only provided models of
prisons but constructed the St. Laurent prison from scratch
on a football field. The stunt people were Spanish, as was
the assistant director, the loyal and efficient Pepe Lopez,
working on his third consecutive Schaffner film, this time

Filming <u>Papillon</u>, 1973:   Steve McQueen (center), flanked by
Dustin Hoffman and Franklin J. Schaffner.

with his brother Juan as another A.D.   Added to the crew
would be their Jamaican counterparts.

The first location was in Spain, where the first problem already awaited the company: the Spanish crew had not
been paid for the work it had done; Schaffner waited for
five days, refusing to leave America until everyone had
been paid.   Dorfmann replied that they were being paid,
but such was apparently not the case when the director
arrived to film the opening sequence.   The company spent
a month in Spain; actual filming took up one week's worth
of time.

The finished film opens with a telephoto shot of
marching feet, belonging to the guards at Saint-Martin-De-
Re prison.   The crusty commandant, portrayed by Dalton
Trumbo, instructs the naked prisoners to forget France and
then tells them to put on their clothes, preparing the viewer
for the cruelty and inhumanity that is to follow.   Papillon

and Dega are given their visual introductions in the prisoners' march through town to the port, where they are to
board La Martinière which will take them to French Guiana.

The boat to double as La Martinière was chartered in
the Caribbean; in Jamaica, the company would be headquartered at Falmouth and shoot interiors at a studio in Montego
Bay. Once again, there was a crew waiting to be paid, including the director of photography. "I went five weeks
without a paycheck," says Fred Koenekamp, "which is very
unusual for a movie." Both Schaffner and McQueen refused
to work until the crews and vendors were paid; they waited
for more than a week. It was in this sort of atmosphere
that Papillon was filmed.

The atmosphere gradually loosened up--soon there
were weekly parties given by the big names before and behind the cameras. But, supervising the picture, executive
producer Ted Richmond was also on hand, maintaining a
proper degree of friction and tension. Ironically, as one of
the prisoners' task at St. Laurent is to chase butterflies--
the blue Morphous from whose wings come the dye used in
American currency--Papillon uses the butterfly hunt as an
opportunity to bribe the Trader and buy a boat for his
first escape; in an appropriate image, one shot of the butterfly chase shows a snake in clear focus positioned in the
foreground. For this sequence, 2500 blue Morphous butterflies were brought in from South America. "Not one of them
survived," the director comments. Neither butterflies nor
anything else were free.

Throughout it all, Dalton Trumbo was in Jamaica trying to keep ten pages ahead of the production. There is
an interesting parallel to Trumbo in the film: during his
first stay in solitary, Papillon, who is sustained by the
coconut strips Dega smuggles in, refuses to name names
when discovered; put on half rations and shut off from
sunlight, Papillon emerges from two years of solitary,
evidently proud of the fact he did not talk. Although this
particular bit of plotting comes from Charrière, one can almost sense the satisfaction Trumbo must have felt in writing the scene; it is only fitting that Trumbo, a survivor of
the blacklist and one of the Hollywood Ten who did not name
names, would write the screenplay about this survivor of
Devil's Island. Papillon would be his last film experience.

In Bruce Cook's biography of Dalton Trumbo, Schaffner recounts his working method with the writer, typically
arising at 4:00 a.m. to begin the day's work:

> This meant, among other things, sitting down with
> Dalton for an hour around five-thirty or six and
> giving a last look with him at the pages to be shot
> that day. Then when shooting was finished, I'd go
> back to the hotel and sometime that evening go over
> what Dalton had written during the day. Depending
> on how many things there were to be dealt with, it
> might be pretty late at night before the meeting
> could actually take place.... And of course we put
> in considerable time every Sunday. [144]

This arrangement continued until it came to tackling the
Guajira Indian village sequence, which, because of the
problems it presented, had been postponed until the end of
the shooting schedule. Writer and director had yet to come
up with the proper conceptualization that would fit the rest
of the film. "It was an awkward inclusion in the movie because it was one sequence which every macho male remembers out of the book--go among the heathens ... and fuck
your way to glory, and you're fed at the same time," Schaffner says. "Grand!" As Papillon cannot speak the native
language and the Indians cannot speak French (or English)
in the book, Charrière conveniently added a character by
the name of Zorillo, an Albino trader, to interpret for both
sides. This would not work in the film; neither would sign
language. Trumbo was as good and as fast a screenwriter
as there was in Hollywood but, before the problem could be
solved, he became ill and had to return to the United
States where x-rays showed he had cancer in the left lung;
he could not continue on in Jamaica.

At this point in production, there was a Writers Guild
strike in America. When they heard what had happened to
Trumbo, several well-known writers, regardless of the
strike, circumspectly offered their services. Trumbo had
another idea in mind: he asked if his son could take over
for him. Schaffner agreed; Christopher Trumbo, without
taking a credit himself, would protect his father's credit,
polish up a couple of scenes, and resolve the Guajira village sequence.

The sequence comes during the second escape attempt
in the film. Energized by coca leaves, Papillon is running
through the jungle when he is hit by poison darts; a high-
speed camera follows him as he runs down the hill and falls
into a river in slow motion. As used in the dream scenes
of the solitary sequence, the slow motion device might well
suggest a fantasy of Papillon's; what follows is much like a
hallucination. There is no dialogue when Papillon awakes;
everything is just perfect and beautiful, a combination of
Walt Disney's Fantasyland and Adventureland. As he has
stumbled into paradise, there is no reason why Papillon
would want to leave, the book's revenge motif notwithstanding; rather than Papillon leaving the village, the village
leaves him in the film. At the end of this pastoral inter-
lude, Papillon is left with a bonus--a bag of pearls.

In the Goldman script, Papillon's stay in solitary
comes near the end, after the third of his escape attempts,
severely impeding the forward motion of Goldman's script;
as there are 20 pages of solitary in his script, it takes a
while before the story can regain its momentum. That
problem was alleviated by moving the sequence up in the
film, after the first escape, which made better dramatic
sense.

The solitary row of the St. Joseph's penitentiary set
was constructed on a soundstage. There are barred ceil-
ings over each cell; guards wear slippers as they pass by
overhead. Papillon is led to his cell to find only a bunk,
mug, spoon, bowl, bucket, and pail for his feces. Measur-
ing the cell, he finds it is five steps wide; Anthony Masters' design makes the cell seem at least a century old, and
humid with its wet-looking walls and mossy green slime.
The first meal Papillon receives contains a dead beetle; as
time goes by, he will welcome any and all additional food.
Time is measured by the occasions when the prisoners get
haircuts, in which a veteran of solitary will ask, "How do
I look?" Papillon cannot supply an honest answer; although
he does push-ups to keep in shape, he grows weaker, sees
a vampire bat in his cell, and, in time, finds himself asking
the same question. Curling up into the fetal position, he
has dream number one: on trial in a Daliesque landscape
of sand and dunes, he is found guilty of the most terrible
crime a human being can commit--a wasted life; the penalty
is death.

When Papillon is put on half rations, a screen is put
over the cell's ceiling, cutting off the light; a thin sliver
of light trickles in to motivate the lighting inside the cell.
Continuing his descent into madness and physical deteriora-
tion, Papillon loses a tooth; a subjective camera blurs. In
a second dream, he and Dega return as heroes to Saint-
Martin-De-Re, riding in an open car: catching sight of his
former fellow convicts Julot (Don Gordon) and Lariot (Bill
Mumy), he runs to them in slow motion, the camera revolves
in a 360-degree angle, and, when he catches up, he finds
they are wearing death masks. Somehow Papillon manages
to survive in solitary, crying out his catch phrase: "Hey,
you bastards, I'm still here."

By nature, the experience of solitary is claustrophobic, which might seem at odds with the aspect ratio of the
Panavision lens; this anomaly is not at all evident in a viewing of the film.   What is evident is Steve McQueen's performance: the sequence offers some of his finest moments
in the film as Papillon tries to maintain his discipline and
sanity, momentarily cracking.   Helped cosmetically with his
teeth and hair, McQueen also changed his gait and voice.
Particularly effective is the use of his eyes: the more haggard he gets the wider his eyes become, giving him a gaunt
and demented look.

So grueling is the solitary sequence that it sets up an
interesting but dreaded expectation when Papillon is sent to
solitary the second time: the audience anticipates yet another long and perhaps even more enervating montage.   The
director subverts that expectation, much to the audience's
relief, by making a couple of straight cuts to St. Joseph
Island vistas, after which Papillon emerges from solitary--
with white hair, wrinkled skin, and lashless eyelids. He is
greeted by the sight of a friend's mutilated body before it
is thrown to the sharks.   Papillon pays his last respects in
a shot encapsulating the solitary experience on the outside:
a thin expanse of sky at the top of the frame melds into
the ocean; a pier extends three-fourths of the way to the
top of the frame; at the head of the pier is the lonely figure of Papillon.

Sophisticated and aloof, Louis Dega, the mastermind
of the counterfeit National Defense Bonds, Series 1928, has
nothing in common with Papillon, an ordinary street criminal.

Schaffner and Dustin Hoffman, filming <u>Papillon</u>, 1973.

Hoffman begins with an unusually eccentric and supercilious
approach to the role; his chief prop is his glasses. In
their symbiotic relationship, Papillon needs money for his
escape plans; the cowardly Dega needs protection. Nearly
total opposites, they make an interesting physical contrast,
one light and the other dark. Ultimately, there is something oddly touching about these two men who, if not for
fate and prison, would never have had anything to do with
each other.

        Their first assignment together at St. Laurent is to
retrieve a crocodile that the guards have shot, only to find
it is still alive. For this scene, the crocodile was fastened
down, its mouth wired, and the director instructed his
stars to ad lib; for the stars' personalities and the action,
the results threaten to become a Laurel and Hardy routine.
Unwilling to participate in any escape, Dega serves refresh-
ments to the ladies and gentlemen gathered on the night of
a band concert, the night Papillon has chosen for his second escape. While the guests listen to the music of a French
tune, Papillon, in a deft directorial touch, hits a guard to
the beat of the song, to drum and cymbals; the music enter-
tains the people there, punctuates the action, and enhances
the drama. In order to help the others, Dega attacks another guard, inadvertently committing himself to the escape;
scaling the wall, he breaks his ankle. On their way to
Honduras, the boat's mast falls on Dega's leg, gangrene
sets in, and once more Papillon sacrifices his freedom to
save Dega's life.

        Because the film was shot in continuity, both McQueen
and Hoffman were obliged to be available throughout the
course of the film's production. In spite of the volatile
combination of two actors with such different backgrounds
and styles, both with reputations for being highly temperamental, and despite the rampant rumors, Schaffner insists
they were not difficult:

        Obviously Steve McQueen was the superstar in
        films. Dustin Hoffman was a star as an actor, if I
        can make that distinction. And they looked
        forward to performing with the other. The fact
        that they fell apart was over enormously petty is-
        sues, but it never affected their own professional
        sense on the set.

Although he had equivocated before finally accepting the role, McQueen was fully committed to Papillon once shooting began. He and Schaffner would meet a couple of times during the week to discuss both the script and the pages McQueen had rewritten; McQueen would eventually agree to follow the script that Dalton Trumbo was presently writing. For scenes involving both stars, Schaffner followed one general method:

> I would always shoot on McQueen first to make him commit and then turn around and shoot on Hoffman. It seemed to work better that way because if I covered Hoffman first, Steve would become restless about what he was doing. The quicker you got him comfortable, the better the scene would play. Hoffman, on the other hand, is a totally electric performer. He comes in with ninety-nine ideas of how to approach a scene. And you're prepared to say, "Hey, look--here in my view is the approach." Usually he'd say, "Okay, let's go right away."

In the final analysis, Louis Dega is essentially a supporting role; the name of the film remains Papillon, not Papillon and Dega. Dega gave Hoffman an opportunity for total characterization, which the director suspects made it rewarding to the actor; the film also gave Hoffman a solid screen presence to work against, giving him the security to immerse himself into the characterization.

Worthington Miner gave an accurate assessment of the director's work with the two stars:

> I thought he did a remarkable job with Steve McQueen and Dustin Hoffman. It was a very tough pair to handle and make you feel that they could have a genuine camaraderie. There was every difference in the world between those two. I thought Frank handled that with extraordinary sensitivity as far as a director's effect on actors is concerned. If he had been weak ... those two could have been at sword's point and the picture would have been critically hurt.

As for the two stars' performances, Andrew Sarris would write in the Village Voice:

What I had not counted on at all was that Steve
McQueen and Dustin Hoffman would be worth every
penny ... doled out to them.... McQueen, the
movies' great mythic exemplar of the escape
syndrome ever since "The Great Escape," here
dwindles and soars from the conventional action
hero to an absurdist Robinson Crusoe trapped in
the settings for "The Count of Monte Cristo." And
Hoffman, less Friday than Sancho Panza caught in
"Endgame," demonstrates once more a flair for comic
characterization. [145]

It is fair to say that each actor's presence on the island of
Jamaica was a stimulus to the other, especially in the case
of the one playing the title role, who, given this type of
competition and direction, was pushed into doing the hardest work of his film career.

Wrapping up in Jamaica a week ahead of schedule,
Schaffner returned to California to begin post-production at
the Goldwyn Studios. Also returning from the location was
Robert E. Swink, whose work and company on The Best Man
had not been forgotten; the editor had the unenviable job
of trying to get the film in shape for its December deadline.
Adding to the complications, there was still a crucial scene
remaining to be filmed--Papillon's climactic leap into the
ocean. There had been no cliff of any suitable height in
Jamaica to accommodate the story's drama--in point of fact,
no cliff on the actual Devil's Island site is even remotely
impressive--so it was up to art director Robert Boyle, ex-
pressly hired for this purpose, to find an appropriately
imposing site.

A comprehensive search in northern California yielded
no results. Time was running out when the solution to the
problem came in the person of Dar Robinson, the stunt man
hired to make the leap: he swore to disbelieving ears that
he remembered a serviceable cliff in Hawaii, on the island
of Maui. At the beginning of October, five days before he
was scheduled to be in Rome, Schaffner ventured to Maui
with Robinson, Fred Koenekamp, and a unit including a
double for Dustin Hoffman. Bad weather prevented any
filming on the first day; the winds moved in the wrong direction on the second; the leap was filmed on the third day
under less than ideal circumstances.

Schaffner immediately flew to Italy, joining Jerry Goldsmith who was recording the score. A film shot outside of the United States is not constrained to be scored in America (Goldsmith estimates he scores 75% of his films overseas because it's half as expensive), and Dorfmann had chosen Rome. When the composer had first received the assignment, Schaffner requested a Montmartre-like theme for the film, an idea Goldsmith strongly opposed. The theme, however, kept evolving as he wrote, until he reached the end with only two men and the unhurried lifestyle on Devil's Island. "Everything is peeled away," Goldsmith says. "The music starts very complex at the beginning of the picture and it gradually goes through a metamorphosis where it becomes simple at the end of the picture. And basically it becomes this simple little tune." In other words, it became the Montmartre-like tune Schaffner had suggested. The composer also recalls an incident during the recording session for the convicts' march in Saint-Martin-De-Re, the prisoners' last connection with the civilized world:

> Frank came over and made one of the dumbest suggestions I've ever heard. He said, "At that point there, why don't you have the accordian play the tune." "What do you mean, Frank?" "Over the orchestra." "That's going to sound terrible," I said, "the piece is atonal, there's no key sound." "I think it'd sound great." I said, "Frank, my name goes on this." "Try it." I tried it. Well, it works sensationally.... I learned after that that he was usually pretty right in what he wanted and what he was thinking. If you can decipher what he's thinking, it works great.

Robert Swink called Rome as soon as he saw the footage to describe Dar Robinson's jump: the man's figure was so tiny, he told Schaffner, he didn't think it would work. The actual jump took two seconds, ten seconds in slow motion; Schaffner informed Goldsmith that the cue for the jump had to have a variable in it between two to ten seconds. Consequently, without either director or composer having seen the filmed jump, the shot worked out very well for the film.

At the start of Papillon's history, when production looked iffy at best, nobody had worried or quarreled about credits; no one was concerned. But as the film was being readied for release, when it looked as though it might have a chance at success, everybody involved in the production suddenly came out demanding credit, larger credits; the list became longer and longer, larger and larger. "Pissed off with everybody's greed," Schaffner says, he placed the stars' names and the film's title in the opening credits, putting all the rest of the names in the end credits. He then returned to work with Swink on the more urgent matter of final editing.

Rushed though it might have been, Papillon was ready by Christmas of 1973, the year of The Exorcist, The Sting, American Grafitti, and The Way We Were. Schaffner was once again responsible for the biggest picture of the year: despite the misgivings some had had about Papillon's box-office potential, it grossed over $3 million in its first week, a record for Allied Artists. The Walter E. Heller money was soon paid back and Allied Artists went into profits in six weeks. The $13 million gamble paid off--and Schaffner had been able to do it his way.

Stuart Byron, the film's chief defender, wrote in The Real Paper:

> It's a big-budget epic that doesn't compromise; it's gloom and doom on such a large scale that it becomes the cinematic equivalent of a Wagner opera or a Zola novel.... To anyone familiar with how softness commonly goes along with Hollywood bigness, the daring of "Papillon" is breathtaking.... Schaffner has made his most personal film, a moving and powerful testament to the life force. [146]

The film displays an individual's will to survive: Papillon is either going to escape or die trying. In the life and death struggle, he gains control over himself and his environment, thereby controlling his own fate.

Typically, Schaffner employs a three-part structure in Papillon, but one composed of divergent moods. The first part--taking Papillon to French Guiana, through his first escape and first term in solitary--is very realistic indeed. The second part--his escape from the hospital on St. Laurent, the Guajira village, the betrayal by the nun--

constitutes a romantic odyssey in which Papillon is larger
than life. The third part, the last 20 minutes, is, in its
director's words: "a bizarre glissade."[147]

The final section begins when Papillon, prematurely
aged, emerges from the five-year term of his second stay
in solitary and is sent to Devil's Island--the Riviera among
penal colonies, where prisoners are free to do as they like,
the sharks and tides making escape impossible. A nobody
among nobodies, he soon spies a familiar face, a face which
has in fact been covertly staring at him: Dega now has a
beard, mustache, and a rather prominent bald spot on his
head. His wife having married his attorney, Dega, like
Candide, is content to live out the rest of his life tending
his garden. He sees ghosts, his only companions are his
pigs; spiritually, Dega is an old man. After all this time,
they--each in his own form of dotage--are the only survivors. Papillon still has the will but not the means to escape; Dega has neither will nor means. McQueen and Hoffman's last moment on screen together comes as Papillon,
preparing for his absurd leap to catch the seventh wave,
turns to embrace and say farewell to Dega. What is noteworthy about it is that McQueen dominates the screen, not
by his superstar presence, which is hidden in make-up,
but by his acting.

Surprisingly and perhaps perversely, both McQueen
and the film received rave reviews from French critics. Inasmuch as Schaffner had coaxed the finest performance of
Steve McQueen's career, it is all the more unfortunate that
the actor passed away at the age of 50 in 1980: the director had a fine working relationship with him; their collaboration could have resulted in several more memorable films.
A superstar's participation enabling a director to obtain financing for a project, McQueen would have provided the
same function for Schaffner that John Wayne provided for
John Ford or Howard Hawks. But, for the moment, they
ended on a note of triumph.

Papillon floats away from Devil's Island on a raft made
of coconut shells in, as Charrière described it, "the final
most idiotic and successful attempt."[148] "Hey, you bastards," he announces to the world, "I'm still here." Over
a helicopter shot of Papillon's minuscule figure out alone in
the ocean, a narrator's voice informs the viewer that

Papillon made it to freedom and lived a free life, Papillon
survived: the voice belongs to the director of the film,
who survived as well. End credits are superimposed over
selected shots of the penal colony, shut down in 1936,
taken at St. Joseph and Royale: the footage of the decay
suggests that, even though the system may destroy men,
the system finally destroys itself; Papillon outlasted the
system.

"'Papillon' is a film as emotionally draining as one by
Bergman or Antonioni," Stuart Byron observed. [149] For all
the unexpected heaviness in an American film, "Schaffner,"
Andrew Sarris added, "has really made an exhilarating movie
out of the most dangerously depressing material." [150] Prais-
ing the emotional commitment and power of the film, Alan R.
Howard concluded his Hollywood Reporter review with a remark as sweeping as the film itself:

> Visually, "Papillon" cannot be faulted, and with it
> Schaffner joins the ranks of screen imagists who
> have turned the resources of epic filmmaking to
> their own private concerns, like DeMille, Griffith
> and Von Stroheim. [151]

Papillon is Franklin J. Schaffner's tour de force.

Dynasty of Western Outlaws

Papillon was released in December 1973; Islands in the
Stream began shooting in October 1975. Schaffner spent
a long time between pictures hunting for the right material,
but the interval was not without activity or event. Towards
the end of 1972, Creative Management Associates (CMA)--
which had put together The Directors Company (not to be
confused with Schaffner and Cook's Directors Company)
at Paramount for Francis Ford Coppola, Peter Bogdanovich,
and William Friedkin--tried to form The United Directors
Company. To be comprised of six major directors, the company was intended to be the directors' equivalent of First
Artists, which was made up of such stars as Paul Newman,
Sidney Poitier, Barbra Streisand, Dustin Hoffman, and Steve
McQueen. As a CMA client, Schaffner would have been one
of the six, also including Arthur Penn and George Roy Hill;
the other three were yet to be announced. In view of what

happened to First Artists and The Directors Company, it is just as well that The United Directors Company never did eventuate.

During this time, Joseph T. Naar of CMA, who had been involved in the negotiation of Patton and later would produce Starsky and Hutch for ABC Television, brought a project named Dynasty of Western Outlaws, based on the book by Paul Wellman, to Schaffner's attention. Franklin J. Schaffner has always wanted to do a western: with his reputation for films featuring strong male action, he and the western genre would seem like a felicitous combination; it's surprising that a director with such a fine eye for filming wide-screen exteriors should never have made a western.

Dynasty of Western Outlaws was actually envisioned as more than a western--it would give evidence on the big screen that when the cowboy outlaw died he went to the city and became a gangster. "It is a fascinating idea," says Schaffner, "this 70 years of bloodline." Centered in the 300-mile radius around Kansas City, the story began with Jesse James and ended with Al Spencer, Pretty Boy Floyd's partner, at the Union Station in Chicago. The film would trace the family lineage--the bond among these American folk heroes, cowboy or gangster.

A home for the project was found at Columbia, where John Gay was brought in to write a couple of drafts of the script. The concept was to have three actors--two males and one female, probably unknowns--play the three major parts in each generation of outlaws; Lee Marvin was sought for a guest role. After the team had spent much time and energy preparing it in 1973-1974, Columbia president Stanley Schneider cancelled the project. It was not viable, he insisted, things were bound to go wrong. Years later, Jennings Lang of Universal considered the project for a television miniseries; nothing came of that either. Since then, as for Schaffner's desire to film a western, the genre has virtually disappeared from sight.

That Championship Season

If not a western, Schaffner, having directed four large pictures in a row, was looking for something intimate. A

project like <u>That Championship Season</u> seemed like a tonic
to him--a small film to be shot in the 1:85 aspect ratio.
William McCutchen owned the rights to Jason Miller's Pulitzer Prize-winning play and had made a development deal
with Columbia in 1974.

Schaffner joined him and spent the next six months
working on the script with Miller, going through draft after draft. According to the terms of the deal with the
studio, the ground rules were that the below-the-line budget could not exceed a million dollars; the actors would be
required to give two weeks free for rehearsal as well as
another week at the end should the production run over
schedule.

Schaffner sent letters to James Cagney and George C.
Scott asking them if they would consider playing the role of
the coach. [152] Although the film adaptation would still be
mostly composed of interiors, there would be a flashback,
of sorts, to the basketball game, set in the living room,
with life-size cutouts of the boys/men as they were in their
prime. Most problematic to the director was the third act:
in the play, the team gathers around the coach to listen to
a recording of their one moment of triumph; there is a momentary reconciliation as they pose for a group photograph.
Accentuating the coach's bitterness, the director would have
had him, recognizing his protégés as failures, walk out on
the team. Schaffner never did get around to persuading
Miller to make this change; by then, the project was cancelled.

Studio president David Begelman was enthusiastic
about <u>That Championship Season</u>, but Columbia's below-the-
line estimate was $200,000, more than Schaffner's. The di-
rector proceeded to make budgetary accommodations to suit
the studio. "I never was able to get them to hit the million," he says. "I could always hit the million, but they
couldn't." The reason became perfectly obvious: the budget estimators had received specific instructions; on the
grounds that the film would do no business overseas, Alan
Hirschfield, the company president, had vetoed Begelman's
go-ahead. "I think at that time, with that concept," Schaffner says, "it would've made a helluva small picture."

Islands in the Stream

Schaffner was deeply committed to making a motion picture
about an emotional adventure. Searching for an adult love
story, he was also thinking about an allegory along the
lines of The Man Without a Country. In Islands in the
Stream, Schaffner discovered his love story and a man without a country allegory. Although it would turn out to be
as physically taxing as his previous films, on paper it was
not the stuff of a screen epic but a more modestly sized
production. An added attraction was that it was based
on a work by his favorite writer, Ernest Hemingway.

Islands in the Stream, published posthumously by
Mary Hemingway in 1970, came from Hemingway's epic "Land,
Sea, and Air Novel" about the Second World War; though
not about war, The Old Man and the Sea was probably intended to be the coda for the larger book. By itself, Islands in the Stream is frequently patchy and embarrassing,
yet parts of it are excellent, containing prose as fine as
the author ever wrote. Importantly, Hemingway had expanded on his hero type: heretofore, the Hemingway hero
would go to his room alone before lifting his mask to cry;
in this book, the Hemingway hero, Thomas Hudson, an artist like the 19th-century Thomas Hudson, will lift the mask
and cry in front of others. Reminiscent of Colonel Cantwell
in Hemingway's Across the River and into the Trees, Hudson is a product of his pain. Tired, no longer enjoying
life, he still lives by the code: "Get it straight. Your
boy you lose. Love you lose. Honor has been gone for
a long time. Duty you do."[153] Thomas Hudson's journey
is a search for moral growth.

Denne Bart Petticlerc was a former newspaperman
who had learned to write by copying Hemingway's works
in longhand. As a reporter for the Miami Herald in the
1950s, he had come to know his hero. Because of his close
relationship with Mary Hemingway, he had in effect a free
option on Islands in the Stream; his first draft of the screenplay closely followed the book. His agent, Mike Medavoy,
submitted the script to another former newspaperman, Peter
Bart.

As a reporter for The New York Times, Peter Bart
came to Hollywood in 1967 hoping to write a book not unlike

The Studio--but from an insider's point of view--and ended
up as Robert Evans' assistant at Paramount; by 1972, he
was vice-president of production at the studio. Given a
producing contract with Paramount in 1973, he joined forces
with Max Palevsky to form Bart/Palevsky Productions.
Former philosophy professor Max Palevsky had founded
Scientific Data, which, when it merged with Xerox in 1969,
made him the largest Xerox shareholder in 1970. Always a
film buff, Palevsky was briefly associated with Donald Rug-
off in Cinema 10 before approaching Bart with the idea of
financing a production company.

Bart/Palevsky acquired the film rights to Islands in
the Stream in 1974. As Petticlerc's script was 240 pages
long, Bart immediately sat down with the writer to work
on another draft. First choice to direct the film, as Bart
explains, was Franklin J. Schaffner:

> I just thought he'd be wonderful. He is absolutely
> a loveable man. He's the only director I've ever

Mary Hemingway and Schaffner during filming of Islands
in the Stream, 1975.

worked with who I have genuine affection for as a
person; I just think he's a wonderful man. I think
most directors are--if you turn over a rock, you'll
find them crawling out from underneath.

Schaffner came aboard as the third of what would be eight
drafts of the script was written.

    With only Schaffner and the script for a package,
Islands in the Stream would be a hard sell; it needed a star.
At the outset, in the back of Bart's mind was the notion of
reteaming Franklin J. Schaffner and George C. Scott; the
reality was that it would be hard to get the film off the
ground with Scott. The producers instead went after the
most bankable name, Steve McQueen, who was more than
acceptable to Paramount, even though Robert Evans was
still studio boss. [154]

    McQueen, attracted by the idea of working with sons
in a film, something very close to him in his personal life
at the time, spent a couple of months working on the script
with Schaffner, Bart, and Petticlerc without really committing himself to the project. It was his idea, for instance,
that the two younger sons should not be killed off in a car
accident; neither he nor Schaffner liked Hemingway's plot
device of Hudson going after the German U-boat's Kapitan
Kehl, who it turns out is slightly older than his son Tommy.
The necessary changes were made.

    Like the novel, the screenplay followed a three-part
format. The book's three sections are entitled: (1) Bimini;
(2) Cuba; (3) At Sea. At the time of its release, studio
president David Picker, for better or worse, titled the film's
three sections: (1) The Boys; (2) The Woman; (3) The
Journey. The novel's "Bimini" actually constitutes the first
half of the film, Cuba was entirely eliminated as a setting,
and "The Journey" was admittedly lifted from To Have and
Have Not. "We struggled for a long time to change that
so-called third act," Schaffner says. "We came up with the
concept that was in the picture that I'm not about to say
works, but it was the best that we could do." This meant
that Hudson, who in Petticlerc's first draft not only sur-
vives but is also rejoined in the end by his first wife, would
have a very different fate in store for him.

The role of Thomas Hudson would have shown a new
side of McQueen, a vulnerable side, as a man with dramatic
conflicts with his three sons, his ex-wife, and himself. For
whatever reason, McQueen inexplicably felt the role was not
right for him. "When he finally withdrew," Bart recalls,
"he said, 'You know, I think you need a better actor than
me.' "[155] Another logical choice was Paul Newman, another
superstar with whom there would be no problem getting financing; Newman, however, didn't think he was right for
the part, instead recommending George C. Scott. Third
but actually first choice, Scott was unavailable when the
offer was made. Then, in another unusual and daring bit
of casting, the script was submitted to John Wayne, an unlikely but, as Schaffner suspects, excellent choice:

> I'm convinced there could have been an absolutely
> fascinating performance by Wayne. At least I was
> vain enough to believe that I could've gotten it
> from him or that he would've brought an entirely
> different mode than what he had always been fa-
> mous for.

Wayne, albeit a mite old, had the requisite toughness and
tenderness, plus the power, to make the story work; the
script, unfortunately, was not to his tastes.

The producers returned to Scott; the problem was
that the actor had retired. According to the story Peter
Bart told in 1977: "Schaffner said, 'Let's send him the
script. If he reads it, he'll unretire.' Scott read it and
sent back his reply: 'Don't change a word. When do we
start?' "[156] Scott probably also took on the role to offset
the debts he had incurred producing, directing, and distributing The Savage Is Loose (1974); the script he accepted was the same one that had been tailored for McQueen.

"Steve was always a difficult man to trap into a project," Schaffner comments. "I'm sorry he didn't make it.
He would have been marvelously interesting." George C.
Scott is a superb actor and bears an uncanny likeness to
Papa Hemingway in the film, but he isn't really a Hemingway hero: as an actor, his style is too verbal, too eloquent. Being the even more extreme Hammett hero type,
McQueen is a Hemingway hero: his screen persona matches
the Hemingway code. The difference between Scott and

Schaffner and George C. Scott enjoy a break during location filming of Islands in the Stream, 1975.

McQueen is tantamount to the difference it would have made had Spencer Tracy instead of Humphrey Bogart played Harry Morgan in Howard Hawks' 1945 production of To Have and Have Not.

"[McQueen] would've been wonderful for the picture," Bart concurs, but from another standpoint. "Scott was not wonderful for the picture, although he gave a wonderful performance. Young people, I don't think, like George C. Scott. They see him as a stern, off-putting authoritarian figure.... He does not play to young people, he just doesn't." With Scott--instead of a McQueen, Newman, or Wayne--the producers had to raise 40% of the money outside the studio, through Connaught Productions Services, a tax shelter group with which Palevsky was involved. "So essentially," Bart says, "we said to Paramount, 'Here's Scott, Schaffner, and 40% of the financing. Do you want it or not? You've got 48 hours.'" Paramount took it.

The highpoint of the novel, the electrifying moment when the book comes to life, begins in a bar when Hudson's

unnamed first wife, his true love, makes her spectacular
entrance: she is a famous actress who is entertaining the
troops for the USO; it soon becomes clear that Hudson married Marlene Dietrich. Regrettably, the Dietrich character
was removed from the script; in the film, the first wife is
named Audrey and modeled after Hadley Richardson, Hemingway's first wife. Casting this small but crucial role was
another major hurdle. On a longshot, although he knew
what the probable answer would be, Schaffner wrote to his
first choice, an ideal candidate, an actress with whom he
had worked several times in live television. He received
the following reply, "George Scott is an excellent choice
for the role of Hudson and will be very moving in the part
I am sure--I am flattered to be asked to play Audrey--
unfortunately it will not be possible and I am sorry to have
to say no."[157] The handwritten letter was signed by the
actress who had performed under the name of Grace Kelly.
In the film, it is the function of Audrey, gracefully played
by Claire Bloom, to tell Hudson their son Tommy is dead.

Another major casualty of the film was Boise, Hudson's
supernaturally intelligent and loyal cat. "Jesus Christ, you
had over 50% of the picture on water, in water, underwater,
three kids," Schaffner explains. "When Boise would come
up my standard answer would be, 'I've got water and kids,
why do I need animals?'" Neither was Roger Davis, the
failing writer, needed in the script: Hudson's own artistic
crisis would suffice; in Joseph (Julius Harris), Hudson already has a confidant in the film. The other man close to
Hudson is Eddy, a character not described in the book:
considering the location, Eddy would probably be British,
younger than Hudson.

Tom Courtenay was the first choice but, when he
proved to be unavailable, a bloated and dissipated-looking
David Hemmings was given the part. Hemmings' Eddy the
Rummy is a far cry from Walter Brennan's in To Have and
Have Not, far more realistic and pathetic. Brennan's Eddie
seems to be crazy, and, if he isn't crazy, at least a very
whimsical eccentric; Hemmings' Eddy is obviously a hope-
less alcoholic. All three parts of the film begin with the
motif of Eddy having been beaten again in a bar fight.
The Hemingway hero in both films refuses to take Eddie/
Eddy on a trip in which he will run refugees, but it is
better motivated in Islands in the Stream: his son has

died, and Hudson takes it out on the drunken Eddy; however, the film shows that Eddy is never less than professional when he is at sea. Hemmings' performance does suggest the man Eddy was before he became a rummy, the man
he was when he first became Hudson's friend.

Curiously, the location search for this picture was no
less extensive than the one for Papillon. The logical place
to shoot was Florida--within the United States, less travel--
but a search of the Keys did not result in any suitable locations. The Bahamas would have been acceptable but it was
politically too unstable; Bimini itself was too small and developed, prohibiting any shooting. Again considered were
Jamaica, the Cayman Islands, and all the little islands in
between. Associate producer Ken Wales, who had worked
there on The Tamarind Seed (1974), found a place in Barbados but a severe logistical problem soon developed.
Charles Bludhorn, the late chairman of Gulf and Western,
parent company of Paramount, suggested the Dominican Republic, where he had financial interests: promising sites
were found, production designer William J. Creber reports,
but problems arose when dealing with the people there--and
with Bludhorn, as he and Schaffner soon learned while using
the company helicopter for a location survey at a moment
when the chairman wanted it.

Schaffner was skeptical when Ken Wales suggested
Hawaii--Bimini was a coral reef island, not a volcanic island
--but, on Creber's recommendation, when he went to Kauai,
the director discovered he could fake Bimini on this the
farthest island west: one small harbor would be isolated
for the shoot; the mountains would never be shown. Since
Kauai was quite clear and clean, meaning there would be a
lot of contrast and the colors would come out brighter,
Schaffner brought Fred Koenekamp over to make tests.
Fuji stock provided the soft pastel look they were looking
for, but there was no guarantee of enough film of the same
emulsion and grouping or of lab quality; being cheaper than
Kodak, Fuji stock had been bought up for television consumption. As he had for Papillon, the director of photography would use Eastman 5254 stock and, as Schaffner did
not want to flash the film, a 1/4 fog filter to mute the color.

Discussing the visual style of the film, Bart told
American Cinematographer:

> Frank and Fred and I all agreed that there should
> be a more austere attitude toward camera movement
> than we usually adopt. They wanted very much--
> and I concurred with them--not to have the camera
> steal the show. This is really an actor's picture,
> and that attitude, I think, reflects itself in the
> way it is being photographed. [158]

Specifically, despite the wide screen and color, the director
was going after the style of the film's period: Islands in
the Stream takes place in the 1940s; the intention was to
make a 1940s type of movie, visually and editorially. The
camera would not move and the editing would be functional
--all the more to accentuate star acting.

The photographs he had taken on the location search
provided Creber with the basis for creating an entire town
in the colorful Caribbean style. "Every stick, every piece
of architecture in the film was put there," he says of the
Kauai location. Hudson's house was built on a low cliff of
a private beachfront owned by the C & H Sugar Company.
"The whole idea of the house was to have it appear to be a
place that grew from a single room," says the production
designer. "We even built it that way." Posts were sawed
so that the roof would sag, the porch was added on, roads
were cut, and a garden created. Schaffner would keep the
camera away from the mountains behind the house; a matte
took the mountains out in the film's only reverse angle of
the house.

For ambience, the director wanted to have a sense of
the exterior no matter where the scene was set: this meant
that the ocean should be present in the frame, even in interiors. This would normally be accomplished through rear
projection, but it was one of those private challenges Schaffner looked forward to handling. Koenekamp had to balance
interior, ocean, and sky; using quarter-inch gels and an
85 correction filter, the cinematographer shot the interior/
exterior evening scenes day for night because, as Schaffner
likes to point out, "You can't light the Pacific Ocean." The
weather was already hot, and, with the brutes, the biggest
light source, the heat was unbearable. "Scott--he hated
it," Koenekamp recalls. "'What are you trying to do to me?'
he'd say." But with the ocean that could be seen through
the windows, with the illusion of moonlight, it was worth it.

Creber's ingenuity is also evident in the final sequence
of the first part of the film: Davy and Andrew have gone
to their New England school; Tommy has joined the RAF in
Canada. In their respective locations, the boys read a letter from their father, who writes: "You moved into a part
of me that, when you moved out, became empty and it has
been bad a long time." Not only was the dorm scene shot
locally, the Canadian airfield was also recreated in Hawaii:
Tommy enters the barracks in the foreground; in the background are life-size cutouts of British Spitfires, complete
with pilots faking the climb into the cockpit.

Schaffner found it pleasant and productive working
with Bart/Palevsky and Petticlerc.[159] Peter Bart had a
good script sense and Max Palevsky had aptitude; both
were strong on casting. Palevsky, however, had had no
practical film experience and was far from being a veteran
line producer; despite his years as a production executive,
Bart also lacked experience as a line producer. Ken Wales,
the associate producer, would have to take care of the actual nuts-and-bolts work. Unfortunately, Palevsky was
continuously ill during the production, hospitalized for hep-
atitis and a second heart-bypass; Bart had to leave Hawaii
before filming was completed to take care of business on
their next production, Fun with Dick and Jane (1977).

Massive changes had been made in the meantime back
at the studio: Barry Diller had been brought in as Paramount's chairman, a move that prompted Frank Yablans'
resignation as studio president. Robert Evans had left in
April 1975 to be replaced by the team of Robin French and
Richard Sylbert as heads of production. Under Evans, the
budget had been set at $6 million, but by September, when
filming began in Kauai under the new administration, an additional $3 million had to be added to the budget to cover
the problems on land, sea, and air. All things considered,
the sea being so unpredictable, it was a relatively low sum
compared with the overages of two 1975 films, Jaws and
Lucky Lady, whose problems on the water were carefully
studied.

Like Schaffner, Koenekamp had been in the Navy and
recalled that landing forces had used steel pontoon floats.
On the basis of Koenekamp's idea, Creber designed a unique
rig that was put together by construction man Don Nobles:

the boat was mounted in a cradle welded to 10' by 20' mod-
ules over which was placed a platform to carry director,
cameras, cast, and crew. An old Navy ammunition carrier
was rented to tow the boat and its accessories out into the
open sea. A Tyler-gyro mount was used for the water work;
sometimes the mount itself would be mounted onto a Chapman boom on the mother ship. Two boats were purchased
for the Tortuga--Hudson's boat, modeled along the lines of
the Pilar, Hemingway's boat--one to be put in the sling of
the rig and the other to be free for shots of the Tortuga
at sea. Fortunately, there was no need for a mock-up; at
36 feet, the Tortuga was large enough to accommodate interior shooting.

Schaffner and Creber worked out the chase sequence
for the final part of the film. "We designed a hypothetical
river," Creber said, "and fit all [Schaffner's] action elements into it, stringing them out so that you could actually
follow the chase through our map."[160] The Wailua River
proved to be serviceable for their purposes; the company
opened up channels and, at one point, blocked the entire
mouth of the river. Because of the constant rain--it rained
from Thanksgiving on--Schaffner had to keep his eyes on
the reeds so that he would know when to get out.

The ocean itself, Schaffner acknowledges, made preparation much more complicated:

> Working on the water is just, I think, the toughest
> experience of all. The result of which we were
> carrying two cameras all the way through, double
> cameraed all the way through. Sometimes we tripled
> cameraed, but always when we went out we double
> cameraed or we simply would not have gotten the
> work done. Just too difficult to set up, too diffi-
> cult to light. Endless days out there.

Then there was the unpredictable weather. Sometimes, if
the director heard that swells were coming up, he could
make a last-minute change and shoot something else; other
times, the company would just get caught in a swell. "The
moral to the story is that whenever waterwork is scheduled,"
Ken Wales stated, "a very large contingency in the budget
should be provided for 'acts of God.'"[161] "Under those
circumstances," the director concludes, "it's not what you
want but what you get."

As released, the film begins with aerial shots establishing this island in the gulf stream, followed by shots of
a rock in the ocean near Hudson's house. Not only does it
serve as bookends for the content of the film, the rock is
also a visual reinforcement of the theme of isolation--physical
and emotional--and a reminder of the words of John Donne,
so familiar to Hemingway, that no man is an island. As the
credits roll, there are shots of Hudson's house: the found-
ry for his sculpture is prominently on view, but the only
visible evidence of his former calling as a painter is inside
the house--a drawing of his first wife, Audrey. The montage takes the viewer to town as George C. Scott saunters
by on the beach; like the film, his pace is relaxed and
casual.

Jerry Goldsmith's score--containing the most music he
has ever composed for a Schaffner film--is highly varied,
at once masculine but also melodic and sentimental, serving
as a vivid counterpoint to Hudson's seemingly cold demean-
or, hinting at all the feelings he has buried. With indige-
nous rhythms mixed in, the music accompanies Hudson as he
encounters his first friend, Captain Ralph (Gilbert Roland,
who was suggested to Schaffner by production manager
Cisco Day, Roland's brother), who, as he is involved in
refugee running, prefigures Hudson's final adventure. In
short order, the viewer is introduced to Eddy and Joseph,
the men with whom Hudson works and plays, and Honest
Lil (Susan Tyrrell), the whore with the heart of gold with
whom he plays.

"The Boys" of the first part share a room at their
father's house and soon get into an impromptu pillow fight
to break the ice, creating a sense of fraternity among these
three sons of different wives. Entering the room, Hudson
is soon drawn in as a participant, but Davy (Michael-James
Wixted) won't stop and begins to hit his father for real.
In a subplot added by Schaffner and Petticlerc, Davy re-
sents his father for having beaten his mother; this conflict
between father and son is established simply, without the
need for dialogue.

The feud continues on a fishing trip, which, when
he hooks a marlin, also provides Davy with his rite of passage. The protracted duel between boy and fish is similar
to the one in The Old Man and the Sea, but there is another
dimension to the struggle--Davy is fighting his father as

well. Close shots reveal that his feet and hands are bleeding, but Davy is determined to stay at it until either he or
the marlin dies; the line tears before it reaches that point.
"I know you love him the most," Tommy (Hart Bochner) will
say of Davy when he tells Hudson his plans to join the RAF,
"and that's right because he's the best of us." The truce,
however, is tenuous at best.

        The fishing sequence is marred by inserted footage of
the marlin. William Fraker had been commissioned to shoot
some footage but had no luck. Instead of waiting half a
year more to get the marlins to cooperate for the cameras,
Schaffner had to buy stock footage--from Australia, which
was blown up from 16mm to 35mm and adapted to the wide
Panavision screen. "It doesn't work," Schaffner admits,
"but it seemed to me that, in balance, the fact of tying the
people together with that ocean was more important than
the disadvantage of that particular imperfection of five
feet."[162] By contrast, the underwater footage, shot in a
studio tank, of the hammerhead shark attacking Tommy (before Eddy, proving himself for the boys at the last moment,
saves the day) slips by, unnoticed by an audience; the
matte shot in the film's marlin sequence is definitely jarring,
disengaging the viewer's emotional link with the action.

        But the emotional intensity is too strong to be more
than momentarily affected; the family drama proceeds naturally and honestly, its simplicity making it powerful. Also
helpful are the actors portraying the sons: Hart Bochner,
spotted at an American Film Institute function by Jean
Schaffner, who noticed his resemblance to Claire Bloom;
Michael-James Wixted, called a "gold mine" by his director,
whose voice had changed by the time it came to loop his
lines; Brad Savage as Andy, who is particularly effective
when he asks Hudson, "Is ten too old to kiss your father
goodnight?" In this conflict and reconciliation of generations, father too must make some concessions: responding
when Davy says he's afraid of the dark, Hudson admits,
"I was always afraid of dying." This is a rare admission
from a Hemingway hero, but then Hemingway had never before ventured into these parts--a father's love for his sons.
Perhaps the highest point in the film comes in the farewell
scene between Hudson and sons, with all the sub rosa emotions running through it.

Claire Bloom, the "Woman" in the brief second act,
must establish her character as the former Mrs. Hudson,
and she accomplishes it quickly, delicately, and poignantly.
Audrey mentions she's heard Hudson has given up painting
--the only reference in the film of the medium that made
Hudson famous; they talk about Davy and Andy's mother,
Joan, who was once Audrey's best friend, much as Pauline
Pfeiffer was Hadley Richardson's friend, but there is more
to her mission than just to announce her impending marriage.
Audrey's visit is underscored by a love theme: the sound
of maracas can be heard in the music on the drive to Hudson's house, causing an effect that sounds like the ticking
of a clock, a subliminal foreshadowing of what will soon be
made known. After she leaves the island, having said what
had to be said about Tommy, Julius begins to cry, and then
Hudson cries. They both look at the isolated rock in the
ocean; there is no music.

"The Journey" of the third act begins when Hudson,
shutting down his house, decides to move back to the mainland. On his way, he meets Captain Ralph, whose ship is
burning, and brings the Jewish refugees on board the
Tortuga, thus becoming involved with mankind again. When
he tries to land the refugees in Cuba, he is chased by a
couple of Cuban Coast Guard boats, action that results in
Eddy's death. Scott is most effective when he says, "He's
dead," reading the line in total astonishment. Still in shock,
Hudson holds Eddy's hand until he is reminded he must
throw the body overboard. In a fine directorial touch, a
blood stain is revealed on Hudson's shirt over the spot
where his heart is.

In his New York Times review, Vincent Canby wrote:

> It's a film that begins so well, with so much genuine
> feeling that, as it goes on, sort of petering out, one
> starts wishing one could control it. Two-thirds of
> the way through, the wish is desperate. It is like
> sitting in the back of a car that is going gently,
> but unmistakably out of control. [163]

The film has peaked twice before with the boys' departure
and the disclosure of Tommy's death. Islands in the Stream
does not recover after Eddy's death; the dramatic intensity

of the scene is not again equalled in the film. "It was one
of those uncalculated suggestions you live to regret," Peter
Bart says of the To Have and Have Not ending he suggested
for the film. Reflecting on the film six years after its release, he opines:

> If you had started with the last third, then done
> the first and second third, I think you would have
> a very moving and interesting film. Or instead of
> the refugee stuff had you used the stuff in the
> book about going from island to island, you would
> have had a picture of the tracks the story builds,
> character, and finally comes this tremendous teary
> ending.

Since no alternate endings for the film were shot, it is hard
to comment on the other possibilities; in any event, the
troubles the creative team had had with the ending in pre-
production were made manifest in the final cut of the film.

In a cat and mouse game with the Cuban Patrol boats,
Hudson and crew pole and pull the Tortuga through the
maze of the river. After he successfully helps the Jewish
women to safety, Hudson is shot. As the hero lies dying,
Schaffner uses a series of overexposed flashforwards to tie
the cycle of life and death together. At his house, Audrey,
dressed in white, joins Hudson, also dressed in white; they
are very much in love. The scene returns to the Tortuga;
at this juncture, to Joseph is given the haunting last line
of the novel, expressing a fundamental weakness of every
Hemingway hero--"You never understand anybody that loves
you." Returning to his reverie, Hudson sees overexposed
close shots of Davy and Andy, his two remaining sons; back
on the boat, Joseph begs Hudson not to die. Hudson winks
and then returns to his dream of the ideal: the Hudson family leaves the house; Audrey has an arm around each son
as if she were their real mother. A medium close shot of
the dying Hudson aboard the Tortuga shows him smiling in
contentment. In the fourth and final flashforward, the Hud-
sons get in a taxi and wave goodbye to Joseph; it is clear
in the overexposure that in these three living people the dying Hudson has all a man needs and can ask for in life--love.

After Robert Swink completed editing the film, Schaffner returned to the Hemingway book to excerpt several of

Hudson's interior monologues, had Scott record them, and
put them over the flashforwards: his journey over, Hudson
recounts the universal truths he has learned. In a more
accepting way, they reiterate the theme of To Have and
Have Not: "A man alone ain't got no bloody fucking
chance."[164] Hudson dies; Joseph cries. The film concludes
with aerial shots of the gulf stream and finally a shot of the
lonely rock. Hudson lived and loved; in death, he has
found what he was all along--a piece of the continent.

Analyzing the commercial prospects of the film in
Variety, Art Murphy wrote:

> The strength of "Islands in the Stream" is simul-
> taneously its commercial failing. It gracefully de-
> molishes those macho posturings that, in the era of
> Howard Hawks, John Ford, Bogart, Cagney and
> their peers, were enough to establish and define
> character. Yet--since we have not yet reached
> consensus on new symbols--it cannot do more than
> lay back an exposed soul. And as practitioners of
> the popular arts well know, exposed souls and nerve
> endings are not surefire box-office. [165]

This line of reasoning worried the front office: the film
wrapped up shooting in Kauai shortly before Christmas 1975;
it was not released until February 1977. During the film's
six months of post-production, Paramount underwent another
change in administration. In January 1976, David Picker
was appointed head of production, becoming the studio president in October. Rumors abounded on the lot that the film
was slow and dull, that it was definitely in trouble because
Hemingway was out of style. But when Picker saw the director's cut of the film, he was prompted to write Schaffner:
"I personally think it is one of the most touching films I
have ever seen. No one can guarantee financial success
but I can guarantee that Paramount is proud to be handling
the picture."[166] He did not guarantee how the sales organization of the studio would treat it; the picture was shelved
for nearly nine months.

Four removes from power, Peter Bart could do little
about the situation. He and Palevsky hired Max Young-
stein and Leon Roth to help sell the film and fight the studio, but the $3 million minimum promotion budget that had

been allocated was cut to a third. Ironically, when the
film was finally released, its ad line read: "How long has
it been since you've seen a really good movie?" In his review of the film, Arthur Knight was moved to speculate:
"Why this eloquent and searching drama has been withheld
from the screen for so many months is one of those questions that makes show business so fascinating and mysterious to any outsider."[167] While it is true the studio did not
get behind the film, Bart doesn't think <u>Islands</u> suffered
from the changes of regimes; Paramount undoubtedly felt,
with some justification, that the film would get lost in a
summer release against action films, that a February release was as good a time as any. Bart concludes:

> A brilliant distribution man could've done a lot more
> with this picture, but how many brilliant distribu-
> tion men are there? It was a tough picture to sell
> .... The picture just didn't get that electricity,
> even in the previews. It didn't connect with the
> audience, it just didn't. I don't think it was fucked
> over, as they say, I think it was the victim of what
> I say.... I always draw an analogy to a soufflé:
> it rises or it doesn't--you know it.

A favorable critical response is always crucial to a
film of this nature, and the New York press was harsh, attacking Hemingway more than the film. Jack Kroll wrote in
<u>Newsweek</u>:

> You know how it is when the lights go down and
> the music comes up and the words on the screen
> say the movie is based on writing by Ernest Hem-
> ingway? It is not a good feeling because the mov-
> ies based on writing by Ernest Hemingway have al-
> most always been very bad. You know they are
> bad because they do not make you feel good.
> <u>Islands in the Stream</u> does not make you feel good.[168]

Not everyone on the east coast went in for the kill. Judith
Crist, for example, wrote in <u>Saturday Review</u>: "The
quintessential--perhaps the ultimate--Ernest Hemingway has
come to the screen at last in <u>Islands in the Stream</u>."[169]
One west coast viewer was deeply affected over a long
period of time. "It was one of those things that everyday
I'd sit down to work and I'd run a scene on the moviola

and I'd start to cry," says Jerry Goldsmith. "I think that's
Frank's best picture. I like Scott better there than in <u>Pat-
ton</u>."

    Beginning with his physical appearance, no one can
overlook the contribution to the film of George C. Scott, a
man about whom John Huston has written, "I have little use
for Scott as a private person but my admiration for him as
an actor is unbounded."[170] Having guided him in his performance as Patton, Schaffner was no stranger to the actor's idiosyncrasies:

> Every time a director got to work with Scott, he'd
> call me, say, "How do you handle him?" So you try
> to lend them what advice you can. When the pic-
> ture is finished, they come and say, "Gee, there
> were no problems--he was a pussycat." "That's
> great, you struck a lode I didn't know existed."
> But then you look at the picture....

In utilizing this great talent to maximum effect, a director
must make certain preparations, not unlike preparing to
work on the ocean. Scott is in virtually every scene of
<u>Islands in the Stream</u> and his performance is a model of
economy: only the tip of the iceberg shows.

    He throws no temper tantrums in the film; when he
cries, he does not do so histrionically. This is the most
subdued performance of his career; in other films, he draws,
if not commands, attention to himself, but Scott is always
giving to the other actors in <u>Islands in the Stream</u>. Perhaps
for this reason Hudson is the most touching character he has
ever played. Most memorable is his scene with Claire Bloom
at Hudson's house: Audrey is getting drunk; Hudson gets
up to fetch another bottle of wine, his back to the camera
that follows him. Suddenly, he intuits the reason behind
Audrey's visit: in a close shot, he touches the back of his
neck with his left hand, turning around slowly; his eldest
and only son by Audrey is dead. There are no tears, no
rage; it is a quiet moment. Emil Jannings was justly famed
for acting with his back in E. A. Dupont's <u>Variety</u> (1925);
in this scene, George C. Scott acts with the back of his
neck. Submerging his own persona in the role to this extent, Scott does not appear to be acting; he just is. "It
was an enormously restrained, deeply felt performance, and

it's not my doing," Schaffner maintains. "That's how he
came on with it and was exactly right." Nonetheless, as
was the occasion of Patton, Franklin J. Schaffner was
there.

Perhaps Dale Winogura was closer to the mark than
he knew when he wrote in Cinemaphile: "This is the closest film to capture the poetic essence of [Hemingway's]
prose of any of them, and Schaffner has inadvertently been
preparing for this in all his films."[171] Islands in the Stream
represents a work by a filmmaker at the height of his powers. It is peopled with rich characters, portrayed by a
uniformly fine cast, led by an outstanding performance from
its leading man. There is an easy camaraderie among men
that is admirable in its seeming effortlessness, and a love
affair between a man and a woman that bespeaks an entire
love story in a brief encounter. On display is the fact that
one of Schaffner's most underused and not inconsiderable
skills is his ability to work with children. Except for the
marlin shots, the film is visually impeccable. Despite weaknesses in the third act, the plot unfolds logically, and the
characterizations are so sound that they evoke deep-seated
emotions. Surely the fate of the film must have been dis-
heartening to its director.

Whether or not the timing was right, the times they
had been a-changing. Andrew Sarris observed:

> In their loving celebration of the Hemingway hero,
> director Franklin Schaffner, scenarist Denne Bart
> Petticlerc, and actor George C. Scott are swimming
> gallantly but hopelessly against the tide of cultural
> history.... Islands in the Stream is a beautiful,
> elegant movie, and a thoughtfully ennobling enter-
> tainment. If it should fail I would have to suppose
> that both Hemingway and Scott are commonly per-
> ceived to be passé, and that the Hemingway hero
> has outlasted his welcome.[172]

Hemingway had had a profound influence on everyone in his
time, but America had moved several generations beyond the
lost generation into a new era of popular culture. A film in
which its hero, speaking of the sea, says, "She is my home,
my religion; she gives life and she ends it," seemed peculiarly out of place in the year of Star Wars and Close Encounters of the Third Kind.

The Entebbe Project

Towards the end of July 1976, Guy McElwaine, Schaffner's former CMA agent who had become the head of production at Warner Bros., called to say that (Schaffner's former agent at Ashley-Steiner) Ted Ashley, the Warner Bros. chairman, wanted to make a film based on the Israeli commando rescue of the 104 passengers of Air France flight #139 who were hijacked by Arab guerrillas. Asked if he would be interested in directing it, Schaffner replied yes.

The incident had only occurred at the beginning of the month. It was a throwback to the Warner Bros. pictures of the 1930s, a film made from current newspaper headlines, a type of project the director had not undertaken since his days in live television. It was such a good idea, however, that two other motion picture projects based on those headlines were announced: Paramount's 90 Minutes at Entebbe, to be written by Paddy Chayefsky and directed by Sidney Lumet; Universal's Rescue at Entebbe, to be written by Loring Mandel and directed by George Roy Hill. Significantly, the studios had sought men whose training came from live television, men who would be able to organize and produce quickly.

Obviously, all three major studio productions would not be made; whoever could first sign with the Israeli government would make the film. Warners had the jump on the other two studios: Ashley had secured the services of Steve McQueen to play the General Dan Shomron character, heading what would probably be an all-star cast, and was willing to spend over $10 million on the production. Already at work in Israel, Ashley would personally be the executive producer of the film.

At this stage of pre-production, Schaffner immediately needed a team of three men. Having been impressed with the screenplay of Fred Zinnemann's 1973 production of The Day of the Jackal, he chose Kenneth Ross to write the script. Alfred Sweeney was hired to be the production designer. Stanley O'Toole, formerly the production head of Paramount's European office and the producer of The Last of Sheila (1973) and The Seven-Per-cent Solution (1976), was brought in on the recommendation of Paul Hitchcock, then a Warner Bros. production vice-president. "I was desperately looking for a producer, and I phoned around

town and his name came up several times," Schaffner explains. "This is a preciously small film community and
everybody's reputation somehow or another precedes him.
It isn't a difficult task to find out." Considered an expert
on European location shooting, O'Toole began work by
rounding up a British crew. Before departing for Israel,
Schaffner alerted Fred Koenekamp and Jose (Pepe) Lopez
Rodero, his favorite D.P. and A.D. respectively, of his
plans.

By August 19, 1976, Ashley had worked out an
agreement with the Minister of Commerce, Chaim Bar-Lev,
in conjunction with the other cabinet members. The government of Israel would receive a $500,000 guarantee and
10% of the profits of the film; furthermore, Warner Bros.
had to put $250,000 into the Israeli film industry and in-
vest in six films over a period of three years. There were
two other important stipulations: (1) the film had to begin
shooting by February 28, 1977, or else there would be a
$375,000 penalty, and released by August 31, 1977--in time
for the October elections--or else there would be another
$375,000 penalty; (2) the entire film had to be shot in
Israel. [173]

The first stipulation gave the company little time for
pre-production; the script had not even been started yet.
Schaffner and Ross came up with a tentative outline and
began research by interviewing hostages, not the easiest
of tasks as, by now, the hostages were receiving money
from the media of many countries for their exclusive stories. Fortunately, a reception held by Prime Minister Yitzhak Rabin, reuniting many of the hostages, worked in
favor of the film. Some cabinet members cooperated, others
did not; even when given permission to interview some of
the people who had participated in the raid, director and
writer were always accompanied by a general representing
the interests of the military and intelligence.

The stipulation about shooting in Israel posed major
problems for Al Sweeney, the production designer: there
was no Lake Victoria or reasonable facsimile in Israel, nor
was there much jungle. The company definitely needed an
airstrip, but there were no reports of the actual size of
the airport terminal where the hostages had been held; the
architect's blueprints were, oddly, missing from the govern-

ment files. Sweeney had to design the main waiting room
and stairwells from hearsay: he knew that the hostages
had slept on the floor; by placing paper cutouts of each
hostage on the tentatively chosen location, he arrived at
the approximate dimensions of the airport's ground floor.
For Lake Victoria, he planned to use reflecting material on
a nearby field and surround it with cutout trees. An airbus similar to the one used for flight #139 was rented for
weight tests on the runway of the landing strip chosen
for the film.[174]

Later during Schaffner's stay, Hill and Mandel arrived in Jerusalem to work on their Entebbe project. It
was an unusual situation, these former partners and collaborators working on the same but separate projects:
Schaffner and Mandel had dinner and talked about every
possible subject except Entebbe; although they did not
have dinner and talk of their respective films, George Roy
Hill says, "There would have been absolutely no tension on
either one of our parts--Frank's a very cool guy." By
now, Lumet and Chayefsky had dropped out of the picture,
and the Universal Entebbe project was far behind Warners'.
"It was apparent that if it was going to be done," Schaffner says, "we were going to do it." Enough progress had
been made so that a budget could be forecast: with costs
escalating from the mandate of shooting only in Israel, the
estimate came to $17 million, a very expensive production
for that time.

Research being so intensive, Kenneth Ross got further and further behind in the script. What he was un-
earthing was the inside story of the rescue, a behind-the-
scenes look at the Masad--Israeli Intelligence. Initially,
Ted Ashley had been able to get Steve McQueen on the
basis of the press releases; as the inside story developed,
emphasis was taken away from the Dan Shomron character,
away from what had been reported in the media. The biggest script development, however, turned out to be the
Israeli government's reluctance to give its approval to what
Warner Bros. considered to be the real and more fascinating
story. Although Yitzhak Rabin was in favor of the film,
many high-ranking members of the government, especially
Chief of Staff Lt. General Mordechai Gur, were strongly opposed. There were six sensitive areas of censorship:
(1) the small plane flights; (2) navigational problems on the

operation; (3) landing and ground operations; (4) disguises
of the assault force; (5) the Kenyan involvement; (6) the
activities of the Masad. Bureaucracy delayed the production for a couple of months; criticism of the possible use of
army personnel and equipment grew louder.

In a memo to Ted Ashley, Schaffner described a meeting he had with General Benny Puled, Chief of the Air
Force, who apparently had more than a passing familiarity
with Hollywood movies:

> Said he was against the making of the film because
> the operation wasn't much--that it was like "casing
> a bank and then robbing it" and that we would
> probably make a film filled with "schmaltz." When
> asked what that meant, he said the picture will
> say, "Oh, look. The Israelis can fight and the
> Israelis can fly, with a lot of music behind it."[175]

"We knew that one of us was going to fall out," says George
Roy Hill. "In fact, both of us fell out." Kenneth Ross had
only completed 45 pages of the Warner Bros. script which,
at this stage, read more like a screenplay for the Airport
series than a docudrama.

In mid-October 1976, the company disbanded; sketches
and plans were confiscated. As it was and still is politically sensitive, Schaffner and company agreed not to reveal or
discuss any information research had yielded. The Israeli
government, however, claimed and received the $750,000 in
penalties. Later, Minister of Commerce Chaim Bar-Lev made
a public statement about The Entebbe Project: "Warner
Bros. did not want to film just a well-documented drama....
They wanted to reconstruct exactly what happened. That
violated our security."[176] For Warner Bros., read Franklin
J. Schaffner.

Ironically, television has the last word in this story.
It is no secret that television can scoop a motion picture:
in this case, the Entebbe story was on television before
the Warner Bros. project, had it been able to secure the
Israeli government's final permission, would even have
started production. Similar to the major studios' rush to
make an Entebbe film, two television productions, after
other projects had dropped out along the way, raced each

other to the air: ABC's <u>Victory at Entebbe</u>, directed by
Marvin J. Chomsky, a videotape production with Kirk Douglas, Burt Lancaster, and Elizabeth Taylor, was finished
first, airing on December 13, 1976; NBC's <u>Raid on Entebbe</u>,
directed by Irvin Kershner, with Charles Bronson and
Peter Finch, was broadcast on January 9, 1977. The former was produced, unbeknownst to Ted Ashley, by David
L. Wolper, whose company had been acquired by Warner
Bros.

The Boys from Brazil

"The Boys from Brazil" are not Astaire, Kelly, and
O'Connor dancing, singing in the rain for M-G-M
or RKO. [177]

--Rob Edelman

In the years following <u>Advise and Consent</u>, Robert Fryer
had become enough of a theatrical force so that Hollywood
would inevitably beckon him. "I came out here when we
did <u>Sweet Charity</u> and <u>Mame</u>," he says, "and I really thought
I'd never do another play on Broadway." He made films to
make a living, he frequently said, and did theatre for love.
Lawrence Carr had passed away, and James Cresson was
his new partner; together, they made a living in Hollywood
by producing such films as <u>The Prime of Miss Jean Brodie</u>
(1968) and <u>Travels with My Aunt</u> (1972).

Having helped cast their film productions of <u>The Bos-</u>
<u>ton Strangler</u> (1967) and <u>Sweet Charity</u> (1969), Martin
Richards joined Fryer and Cresson to co-produce the stage
production of <u>Chicago</u>; partnered with his wife, Mary Lea
Johnson, Richards would later be a producer on Stanley
Kubrick's film version of <u>The Shining</u> (1980). In 1976,
Fryer, Cresson, Richards, and Johnson formed Producers
Group; when they learned that Robert Wise already had a
claim on that title, they named their company Producer
Circle.

Producer Circle optioned a property that Fryer, who
would be the film's executive producer, strongly wanted to
make, a best-selling novel by Ira Levin. His first choice
for director was the man who had directed <u>Advise and Con-</u>
<u>sent</u> on Broadway. "Didn't think he'd do it," Fryer admits.

Executive producer Robert Fryer with Schaffner, filming
<u>The Boys from Brazil</u>, 1977.

"I went to see Frank, and he was editing Islands in the Stream at Paramount--it was a hot day." Schaffner had heard about the property: Ira Levin was asking so much for it, in addition to a percentage--as well the author of Critic's Choice, No Time for Sergeants, and Deathtrap might --that many studios had already turned it down. Fryer, who had brought a copy of the novel with him, asked the director to read The Boys from Brazil.

In 1974, seven German men gather at a Japanese restaurant for some nefarious purpose: Aspiazu, the man dressed in white, is actually Dr. Josef Mengele, the infamous Nazi war criminal responsible for the deaths of 300,000 Jews at Auschwitz. He announces a plan for the hope and the destiny of the Aryan race, for the future of the Fourth Reich: on a two-year timetable, it involves murdering 94 men in Europe and America, stable family men and civil servants who are all 65 years old. "It's a holy operation you're taking part in," he proclaims.[178] Mengele's antagonist is an aging Viennese named Yakov Lieberman, plainly modeled after Simon Weisenthal. In this book, Ira Levin recapitulates the themes from two previous novels: biological engineering (The Stepford Wives) and the rebirth of the devil (Rosemary's Baby). Specifically, the boys from Brazil are clones of Adolph Hitler.

Schaffner accepted; that it would give him the opportunity to work in the suspense/mystery genre was attractive, but the big challenge would be in the casting of the film. In particular, this meant the two old wolves, Mengele and Lieberman, the two long-hating antagonists. "I would like to say rather fondly," the director declares, "that here I was faced with casting a geriatric movie." This, in fact, was one of the reasons that had made the property such a hard sell: studios, courting the younger audience, were leery of a film with an older cast. Financing became available when Producer Circle made a deal with Sir Lew Grade and ITC.

On the basis of his experience on the Entebbe project, Schaffner brought in Kenneth Ross to write the screenplay. Ross proceeded to write six wildly different drafts of the script, the second serving as an example of the different approaches he tried out: Lieberman is cornered in Miami by Morris Koehler, who hires him to fetch his errant

son, Barry; in Paraguay, Lieberman and Barry learn of
Mengele's plot; after Barry is killed by the Nazis, lawyer
Eileen Lowell visits Lieberman in Vienna to learn the circumstances behind young Koehler's death and stays to help
out; in the end, after Mengele is killed by the Wheelocks'
dogs, Lieberman, discovering Eileen is a neo-Nazi, kills
her and is himself murdered by Beynon (Denholm Elliot in
the film), his newspaperman friend at Reuters. The denouement takes place a few years later on an athletic field
in Nuremberg, where 18-year-old Bobby, joined by eleven
other young Hitlers, frolics in an unqualified triumph of
the will.

Try as he may--he even had the Doberman Pinschers
kill Lieberman--Ross could not come up with an approach
that was satisfying to the company. Finally, he returned
to the book, tried it Levin's way, and dropped out of the
project. Heywood Gould was invited in by Martin Richards,
who had purchased his Fort Apache, the Bronx, a script
that wouldn't be produced for another four years. Gould
began work at The Boys from Brazil's offices at 9200 Sunset Boulevard in Beverly Hills: "[Schaffner] kept that
poor man in that room ... the guy would do anything to
get out of the room, and Frank would bring him right in,"
Fryer recalls. "He was really like a caged animal." As
soon as Gould's first draft was completed, the director went
over it with him sentence by sentence, covering each and
every detail. "The end result was good," Fryer says, and
as for Gould, "He was crazy about Frank finally."

In casting, emphasis was on first finding the right
actor for Mengele. Laurence Olivier was an obvious candidate but, since he had already played that role in Marathon
Man (1976), there would be no challenge either to him or
the audience; Gregory Peck, on the other hand, had expressed interest in playing the Lieberman role. Schaffner
had a sudden idea: it would be casting against type but
Gregory Peck would make an interesting Mengele; the company had a recent photograph of Josef Mengele, and Peck
could be made to resemble him, even if Mengele stood only
5'6" tall. Olivier would make a splendid Lieberman; furthermore, the actor was interested in the role, something
particularly gratifying to Robert Fryer, whose first job out
of the army in 1946, when the Old Vic visited America, had
been to run errands for Olivier. The two stars were signed

almost simultaneously; each looked forward to playing against
the other.

    In Gould's script, Lieberman's first name was changed
from Yakov to Ezra, who is further linked to Simon Wiesenthal when Mr. Wheelock refers to him as the man who caught
Adolph Eichmann; in the course of production, Olivier would
be able to host a cocktail party for Wiesenthal. Lord Olivier's health, however, was the cause of many anxious moments: in recent years, he had been afflicted by a host of
diseases--cancer of the prostate, myositis, a kidney operation, and thrombosis, and during The Boys from Brazil he
was recuperating from cancer, nerve tissue disease, and
pneumonia. "We started our meetings with Greg," Fryer
recalls, "and Greg started his voice lessons, the accent
lessons, and worked very hard. He did the make-up tests.
Olivier was ill in a nursing home in Brighton, and the doctor said, 'He can't travel.' " As he had for Nicholas and
Alexandra, Schaffner rearranged the shooting schedule to
accommodate Olivier.

    For the icy, efficient, but not unhumorous Nazi Colo-
nel Eduard Seibert, Schaffner wanted James Mason, who
in turn had sought one of the two leads. Thinking that
Max von Sydow would make a good bad Nazi, the English
backers had to be persuaded Mason was worth hiring;
Schaffner had his way, and the actor who had played Field
Marshal Rommel in two films was again employed to play
a Nazi. As security chief, Seibert is a hatchet man and
an enemy of the enemy, but the role is little more than
a device for exposition, like a maid in a play; one of the
luxuries of the film is that so gifted and urbane an actor
could lend his considerable style to so little.

    Martin Richards was set to receive producer's credit;
his forte being casting, a more production-oriented producer
was necessary. Remembering his work on the Entebbe project, Schaffner brought in Stanley O'Toole to co-produce
the film--the bulk of the film would be shot on European
locations, areas this producer knew well. Since taking an
American crew to Europe would be expensive and, because
an outside crew could not be brought into England, use-
less, Schaffner and O'Toole decided on a British crew: even
if the bulk of the filming would be outside Great Britain,
the director maintains that "an English crew on location
is always very good."

Schaffner, however, wanted a French cinematographer.
He felt a French cameraman would work more freely than
his British counterpart, and, as long as he used a British
crew, he could bring a non-British cameraman into the
country; believing that multi-nationals tend to stimulate
each other, Schaffner has always enjoyed working with a
mixed crew. Several directors of photography were considered: at the top of the list was Henri Decae, whose
reputation (Bob le Flambeur, 1955; The 400 Blows, 1959)
had long preceded him; Decae accepted the offer. To prevent the possibility of the wide screen detracting from the
drama, Schaffner, as he told Films and Filming's Ralph Appelbaum, chose the 1:85 aspect ratio:

> There is something very romantic about the size of
> that screen. And also, you tend to get very artsy-
> fartsy in Panavision by staging what is essential
> stuff off-centre. And the fact is that a lot of peo-
> ple tend to miss that, because they look at the cen-
> tre of the screen. [179]

In addition to the narrower aspect ratio, the visual conception was to give a documentary feel to the film.

The production designer was Gil Parrondo, Schaffner's
first choice when it comes to European filming. A research
team was sent to photograph people and places in Paraguay,
but due to its inaccessibility, lack of suitable facilities, and
general political hostility, the country had to be eliminated
as a possible location. Spain was considered to double for
Paraguay, but, in the half dozen years following Nicholas
and Alexandra, it had become too expensive; besides, no
jungle atmosphere could be found.

The next tactic was Central America. Beginning in
Yucatan, the location team (Parrondo; Jose Lopez Rodero;
Scott Woodhouse, the location manager) would journey south
until the right terrain was found. After the team had finished scouting a pair of countries, Schaffner would fly down
to take a look; in all, he made three trips. Panama seemed
the most appropriate: there were the requisite river, jungle,
and a city that could be used for Asuncion, and it looked
right; construction on Mengele's house and laboratory commenced in the jungle. The company knew there would be
rain, but the amount was grievously underestimated in a

study of the rain tables; consequently, only four hours a
day could be spent on construction. At least as damaging
as the rain was another major obstacle: the Panama Canal
Treaty vote was coming up in the United States Senate,
and the political forecast did not look too promising for location filming. For a combination of reasons, the company
decided it wisest to leave Panama in September 1977.

Construction resumed across the Atlantic Ocean. Outside of Lisbon, Portugal, art director Peter Lamont had
found a salt marsh with hills around it that had the look of
a jungle. Happily, it was found that Lisbon, if carefully
photographed, could pass for Asuncion, Paraguay. "They
had good photographs," Fryer insists, "and you couldn't
tell the difference. You really couldn't." Production commenced in Portugal at the end of October with Gregory
Peck and James Mason on hand. Over 400 Portuguese were
employed as extras for The Boys from Brazil, making it the
largest production that had been filmed in that country.
"It was very hard to control the crowds," Fryer says of
the understandable confusion. "We shot very late at night
very often, and it was cold and miserable."

Fortunately, communication was good among the various national groups at work, a quality that is evident whenever Pepe Lopez is involved as the first assistant director
on a production. Schaffner was able to pick up the necessary shots, including a pan that moves across Mengele's
lab to young native boys who have brilliant blue eyes; also
seen in the Paraguayan panoramas are human creatures who,
thanks to Dr. Mengele, look like strays from Dr. Moreau's
island of lost souls. In the last scene shot in Portugal,
Seibert, under orders from the Comrades Organization, the
group plotting the rise of the Fourth Reich, burns down
Mengele's compound--much to the chagrin of the salt marsh's
owner, who had insisted the company turn over the buildings to him once filming was over.

The company moved to Pennsylvania, where in anticipation of its arrival, Franklin and Marshall College in Lancaster was prepared to confer honorary Doctor of Humane
Letters degrees upon Schaffner, Peck, and Olivier. The
last was awarded in absentia, as Olivier's doctors would not
allow him to travel to America and be exposed to the cold
weather. Olivier, it was said, would be able to work when

the company got to England, but, in the meantime, a double
had to be used for the shot of Lieberman walking to the
Wheelock house in New Providence, Pennsylvania for his
climactic encounter with Mengele. The company also took
advantage of its stay in Pennsylvania by filming exteriors
that represent Massachusetts in the film, when Lieberman
meets Mrs. Curry and her son Jack.

The company shut down for two weeks over Christmas
before resuming for a week's shooting at Shepperton Studios
in London. The doctors vouching for his health, Olivier
performed his scenes with Anne Meara as Mrs. Curry and
Uta Hagen as Frieda Maloney before the company moved to
Vienna, where interiors were waiting at the Wien Studio.
Regarding Olivier, his health, and acting, Schaffner observed:

> He was sickly, he was in pain, but yet he was
> there for every call through every working day in-
> volved; never requested any release. And you
> could tell when he was having a good day physical-
> ly and when he wasn't. You could read in his eyes.
> On a bad day, he would just train his mind to what
> we were doing.... On a good day, he'd feel so
> great--such relief--that he would blow lines all
> over the place.

Even though Olivier was down to 140 pounds, not one day
was lost to his health. "The sum of the thing," says Fryer,
"was that Larry became crazy about Frank during the shooting of the picture."

Lieberman consults with Dr. Bruckner, complaining
that Mengele is a sadist with an M.D. and a Ph.D.: a good
definition of a scientist, his learned colleague replies.
Bruckner, played by Bruno Ganz, the versatile actor best
known to American audiences for his work in Wim Wenders'
The American Friend (1977), is on hand to provide an explanation of cloning, screening a short film as an audio-
visual aid; the 16mm film was made by Dr. Derek Bromhall,
an Oxford biologist serving as technical adviser on the production, who had cloned rabbits for his film. Lieberman
goes over and over the clues until he finally realizes, if
the audience has not already guessed, that it is Hitler who
has been cloned; the discovery is made in a lecture room,
Schaffner effectively revealing it in an extreme long shot.

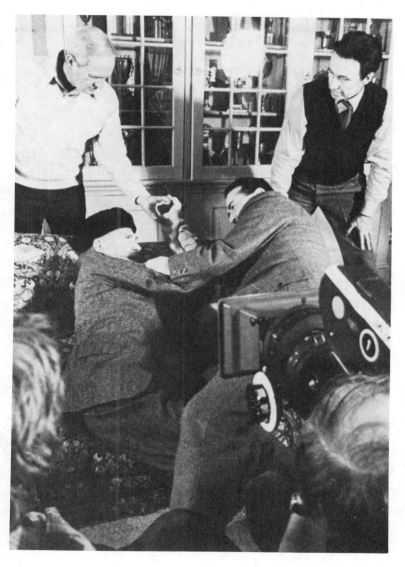

Filming the showdown of the two old wolves in <u>The Boys</u> <u>from Brazil</u>, 1978: Schaffner, Laurence Olivier, Gregory Peck, and stunt coordinator Eddie Powell.

Peck and Olivier worked together for the first time
in Vienna. As dictated by the script, the long-time ad-
versaries meet just once in a showdown from which only
one man will survive. The fight scene plainly had to be
shot in very short sections to accommodate Olivier; as the
film shows, the fight is violent and strenuous--they bite,
scratch, and gouge. Everyone was concerned about Olivier's condition, but Bernard Drew, an eyewitness, re-
counted something he saw on the set: "Peck murmurs to
Olivier, 'Nice faking.' Olivier, still flat on the floor, looks
up at Peck, bats his eyes flirtatiously, and says, 'Just
like Tristan and Isolde.' "[180]

Six Dobermans, the veteran stars of The Daring Dobermans (1973) and The Amazing Dobermans (1976), were
carted from their home in the San Fernando Valley to Pennsylvania and finally to Vienna--the last move necessitated
because a Doberman's ears are not allowed to be cropped in
England and, in Germany, Dobermans are trained through
pain. Supposedly taking instructions from Bobby Wheelock,
the male lead dog actually looked to its trainer--who with
buggy whip in hand stood to the side of the camera--and
moved according to silent commands, followed by the five
female Dobermans. "The only advantage we have on this
particular picture," Schaffner quipped with the memory of
his previous film in mind, "is that we were not working
with animals and children on water."[181] As filmed, Mengele's fate is all the more harrowing for its realistic treatment, playing off an almost universally deep-rooted fear.

The last scene filmed takes place at a dam in Sweden:
Mundt (Walter Gotell), one of the Nazi underground agents,
arrives to kill a man who was his major in the Second World
War, and, in an extreme long shot, embraces him before the
major's body is seen falling off the side of the 600-foot-high
dam; a cut to an even longer 19mm lens shot reinforces the
feeling that these casual murders are committed most im-
personally. The original location was snowed in; as a last-
minute replacement, Schaffner, who had never seen it before, used the Malta Dam outside Salzburg, Austria, and
managed to get all the necessary shots in the single day
that had been alloted to him. After 13 weeks of shooting,
filming was completed on March 14, 1968.

Lew Grade had arranged a distribution deal with

Twentieth Century-Fox, ITC's first link with the Hollywood
studio, which meant Schaffner could go back to the "campus" where he would work on the editing of this $11 mil-
lion motion picture with Robert Swink, as was his wont.
Jerry Goldsmith was brought in to compose the music. "We
met in Vienna," Goldsmith recalls, "and he said, 'Think
3/4' "--which could only mean a waltz. Accordingly, he delivered Viennese and German waltzes, contrasting the opposing sides. He also wrote his first song for a Schaffner
film, "We're Home Again," a ballad that accompanies two
murders in England. "Frank wanted Mengele to be very
Wagnerian," the composer says, "so I gave him Wagner."
Since Lieberman should be correspondingly Austrian, Goldsmith ended up "borrowing" from Richard Strauss and Gus-
tav Mahler.

        The film was released in October 1978. Intended as
"a pure theatrical adventure," The Boys from Brazil opens
with a waltz on the soundtrack; in their own way, Goldsmith's waltzes are as effectively ominous as the cello theme
in Jaws. A title establishes the opening location--Paraguay.
In a parade featuring goose-stepping soldiers, Barry Kohler
(Steven Guttenberg) spies a group of men he suspects are
ex-Nazis climbing in a Mercedes; he follows in his own car,
which, in a nice touch, is a Volkswagen bus.

        Introducing the protagonist, the scene shifts to Vien-
na: making a protractedly grand entrace as Ezra Lieberman, a weary and battered old man, Olivier walks into what
obviously is a real building, to be met by Strausser, the
landlord, who demands the rent; Lieberman takes the elevator up, while Strausser climbs the stairs and yells at
him. They are still arguing when they enter the cluttered
Lieberman apartment: Esther (Lilli Palmer) has received a
phone call from Barry in Paraguay; Strausser complains
that the heavy file cabinets are causing the floor to sag
and demands that they be removed; in return, Lieberman
complains about the plumbing. Not until Lieberman's character has been fully sketched does he answer the long-
distance telephone call: he talks on the telephone in the
mid-background of the frame while Esther, taking over for
him in the foreground, continues the argument with the
landlord.

        The antagonist is given his own kind of spectacular

introduction: a seaplane lands at night in Paraguay; dressed in a white suit, Dr. Josef Mengele emerges from the plane, bathed in white light--the Angel of Death is none other than Gregory Peck. Discovering that Barry has tape-recorded the disclosure of his secret plan, Mengele and his henchmen track him back to his hotel where the amateur spy, talking to Lieberman on the telephone in a mirror shot, is knifed to death. Mengele picks up the receiver and listens momentarily; now it is up to Lieberman to play sleuth and find the man whose cold presence he has felt over the phone.

When the two finally meet in their New Providence confrontation, Mengele shoots Lieberman both in the arm and the back of the hand. As he continues to fire, there are close shots of bullets hitting the door and the trophy case, creating a rhythm that brings the audience closer to the fateful encounter with the Dobermans. Actually, the fight scene is ludicrous--Mengele is still healthy and Lieberman, who is not, has three bullets in him--yet the fight is so well staged that any lapse in logic is overlooked. When Bobby comes in to take pictures, Mengele stops to admire him, telling him he's Hitler; "Oh, man," Bobby can only reply, "you're weird." Hitler was 14 when his father died, the same age of Erich, Simon, Jack, and Bobby--all played, properly sneeringly, by Jeremy Black in the film.

In his Newsweek review of the film, Jack Kroll wrote:

> Mengele must be destroyed, but what do you do about 94 children who are a grotesque compound of natural innocence and implemented evil? That is the real horror. Heywood Gould's reasonably suspenseful screenplay blows it by turning Lieberman into a kindly old Jewish uncle instead of a man who is willing to face the tough paradoxes of good and evil.[182]

Kroll refers to the hospital scene with Lieberman and David Bennett (John Rubinstein) of the Young Jewish Defenders, a group somewhat like the Jewish Defense League, an organization Lieberman terms a bunch of fanatics. The old man lights up a long-postponed cigarette and, much to David's dismay, burns the list of the 94 clones. In the book, Lieberman says, perhaps self-righteously, "This was

Mengele's business, killing children. Should it be ours?"
and then tears up the list and flushes it down the toilet.[183]
Lieberman may similarly refuse to slaughter the innocent in
the film, but a reading of this scene, according to the
Schaffner theme of heroes with feet of clay, changes that
meaning: Mengele's hubris was in thinking Lieberman a
harmless old fool--he easily could have killed him earlier;
in turn, Lieberman's flaw is that he believes the clones are
free of evil and should be spared.

    In the European version (that now appears on Ameri-
can television), the film ends with Bobby, alone in his
darkroom: everything is blood red as he takes the prints
from the fixer and admires the pictures of the mutilated
Mengele. Contrary to the current motion picture practice,
Twentieth Century-Fox objected, insisting the filmmakers
were deliberately aiming for a sequel. Therefore, in a
somewhat peculiar move, further confusing the ending, the
studio cut out the last scene: the film concluded with
Lieberman's act of faith in the hospital, then segued to the
final rack focus shot of the foreground object in all the
blurry red of the darkroom--the bracelet of animal claws
that Mengele took from his lab and brought with him to
America.

    Noteworthy in a film entitled The Boys from Brazil
are the vignettes featuring the work of four actresses, including Rosemary Harris as the flirtatious Widow Doring who
greets Lieberman in Gladbeck, Germany and Anne Meara
who plays the distressed widow of Jack Curry with full an-
xiety. "In the casting," Schaffner asserts, "we had the
opportunity to avail ourselves of some of the most exquisite
actors and actresses in the world." Lilli Palmer is further
proof of that. It is apparent that the nervous and chain-
smoking Esther, herself a survivor of a concentration camp,
can communicate well with Lieberman--especially since she
doesn't have that many lines of dialogue--nonverbally.
While arguing with the landlord, she says, "Leave my
brother and me alone," the only reference in the film to
her relationship with Lieberman; without it, Esther would
seem for all the world to be his wife--a most interesting
approach to a relatively small role.

    Lieberman goes to the prison in Dusseldorf, West
Germany to interrogate Frieda Maloney, who, at the behest

of the Comrade's Organization, worked in an American adop-
tion agency, finding the proper homes for the infant Hitler
clones; she was the one, when he caught her, who made
Lieberman famous. The verbal battle between Lieberman
and Mahoney constitutes seven pages of script--a scene so
important that the director covered it with four master
shots. Frieda is played by Uta Hagen, the gifted actress
who created Martha in Who's Afraid of Virginia Woolf? and
yet has been virtually overlooked by the film world. Hagen
takes maximum advantage of this cameo role: kissing a female guard when she enters, Frieda has a most deadly smile
but remains civil, becoming angry only at the mention of
Lieberman's name--in one sudden moment, her face is trans-
muted into hate; it is remarkable how the actress was able
to generate such intensity in so little time. "You lying
Jewish swine," she spits out at Lieberman. Recoiling, the
Nazi-hunter replies, "You are not a guard now, Madame.
You are a prisoner. I may leave here empty-handed, but
you're not going anywhere." This particular speech by
Olivier was featured in all the trailers and promos for the
film; it is probably his finest acting moment in the film,
certainly his most effective. What most of the promos didn't
show was Uta Hagen: Olivier was playing against a superb
actress; she made him work that much harder, eliciting that
reaction.

Olivier is consistently good as the battered little man,
the David against the Goliath of Mengele. "Without help,
without money," he moans. "What else is new?" After visiting Mrs. Curry, he returns to his motel to make a phone
call. Schaffner stages the scene so that Lieberman's back
is to the camera, making him look like a lonely and pathetic
figure. Olivier plays Lieberman as an old man who works
himself up to a fury for one last mission; just as his struggle revitalizes Lieberman, performing in this film revitalized
Olivier--acting was truly the best therapy for him. Since
this film, Olivier has appeared almost indiscriminately in a
variety of films for an ever-escalating salary, and his work
seems to have become proportionately sloppy: the same accent he employs in this film can be heard in later films--as
a German in Dracula (1973), a Frenchman in A Little Romance (1979), and an American Jew in The Jazz Singer
(1980). Not since The Boys from Brazil has one of his performances been as disciplined; surely Schaffner can take
some of the credit for this, having been a restraining as
well as encouraging force.

Gregory Peck, on the other hand, has seldom had such an interesting screen role since <u>Duel in the Sun</u> (1946), in which he also played a villain. His best scene occurs in the Paraguayan hotel ballroom, for which a Portuguese casino was used: when he sees Mundt there instead of on assignment, Mengele goes beserk and tries to kill him. Performing his own stunt, Peck crashes into a table; a bystander calls for a doctor. "I am a doctor, idiot," Mengele snaps. Removing the glass fragment's from Mundt's head, he turns to Mundt's wife and snarls, "Shut up, you ugly bitch." Later, when Seibert arrives to tell him that the operation has been terminated because of Lieberman's investigation, Peck is allowed a temper tantrum as Mengele rants about his nemesis, "Kill him! Kill him!" For this role, Gregory Peck, who made his reputation playing forthright men of integrity, had his hairline altered, his head partially shaved, his hair darkened and restyled, eyebrows trimmed, wore contact lenses and pallid make-up, and had a triangularized mustache; throughout the film, he displays a credible German accent. "Peck is a revelation," wrote Rob Edelman in <u>Films in Review</u>. "Here made up to look like a cross between a banana republic dictator and a rodent, he is superb."[184] There are moments when Peck seems actually to believe in this master race business.

Schaffner had successfully tackled another genre-- so successfully that it is easy to overlook the fine performances in the film, for which the director can claim some responsibility, having participated in all casting from stars to extras. Despite the 1:85 ratio, Schaffner's style is still grand and majestic, which suits the material very well, lending a measure of subjective realism to the interpretation of Levin's tale. Schaffner's more thoughtful pace and visual sense add weight and substance to what was originally more of a light entertainment. "Mark down 'The Boys from Brazil' as Exhibit A in how to make a first-rate espionage thriller," Robert Osborne wrote in <u>The Hollywood Reporter</u>. "The result, in this case, is a crisp, fascinating and involving chiller.... In a word, it's terrific."[185]

<u>Sphinx</u>

In 1978, the newly-formed Orion Pictures was headquartered at the Burbank Studios, run by the same executive team

(Arthur Krim, Robert Benjamin, Eric Pleskow, Mike Medavoy, Bill Bernstein) which had successfully headed United
Artists until the parent company, Transamerica, began to
meddle in its affairs. Dubbed a mini-major, Orion, with a
$100 million credit line through Warner Bros. and complete
access to the Warner distribution system, had all the advantages of a studio and all the advantages of an independent; as had been its policy at United Artists, the company's
management would not interfere with the filmmakers or even
look at the product until it was edited. In order to establish itself in the Hollywood firmament, Orion needed properties that would make profitable motion pictures. In September 1978, Orion made a deal with International Creative
Management agents Bob Bookman and Erica Spellman, representing film and book rights respectively to an untitled
novel by Robin Cook to be published by G. P. Putnam's
Sons.

Robin Cook--the Boston ophthalmologist who had
written The Year of the Intern about his medical experiences and, more successfully, Coma, a novel with a medical
background--was being compared with Michael Crichton as
another doctor who wrote best-selling books and had a potential Hollywood career. His first love had been archeol-
ogy, and Cook was still interested in Egyptology; his manuscript in fact was tentatively titled Tombs and described as
a contemporary thriller set against an Egyptian background.
At that time, the King Tutankhamen exhibition had been
the surprise rage of every city it visited, and a story with
an Egyptian setting had a great deal of currency. Even if
Cook wasn't planning to deliver the manuscript to his editor
for another month, and the book itself was not scheduled
to be published until April 1979, Orion bought the book
sight unseen. The exact sum is not known, but a reasonable guess is that the price went into the high six figures.

The Cook book was indicative of how highly inflated
sums of Hollywood money were going into publishing: the
author would receive about $1 million for the hardback
rights, $3 million for the paperback rights from the New
American Library; in addition to the purchase price, Orion
would give Cook 5% of the film's gross once it reached the
breakeven point, $5000 for each week the book was ranked
1 through 5 on the best seller lists, and $2500 for each
week it was ranked 6 through 15. Altogether, as a literary

property Sphinx was worth in the neighborhood of $5 mil-
lion. Lucrative as his medical practice might be, it could
not begin to compare with the money Cook could make in
writing.

Orion sent the galleys of Sphinx to Franklin J.
Schaffner in February 1979. Its story concerns an Egyptologist with the intriguing name of Erica Baron who goes
to Cairo, proving Egypt is as important to her as medicine
is to her fiancé, Dr. Richard Harvey of Boston; there, she
inadvertently gets caught up in a black-marketeering ring.
She is immediately romanced by a mysterious Frenchman
named Yvon Julien de Margau, who has a great interest in
the statue of Seti I that Erica has seen in a nearby shop,
a work of art that surpasses any of Tutankhamen's treasures. Stephanos Markoulis, a sinister travel agent, also
has designs on it because there is another Seti statue in
Houston, the personal property of Texas millionaire Jeffrey
Rice, who would dearly love to have his hands on both
statues. Ahmed Khazzan, Director-General of the Egyptian
Department of Antiquities, is interested in the statue for
obvious reasons and, for other obvious reasons, is interested in Erica. Cook mixes love, intrigue, and violence; a
liberated woman becomes a damsel in distress, the drama
coming to its climax when Erica is trapped in Seti I's tomb.

Although the Cook book will never be mistaken for a
work by Dostoevski, it is a cunningly written work calculated to be an instant best-seller. The following exchange
between Yvon and Erica typifies the style and the spirit of
the book:

> "The fact that you are trained as an Egyptolo-
> gist," continued Yvon. "I find fascinating, because
> --and I mean this as a compliment--you have an
> East European sensuality that I love. Besides, I
> think you share some of Egypt's mysterious vibran-
> cy."
> "I think I'm very American," said Erica.[186]

The tales of Erica Baron are somewhere in between The
Perils of Pauline and Nancy Drew, but Tutmania was at its
peak, and Orion was anxious to sign Schaffner; the director accepted the project in March 1979.

If Ira Levin was a far cry from Ernest Hemingway, Sphinx is a far cry from The Boys from Brazil. At 600,000 copies sold, the Cook book was a best-seller, as far as best-sellers go, but not the must-read novel that becomes a household word. More to the point, this was not the type of material Schaffner's name had become associated with-- neither a serious nor a thought-provoking work with big themes. "Aside from The Double Man," Schaffner says by way of explanation, "I had never done an out-and-out melodrama." Somewhat dissatisfied with the circumstances and results of the earlier film, he would again try his directorial hand at the form with Sphinx. There were other important considerations as well: the lead happened to be a woman, "which," as the director points out, "was and to this day is a rarity"; in Yvon de Margeau and Ahmed Khazzan, there was the potential for two intriguing male roles; moreover, the story didn't take itself too seriously--it was a romp, an entertainment with humor. Finally, and perhaps most persuasively, the property had an exotic background, a truly unique setting. "He does a lot of films out of the country," George Roy Hill observes, "but that's a way of getting away, when you think about it." Sphinx afforded Schaffner the chance of going to Egypt.

Immediately after signing with Orion, Schaffner brought Stanley O'Toole into the picture: Sphinx would be a Schaffner-O'Toole Production, O'Toole serving as producer and Schaffner as director and executive producer. In preproduction, O'Toole, based in London, rounded up a veteran crew consisting of many people who had worked before in Egypt and knew the problems involved in filming there; Schaffner, based in Los Angeles, began work on the script.

According to his contract, Robin Cook had the right to do two drafts of the script. After discussing the project with Schaffner, Cook predicted, much to the director's surprise, that he could write the screenplay in four weeks. He did precisely that but, as is often the case when novelists tackle screenwriting the first time, the end results were not really filmic; it appeared evident that Schaffner would have to find another writer. John Byrum, who wrote Mahogany (1975) and wrote and directed Heart Beat (1980), was chosen primarily on the basis of his screenplay for Harry and Walter Go to New York (1976); Byrum

could write comedy and he was fast. The first move was to
cut down on the number of sidekicks surrounding the principal characters and cut out Jeffrey Rice completely; Erica's
fiancé Richard, who functions as a <u>deus</u> <u>ex</u> <u>machina</u> in the
book, was in and out of the script, and finally eliminated in
the November 29, 1979 script. Byrum wrote four drafts before Schaffner was satisfied and started thinking about the
production.

Schaffner had no background in Egyptology, but then
neither did he have a background in Russian history or the
French penal system; research always makes the big difference on a motion picture, especially when the production designer goes to work and draws sketches. Hired in that capacity was Terence Marsh, who had worked with John Box
on <u>Doctor Zhivago</u> and <u>Oliver</u>. Marsh had but one meeting
with Schaffner in Los Angeles before returning to London to
do his job. In a procedure unusual even to Schaffner, the
designs for the interiors came through the mail or by telex;
working off the floor plans in Los Angeles, Schaffner made
long distance changes and corrections with Marsh over the
telephone. "I didn't see any of those sets until sometime
around the first week in December," the director adds.

Original plans were to begin shooting in October 1979;
by August, it became clear that an October start was impossible. Production was postponed for another ten weeks,
enabling Schaffner to iron out problems with the script and
casting: Orion president Eric Pleskow offered the role of
Erica to Jill Clayburgh in August; Schaffner offered the
role to Jacqueline Bisset and the role of Yvon to Alain Delon
in September--to no avail. It was decided, while the script
was again rewritten, not to go after strong screen personalities but rather cast the leads to balance the story. In
short order, the services of Lesley-Anne Down as Erica,
Frank Langella as Ahmed Khazzan, and Maurice Ronet as
Yvon were secured.

The <u>Sphinx</u> company had to base its operations somewhere in Europe; Egypt was out of the question, despite its
annual production slate of 150 films, because its facilities
were minimal at best. Headquarters had been planned at
Pinewood Studios, but England was too costly; Spain was
no less expensive, and the Sevilla Studios, where <u>Patton</u>

was filmed, had already been torn down. Schaffner's experience on The Boys from Brazil had taught him that an
outside company would be overloaded with local film workers in Vienna; Munich was also considered and rejected.
The company finally settled on a seemingly unlikely spot--
Budapest.

        This was the doing of O'Toole, the European expert.
With the ever-changing situation in international filmmaking,
the only inexpensive places left to film on the continent were
in Eastern Europe--Hungary, Bulgaria, Czechoslovakia, and
Yugoslavia. Sofia had large studios that were technically
advanced but reasonably priced; Schaffner and O'Toole
wanted to recreate Egypt in Czechoslovakia but, for all the
activity at Sofia, couldn't book the necessary space. Fortunately, Hungary's Mafilm was aggressively seeking productions to bring to its studios; the facilities in Budapest
were more than adequate, plus there was the distinct advantage of being located in a capital city.

        A deal was made for four large soundstages at Mafilm;
by his estimate Schaffner figures the company saved $750,000.
That sum might be a bit conservative, according to O'Toole,
who told Daily Variety: "To build that much as we do in so
many studios would cost three times as much in England,
even more elsewhere"; the centerpiece of the production
alone, the tomb of Seti I complete with 900 artifacts, was a
million-dollar set. [187] As it turned out, Sphinx needed more
space for its 26 sets than the four soundstages allowed. A
television studio was rented; scenes involving underground
tunnels and passages were shot, without sound, in a warehouse outside the city.

        Schaffner visited Egypt a handful of times during
pre-production to chose locations in Cairo, Luxor, and the
Valley of Kings; he also secured permission to shoot the
Tutankhamen exhibit at the Egyptian Museum in Cairo. Be-
yond that, the most important reason for the trips to Egypt
was the troublesome matter of casting. The picture called
for split casting: Maude Spector cast the European and
English-speaking roles in London; Mike Fenton of Fenton-
Feinberg went to Egypt with Schaffner to cast Egyptians.
Knowing that the interiors would be filmed in Budapest,
Schaffner decided it more prudent to take Egyptian actors
to Hungary than carry Hungarian actors in Egypt; he and

Fenton spent five days in Cairo searching for the right
Egyptian character actors. Casting in Hungary was held
to a minimum; casting extras on a location is never an easy
proposition. John Gielgud, who in his only scene as Abdul
Hamdi has a dual function to reveal the statue of Seti I to
Erica and then to die, had to film his interiors in Hungary
and exteriors in Egypt.

Pleased with the director of photography's work on
The Boys from Brazil, Schaffner again sought Henri Decae,
but this was not to be: during Sphinx's August postpone-
ment, Decae accepted another assignment. Schaffner hired
instead an equally distinguished French cameraman, who had
also been considered for The Boys from Brazil, Claude Renoir,
perhaps best known for his work on his uncle's Grand Illusion (1937) and The River (1951). On Christmas Eve, a
week before shooting was to begin, the director received an
urgent telephone call from Stanley O'Toole informing him
that Renoir, while visiting his farm outside Paris, had fallen down the cellar steps, injured his eye, was in a hospital, and the doctor didn't think Renoir would be able to
work. "For God's sake, the cinematographer only needs
his one eye for this," the suddenly exasperated director
said. "Isn't there some way the doctor can stabilize the
condition so he can use his good eye?" To which the equally disconcerted producer replied, "It was his good eye."

Schaffner had little time to find another cinematographer; hoping Decae might now be free, he asked again, but
the cinematographer was already committed to another project. The search for a French cameraman ended, and Schaffner turned his attention to Great Britain: Ernest Day,
Freddie Young's camera operator, had now become a lighting
cameraman; knowing Day to have been an outstanding operator from the Nicholas and Alexandra experience, Schaffner
hired him at once.

The film was scheduled for a twelve-and-a-half-week
shoot: five weeks in Budapest, three in Cairo, and four-
and-a-half in Luxor. The company brought in all the lead
craftsmen and technicians; once again, Schaffner would work
with a mixed crew of English, Spanish, and, because of the
location, Hungarians; the reliable Jose Lopez Rodero was
again on hand as first assistant director. Production commenced after New Year's, 1980.

Foreign production being new to Mafilm, three Hungarians were quickly dispatched to Pinewood to learn about
production methods on an English-language film; Sphinx's
production designer, set decorator, property and location
people were obliged to come earlier. They found the hotel
accommodations and food fine, but direct transportation in
Budapest, it turned out, was only a rumor. Inevitably,
there was some stiffness getting started, exacerbated by
the language barriers and the six teams of interpreters.
"Basically three things happen," Schaffner says of working
in this kind of environment, "you compromise a little, you
learn a little, and you teach a little."[188] Eventually the
Hungarian crew took everything that was given and more.

On a film involving a female protagonist who questions the traditional role of women, the men of the crew
only had to turn their heads to see women working alongside them. Assigned to the films by the state, women assistant directors or production managers were an everyday
sight at Mafilm; the executive vice-president at Mafilm who
had brought Sphinx to Hungary was a woman. Women were
conspicuous in the Hungarian film industry, on and off the
set.

In one of the key sequences shot in Hungary, Erica
is trapped in the tunnel: the scene was originally shot
with no other lighting than the flashlight Erica carries; five
days later, when the dailies were ready to be seen, Schaffner and Day found the footage too dark and had to reshoot,
this time bouncing light off of styrofoam. Further on in the
tunnel, Erica kicks a hole open in a wall, jumps down, bangs
her head on skeletons, and lights what she believes to be a
torch, finding it actually to be the remnants of a human arm;
then she is attacked by bats. For this bit of business,
250 bats had to be warmed up to attack Down, special effects man Roy Whybrow's major contribution to the film;
five days later, the dailies revealed a problem with the
scene--not enough bats. It had to be reshot with 275 bats:
as an endangered species, the bats could not be out of hi-
bernation over four hours or be on the set more than two
hours at a time; as she had the first time, Down did the
retake by herself, without the assistance of a stunt person.
To achieve the intended effect, real bats were mixed with
mechanical bats, dead bats, and twisted kleenex blown at
the actress by wind machines; for all the stunts she under-

Recreating Egypt in Hungary: Lesley-Anne Down, Schaffner and Maurice Ronet, filming <u>Sphinx</u>, 1980.

took in this film, one can only term Lesley-Anne Down a
very good sport indeed.

Once the filming of the interiors was completed in
Budapest, the company moved to Egypt, Hollywood's first
production to enter the country since Howard Hawks' <u>Land
of the Pharoahs</u> in 1955. In a not too surprising occurrence, the company was held up for three days waiting for
the equipment to pass through customs. Another fact of
Egyptian movie-making life was the two censors who were
always on the set; their job, always highly subjective, was
to make sure that the country didn't look dirty or poverty-
stricken in the film, that Egyptians were not shown in an
unfavorable light, and that undesirable types were not portrayed as representative of Egypt. Schaffner brought a
rough assembly of the Mafilm footage to show what he and
the film were up to, but the company was persistently
hounded by the chief censor, by happenstance a woman.
"You have to make a certain amount of compromises when
you go into a different country to work," Schaffner under-
states. The value of O'Toole's hand-picked crew was that

each member shared the director's perspective and would
not yell, scream, curse, or add to the problems. "Analyze
the situation," Schaffner continues, "then find some way
just to get around it without wasting anybody's time and,
hopefully, wasting any more money than you're entitled to."

     Although a reasonable number of local film workers
were added to the crew, Schaffner, as he had anticipated,
found shooting in Egypt to be more difficult than in Hungary. The film negative was shipped to London and processed at the Rank Laboratories, but something would happen on the way back, and the film would bounce back and
forth between customs and the brokers; sometimes the company saw no dailies for three weeks. Another constant
problem was that the exterior scenes always attracted enormous crowds; to get rid of the crowds, the company had to
resort to early meals when shooting night scenes. One unpleasant and all too true detail is recreated in the film: the
highly visible Erica Baron becomes the focal point of a curious crowd everywhere she goes in Cairo; the narrow streets
and alleyways become positively claustrophobic as she is
touched and harassed. In these scenes, contrary to the
censors' efforts, Egypt is depicted in far from the most
flattering light.

     The final stop was Luxor, which, Robin Cook ac-
knowledges in his novel, "is to Egypt what Florence is to
Italy: the jewel"; [189] as such, Luxor was overrun by tour-
ists. It was impossible to book rooms for more than ten
people throughout the one-month stay; the M.S. Annie, the
Sheraton Hotel boat, had to be rented to lodge 75 crew members. The set for the Qurna Mosque, where Erica goes
looking for Sarwat Raman, was built for the film; new roads
were carved out, a refreshment stand and entrances to the
tombs were also constructed; other structures already ex-
isted. An establishing shot of the Winter Palace Hotel looks
artificial in the film: it very much appears to be a set on
a soundstage until the camera booms nearly 180 degrees in
the air to reveal a busy street and the Nile River beyond,
creating an interesting mixture of movie make-believe and
film reality.

     The company and its publicists may have talked about
the curse of the Pharaohs, but it is common knowledge that
sick actors, injuries, camera malfunctions, inoperable props

and effects are endemic to all motion picture productions. Yet in April, on the last day of production, something happened in Luxor that was decidedly unusual: Schaffner had a hectic day, involving two camera teams, an aerial unit, and 300 extras; a total of 2700 feet of film was exposed that day, and, suddenly, the footage disappeared. Nobody ever saw that negative again. The thief was never found; if it was a member of the crew, he or she never asked for ransom. It might have been customs, but, for all the other difficulties, everything else had eventually gone through. The missing 2700 feet still remains a mystery.

There was no way the film could be edited around the missing scenes--they were absolutely crucial--but there was always a chance that the footage might show up at the last moment, and so the director decided to wait. The upshot was that in August, deep into post-production, Schaffner had to return to Luxor and reshoot the missing scenes in the hot season. "It's not comfortable," he told a reporter, "but we ain't paid to cry about it."[190] For all the inconvenience and the $80,000 cost of retakes, some of which was covered by insurance, it could have been worse.

Robert E. Swink, who had once again been summoned to do the editing, accompanied the production to Hungary and Egypt, but, after completing a first cut, had to leave the job for reasons of health. Michael F. Anderson came in to finish editing Sphinx. "It was a stroke of luck, it was just an ideal situation for me," Anderson says, despite the obvious difficulties he encountered, not having had the chance to see the dailies. In the past, working at Twentieth Century-Fox, the editor had had the opportunity of seeing Schaffner, a director he particularly admired; now he was on the lot working with him.

Schaffner returned to London for the looping and the music scoring. When Jerry Goldsmith proved to be unavailable, O'Toole brought in an English composer who came highly recommended, Michael J. Lewis, to write the rousing score. In September, post-production resumed at Fox with the rerecording: Sphinx was Schaffner's first experience with Dolby stereo, which he found difficult, especially as the studio policy was to mix the Dolby track first and the monaural track separately; when segments had to be redone, it took a third again as much time as non-Dolby

stereo. The film was brought in for $10 million, ready for
a February 1981 release.

There were good feelings about the production. After
an advance screening, Henry Rogers of the Rogers and
Cowan public relations firm sent a letter to Lloyd Leipzig,
Orion's vice-president of advertising and publicity, stating:
"We really believe that the subject matter and the quality of
the film gives it the opportunity to break through as a
blockbuster."[191] Unfortunately, the critics did not share
Rogers' enthusiasm for the film; Sphinx was met by a rather
hostile reaction. Indicative of words to come was the Daily
Variety review:

> The film is an embarrassment of the first order,
> one of those dreaded misfires at which the unin-
> tentional laughter builds to a heady hilarity by the
> time the frenzied climax rolls around.... Franklin
> J. Schaffner's steady and sober style is helpless in
> the face of the mounting implausibilities, and one
> hopes this will be a momentary lapse in a generally
> distinguished career.[192]

The film opens with a silhouette shot of a dog on a
ridge; the prologue takes place in the Valley of the Kings,
1301 B.C. Recreated by scholars for the film, the language
spoken is authentic; English subtitles translate. Menephta,
the royal architect, has caught grave robbers: as punishment for the crime, setting the scene for the intrigue and
violence that is to come, each of a robber's four limbs is
tied to a separate horse, and, when whipped, the horses
literally tear him apart.

After the opening credits, Lesley-Anne Down, "the
world's prettiest Egyptologist,"[193] establishes her feminist
credentials in short order, discussing the plight of women
in academia, and recounts how her parents read three
pages of her thesis on "Syntactical Problems in Late Egyptian Stories and Love Poems" before stopping to ask when
she would get married. Whenever she mentions Egyptology,
she says, people start talking about Pyramid Power. Complaining about being routinely passed over in her field because she is a woman, she insists:

Because of an accident of fate 10 million years ago,

when somebody had to finally get up and go out of
the cave and strangle an animal for dinner, their
gender and not mine was the one that was big
enough, hostile enough, and dumb enough to do it!

When Yvon de Margeau (Ronet), claiming to be a friendly
journalist, slaps her to help her regain her senses, Erica
is independent enough to slap back, snapping, "I don't
like being slapped, even when I'm hysterical." To her
credit, Erica is hip enough to say that whenever she talks
about Menephta, "it makes most people look like they've
swallowed a Quaalude."

At the Antica Abdul, Abdul Hamdi (played by, as the
credits read, Sir John Gielgud) discreetly reveals the price-
less statue of Seti I, and the first close-up of Down in the
film follows: Erica lights up, she looks transported; when
the statue is put away, another close-up reveals her darkened face.   "When Gielgud's name is listed that far down in
the credits," Arthur Knight observed, "you know he isn't
going to be around very long."[194] Gielgud's death scene
is also instructive of Schaffner's style.   Hamdi is beheaded
by a scimitar in two shots: (1) Gielgud's face as he lies
with his back against a glass case; (2) a reverse low angle
under the case, showing the blood, broken glass, and finally Hamdi's head as it slumps down.   Similar to the grave
robber's execution in the prologue, the violence is neither
romanticized nor embellished: there is blood, but not a
copious amount; no slow motion poeticizes or exploits the
bloodshed; the camera does not linger on or back off from
the deed.   Schaffner's film violence is very realistic, and,
as opposed to other styles of screen violence, realistic violence is often more difficult to watch.

Ahmed Khazzan (Langella) is introduced by a mirror
shot in Erica's room.   Purportedly representing the Egyptian
government, he is the tormented, brooding romantic type.
"Egypt's one great national resource," he intones, "death."
He will take Erica on the grand tour of Luxor, visiting the
actual tombs of Seti II and Tutankhamen; although there is
a definite attraction between them, he tells her to go, a
Yale student has already been killed trying to uncover what
she seeks.   In a moment with the unabashed romanticism
and the Anglo-American Technicolor look and atmosphere of
Albert Lewin's Pandora and the Flying Dutchman (1950),
Erica slaps her horse away, to stay the night with Ahmed.

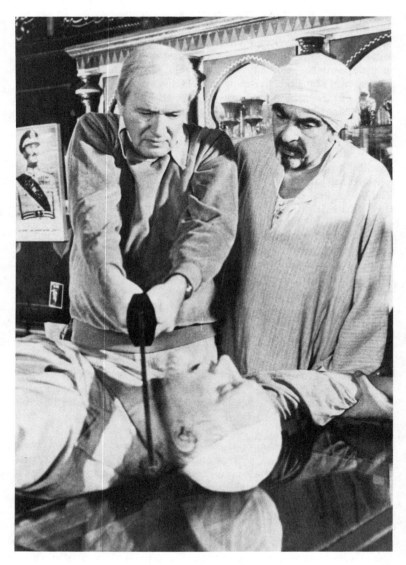

Realistic violence: Schaffner, John Gielgud (horizontal),
and Martin Benson, filming Sphinx, 1980.

Schaffner was right in eliminating most of the accom-
plices; even as it plays, with fewer characters, Sphinx can
be confusing. Stephanos Markoulis (John Rhys-Davies) is
clearly a heavy according to a film code that goes back at
least to Henry King's Tol'able David (1922): in his first
screen appearance, Markoulis tries to kick a dog. What he
wants is clear, but why and for whom are less easily dis-
cerned. When Erica goes to the Museum to translate Menephta's inscription on the Seti I statue, she is held at
knifepoint by Markoulis; she manages to escape when his
face is sliced by the evil-looking Khalifa (Vic Tablian), the
assassin who killed Gamal, Ahmed's assistant. Due to the
plot and the presentation, all this intrigue is perplexing to
an audience.

The second flashback to Menephta establishes that the
architect had a secret plan to ensure the safety of Seti I's
tomb. Like the prologue, it is so rich in detail and atmosphere as to suggest that the director would have felt more
at home making a film about Menephta, and that it would
have been superior to the film about Ms. Baron. Regrettably, the scene returns to the present, catching Erica's
reflection in a mirror shot when she has the brainstorm that
solves Menephta's riddle about the tomb.

Betrayed by the man in the burnoose at Qurna Mosque,
Erica slowly crawls her way to the secret tomb, finding, by
turning on electric lights, that a later generation of grave
robbers knows the secret too. When she sees the treasures,
a close-up of Down displays the same transported smile Erica
had in her first close-up. Somehow, she manages to return
to her hotel, where she is chased by Markoulis, who is killed
by Khalifa, who works for Yvon, also a black marketeer.
This is an adventure movie, and there has to be a chase:
Erica jumps into an old truck loaded with men in the rear
and drives madly away, pursued by Yvon and Khalifa;
prominent in the chase montage are such ingredients as a
clothesline, mud, chickens, and cars that smash into each
other. Although the truck manages to knock Yvon's car
into the river, Erica can't prevent it from crashing through
a wall; conveniently, she just happens to have arrived at
Ahmed Khazzan's house. Awaiting her is the man in the
burnoose (Martin Benson), Ahmed's uncle--their family has
been looting the tomb for generations. Drawing a gun on
her, he prompts a nearly operatic gunfight reminiscent of

the multiple gunfight in Nicholas Ray's Johnny Guitar (1954)
in which everybody manages to kill everybody else, leaving
only Ahmed to flee down the Nile.

At the end, as if moving back in time, Erica rides the
white stallion to the Valley of the Kings, joining Ahmed in
the secret tomb. That she should love him so soon and so
passionately comes as a bit of a surprise--a scene further
developing their romance was cut from the film--but such is
a convention of the genre. Despite her strong protestations
of love, he sends her away to the safety of the shaft, and,
with the help of a sledgehammer, like a Brontean hero, Ahmed Khazzan literally brings on the fall of his house.

"Franklin Schaffner, I'm fairly certain, did not intend
that his epic adventure film 'Sphinx' should emerge as an
instant example of high camp," Barry Brennan wrote in the
Evening Outlook. "He did not intend it. But he achieved
it."[195] The film was not intended as an epic nor was the
humor unintentional, but the film's levity was not designed
for the response with which it was greeted. When the initial public reaction to Sphinx proved to be apathetic, Orion
Pictures withdrew its support and turned its corporate attention elsewhere. More puzzling, considering its investment in the Schaffner project, Orion, two months earlier,
had released another mystery-adventure movie with an
Egyptian background, The Awakening--a picture starring
Charlton Heston that also died at the box office. Yet in
the summer of 1981, Paramount released Raiders of the Lost
Ark, whose resemblance to Sphinx, including the white
horse and John Rhys-Davies, was noted:

> Since all cakes have the same ingredients, it must
> be the mixing that matters. It's the same thing
> with adventure films. Sphinx has every one of the
> elements that made Raiders of the Lost Ark such a
> smashing success, yet it fizzles. Like Raiders,
> Sphinx follows an attractive archeologist to the
> mysterious Land of the Pharaohs. While Raider
> Indiana Jones gets into all kinds of trouble he
> usually finds some spectacular way out of it.
> Sphinx heroine Erica Baron ... just seems to plow
> deeper in.[196]

The critics and public accepted one film, helping it to

become the biggest moneymaker of the year, and rejected
the other.

   True, a critic can find fault with Sphinx: the element of European intrigue could have been further developed; the same applies to the love triangle of Erica, Ahmed, and Yvon. Yvon is played by the suave and debonair Maurice Ronet, who is curiously unconvincing playing
a Ronet type, perhaps most attributable to his voice that
must speak English in the film. As Ahmed, Frank Langella
speaks with a semi-British accent, which is acceptable if
John Gielgud's accent is acceptable--probably more so,
since Khazzan is the type whose British education has only
strengthened his loathing of the colonial mentality. "You're
the rudest sonofabitch I've ever met in my life," Erica tells
him soon after they first meet. Ahmed's assistant Gamal is
quick to concur: it is the type of part that has become
Langella's forte.

   In spite of her hairstyle, with its punk look and unnaturally red tint, making her look like a fugitive out of a
Michael Powell film, Lesley-Anne Down is quite appealing.
She is somewhere between Audrey Hepburn and Jacqueline
Bisset--not as charming as the former but not as sullen as
the latter--and she is prettier than the statue of Seti I;
the film also gives her ample opportunity to show how well
she can run. She is particularly affecting in the denouement, when an American girl asks if she's found anything
digging, and Down dejectedly replies, "Nothing to write
home about." Sphinx, however, did not make her a major
star, as was predicted. Part of the problem was that, for
all their individual strengths as screen personalities, Ronet,
Langella, and Down did not mesh well together, something
that detracted from each performance. Secondly, Down does
not have sufficient depth to be convincing as a scholar who
makes feminist pronouncements: by way of comparison, Harrison Ford as Indiana Jones was given no hard sell to establish his credentials as a professor; the trouble was built
into the role of Erica Baron. In a detail no one familiar
with the modern university can carp at, the film shows that
the Egyptologist cannot speak the Egyptian language. Looking for Sarwat Raman, the only Egyptian allowed in the
tombs when Howard Carter made his discoveries, she instead comes across his widow, Aida (Eileen Way), who tells
Erica she's just like all the rest who come to dig holes in

Egypt. When Erica denies the charge, Aida points out that
she is now in fact growing academically greedy. This kind
of insight does not easily blend with the melodramatic high-
jinks of the role and the overall film.

Still, nothing in the film warrants the critical pasting
it took. Schaffner is incapable of making anything but a
handsome-looking motion picture; overlooked in the flak was
how he had managed, through some sleight of hand, to get
so much production value on the screen, with the inflated
dollars of the 1980s, at such a low cost. Perhaps people
had come to expect something more from a film signed by
Franklin J. Schaffner. "I think I was held hostage by the
critics," Schaffner says evenly, "for doing what I thought
was a romp and they thought a thin and unimportant picture."

Yes, Giorgio

In the early days of CBS Television, every staff director
spent some time working on Blues by Bargy, a musical program featuring singer-pianist Jeane Bargy that ran from
1949 to 1950. Somewhere along the line, each director, and
Franklin Schaffner was no exception, would invariably super-
impose a shot of tapping feet over Bargy's head. Franklin
J. Schaffner has always wanted to do a movie musical, but,
inexplicably--since the advent of CinemaScope and rock and
roll, which would seem a natural combination--the genre was
on the wane. With the exception of a big-budget adaptation
of a successful Broadway musical, on occasion prompting a
short-lived cycle, Hollywood studios were reluctant to tackle
the genre.

Ironically enough, the closest Schaffner had come to
the form on the big screen was in a scene near the end of
Patton--the banquet for American and Russian generals in
which Patton's contempt for the Russians intensifies. A
high-angle shot establishes the evening's entertainment, a
Russian dance, followed by a dolly shot behind the orchestra on the mezzanine intermittently catching the dancers
below; rather than the time-honored method of using long
takes of full shots to follow the dancers, Schaffner heightened the motion and added to the vigor of the dance through
montage. Patton proved the director could handle large-scale

action; the banquet scene suggests Schaffner would be quite
adept at action on a dance floor, given the right opportunity. When the chance came, however, it would not be a
dance musical; the music wouldn't be the stuff of Tin Pan
Alley but of Lincoln Center. From Blues by Bargy to opera
by Pavarotti, Schaffner and the musical genre had traveled
a tortuous route.

On June 2, 1980, David Begelman, president of the
M-G-M Film Company, announced that Luciano Pavarotti
would make his film debut in Yes, Giorgio. It seemed appropriate that the Italian tenor should work for a studio
that was the home of motion picture musicals in the 1940s
and 1950s, especially with the Arthur Freed unit's productions of Meet Me in St. Louis (1944), On the Town (1949),
An American in Paris (1951), and Singin' in the Rain
(1952).

Hollywood has long been enamored of celebrities in
other fields, particularly in the more cultured arts. Pavarotti had already achieved great fame in his own right,
having made the covers of both Time and Newsweek and
published a premature autobiography, Pavarotti: My Own
Story; able to command $40,000 and up for a two-hour con-
cert, he couldn't be seduced by offers of big money. In
addition to the PBS opera specials, Pavarotti had also done
well on network television, making pasta with Dinah Shore,
singing with Loretta Lynn, and talking about diets and getting bleeped for saying "tits" with Johnny Carson. Most
noteworthy was his American Express credit card commercial
in which he displayed a most engaging persona.

Opera singers had come to Hollywood in the past:
paradoxically, Enrico Caruso, Mary Garden, and Geraldine
Farrar appeared in silent films; John McCormack, Feodor
Chaliapin, Lily Pons, Ezio Pinza, Rise Stevens, and Lauritz
Melchior had all made films, but, with the possible exception of Grace Moore, who enjoyed popularity in the 1930s,
no opera singer had become a genuine motion picture star.
To be sure, Mario Lanza, with whom Pavarotti would inevitably be compared, was a major movie star. Excellent
as his voice was, it was untrained, and that was the outstanding difference: Lanza was essentially a creation of
motion pictures--an M-G-M property, at that--whereas
Pavarotti was a genuine opera star, the world's number
one tenor, the King of the high C's.

A well-known music critic was prompted to note:
"The moguls of the '50s would, no doubt, have cast Pavarotti as the hero's good-hearted best friend or amusing
uncle, not as the fellow who gets the girl."[197] No less a
singing phenomenon than Frank Sinatra had spent a dozen
years playing juveniles; even Elvis Presley had played the
second male lead in his first film, Love Me Tender (1956).
Pavarotti, instead of singing a specialty number or two and
gradually being groomed for starring roles, would play the
lead his first time out in films.

He was not completely without experience: he had
had to do some acting in opera, and he had learned a thing
or two about appearing before cameras from his television
work. That he was a native-Italian speaker posed no major
problem; immediately problematic, however, was his egre-
gious size--Pavarotti is of the same proportions as Sidney
Greenstreet. There had never been a leading man of that
size; avoirdupois had led to the ruination of Mario Lanza's
career. Peter Fetterman, the English producer of Yes,
Giorgio, was quoted as saying, perhaps somewhat ungal-
lantly, "In England, no one would hear of doing a picture
with a fat man as the romantic lead."[198] But things were
different in America: a generation ago, it would have been
unthinkable for Woody Allen to be a leading man; if the
diminutive Dudley Moore could become a star, it wasn't inconceivable that the no less cuddly Luciano Pavarotti could.

Fetterman, who had earlier produced The Haunting of
Julia (1976), found the idea of Pavarotti and a Hollywood
musical irresistible. To him, the ideal vehicle would be a
film biography of Enrico Caruso, but that had been done by
M-G-M with Mario Lanza in 1950. Instead, when he came
across a copy of Anne Piper's novel Yes, Giorgio, Fetterman
found the raw material for a film. With the help of his new
partner, Alain Bernheim, a former literary agent, Fetterman was able to meet Pavarotti, who was intrigued by the
possibilities of film--if nothing else, a film appearance would
attract more people to opera.

Alain Bernheim had an in with M-G-M, having brought
to the studio Francis Veber's L'Emmerdeur, an eight-year-
old French film directed by Edouard Molinaro which was on
its way to becoming Billy Wilder's Buddy, Buddy. As soon
as the project was mentioned, David Begelman, being a great

fan of Pavarotti's, jumped at the idea; a deal was made in short order. Fetterman would be producer and Bernheim executive producer, the same credit he was receiving on Buddy, Buddy; for his participation in setting up the package, Herbert H. Breslin, Pavarotti's manager, became co-executive producer. Begelman then gave Fetterman the green light to purchase the Piper novel.

The book concerns an Italian professor of International Law who is invited to the United States to give a series of lectures; Yes, Giorgio refers to what he is accustomed to hearing from women--until he meets a strong-willed Welsh woman named Rose Williams, the narrator of the book. Married for ten years to a socialist, Rose has come to America to study on a scholarship; she and Giorgio drive off in a blue convertible, leaving New York to explore America on a motel trip not unlike the one in Vladimir Nabokov's Lolita. The romantic journey gets as far west as New Mexico, where they meet 20-year-old Patsy, causing Rose to reflect:

> I don't even know the name of Giorgio's wife. Every day I could have asked him, but she was there so strong without one. No name and no face but always more alive than I was. He punished me for her and now he's punishing Patsy for me. [199]

Rose returns home to her husband, a sadder but wiser woman.

In a letter to Adolph Green, a prospective screenwriter for the film, Alain Bernheim wrote: "David Begelman says it should be a mixture of SUMMERTIME, ROMAN HOLIDAY, and TWO FOR THE ROAD." [200] The final script would not be as sophisticated as Begelman's models, nor would the film be graced by the presence of a Hepburn. John Tarnoff, the M-G-M vice-president who would supervise the film, brought in Norman Steinberg, theretofore best known for his work on Blazing Saddles (1974); Steinberg would later stay on the lot to work on the script of My Favorite Year (1982), but not before he and Fetterman first went to Europe to meet Pavarotti, get the flavor of the man, and come up with a story. Piper's plot was thrown away, the Italian professor of International Law became an Italian opera singer, and soon the only thing remaining from the book was its title.

Franklin J. Schaffner did not attend the June 2 reception for Pavarotti at the Beverly Wilshire Hotel. He had heard there was a film in the works, but didn't know much about it or what its progress was; he was otherwise occupied. In October 1979, Schaffner, Martin Manulis, and Stanley O'Toole had optioned John A. Nist and David Kranes' Dealer, a story about a baseball player turned dealer; the option expired in May 1980, before they could do anything with the project. Then Schaffner and producer David Foster tried to develop an idea they had, Titles, with Alan Swyer; nothing mutually satisfactory resulted. After the successful New Orleans sneak preview of Sphinx in November 1980, Schaffner began looking around for a new project: beyond the expected western, political or historical drama, he was looking for a romance, a comedy, and something with music; in the Pavarotti project, there was the possible combination of all three elements. He asked his agent George Chasin to call his former agent David Begelman and inquire if a script was ready and if he could read it--without any obligations on anyone's part. Shortly thereafter, Schaffner had a meeting with Begelman, Fetterman, and Bernheim, and was signed to direct Yes, Giorgio.

Although he had no professional experience in opera, Schaffner had been a frequent patron of the Metropolitan Opera and possessed a solid background in music; furthermore, in 1966, he had toyed with the idea of making a film biography of Tito Schipa, another tenor. Yes, Giorgio may not have offered him material with the scope of his other films, but it did provide a definite challenge: having worked with the likes of Steve McQueen, Dustin Hoffman, and George C. Scott, Schaffner would now be working with a temperamental opera singer, Luciano Pavarotti.

The director first met his star at the Bel-Air Hotel. Typical of meetings of this sort, the place abounded with other people's assistants; even if possible, it would have been pointless to make any attempts at meaningful conversation. Because nothing productive could be accomplished inside, Schaffner took Pavarotti for a walk outside the hotel; they talked together for over an hour. To allay the fears of the first-time film actor, the director explained how he worked; as the meeting came to an end, Schaffner recalls, Pavarotti said, "I am in your hands entirely, but when it comes to music you must listen to me."

Schaffner soon discovered that Fetterman and Bernheim were not the most experienced of producers; he needed
a producer to take care of the nuts-and-bolts work. "To
his great credit," Schaffner says of Pavarotti's manager,
"when I sought to bring in Stanley O'Toole, Breslin stepped
aside, so that if the whole thing had worked it would've
been Bernheim and O'Toole, executive producers." Fetterman and Bernheim were not very enthusiastic about the
idea. "A political situation arose," the director comments,
"that made it impossible for O'Toole to remain."[201]

Steinberg's script was 140 pages long--without ac-
counting for the songs the star would sing. With an assist from M-G-M, Schaffner persuaded the writer to pare
down the script: one of a distribution company's standard
demands is that no film be longer than 135 minutes. An
average script is approximately 120 pages, and Schaffner's
aim was to get Steinberg's screenplay down to 100 pages
and, in the best tradition of integrated musicals, let the
music tell the story and move the plot forward. The choice
of songs would be crucial to the final script: Turandot,
for example, was always set for the opera sequence--just
how much would be used was undetermined; up until the
start of production, Herbert H. Breslin received frequent
phone calls asking him what numbers Pavarotti was either
fond of or proficient at singing.

Schaffner and Steinberg worked furiously to adjust
character attitudes and reactions, and redesign the content
before the impending Writers Guild strike in April 1981.
Normally, Schaffner likes to have the attention of his writer until the moment he begins filming; during the two-month
interval between the strike and the beginning of production,
Schaffner, according to the Writers Guild contract, did not
talk to Steinberg about the script. However, he cast Steinberg in the role of Dr. Barmen, the Giorgio Fini fanatic.
"It was not a device," the director insists, "to get him on
the set."

A far more damaging strike was on the horizon--the
Directors Guild of America had tentatively set a strike for
June. Schaffner was asked if he could begin shooting in
April and finish before the strike. Realizing the studio
might cancel the project if he replied no, Schaffner an-
swered truthfully: it was possible, but the added pressure

on the schedule would be expensive; more people would
have to be hired. There would be new complications: as
Boston would be too gray and blustery, should the concert
scene be cancelled? As the grapes would not be in season,
what would the company do about the Napa Valley sequence?
These turned out to be secondary problems; the film did not
begin production in April because Luciano Pavarotti's schedule prevented it. So, when April came, Schaffner got Pavarotti's final reaction to the script; the following month, he
traveled to Miami for more discussion, bringing with him
the costume designer, make-up artist, and hairdresser who
took care of their respective film chores in Florida.

    Scoring the film would not be a simple or rewarding
task: rather than write his own music, the composer would
have to integrate and arrange other people's music. Schaffner had two people in mind for this unenviable job--Jerry
Goldsmith or John Williams, but both were busy on other
projects. Best known for his epic film scores, Williams,
however, expressed interest in trying his hand at an original love song for the film; the result was "If We Were in
Love," co-written with lyricists Alan and Marilyn Bergman.
"The number was obviously wrong as the very opening kind
of 'up' Broadway piece for the picture," Schaffner says.
Leoncavallo's "Mattinata," originally set for the San Francisco sequence, was moved up to the opening credits.

    Based on his work for Sphinx, Michael J. Lewis was
the composer selected for the thankless job of writing the
score for a film featuring music by a variety of classical
composers, John Williams, and a song made famous by Tony
Bennett. "It takes a balanced ego to accept that kind of
assignment," Schaffner opines. "It takes an English type
of temperament to do that kind of thing." Contributing a
mini-score, including an overture as lovely as any music in
the film, Lewis also made musical alterations in post-
production, recording new musical tracks and introductions
for pre-existing material. In June, Pavarotti prerecorded
the numbers that had been selected, and the songs were
finally locked in: conducting the orchestra at Twentieth
Century-Fox was Emerson Buckley of the Miami Opera, the
man who had first brought Pavarotti to America a decade
earlier; Buckley would more or less play himself in the Boston Hatch sequence in the film.

Sven Nykvist, then completing <u>Cannery Row</u> (1982) on the M-G-M lot, was considered for the cinematography, but Fred J. Koenekamp got the job. On his fourth collaboration with Schaffner, he would be working with material that lacked the size and scope of the previous films: the 1:85 aspect ratio was chosen accordingly; the wide screen, for some reason, seems to run against the spirit of comedy, and would only have made their job more difficult. For the visual look, Schaffner and Koenekamp decided on soft full lighting, a very fashionable style of late (e.g., <u>On Golden Pond</u>, 1981); if neither man particularly cared for this lighting style, they both agreed it would best suit the purposes of the film--make everything look good.

In one of the few breaks the film would get, the actors had already had their strike, but still remaining to be solved was the delicate problem of casting a leading lady. Gone were the days of the studio system when M-G-M could make Lana Turner, whether she wanted to or not, appear in <u>Mr. Imperium</u> (1951) with Ezio Pinza. "We had tried to build a script that was a two-hander," Schaffner says, "but there isn't any question about who was going to be the dominant force in the film." Matters were not helped any when one of the producers in his eagerness sent copies of the script, before it was ready and without the director's knowledge, to several actresses who were possible candidates for the role of Dr. Pamela Taylor. Schaffner's personal and realistic choice was Blythe Danner, an actress of intelligence and maturity, but M-G-M wasn't that excited about her and refused to make a deal over a small difference in money. Discussions with Sigourney Weaver were cordial, but in the end she refused. Kate Jackson accepted the role, but grew concerned about the script and, at the last moment, decided she'd be more comfortable not playing the part. Kathryn Harrold, the rising young actress of <u>The Hunter</u> (1980) and <u>Modern Romance</u> (1981), had been a contender for the role, except that Schaffner had envisioned Pamela as a slightly older woman; she was still available and was signed by the time production commenced.

San Francisco as one of the script's chief locations was a source of discomfort to the director; the city's scenery had become too familiar from films and television shows, and the <u>Giorgio</u> script called for the standard tour. He had

instead wanted to shoot in such less familiar but picturesque
cities as Seattle, Denver, or Santa Fe, where the Giordano
ranch was originally set. "In the end, because of the now
looming inclusion of the balloon sequence," he says, referring to the colorful means of transportation that takes the
principals to the nearby Napa Valley, "we decided to go
into an altered version of San Francisco." No less significant a determining factor was that Pavarotti had already
committed himself to a June 13, 1981 benefit at the San
Francisco Civic Auditorium for the Morra de Sanctis earth-
quake victims. M-G-M made a $25,000 contribution, and
the concert, with the San Francisco Opera Orchestra under
the direction of Kurt Herbert Adler, was filmed by six
cameras in its entirety.

The problem of lighting the auditorium--compounded
by the heat of the lights and the cables on the floor that
were sure to make the distinguished audience uncomfortable
--was solved when the house lights proved to be sufficient.
Although rehearsals were impossible, the director had a
choice of three lighting schemes: full house lights, medium,
and stage lights only. On the night of the concert, Schaffner and Koenekamp sat in the booth for three and a half
hours, the former cueing the cameramen by radio and the
latter taking care of the house light changes, unbeknownst
to a delighted audience of 14,000. Puccini's "Donna Non
Vidi" had been pre-determined for Giorgio's San Francisco
concert in the film; when the company later returned to the
city, bringing in its own lights, the close shots of Pavarotti
were picked up in a minimum of time.

In spite of the directors' strike, now scheduled for
July 1, Schaffner took the company to Boston and began
production: first on the agenda, scheduled for Thursday,
June 20, was the concert at the Hatch Shell on the Charles
River; as scripted, since concerts are usually given in the
evenings, it took place at night. On an inspection of the
Hatch Shell, the director realized the pitfall of night shooting: the more than 100,000 anticipated spectators had to
be lit; although this was technically possible, only the concert area itself would be seen. Gone would be the view of
the Charles River, the boats, the skaters, and the picknick-
ers; but in a day concert, helicopter shots would also be
possible.

The trouble with shooting Thursday afternoon was twofold: heavy traffic--a state highway runs by the Hatch Shell; and the Boston Red Sox were playing a day game. With the help of the Massachusetts Film Commission, the concert was rescheduled on Saturday, when traffic would be rerouted for two hours. In the remaining time, the concert had to be promoted: if it were too heavily promoted, too many people would turn up; if it weren't promoted, nobody might show up. As a compromise, the concert was mildly promoted; even then, people started arriving Friday night to wait for good seats.

The crew was ordered to arrive at 8:00 a.m. to film pick-up shots, before the crowd became too dense for the 4:00 p.m. concert; the reactions of all the principals were filmed long before Pavarotti went on stage. An additional six cameramen were brought up from New York, Boston being within the New York jurisdiction, also instructed to arrive early at the Esplanade--or they wouldn't have been able to get their equipment in position, the crowd had become that heavy. Fortunately for all, the audience was well-behaved; all in all, over 110,000 people showed up, making this the largest event of its kind since Woodstock.

Schaffner had everything worked out in detail before the concert began:

> I would pre-brief all the cameramen as to what lenses they were going to be on for a particular number, and I would use a cueing system which told them that at a certain point they would go from a 35 to a 75, or at a certain point they'd be on a 125 and they would come back to a 50--that kind of stuff. So I sat on one camera platform, you know, just number by number, would talk to camera 1 and 2, 3, 4, 5, 6. In between the numbers, during the applause, you would pre-set everybody for his opening shot.

Along with the San Francisco concert, this was not unlike his experience decades earlier in the control booth at CBS. A significant difference was a sync problem that did not exist in live television; this was worked out in advance with digital readouts that timed the concert from beginning

to end. Another difference was that the maximum load of a
film magazine is 1000 feet--or about eleven minutes of shooting time; the cameras started rolling at staggered intervals
so the cameramen, while they were reloading, would know
that at least four other cameras were covering Pavarotti.
After reloading, each cameraman would photograph a few
frames of the digital timer so there would be no trouble
when it came time to synchronize the sound and the picture. But no matter what the medium, a live concert is a
one-shot affair, and the director admits: "It did feel like
the old days of television."

     As a hedge against the Directors Guild strike, an
enormous amount of footage was shot for the San Francisco
and Boston concerts. If there was a strike, the film would
probably be cancelled because Pavarotti was solidly booked
for years; in that event, the footage from both concerts
could be combined for a television special. Although Schaffner would not be involved, it could help defray some of the
monies that had been put into the production; certainly a
decent one-hour television show could come out of the 26
hours of film. If there wasn't a strike, the concerts were
still an integral part of the film. The Directors Guild of
America settled with the producers, and the strike was
called off on Sunday, June 28. Not only would there be a
Yes, Giorgio but Schaffner, who was committed to working
up until the last moment before the strike, had a head
start on the other studios' stalled productions. His gamble
in going to Boston had paid off.

     In working with Luciano Pavarotti, Schaffner had
three major areas of concern: (1) how to make him look as
if he fit on the big screen--hiding his size, in other words;
(2) how the star would cope with the filmmaking process--
how long a scene he could handle, how he would manage
doing scenes over and over, how he would fare with sync,
performing to prerecorded numbers; (3) how skillfully the
two of them could communicate, given that Pavarotti was
not a film actor, English was not his native language, and
the director spoke no Italian.

     Regarding the first area of concern, Kevin Thomas
observed:

     Schaffner was a shrewd choice. As the director of

such epic-scale films as "Planet of the Apes" and "Patton," he's used to thinking big, and he and cameraman Fred Koenekamp place Pavarotti in spacious settings appropriate to his size.[202]

Another important collaborator was Rita Riggs, the costume designer, who selected cuts of clothes to make the leading man look more svelte, dressing him most often in black. Light backgrounds were avoided when photographing Pavarotti as they tended to make him look larger; Koenekamp half-lit him so that one side of his face was darker. For close shots, where Pavarotti's body would not be seen, the cinematographer resorted to the classical cinema style of glamour lighting to make the leading man look as handsome as possible.

Pavarotti's biggest problem was memorizing his lines. For the dining room scene at the Copley Plaza (the actors, in the best manner of movie magic, walk through the bar in Boston and enter a room at Cal Tech in Pasadena), for example, Schaffner wisely used two cameras, not only saving wear and tear on the actors in the oppressive heat of the location, but also providing, for editing purposes, footage of different angles in which Pavarotti delivered his lines identically. The anticipated sync trouble turned out to be no problem at all: Pavarotti is a natural-born performer whether singing live or to playback.

As for the third area of concern, Pavarotti's Italian attitude regarding an American situation immediately manifested itself, but, after three days, there was close communication between director and star. "He sensed immediately what would work for the camera and what wouldn't," Schaffner says. "Really, to get him keyed in on the direction of a scene took no more than 45 minutes--and that's not bad."

Yes, Giorgio posed some interesting problems for the production designer. Usually, the set reflects or reinforces the personality of the character--the Hudson house William J. Creber designed for Islands in the Stream is a prime example. Yes, Giorgio has no sets that reflect on the main characters: the leads are never seen at home, but in hotels or other people's homes; even the opera set, because of its unruly dragon, does not make Giorgio feel at home.

Schaffner and Luciano Pavarotti at the Met, filming <u>Yes</u>, <u>Giorgio</u>, 1981.

Creber's task was to give the film elegance and select the right-looking hotels. "The idea was to give it as much production as we possibly could," he says, "make it just worth going to all those places."

The company moved to New York for the final sequence in the film, <u>Turandot</u> at the Metropolitan Opera. This night at the opera cost M-G-M $125,000. The Met only goes dark once a year for inspection and renovation, which gave the company exactly five days to work. According to the Met's contract with the International Alliance of Theatrical Stage Employees, whenever a different form of entertainment moves in, the workers receive a big increase in their hourly pay rate in lieu of residuals. It was more economical not to shoot the entire opera sequence at the Met but to marry the footage shot there with footage shot on Stage 27 at M-G-M; even then, Schaffner barely managed to finish up at the Met before running into penalties.

While in New York, Schaffner was obliged to use a
local crew; in the meantime, his regular crew returned to
M-G-M to experiment with the lighting of the enormous
gold-fanged dragon on the half-million-dollar Turandot set.
Lofti Mansouri, general director of the Canadian Opera
Company, had been brought in to stage the opera--just as
he would if no motion picture camera was there. The two
days of work on Stage 27 marked the first time Schaffner
had done any filming on a Hollywood soundstage in 12 years.
"Just amazed at what seemed to be an extraordinary number of people that you don't really need," he has commented.
"But then, I'm astounded that a major motion picture studio
needs so many people to administrate it."

Yes, Giorgio was but a small story at M-G-M. In
1981, the studio purchased United Artists for $380 million;
added to its own $235 million debt, the total M-G-M/UA debt
was a staggering $650 million. For Christmas 1981, the stu-
dio banked its hopes on an old pro, a middle-aged pro, and
a young pro--Billy Wilder, Herbert Ross, and John Badham;
their respective films, Buddy, Buddy, Pennies from Heaven,
and Whose Life Is It Anyway? were all box-office failures.
M-G-M/UA was in trouble; in the hot seat was David Begelman. Just as it had on Schaffner's first picture, corporate
warfare and studio politics continued as normal policy on
his most recent picture.

Michael F. Anderson again served as editor: since
the shoot had so many different locations, he did not get
to travel with the company and was unable to receive immediate feedback from the director about the dailies; as it
turned out, that did not much matter--the film spent an unusually luxurious nine months in post-production. His immediate task was cutting a performance from the footage of
a novice actor, but, in the editing, Anderson found himself
more concerned with something else:

> In some cases, we compromised to a certain extent
> in scenes that I felt would've played perhaps a lit-
> tle bit better, maybe had a little more production
> value, because we had to choose angles, close-ups
> where we wouldn't have normally wanted to, had he
> not been of that size.

He saw no problem in the footage with the star's acting.

In January 1982, Pavarotti returned to Hollywood for looping, a process even experienced actors find difficult; he had 32 loops to do, a low to moderate number by any standard. "Now I understand why some actors are good at it and some are not," Schaffner says, referring to the Automatic Dialogue Replacement process. "An actor who's got a sense of rhythm understands almost immediately the problem of synching--Pavarotti had a sense of rhythm." The director had also eliminated the need for a lengthy looping session by choosing to shoot a lot of footage of the star, virtually covering him line by line.

Unexpectedly, more troublesome was the prerecording that had been done at Fox: the quality turned out to be so bad, fatal for a Dolby stereo film of this nature, that long hours and major surgery were required to patch up and salvage the crucial music. Then, despite the dangers of optically blowing up the 1:85 aspect ratio, Schaffner requested and received permission to prepare 70mm prints for the New York and Los Angeles openings. Much to the relief of those who worked on it, as testimony to the excellence of M-G-M's lab, the 70mm print turned out to be visually handsome, albeit with approximately a 2:1 aspect ratio. Schaffner brought Yes, Giorgio in at $12.4 million.

The marketing campaign had begun as early as the 1981 Academy Awards telecast, when Pavarotti sang "Torna a Sorrento" and it was announced he would star in Yes, Giorgio. On the same evening when it broadcast the Academy Awards show the following year, ABC televised a special, Pavarotti and Friends: accompanied by John Williams at the piano in a movie soundstage, Pavarotti sang "If We Were in Love," and a portion of the film's food fight was shown. Around the studio, the word of mouth about the film was good, but a down-to-earth observation was made by Michael Anderson, who commented that the reaction to Sphinx had been similar at a comparable stage in post-production. To discover what the public would think, a sneak preview was held on May 1, 1982 in Seattle, a requisitely cultural community where Pavarotti's name was known. The results were encouraging: 44% of the audience found the film excellent, 32% very good; females of all ages liked it, and, not unpredictably, males under 25 were the least enthusiastic about Yes, Giorgio.[203]

On September 19, 1982, the film was premiered at the
Kennedy Center for the Performing Arts in Washington, D.C.
in a benefit for the American Film Institute. The triumph
of that particular evening in no way anticipated the critical
drubbing the film would receive the following week. Stanley
Kauffmann would be moved to observe:

> What's amused me almost as much as the film is its
> critical reception. Reviewers have been lambasting
> the script for being tacked together and trite--just
> as if they had expected a screenplay that was car-
> pentered for an opera star's film debut to reach
> Chekhovian depths or Shavian heights. [204]

Yes, Giorgio's script is no less flimsy than an opera sce-
nario, its plot no less thin; except for the inclusion of the
food fight, the story is in fact operatic. The point is to
get the opera star to sing; an encore at the Met may be
taboo, but Yes, Giorgio quite evidently is a movie.

The film begins with some spectacular aerial footage
of Capodimonte, Italy, shot from a helicopter by Fred
Koenekamp with a hand-held camera. Giorgio Fini has come
to sing "Ave Maria" at a friend's wedding; lest the proceedings seem too solemn, Schaffner cuts to a young boy as he
yawns. After the ceremony, Giorgio gets into his limousine
and, surrounded by a throng of admirers, makes a grand
exit through the town's square. Unfamiliar terrain to American audiences, Capodimonte is the picture-perfect story-
book Italy, immediately setting the mood for the film. The
combination of the scenery, music selection ("Mattinata"),
and Pavarotti's voice creates a lot of forward momentum before the credit sequence is over.

On his way to Rome, Giorgio encounters a group of
nuns whose car has a flat tire; rather than stop and help,
he takes Sister Theresa to the airport, giving her a mini-
concert along the way to prove who he is. Thus setting
the ground rules, the first nine minutes of the film establish that this is a musical comedy set in the romantic world
of Giorgio Fini, who, like Luciano Pavarotti, is larger than
life, the world's greatest tenor; the film will later show him
to be a great lover, chef, gourmand, and all-around bon
vivant. "Though not at all a believable film," Boxoffice's

David Linck noted, "'Yes, Giorgio' succeeds much like the
Mario Lanza films of old. The main attraction is there; surround him with a workable romantic story and his talent will
do the rest."[205] In anticipation of a reaction to the star's
proportions, the filmmakers beat the audience to the punch
by having James, a patient at Massachusetts General Hospital and a rather hefty young person himself, poke fun at
Giorgio's size. He is not as kinetically mobile as the great
film stars of the past, but Pavarotti standing still displays
a natural and likeable personality for the big screen; the
audience also knows that every ten minutes he will sing.

In the best tradition of Hollywood movie comedies, the
romantic leads of Yes, Giorgio meet cute. When Giorgio
loses his voice while preparing for the Hatch Shell concert,
Boston's finest throat specialist is immediately summoned:
Dr. Pamela Taylor arrives, and Giorgio mistakes her for a
nurse. The situation suggests the potential for a Tracy-
Hepburn type of relationship; in the script, Pamela is in
fact described as a graduate of "The University of Katherine [sic] Hepburn."[206] Unfortunately, the script thereafter
is not set up for a Katharine Hepburn; there is none of
that appropriately witty badinage between the lovers. The
billing of the film tells the story: Pamela is more a supporting role; the actress' function is to make Pavarotti look good.
It is a highly unrewarding role, and Kathryn Harrold doesn't
help matters much. Although there might be a slight hint
at what life must be like for a woman doctor (who undoubtedly must also teach at Harvard Medical School), Harrold's
appearance seems out of character: she may or may not be
too pretty, but she definitely does not look as haggard as
Dr. Taylor should; but then, this is a movie. Harder to
overlook is that Kathryn Harrold seems to lack the requisite
warmth for the female lead in a musical comedy; with a little more heat and passion in the Pamela role, Pavarotti
would have come off looking much better.

Giorgio sings "I Left My Heart in San Francisco":
not only is this a ploy to ingratiate himself with the people
of the city, it is also an attempt to win over the remaining
members of the movie audience still resistant to Giorgio/
Pavarotti. In the midst of the song, Giorgio loses his
voice, and, after the question of a doctor being in the
house is raised, the crowd parts to reveal Dr. Pamela Taylor, who now begins her fling. There are no real love

scenes in the film; a food orgy at the Pacific Heights man-
sion serves as a substitute for a sexual one. All through
the night and early morning, Giorgio and Pamela move from
garage to wine cellar to sauna to bedroom, eating; discreetly enough, the actual consumption takes place off screen.
The topper to the night of pleasure comes when the tenor
takes the doctor "for a glass of wine." If Giorgio were a
play, "If We Were in Love" would be the show stopper:
while Pavarotti sings the love song on the soundtrack, the
helium balloon wafts its way to the Giordano's farm in Napa
Valley. It is the only moment in the film to take advantage
of Schaffner's skill at filming panoramic vistas, and the
view makes the trip worthwhile; furthermore, the balloon
cunningly dwarfs Pavarotti's size.

After the lovers have their food fight, Giorgio is
persuaded into returning to the Met.[207] The opera sequence concludes the film: appearing as herself, Leona
Mitchell plays and sings the part of Turandot; the plot
leads up to the moment when Giorgio as Calaf sings "Nessun Dorma," a Pavarotti specialty, coming to the key line,
"Vincero, vincero"--"I shall conquer, I shall conquer."
Giorgio conquers.

This is the build-up to a calculated tear-jerker ending. As established, Giorgio and Pamela's romance is
doomed because he has a wife and two children, and will
not leave them; she can send a kiss, they agree, and leave
--there are to be no goodbyes. During the Met encore,
Pamela blows a kiss and leaves with tears in her eyes; she
looks back to see the tears in Giorgio's eyes. With the
synesthetic assistance of Giacomo Puccini's music, it is an
effective updating of the ending to The Jolson Story (1946),
in which Larry Parks mimes as Jolson singing "April Show-
ers" while Evelyn Keyes as his wife leaves. "A high-class
soap opera," as Ginger Varney pointed out in the L.A.
Weekly, "made with a sincere effort at Good Taste (for the
culture buffs), complete with an Elevated Moral and an
Adult Ending is more for your money than most movies try
for these dreary days."[208]

However, during Yes, Giorgio's post-production,
David Begelman was replaced at M-G-M by his former CMA
partner Freddie Fields, and was moved over to United Artists as chairman. Rumors of his impending fate in his new

position were only fueled by the publication of David
McClintick's Indecent Exposure, an account of the scandal
Begelman had been involved in at Columbia Pictures; by
July 12, 1982, he was gone from M-G-M/UA. In David
Begelman, Yes, Giorgio had lost its staunchest supporter,
the sine qua non in getting the film made, the man who,
when faced with the possibility of cancelling production due
to the cause and effect relationship of the threatened directors' strike and the star's schedule, had simply said,
"We will buy Mr. Pavarotti out of his concerts if need
be."[209] It would not be unfair to assume that the film got
hurt in the ensuing shuffle.

     Yes, Giorgio was originally given a generous advertis-
ing budget: $4 million for eight weeks, the bulk of which
would be spent in the print medium; there was no reason
to make buys on national television when the film would
only open in five cities (New York, Los Angeles, San Francisco, Washington, D.C., and Toronto). "I agree wholeheartedly with the M-G-M concept of marketing the picture
... Slowly," Schaffner was quoted as saying before the release of the film; he had made a picture deliberately aimed
at the Sound of Music crowd. "This is not the kind of picture that you throw out into a thousand theatres."[210] He
had been under the impression Yes, Giorgio would open in
small houses in each of the five cities; in Los Angeles alone,
it opened in 17 theatres. M-G-M made three national television buys in the second week of the film's release, but
Giorgio's future had already been decided. The director
can only comment:

          What inevitably happens the minute when people
          don't break down the door immediately--there are
          very few people in this business who understand
          the concept of a slow build--they immediately cut
          the advertising budget. And that's what happened.

     The year 1982 was not congenial to movie musicals:
Francis Coppola's One From the Heart (which had begun at
M-G-M) was savaged by the critics, opened to poor busi-
ness, and was quickly withdrawn; perhaps premature, M-G-
M's reaction helped Yes, Giorgio meet the same fate. "[Yes,
Giorgio] is a handsome and lush package of romanticized
glamour," Robert Osborne wrote in The Hollywood Reporter.
"[It] neatly answers a cry from those who constantly berate

Hollywood because 'they don't make 'em like they used
to.'"[211] Admittedly, the film falls short as a cross between, say, Casablanca and Singin' in the Rain; nevertheless, the director succeeded in achieving all he had set out
to accomplish--if not more, certainly not less.

A snowballing critical trend had begun with "The
Wasting of Pavarotti," written by Alan Rich for the May
1981 issue of New York. In the article, published on the
eve of the film's production, Rich asked the rhetorical question, "When was the last time you didn't see Luciano Pavarotti?" and proceeded to quote Rudolf Bing: "Seeing that
stupid, ugly face everywhere I go is getting on my nerves.
It's all so unnecessary, so undignified."[212] The press, having created the Pavarotti legend in the first place, became
the great leveler. The critical reaction may not have hurt
him professionally, but it is unlikely that Pavarotti will
ever star in another motion picture.

In the final analysis, Luciano Pavarotti was the raison
d'être of Yes, Giorgio: he was the one to attract Franklin
J. Schaffner's attention to the project, provide him its
challenges and rewards. It may never be seen again on
the big screen, but Schaffner was able to draw out and
display a genuinely charming screen presence from Luciano
Pavarotti. It was a much more difficult job than the director will let on. "Working with him is kind of like playing
poker with silk covered cards," Schaffner will only say.
"It was really quite satisfactory."

4. CONCLUSION

A Review of Schaffner's Working Method

> Frank brings a lot of intelligence to whatever proj-
> ect he's doing, he's always very well prepared. He
> communicates very well, which most directors do
> not. He knows what he wants. And he has style
> and class--he's probably one of the classiest men I
> know. I hate that word "classy" but I can't think
> of another appellation about Frank other than that.
> --Robert Fryer

From the inception of the motion picture art form, American
cinema has set the standard for the well-made film: narrative strength, moving in linear fashion with a beginning,
middle, and end; solid craftsmanship and state of the art
technology; and, not least of all, movie stars. As practiced by the pioneers of silent movies, the masters of the
golden age, and the present-day high-tech wizards, from
studio system to independent production, this type of filmmaking is synonymous with Hollywood. Franklin J. Schaffner, like other Hollywood directors who preceded him and
will follow after him, represents the best in the tradition of
American films and filmmaking.

In recapitulating a major director's film career, it is
always helpful to examine the various stages and components
of the filmmaking process, from pre-production through production to post-production. As do most feature films, this
section begins with the agents.

Agents

Starting from 1956, when he lived in New York, Schaffner's
agents have included Ted Ashley and Jerome Hellman of the

Ashley-Steiner Agency. Then he was represented by
Ziegler-Hellman-Ross, which was acquired by Marvin Josephson, who also purchased Rosenberg-Coryell to form Artists
Agency, whose Robert Coryell next represented him. After
moving to California, Schaffner joined Creative Management
Associates, represented, in order, by Richard Shepherd,
Guy McElwaine, David Begelman, and Freddie Fields, who
sold the agency to Marvin Josephson Associates. Josephson
also acquired Chasin-Park-Citroen, the agency Schaffner
joined in 1976, where he was represented by George Chasin.
Six years later, Schaffner moved over to Creative Artists,
whose president, Michael S. Ovitz, served as his agent. In
1984, he returned to CMA, and he is currently represented
by Jeff Berg.

     Part of Hollywood folklore are the tales from the hey-
day of the studio system, when clients would abuse their
agents. That changed in the 1950s when stars joined their
agents to become independent producers. As Hollywood
further evolved, the agent was to assume even greater power. The list of Schaffner's agents is a case in point--the
majority of them went on to become studio heads. The lesson is obvious: in contemporary Hollywood, one should be
very nice to one's agent; it is possible that he/she will
someday be in a position to offer jobs. (Parenthetically,
it must be added that Schaffner's deportment with agents
was motivated more out of breeding than ambition.)

Property Selection

Film critics Andrew Sarris, Kenneth Geist, and Sharon
Russell have written persuasively on power as the unifying
theme in Schaffner's films.[1] Although the theme can certainly be seen in his films, more relevant to Schaffner's
personal concerns is an ironic aside in a Vincent Canby review:

> Someone in "Nicholas and Alexandra" describes Rus-
> sia as an 18th century country in a 20th century
> world [sic]--which may well prompt a few theses
> about the director's hang-up with people and things
> outside of their own times.[2]

It is no secret that Schaffner loves historical films: "It is

more effective to make a comment from a removed plateau,"
he has said, "than it is from the one on which one is standing."[3] Drawn to quixotic and obsessive characters, he ap-
lies his concept of history-telling to the film medium. "I
guess I'm really fascinated by the study of giants [with
feet of clay]," he will admit, "rather than ordinary people
with heads of clay."[4]

    Perhaps best known for his big films about big sub-
jects on the big screen, Schaffner has nonetheless worked
in a wide variety of genres--with the notable exception of
the western. What he first looks for in a script is entertainment, yet there has to be something that goes beyond
the simple entertainment value of the story--it must have
believable characters; he must finally feel qualified to work
with the material. Schaffner may choose a script for the
challenge it offers, be it an unfamiliar subject or an untried
genre; potential relationships with people in the screenplay
or on the set can make it attractive; difficulties built into
the script can be enough for him to risk failure, under conditions that are not apparent on the screen. "Nobody knows
what kind of sow's ear you had coming in, going in, and
managing to turn it into a silk purse," he says, "which may
or may not have been good enough." He might choose a
script as a whole or because of its theme; there might be a
single element that catches his fancy, a sequence, or "a
moment on the screen that may be 15 seconds long, which
is really what the French love to call a coup de cinéma."

    Unlike most directors, Schaffner does not juggle a lot
of properties in various stages of development; lest it interfere with his concentration, he will not commit to a new
project while working on another film. The selection process
sometimes takes a while for a man with exacting standards,
who is both cautious and realistic when approaching a new
project:

> I don't think any picture is fun to make. And if a
> director says that it was a fun experience making
> that film, I've got to know that something's wrong.
> The only fun time in a director's life is the day he
> commits to a project.[5]

A commitment involves at least a year and a half of his life;
he must be careful.

Getting started is never easy.

Producers

As director, Schaffner's duty is to the film and the film
only; his relationship with the producer will help determine
how that duty is realized. Like him or not, the director
has to get along with the producer. "You had better be
fairly sure not only that you want to make that film with
all its faults and with all the problems," Schaffner has
said, "but that you're going to be able to live with this
guy. He's got a certain point of view too."[6]

In his film career, Schaffner has been exposed to
nearly every type of producer: some were good with the
script; some skillful in production, casting, or finding the
property and making a deal; some were incompetent; others
were a combination of both strengths and weaknesses. For
the most part, Schaffner has worked harmoniously with his
producers, something evident in the words of Robert Fryer:

> I've worked with a lot of directors in my life--
> television, theatre, and film. There are rare times,
> I must tell you--I don't flatter, it's true--when you
> look forward to the next day's work. And Frank
> makes you feel that way. It's a rare quality in peo-
> ple. And at the end of the day, you'd like to have
> dinner with him because he's a charming, delightful
> human being.

As a consequence of independent production, many
established directors, if not actually producing, began to
get producer's credit on their films. If a director is comfortable with the material, Schaffner sees no reason why he
shouldn't produce. "You do what you normally do," he
says of his functions as a producer, "and a little more."
Those chores, as Fred Koenekamp has observed, are part
of his normal preparation anyway: "As far as I'm concerned,
Frank always produces his pictures." Fielder Cook elaborates:

> I think Frank is probably the finest single producer
> that I've ever known. Not only is he enormously
> capable of producing, but he produces so quietly

that, most of the pictures he does, he produces
and nobody knows it--including the producer, and
he's enormously grateful for that.

If a director is unsure of himself and/or the material, he
needs a producer. The size and scope of the picture is
also a determining factor:

> Once an enormous amount of money is involved,
> somebody has to isolate the director from the pres-
> sure of those who want to tell him how the money
> should be spent. In that respect, a producer can
> be an enormous help. [7]

Schaffner has only taken producer's credit on two
films, first as co-producer of Papillon, when he was totally
at sea as far as financial matters were concerned. "I don't
know what's happened to those receipts," he says by way
of illustrating the control he had in that role. "I have no
idea how Papillon did overseas." He was billed as executive
producer on Sphinx, when he could have easily claimed sole
producer's credit on this project handed to him by Orion.
With Stanley O'Toole producing, the film only cost $10 mil-
lion, the average Hollywood budget for 1980-1981, a rather
modest sum for what was put on the screen. Skillful and
efficient, Schaffner performed the actual producing chores
on Yes, Giorgio, receiving no credit. A producer's credit,
as these examples demonstrate, can mean any number of
things in Hollywood.

Evidence suggests Schaffner functions better with a
producer. Frank McCarthy's military experience in no way
could have hurt a film like Patton; it would have been a
lesser film had anyone else produced it. Schaffner has
recently worked harmoniously with Stanley O'Toole, who
brings practical know-how to the production and leaves the
creative end to the director. A director like Schaffner
probably functions best with a strong, creative producer.
In an extraordinary quirk of fate, the producer of Schaffner's first film was Jerry Wald, who unfortunately passed
away before The Stripper was completed. It might have
been fruitful if Schaffner could have worked more with
Wald, who had the clout to protect a director and the vitality to inspire him; in return, Schaffner could have buf-
fered Wald's excesses. It would have made a potent com-

bination: Schaffner would have played Fred Astaire to Wald's Ginger Rogers. The resulting films would have benefited from the synthesis of Wald's show business vulgarity and Schaffner's never less than impeccable good taste.

Writers

Following the demise of the studio system, motion picture directors began to work more closely with writers. For someone whose background is in television and theatre, this is a fine and natural thing. From his training under Worthington Miner and Felix Jackson, Schaffner fully appreciates the value of the written word and its paramount importance to a film; he deals with the writer as carefully as he would an actor. "Anybody with his intelligence is going to tailor his approach to the characteristics of the writer," Loring Mandel points out, "some must be bullied, I suppose, and some confronted, there are egos and ids to be dealt with."

On a Schaffner film, director and writer work on material that follows a linear, three-act structure, perhaps best described by noted screenwriter Ernest Lehman:

> In the first act, who are the people, what is the situation of this whole story? Second act is the progression of that situation to a point of high conflict and great problems. And the third act is how the conflicts and problems are resolved.[8]

Once the essential structure of the script has been established, Schaffner will spend most of his time with the writer developing characterization. Mandel recalls:

> He wanted to know my reasons for attitudinal changes of my characters, their motivations, why they would communicate thoughts with particular language rather than other language: in short, he wanted as clear as possible a view of the writer's intent and understanding of the material and character.

The daily grind, as Mandel describes it, is a long and arduous process:

> Each page was examined. He was extremely

> methodical, just as I believe he is in almost every-
> thing in his life. He didn't cultivate surprises (as
> I remember), preparation was very important. And
> he was easy about trying new things and slow to
> cast things away. But when something evidently
> didn't work, he would summon me (a call, or a
> flick of his eyes and a nod), in the spirit of "What
> can we do about this?" We would discuss our feel-
> ings about the problem, cause and possible cure,
> and he was quick with suggestions and not pro-
> prietary about them.

As work progresses on each draft, Schaffner makes notes
on character, drama, plot, and editing, and enters them
into separate copies of the script.

Along the way, something interesting happens that
never ceases to astound the director: "There isn't any
question that in each draft you're starting to discard baggage you thought was absolutely essential for the trip."
A director and writer usually spend six to eight weeks trying to come up with a mutually acceptable script, which is
then sent to the front office. Schaffner has observed:

> Their response always is, "Well, you haven't really
> changed it a lot." And that's probably true--you
> haven't really changed it a lot. You haven't changed
> the story a whole lot, but you've made it work di-
> rectly in terms of characterization, and that's what
> motion picture executives don't understand. They
> invariably read plot line, not character.

In the front office, script changes are made according to
the plot line; similarly, as Schaffner learned on The Stripper, when editorial changes are made by executive order,
character is sacrificed at the expense of the plot line.

Following the time-honored method, Schaffner does
not retain his writer's services during production nor does
he call upon him when the film reaches the editing phase.
The collaboration finally reaches a point where it must end.
"The way it works," Schaffner says of the normal procedure,
"the writer makes his contribution and you respond until
the time where you both think it is what you want."[9] The
end result, as Reginald Rose attests, can make this period
in pre-production worthwhile:

Frank is one of the two or three best directors I've
ever worked with when it comes to constructive suggestions on scripts. He sees the entire script
clearly as a whole and as an aggregate of its individual scenes; he understands character and motivation far better than most directors I've known
and is always able to make insightful suggestions
which improve one or all of these elements. I always know that Frank's assessments of what any
given script needed to strengthen it would be valuable and would work both visually and intellectually. That is a rare talent and I was always grateful for being on the receiving end of it.

Temperament never comes into play; Schaffner's relationships are always warm and considerate. "When things went
well, he'd wrap an arm around my shoulder," Loring Mandel avers, "and I felt his respect and I glowed. That's no
small part of Frank's talent."

Preparation

A director must have good health and a lot of stamina to
make a film. Before making the move to the big screen,
Franklin Schaffner never missed a turn directing live drama
on television; he has tackled some of the most arduous film
assignments in the most trying circumstances. But the successful completion of any project goes beyond vitality--it
involves careful preparation.

A point that cannot be underestimated is that the
director must learn to protect himself. Schaffner tries to
anticipate all the problems that will arise in production by
coming up in advance with solutions or shortcuts; in the
planning of a film, he creates a firm foundation for himself.
Not particularly influenced by the size of the budget--
figures are most intimidating on paper--he maintains, "The
devotion, skill, responsibility and creativity are not affected by accountants."[10] More crucial is budgeting time,
"so that when the moment comes when you have to really
spend the time for the magic moment, you've got the time,"
he says, "and can still cope with your schedule."[11]

As each film is an entirely different experience, there
can be no precise pre-production formula but, in a rough

generalization, Schaffner's schedule might be something like this: 30% with the writer, typically two or three months; 30% with camera and crew, including production design, costumes, and make-up; 20% with casting; 10% correcting mistakes, and 10% by himself. Correspondingly, the five key people he needs the most at this stage are the writer, the director of photography, the production designer, the first assistant director, and the casting director.

Thoughts pertaining to the design or look of the film form in the back of his mind while he works on the script. He begins to think in terms of the budget--and its parameters--figuring out, for instance, how many mattes or matte paintings or opticals should be used; these types of thoughts will only end when he has found his editing scheme in postproduction. Only after the script is complete and he has met with the production designer, months before shooting commences, does Schaffner begin to visualize the film. He does not use a storyboard; the only time it is of use to him is for an action sequence, so that copies of it can be distributed to the various departments involved, informing them what will be expected. Even with action sequences, he finds the storyboard has its limitations. "By the time you come to shoot it," he explains, "it's always changed." Rather than break the script down in specific shots, he tries to come up with a visual concept--whether or not it will be in color, what aspect ratio will be chosen, what he will expect from his cinematographer, what the pictorial and dramatic rhythms for the film will be. "That obviously is a function of preparation which can never be 100% complete," Schaffner realizes, "because things happen on a set that develop a scene."

Only recently has a director had approval of his production manager, a fortunate development considering the length of involvement that position entails. By tradition, production managers were responsible to the studio or producer, but now the responsibility is more to the film; needless to say, a production manager who shares the director's philosophical concept of the film can be an enormous asset. Schaffner has found European production managers most helpful; in America, Terry Carr and Joan Bradshaw have been most valuable to him.

If he has checked with the different departments, gone over the script with the assistant director, studied the schedule with the production manager, and agrees to a 90-day shooting schedule, the director, as a professional, has in effect given his word:

> Once you commit to that, then it is your total re-
> sponsibility.... There is no reason why you
> shouldn't be responsible for doing it in 90 days,
> even if you have weather problems, because no-
> body forgives weather problems. Nobody forgives
> actors being sick. Nobody forgives the fact that
> there have to be retakes for technical reasons.
> You said 90 days. [12]

Including research, Schaffner's preparation is pains-takingly thorough, comparable with Alfred Hitchcock's or Ernst Lubitsch's--except, once production begins, Schaffner is the more flexible. His is a habit that can be traced back to his days in live television, when he tried to cover every possible contingency for a program being broadcast as it was shot--knowing there still would be surprises. Even though scenes for film can be reshot, a similar logic exists behind Schaffner's film planning: the better the prepara-tion, the more likely the production will keep to its sched-ule and budget; the editor will have enough of the right footage to work with, eliminating the need for costly re-takes.

Only after such intensive preparation can Schaffner make everything look so easy.

Art Director

Generally speaking, the art director is the architect of the film. Today, the term production designer is more fre-quently used--suggesting an art director with more influ-ence in the look of the film and coordinating a studio's de-partments to achieve that end. "The art director," says William J. Creber of his responsibilities, "does what nobody else wants to do." He designs the set to fulfill the author's intent and to fit character. "A set designer obviously de-signs with a certain amount of artistic eye for a scene,"

Schaffner has said. "He's got to function beyond that,
well beyond that, and that's to design for the drama of the
scene."[13] If the scene needs special effects, the art director is usually the first to think about it. He also must
be practical. "You can design anything, but is it workable
from a motion picture standpoint?" says Fred Koenekamp,
pointing out how Creber built the Hudson house in Islands
in the Stream with a pointed roof and beams, enabling the
camera crew to hang lights.

As is the case with the other key people, the choice
of art director depends on which part of the world the
director is working in, who is available, and who is right
for the job. Schaffner usually meets the art director four
or five months before filming begins. "We talk about who
the actors are and who the characters are," says Creber,
"and what the set should look like, and the kind of key--
whether it's rich, how much aging, whether it's clean."
Schaffner's relationship with his art director is consistently
casual and friendly during their lengthy collaboration--
the art director remains throughout production, trying to
maintain the right values on the set; the director must keep
the art director on the right track and still allow him his
freedom.

Taking photographs of the set is another important
task for the art director: he will take pictures of an exterior, for instance, to see how the light affects its look
during different hours of the day; the handsomely backlit
sunset shot in Islands in the Stream of the drunken Hudson
and party celebrating the Queen's birthday in a rowboat
was the result of one of these photographs. Creber observes:

> It's interesting, you know, when you suggest things
> to directors, sometimes they can't understand the
> mechanics if you suggest a shot or a matching cut
> of film or something like that. It never has been
> for Frank, and he'll just talk as if that's the way
> we're going to do it.

Often an art director builds too much--meaning more time
and money--because the producer or director doesn't know
what he wants; sometimes an art director builds a set that
either can't be shot or the director will not know how to

shoot it. These are the kinds of problems that never occur
on a Schaffner film.

      Schaffner works with Gil Parrondo on projects he
films in Europe:

> Creber does the kind of work that I don't think
> that Parrondo is technically qualified to do. Part
> of Creber's forte is a lot of special effects....
> He's extraordinarily good in this kind of milieu.
> Not so Gil. Gil's forte is I think that he's a mar-
> velous location production designer--great taste
> and a great sense of history.

Location shooting--including filming in actual interiors--has
caused the job to evolve: an art director must have the
patience and the propensity for a location search.

      The art director tells the location manager what he is
looking for and together they search for the proper terrain
or building; if a site offers possibilities, the director will
look at it. The art director makes sketches of how that location will look with sets, as converted for the purposes of
the film. No place is ever perfect. "If you find a location
that will accommodate 70 per cent of your visual and production needs," Schaffner has said, "you're batting a pretty
healthy average, because you make do in the area of the
other 30 per cent."[14] Once committing to a location, Schaffner will return three or four times, bringing the director of
photography, to complete his preparation.

      A filmmaker must always submit the script to the
local government, lest its content reflect poorly on the
chosen country. In Papillon's case, there was no real difficulty as the subject did not take place in Jamaica; however, such countries as Egypt, Israel, Tunisia, Morocco,
and Turkey are not interested in film, making an outside
company's work all the more difficult. Even a politically
innocuous film script like Yes, Giorgio had to be submitted
to the Italian government. The voice of experience warns
about dealing with ministries and bureaus in foreign countries: "Once you commit you'd better not depend on anybody," Schaffner says, recalling what was actually delivered,
"because all the reassurances and cooperation and promises
of help all seem to disappear." As a precaution, motion

picture companies bring in money to pay under the table
when certain difficulties arise--this payoff money is built
into the budget--a practice that applies, in a similar way,
to shooting on American locations.

Creber remembers an incident that happened on a location shoot that, even if there were no political problems,
was no less difficult for physical reasons--the stay in Utah
for Planet of the Apes. Schaffner was already thinking
about a scene at the end of the production, the crucial denouement at the Statue of Liberty; wanting maximum impact
from it, the director asked for some sketches. Creber recalls:

> He looked at the sketches and said, "Good, we'll do
> them all." I said, "Well, Frank, you know, maybe
> we can do a couple." "No, we're going to do them
> all," he said. "You get ready to do it and let me
> worry about the money." And that was the last I
> heard of it. We just went out and got the shots.

Including the over-the-shoulder shot of the Statue of Liberty, the camera move past its arm to Taylor on the beach,
Taylor's reaction shot, and the reverse-angle zoom out revealing the Statue of Liberty in a wide shot, Creber's
sketches were used to great effect in the film.

Assuming that Schaffner collaborated with him on the
creation of the sketches, Creber's anecdote still reveals
much about the role of the art director and the overall influence he can have on a film--provided, of course, the director gives him that leeway. "Frank's one of my favorite
people," Creber says. "I consider him one of my friends.
I like the relationship of making a film with him--that's the
best way of putting it."

Casting

With the exception of the screenplay, Schaffner spends more
time on casting than on any other phase in pre-production.
There is, as he noted at an American Film Institute seminar,
a good reason:

> Every director will tell you that somewhere between

> 70 and 80 per cent of your problems are solved
> when you have cast the picture correctly, which
> indicates why there is a great deal less daring
> casting done in motion pictures than there is in the
> theatre, for example, because that person has to
> be right in a motion picture--you can't turn back
> once you've started. [15]

Many of the roles in his first film were filled by actors under contract to Twentieth Century-Fox; casting was much
more of a clear-cut issue in the days when studios had
rosters of contract players. "When I think back over a
whole host of--a host!--a dozen films that I've made,"
Schaffner says, "I cannot think of one single film where
there haven't been extraordinary problems with casting--
there always are." Not since The Stripper has there been
a film he's worked on that, somewhere during pre-production, that he didn't think would be cancelled because of the
impossibility of casting.

A director like Schaffner feels an absolute obligation
to casting--from star roles down to bit parts--a tendency
developed in his television days. Casting problems multiply
proportionately with the addition of other participants: producers have definite ideas about casting, as do writers and
agents; a major star has approval of the rest of the cast;
not least of all, a studio will have a strong say in the casting. Sometimes an actor is absolutely right for the part
but unavailable, or the right actor won't like the script, or
there are times when salary demands create an impenetrable
barrier. Schaffner himself has been known to change his
mind during casting and look for a different type. "There
is always the haunting attitude there is somebody you
haven't thought of," he says, "no matter how detailed, complete your notes, research, investigation." If numbers may
again be used, Schaffner is looking for a person who brings
a minimum of 70 per cent to the role.

Schaffner studies the actor in casting sessions to see
if he/she considers the role a challenge, enjoys playing the
part; then he tries to determine what kind of contribution
the actor will make to the whole. "Actors are notorious,
generally speaking," he comments, "in that they tend to
read only their own role, and they tend to react to that--
and that's perhaps justifiable." But not necessarily what
he wants.

A good casting director is essential to the success of
any Hollywood movie; it is such an onerous yet such an important job that casting directors have begun to receive
their own separate title cards in the credits. Alixe Gordon,
Maude Spector, Jennifer Schull, Mike Fenton and Jane Feinberg are among the casting directors he likes, trusts, and
admires. "My experience is that the good casting director,"
Schaffner says, "in a reading situation, is not one who
looks for my reaction but is one who can give me a reaction
as to what he or she has heard." Unfortunately, he refers
more to England; a problem with Hollywood casting is that
actors of any stature won't do readings.

Given the difficulty and frustration of casting, it is
no wonder that Schaffner can take some pride in The Boys
from Brazil. (That two of its producers were themselves
former casting directors could not have hurt.) From top
to bottom, there's not a weak link in the cast; this is as
satisfying as it is rare.

Director of Photography

Historically, the director of photography was part of the
production department, often the director's enemy; because
of this, many directors were reluctant to communicate with
their cameramen. Schaffner worked closely with cameramen
in his live television days and continues that practice in
film. A complicated camera move can often be revealed in
the following day's dailies to be far different from what a
director expected, and so the need for communication becomes especially critical. As Schaffner has pointed out,
"When you say to him, 'Did you get it?' and he says, 'Yes,'
and you say, 'Next setup,' you've got to believe him and
trust him."[16]

Like many directors, Schaffner tends to use people
he trusts, because of the ease in communication. The cinematographer he has worked with most often is Fred J. Koenekamp. "He is a very gifted technician who knows an incredible amount about the art of cinematography," Schaffner
says. "I have had a very close professional relationship
with him.... He's fast and he's good and he contributes."[17]

"You have to--in today's market--be conscious of

Cinematographer Fred Koenekamp and Schaffner.

production problems," Koenekamp says. "Production problems mean time and money. And time and money, they are
the name of the game." Film productions are usually rushed;
except for an occasional super-production, everything has
to be shot fast, leaving little time for dialogue between director and cameraman. Koenekamp believes a cinematographer is only as good as his director: filmmaking is usually
a confusing rat race, but working with Schaffner is a different matter. This director never pressures him and,
moreover, is open to suggestions that will improve the pictorial quality of the film:

> This is one thing I can say about Frank Schaffner
> more than any other director I know--Frank will sit
> down and go through the script with me, and we
> will discuss all the aspects, scene by scene. Not
> many directors want to take that time out and deal
> with the cameraman.... On Patton, Papillon, Islands
> in the Stream, I almost felt like I knew every day
> what Frank was thinking and was going to do, be-
> cause that's the way he works.

Schaffner has managed to work effectively with cinematographers on both sides of the Atlantic ocean, adapting
comfortably to the system in Great Britain where a director,
who shouldn't even look through the camera, sets up a shot
with the operating cameraman—not the British equivalent of
the director of photography, the lighting cameraman, who,
by virtue of his title, is more involved with the lighting
process, doing much of his own work, which often is time-
consuming. An American D.P. tends to work more quickly,
setting up the lights with his gaffer. On an international
production, an American cinematographer is allowed to take
his key people: camera operator, gaffer, head electrician,
key grip, camera assistant or technician; due to their experience working together as a team, communication is quick-
er within the crew. "We do a lot of things without even
telling each other what we're doing," Koenekamp says.
"That's one reason I can go fast."

Koenekamp watches Schaffner rehearse the actors on
the set. "As a cameraman," he says, "you can pretty well
know what the coverage is and what the shot is and what
he wants." Schaffner might discuss the scene with him and
the camera operator, refining the shot, detailing what kind
of moves are required; he will look through the camera and
inform the operator where the shot should begin and end.
Sometimes the shot is so obvious, Koenekamp will lay it out,
getting tracks if needed, light the set, and bring Schaffner
back to see if it is satisfactory. "We don't have to spell
out everything in detail now to each other," the cinematographer says. "A lot of times it's just a look at each other
and 'Yes,' 'No,' or 'Crank,' and that's all there is to the
conversation."

If a director is interested in the look of a film and
the cameraman's problems, a Fred Koenekamp will work that
much harder:

> There is no other director I would rather work with
> than I would with Frank--strictly because I always
> felt so close to him and what he wants. I always
> felt that Frank was interested in giving me a chance
> to do what I needed to get the job done.

Despite his Academy Award for The Towering Inferno, the
films Koenekamp most enjoyed doing and felt the best about

--<u>Patton</u>, <u>Papillon</u>, <u>Islands in the Stream</u>--were directed by
Franklin J. Schaffner.

Actors

The main value of rehearsal is that communication is improved and people are enabled to come to a level of understanding. Unlike the theatre or live television, there is
seldom a rehearsal period allotted to films; only in his first
two films was Schaffner given this luxury. It is too costly
to carry actors on a rehearsal period; besides, not all actors like rehearsal. Schaffner has mostly directed productions on the move, making rehearsal impossible. If feasible,
he will have a day or two of readings to express his point
of view and let the people get acquainted. Thereafter, rehearsal goes on a day to day basis as the film is shot; sometimes, if circumstances are right, he will rehearse at night.
Using a technique he perfected in his television days, he
works with actors individually, drawing them aside for private conversations.

Schaffner tries to create an atmosphere on the set
that will foster creativity. It is a subtle help for the actors to know that Schaffner runs a calm and professional
set; that he has assembled a proficient crew is reassuring
to them. Schaffner gathers the actors on the set to block
the scene technically before they attend to their wardrobe
or make-up; the set is then handed over to the crew, and,
when it has finished (which helps explain why actors don't
appreciate cameramen who spend more time on the set than
they), Schaffner brings the cast back to work on the scene.
Hardly an ideal method, it is nonetheless the most practical
way for him to work in film. Consequently, Schaffner considers the master shot as his dress rehearsal; at this point
he has a clear idea as to the dramatic punctuation, action,
and reaction.

Occasionally, Schaffner will work with a Henry Fonda,
a George C. Scott, or a Laurence Olivier, any one of whom
has the concept of the role and its characterization fully
developed before he sets foot on a set. In most cases,
however, the actor needs a director more in film than in
any other medium: a film is not shot in sequential order;
the actor has not had a chance to test his interpretation,

character changes, or the scene's tempo. A director provides the general continuity and an overview of the role to
help the actor bridge gaps in time and emotions. Schaffner
seldom has his actors improvise, but concedes, "There is
some 'improvisational direction' in every scene one tackles."[18]
There are many matters to consider: some actors are only
effective in the first take, some after the fifth; actors have
different energy levels; some will not put out in reverse
angles. There are endless combinations.

Applying a military metaphor to film, Charlton Heston
has said: "The director is a field marshal but the creation
of a role depends on creative give-and-take."[19] With
Schaffner there are no long discussions; conversations are
pragmatic. He may mention something about the character,
have the actor work with a prop, or suggest another movement within the frame. Heston continues:

> Without being dogmatic, without by any means clos-
> ing off various options open to the solution of the
> scene, he gives you a way to begin, a way the scene
> will work. This is enormously reassuring. If in
> exploring the scene you find it doesn't work, fine.
> You change it.[20]

Schaffner is not especially concerned about actor-directors,
actors who would direct:

> An actor is there to do, to perform a particular
> function, and very infrequently will an actor sug-
> gest that his staging solution is better than yours.
> And the reason that that does not happen is be-
> cause he is a professional and he knows that all
> sorts of things are going to happen in the editing
> room.[21]

If the actor insists on his way, Schaffner will discuss the
scene one more time; if the actor is still adamant, he will
film it both ways.

Schaffner's comment about editing reveals the biggest
adjustment he had to make to the film medium--a performance
first comes to life in the editing room. "Generally speaking," he says of film acting, where often it's most important
that an actor make a good face for the camera, "I have found

that most of the performances change in the close-up, or
are most fully exploited in the close-up." [22] Indeed, the
most valuable part of an actor's anatomy are his eyes.

Sometimes his work with actors goes beyond verbal
communication. Peter Bart, a keen student of the dynamics
between director and actor, describes the phenomenon of a
fine actor at work with a fine director:

> It was very interesting to see George Scott and
> Frank communicate.... Scott would go up to Frank
> and he'd say something like, "Unnh." And Frank
> would say, "Ehh, what do you think, George?" ...
> There never would be an exchange that went beyond
> two words.... If the picture had been a big hit, I
> would've put out a book just between us called The
> Schaffner-Scott Dialogues, which would have con-
> sisted of "Mmph," "Shucks."

Bart surely exaggerates; the results, however, speak for
themselves.

Heston maintains Schaffner is never too enthusiastic
about anybody's performance, never overly appreciative of
anyone's work. That is fine for actors like Heston who
prefer this kind of direction; Schaffner gets his point over
through his patience, understanding, and indirect approach.
For other actors, he can be an intimidating sight on the
set, at once a very attractive man and one who looks for-
bidding in his silence. It is part of his personal style.
"He tends to say less than other people," Mayo Simon observes. "He tends to make actors want to please him by
saying less to them, so they're not quite sure what he
wants, and they offer things up to him."

It has been noted that Schaffner's giants are all men.
Commenting on the absence of women in Schaffner's film
world, Sharon Russell wrote a rather curious defense:

> This lack of strong women would seem to indicate
> an understanding of the difficulty of finding women
> who have power positions in their public worlds.
> Schaffner does not take an anti-feminist position,
> but rather he indicates an awareness of the true
> situation of women in the world today. [23]

Today, to continue in this vein, there are few scripts written for women, fewer bankable actresses. Joanne Woodward
gave an exceptional performance as The Stripper, but her
efforts were incalculably damaged in the truncated version
that was released. Even so, the days of a Lila Green--who
calls herself a "girl," whose idea of a "decent job" is being
a secretary--are past. Working with actresses becomes
more problematic as Schaffner does not accept material that
exploits a woman from a physical rather than a character
standpoint.

   Mayo Simon points out Schaffner's characteristic reserve with actors: "This inhibition is fine with men--it
comes out as restraint." Schaffner's demeanor, it follows,
works less well with women. From an empirical point of
view, mostly based on his television work with such actresses as Margaret Sullavan, Schaffner's deportment would
have been a great asset had he worked with Bette Davis in
the 1930s and 1940s; his decorum could have been effective
working with Greta Garbo or Katharine Hepburn. True,
these statements can never be proved; Claire Bloom's appearance in Islands in the Stream and the ensemble acting
of Lilli Palmer, Uta Hagen, Rosemary Harris, and Anne
Meara in The Boys from Brazil, however, exist as proof of
his way with actresses. Further evidence is the way he
worked with the likes of Grace Kelly and Jacqueline Kennedy; yet, for better or for worse, these types have entirely disappeared from the contemporary film scene, replaced by a new breed of leading lady who jibes less well
with Schaffner's courtly style.

   Robert Fryer, a Schaffner observer for over 30 years,
sees a consistency to his friend's dealings with actors
through the years:

        The actors loved Frank; they still do. Until they
        get to know him, they're terrified of him.... He's
        warm to supporting actors though. The smaller the
        part, the nicer he is to them. I think he's quite
        calculated, actually.

So it would seem. The excellence of the performances he
has directed comes from something beyond preparation. This
personal idiosyncrasy--his detached air--combined with his
good looks, helps explain his success with actors: as

director he is like a withholding father to the actor, who as
the child becomes the more eager to please him. Something
about Schaffner cuts through every level of success or reputation: he elicits fine acting from superb actors, and has
guided George C. Scott, Charlton Heston, and Steve Mc-
Queen to their finest screen performances.

The Shoot

Once the final screenplay is completed, Schaffner goes
through the previous drafts, transferring all his important
notes to a new script. A month before shooting begins, he
reviews the annotated script and plans his day-to-day, week-
to-week work in a clean script; he will carry the old annotated script for reference. Visualization develops slowly:
if the script is right, action and reaction will arise naturally from character, not incident.

The creative periods of the filmmaking process come
for Schaffner in pre-production and post-production; once
filming begins, so many different matters need supervision
that production often becomes a technical exercise. Schaffner rarely creates on the set; what he tries to do is establish the right environment, and then deal with the 150 people around him who are clamoring for his attention.

"My method of work is, I don't suppose, dissimilar to
a lot of people who came out of television," Schaffner maintains. On the weekend before filming, he goes through the
week's work, trying to lay it out visually. "And it's not
final," he says. "There's a lot of looseness to it." He
knows, for example, that no matter what the script problems are or how chaotic pre-production has been, once
shooting starts certain difficulties will tend to disappear.

A director can be helped immeasurably by a good first
assistant director. All too often an A.D. will yell and push
his weight around the set; a good A.D. is worth his weight
in gold. It has been Schaffner's good fortune to have worked
with Jose Lopez Rodero on each of his five European-based
productions, beginning with Patton, which Fred Koenekamp
considers the best coordinated picture he has ever been on,
giving due credit to Pepe Lopez: "He ran things with an
iron hand." Starting in pre-production, a good A.D.

Schaffner and assistant director Jose (Pepe) Lopez Rodero.

relieves the director of administrative duties; for the big
Schaffner films, involving diverse languages and cultures,
this cannot have been a simple job. "I personally think,"
Lopez has opined, "the Assistant is the one who has the
worst part, acting like a Judge of Friendship in this kind
of Movie making United Nation [sic] ... (A pain in the
neck)."[24] An A.D. like Pepe Lopez brings more to a production than his considerable coordinating skills, as a call
sheet from Sphinx will attest. When the company found itself shooting in Budapest in the middle of winter, Pepe
Lopez wrote an additional message:

> Sore Throat Note: To increase the humidity in your
> room, adopt the following Spanish peasant remedy,
> 1 wet towel over radiator at night does wonders.[25]

On a shooting day, Schaffner arises at 4:00 a.m. to
spend a couple of hours planning the day's work--considering
possible cuts in the script or in the editing room, visualiz-
ing every shot in the two or three pages of script to be
covered, and writing his ideas down in sequence on a yel-
low legal pad. In addition to this list, when he is on location Schaffner will walk onto the set carrying another shot
list, the "in the event of" list. Sometimes, if there is a
possibility of rain, he will have in his briefcase a third
shot list of things to do on a cover set--usually 100 pages
ahead of or behind the material on his first shot list. On
Sunday, his only day off on location, he prepares the next
week's work.

Schaffner does not wear a viewfinder around his neck
when he is on the set; he has never found one that was
completely accurate, and, having thoroughly studied the
floor plans, does not need one for interiors. Neither does
he carry a bullhorn; he is quite the opposite type. Fred
Koenekamp comments, with some amusement:

> He's not a man of many words. And he also talks
> so darn quiet, if you don't listen to him like this,
> you don't hear it, you know? There's many many
> times even the assistant director will come to me
> and say, "What'd he say?"

"Frank never used to want to tell the crew what he
was going to shoot next," Mort Abrahams recalls of the

Planet of the Apes experience. Instead of lining up the
shots in advance with the A.D., as is the custom, Schaffner would reach into his pocket for his list, take a look at
it, put it away, and then call his shot. When asked the
reason why, Schaffner replied, according to Abrahams, "I
don't like to work that way, Mort, I like to have freedom.
I feel if I tell him the next shot, then I can't change my
mind." Schaffner still works this way--it is part of his
directorial personality--endlessly supportive but mysterious.

The balance is effective: he is in charge of the set
and his responsibility is to get the work out of the people
around him so that the film can come in on time and on
budget. There is also an artistic reason behind his efficiency:

> You are paid to make this machine run so that you
> are using all of these devices, shortcuts, etc. so
> that when the moment comes when you have to real-
> ly spend the time for the magic moment, you've got
> that time, and can still cope with your schedule. [26]

"He starts with the absolute best shot his preparation
can arrive at," Charlton Heston observed at an American
Film Institute seminar, "but he's able to keep himself open
for creative developments during shooting." [27] Schaffner
first sets up the master shot; according to this method, as
the day goes on, he works his way to a close-up, the last
in a series of move-ins, and then he will reverse angles.
This way, everyone on the set has a pretty good idea of
what will happen during that shooting day; however, as
Heston noted, Schaffner allows himself considerable flexibility. Having had similar experiences in television, he
knows his collaborators can make valid contributions on the
spot:

> There are many striking moments in this wonder-
> world where you are responsible for being prepared
> for everything that can possibly happen. And sud-
> denly, you discover you have staged a master be-
> cause, goddamn it, that's the way it really has to
> be. And an actor will come up with a moment which
> changes the texture, and intent of everything you
> have planned. He's right. And now suddenly you
> have to scurry to accommodate that. [28]

To be sure, this is not an everyday occurrence. Although
to some it may seem like a waste of time, Schaffner will
stick to his master shot, occasionally breaking a scene into
two or three masters, or shooting reverse masters; it is
nice to have that footage in the editing room when a close-
up doesn't work.

The amount of footage he shoots differs from film to
film, depending on the situation and how many cameras are
used: the shooting ratio on Yes, Giorgio, for example,
was nearly 40 to 1 because a couple of two- to three-hour
concerts were filmed in their entirety by six and seven
cameras; in an average situation, Schaffner's shooting ratio
is approximately 10 to 1. He does not normally exceed
eight takes, which he considers "a heavy commitment"; if
he goes beyond eight takes, it's more for a technical, not
a performance, reason.

Schaffner is perfectly willing to cheat on an exterior
--shoot actors against different backgrounds to adjust to
the changing light--but, if the situation calls for it, he will
more often use double cameras on basic dialogue scenes in
deteriorating weather or light conditions. He carried two
cameras throughout Islands in the Stream for an obvious
reason, the ocean; just as obviously, he will use multiple
cameras on an action sequence. Generally, he does not
employ more than one camera on an interior set, a rare exception being the food fight scene--an action sequence of
sorts--in the kitchen set for Yes, Giorgio.

Carefully composed mirror shots occur repeatedly
throughout his films: by circumstance, Lila's suicide attempt, the crucial mirror shot in The Stripper, was excised
from the film; in its own way, Planet of the Apes was designed to be an ultimate mirror shot. Patton's suitably dis-
orienting entrance into his London flat is captured through
a wall mirror; his bedroom has a mirrored ceiling, prompting him to comment that he feels like he's in a cathouse.
As in his television career, it is not impossible to read
"recognition" into Schaffner's mirror shots, but such was
not his intention: Schaffner shot into those mirrors because, based on research, the set was designed that way.
An accomplished visual stylist, Schaffner uses mirror shots
to produce some offbeat and compelling images.

Schaffner favors an exterior over an interior, prefers
shooting on location; he has a natural talent for working
outdoors and staging action, proclivities that lend themselves to the wide screen. Always prepared, never excit-
able, he tells the crew what he is going to do and what he
wants done. Fred Koenekamp can only say: "He can take
things and say, 'All right, now fellows, we're going to do
this and do this.' And it'll all work!" Schaffner will get
the shot.

"I feel perfectly comfortable working in CinemaScope,"
Schaffner says, referring to his hallmark as a director. "A
lot of people don't." It was not always so: in his first
film, Schaffner used more close-ups than he needed and did
not take advantage of the depth of field available to the
medium. True, the material was based on an intimate stage
play that had no need of the wide screen--if he had his
say, he would not use black and white with the wide screen
either--but he was just beginning his film career. With a
little experience, taking advantage of wide-angle lenses and
carefully panning the camera, Schaffner found himself at
home with the wide screen. "I like it," he can say. "I
think it is perhaps overwhelming for some kinds of storytelling, but it can be just as flexible as the standard ratio."
For example, in an extreme long-shot of the convicts' march
in Papillon, the camera slowly booms up over a gate grill;
on the wide screen, the effect is not unlike an optical wipe
from top to bottom. For a television director whose tracking shots could be compared with Max Ophuls', Franklin J.
Schaffner, because of the wide screen, no longer moves his
camera as much in films.

In staging for the camera, Schaffner was most influenced by another director noted for his splendid pictorial
sense, John Ford--who, instead of moving the camera to
them, had the actors move to it. Schaffner only moves the
camera when he feels it dramatically right; his characters
move within the frame from shot to shot, creating and maintaining a fluid style.

"He knows how to make a beautiful motion picture," a
critic once wrote. "The vista does not exist that can evade
his unblinking gaze."[29] Schaffner's films have been justly
praised for their impressively rich and expansive look.
Sometimes he will talk about his visual compositions coming

from character, almost as an extension of character, or
secondarily of the situation, but Schaffner has good instincts. Editor Michael F. Anderson compares directors
to painters:

> Some lend themselves to different areas: he has
> an eye for the epic; he has an eye for the full
> frame. Time and time again--an extra who's over
> at the side, or someone's entrance, where your eye
> would never usually get directed--he has a sense.

In the final analysis, his command of the wide screen is not
unrelated to something he once said about staging for the
camera: "It's going to depend in the end upon your subjective judgment and upon your taste." [30]

Editing

Production is always exhausting; after production, Schaffner
usually takes a brief vacation to recuperate and steel himself for the psychological rigors of post-production. As an
index to the importance he attaches to this phase of filmmaking, he now sets up his offices in the editing room.
Post-production is a relatively orderly process, following a
basic pattern: typically, a director is contractually obli-
gated to deliver an answer print 24 weeks after principal
photography has been completed; the release date is the
end target. He ordinarily spends the first 12 weeks editing the film.

Due to the peculiar nature of the film medium, Schaffner considers editing as his rehearsal time: he examines
the structure and characterizations, checks if emotions have
been dramatized as he wanted, discovers whether or not his
concept works. Within the limitation of working with raw
material that has already been captured on film, he has the
time and luxury of trying out different tactics, refitting
parts to strengthen the whole.

A live television director was his own editor, watching
the monitors, cutting to prearranged cues as the program
aired. When he moved to film, Schaffner wanted similar involvement in the editing process: the way his old habit
translated best to the new medium was to stand all day

behind the editor at the moviola; a not uncommon practice, this system works best for him. Because of the physical setup, the director and editor have a most intimate working relationship, often beginning in pre-production: not only must they respect each other's opinions, it is absolutely necessary that they like each other--if they are to work in close quarters. Schaffner worked most frequently and intimately with Robert E. Swink. Before Swink's retirement, Schaffner was heard to remark at an American Film Institute seminar:

> He is a superb editor.... He knows it all. And he is very objective and very stubborn and rightfully so. But I am the kind of director who is a pain in the ass. I stand in the editing room all day long behind the editor and keep hitting him on the back. It takes an accommodating personality to put up with that. But beyond the fact of just editing, I enjoy being in that room with him so that we have, I think, a very advantageous flow and interchange of ideas for the picture. [31]

That Swink should share these sentiments is noteworthy in that he was accustomed to the old studio system, when a director seldom set foot in the editing room. "Usually I prefer working in the cutting room alone," Swink says. "Working with Frank was a very pleasant experience."

The editor puts the first assembly together as the director shoots. Occasionally they discuss the footage: Schaffner will tell the editor how he visualizes a scene or what he had in mind when he shot it. On his own, Swink's working method was simple and uncomplicated:

> In looking at the rushes each day I would look for the moments in the scene which affected me in some way. I would remember those moments when sitting at the moviola with the film and incorporate them into the edited version. I never would try to pre-edit a scene. I let the material lead me. There are exceptions to this and that would be when a scene is badly written, or poorly acted, or badly photographed, or some such thing. Fortunately I had very few instances of this with Wyler and Schaffner.

Schaffner has one fundamental ground rule in editing: for
future reference, the editor should use something from
every take; later, when he sees the pieces from each take
and remembers what and how he did it, the director can
use something from any of those takes if he thinks it worthwhile. In planning a film, he already knows where the
problem areas will be; during production, he overshoots
these scenes as a precautionary measure. His homework
pays off once the film reaches the editing phase: "His
staging of scenes was good, and his coverage was good,"
Swink recalls. "There were not many unused shots left in
the cutting room."

        Approximately three weeks into the editing, the first
cut is ready to be seen. "Invariably it's a disaster,"
Schaffner has said of a director's worst moment in the filmmaking process. "Awful. And it's the kind of traumatic
experience where you want to lie down for five days." [32]
Running about three and a half hours, the film contains
nothing that seems to work; the director can only see his
mistakes. Returning to the editing room to put together
the next cut, the director begins to eliminate things that
don't work structurally, dramatically, or emotionally, coming to know his film better. "Editing is a form of music to
me," says Michael F. Anderson. "It takes on a certain
rhythm; the cuts take on a certain rhythm." Together,
director and editor make transpositions, refinements, cut
performances, and try to establish a visual pattern.

        Discussing the times he spent in the editing room with
Schaffner, Swink says:

> We would run all the film and edit it together. This
> way we both had our input on the scene together
> and would try many ways of cutting a scene and
> hopefully end up selecting the best version. It was
> fun and I think the picture was better for it....
> There were games I played on him to get my way,
> and I'm sure he did the same with me.

No matter how heavy the pressure is, the cutting room never
becomes too somber. "Franklin is Franklin," Anderson says.
"He has a way of breaking the tension, his moments of silli-
ness.... He likes to bellow, with his very deep loud voice,
catch you off guard."

Once the visual pattern is set, the dialogue is
trimmed, which is a sobering experience for a director who
remembers the hours of hard labor spent with the writer
coming up with essential lines of dialogue, only to find how
easily they can be eliminated. "It's amazing how much the
visual impact tells the story, and how much there is that
visually influences the story," Schaffner has observed.
"And you can only think to yourself, 'What was I doing
months ago, wasting my time?' "[33]

The more he worked with Scope, the less Schaffner
began to cut, thereby accommodating the larger aspect
ratio--something he learned almost automatically as he acquired more experience:

> When you start into post-production, you keep re-
> minding yourself of the size of the screen. You've
> got to watch the rhythm of your cutting because it
> is so large; it is so larger than life in its size that
> where you think you might want to put in a close-
> up, a two-shot might do just as well, simply because
> of the size of it.... As I start the editing phase,
> I keep reminding myself of it and then I discover
> that I'm editing it for the dramatic content anyway
> --and end up paying no attention.

Unlike today's producers, who figure audiences weaned on
television might insist on a more rapid editing tempo, Schaffner, believing his method effective, remains faithful to his
vision of the film.

Schaffner is a perfectionist; he knows exactly what he
wants in the editing room. Anderson comments:

> He really has very strong feelings on what he wants
> out of a scene, how he wants different characters
> to come off, whose scene it is.... If a scene works
> for him and we've got it down, then he won't keep
> picking at it needlessly. But, on the other hand,
> if he's not happy with a scene or sequence, we'll
> go through it and go through it and go through it,
> and put it aside and come back to it.

After the film has been edited at least a handful of times,
with trips to the projection room following each new version,

the director's cut is completed by the twelfth week of post-production. The film's length has been reduced to a little over two hours, and the time has come for sound effects, looping, and scoring.

Music Score

Schaffner is not especially concerned about the music score until post-production; unlike George Roy Hill, who will design sequences to music in advance, he has never choreographed action to music in pre-production. When the time comes, however, he works very closely with the composer—and is even on the music stage when the score is recorded —to ensure that he gets the best and most out of the music.

The function of the music score is to support the drama: ideally, as far as Schaffner is concerned, a composer will bring out the drama in a very different but no less important way than a writer or director. In film music,

Schaffner (center), flanked by two favorite collaborators: Jerry Goldsmith (l.) and Robert E. Swink.

his wants and needs have been supplied most frequently
and successfully by Jerry Goldsmith, with whom, in a working relationship that spans three decades, he collaborated
in television and on six films. Expressing his thoughts on
film music, Schaffner once wrote:

> In the film form, the composer must use his music
> as an interpretative reaction to the force of the
> drama, and in mirroring the mood of the picture
> the composer must use constraint, never dominate,
> always enhance.... In such an extensively col-
> laborative effort as a motion picture, personal
> statements don't work because they fail to support
> the film and its characters. To sublimate oneself
> is about the toughest demand you can ask of a gen-
> uinely talented individual. Jerry Goldsmith is an
> artist who meets all the demands upon the composer
> in film. He communicates, integrates, subordinates,
> supports and designs with discipline.[34]

"Music is trying to convey what the audience is supposed to feel," says Jerry Goldsmith, a firm believer in
music as the most emotional of the arts, "and what you want
them to feel more. I'm trying to help an unseen thing."[35]
His music is nothing if not subtle, changing from film to
film; it does not, however, pass by completely unnoticed.
For a composer as well known as he, it is interesting to
note that one of his hallmarks is his sparseness, his brev-
ity; there are only 30 minutes of music in Patton.

"Franklin Schaffner is one of the few directors I've
worked with who has a true understanding of music, a
knowledge and awareness of the dramatic value of music,"
Goldsmith has said.[36] "He's probably the most musical director who I've worked with." Thus, the two men can talk
shop in a common language and with total candor, since
theirs is a friendship that goes back to the beginnings of
their respective film careers; they have their own chemistry. Another similarity is they both stress the importance
of character--the basis of their work. "I do my best when
I have a strong leading character that I can get inside of,"
Goldsmith has said, "and all of Schaffner's films are built
that way."[37] At any given moment, his music will reflect
a character's feelings in a particular situation, probing
psychological elements that go beyond the character's actions on the screen.

Goldsmith normally works on a ten-week schedule: his task begins in post-production, when he sees the film for the first time and receives a direct positive dupe of the film which he can run at home until he gets a feel for the picture. Then he meets with the director: "We discuss character and that's about it," he says of his meetings with Schaffner. "We don't usually discuss a picture really in depth because Frank says a lot in one line.... He can say what he wants or what he feels in a couple of words, and that's it." Some directors verbalize at length, but "Montmartre" and "Think 3/4" were all Schaffner needed to say for Papillon and The Boys from Brazil respectively.

When the director and the composer spot the film-- choose where the music will go and what kind of music it will be--Schaffner, like many directors, will ask for more music than he can use. Once spotting is completed, the music editor gives the composer a cue sheet with the dialogue and the timing of the selected sections to be scored. Working at home, Goldsmith gives his music a beginning, a development section, and a recapitulation--not unlike the three-act structure Schaffner employs. Although the director does not hear the score until it is recorded, he is free to make suggestions, as Goldsmith says, recalling his experience on Papillon:

> Frank calls everyday when I'm writing--8:00 the phone will ring and it's Franklin. He'll have his little one-liners and his funnies and all that, and then: "What scene are you writing today?" "I'm working on the tattoo scene." "Get some fear in there too." And I must say I got so caught up with the bucolic quality of it all, I forgot that-- hey, wait a minute, this guy's in a strange situation, he doesn't know what the hell is going on. He sees these people hung up on posts and all that, and what are they going to do to him? I forgot about that. And then Frank goes into his one-liners, urging me on. But that's how Frank does work.

Another Goldsmith story illustrates Schaffner's working method with the composer. For Patton, Goldsmith had the notion of composing music so sympathetic to Patton that when he slapped the soldier it would come as a dramatic surprise; Schaffner, who originally wanted no music for the scene, let Goldsmith try it. Only in the dubbing stage, with all the dialogue and sound effects in, did Goldsmith begin to have misgivings about his work. The music made it seem as if Patton was right--that the soldier deserved to be slapped. After careful deliberation, Schaffner had to agree but, as Goldsmith tells it, still wanted to make an effort to salvage the scene with the music intact:

> We spent almost a day starting it at different places, bringing it in later, taking it out sooner, eliminating this part of it. Finally I said, "Franklin, it just isn't going to work. Take it out and be done with it." There was no music. That's the way we resolved it. But Franklin, because of his respect for me and what I was trying to do, believed there was a validity in my [original] theory, that it was worth trying to make it work. [38]

His colleagues find the latitude Schaffner gives them rewarding, and he, in turn, is rewarded by the fruit of their labor. It is the specific combination of the man and his films that makes the collaboration so enriching for Jerry Goldsmith:

> It's a funny thing, my working relationship with Franklin. My orchestrator Arthur Morton always says, "Frank puts a hex on you." I suffer so much when I work on his pictures. But he means a great deal to me. Somehow, I can measure my career and artistic growth on his films. Each of his pictures that I've done has been a new step for me, have led me in different areas. I can sort of pinpoint each one and see a period of growth, a foundation for a new growth period in my own creativity.

Finishing Up

At this stage of post-production, the director and editor work in more of a supervisory capacity. In addition to fine tuning the film, the editor acts as liaison among the director and the composer, music editor, sound editor, title designer, optical house, and lab. By this time, the sound effects and loop lines have been built and recorded.

A believer that actors cannot truly recapture their performances after the fact, Schaffner tries to avoid as much automatic dialogue replacement as he can; looping, he feels, is
always difficult to judge while it is being done, and the results can often be disappointing.

Hollywood movies are renowned for their elaborate
special effects, but equally impressive, in their own way,
are the unobtrusive effects that go unnoticed by an audience. The Met sequence in Yes, Giorgio serves as an il-
lustration. Schaffner had only two days to shoot in the
actual Met. On the first day, he brought in 100 extras to
serve as the portions of the audience that had to be seen
in the reaction shots of Giorgio's lover (Kathryn Harrold)
and manager (Eddie Albert). The second day, 690 extras
arrived: the audience shots were filmed towards the stage,
where the matte of the studio opera set would go; the
camera was then turned around, shooting across Luciano
Pavarotti to the audience. Later, in post-production, the
standing-room-only audience was created with a five-way
matte: the 690 extras were used for the center aisles, then
to the left, to the right, to the first balcony, and finally
to the second balcony. None of this is in the least apparent in the film: the combination of M-G-M's Stage 27 and
the Metropolitan Opera House footage looks as if there is
no marriage at all--as if it were all shot on location. It is
a fine example of Hollywood's expert yet seamless craftsmanship.

By the sixteenth week, the dialogue, sound effects,
and music tracks are mixed reel by reel. Schaffner, as
Jerry Goldsmith can attest, has an excellent ear: sound
was important to him when he was directing live television
and no less so in film; he has spent hours agonizing over
the soundtrack, even longer working with Dolby stereo.[39]
When the first reel is finished to his satisfaction, it is sent
off for negative cutting; by the time, say, the twelfth reel
is rerecorded, the negative cutter should be completing the
eighth reel.

The work becomes more tedious. The director of
photography returns for the timing process, in which the
densities and colors of the original footage are improved
to obtain the most satisfying print possible. "I probably
time more with Frank than any other director," Fred

Koenekamp says. "It's a matter of wanting everything as
perfect as possible and knowing that Frank is still not
happy--I can sense Frank now and pretty well know when
it's got to be changed."

    At this point, the film is taken from Schaffner's
hands and given to the advertising, marketing, and distribution people. Directors normally don't get involved in
the trailers and promos for their films, but on Yes, Giorgio,
Schaffner was so dissatisfied with what was provided by
Kanew-Manger-Deutsch, the company M-G-M had hired to
do the job, that he ended up supervising the preparation
of seven promotional pieces for film, television, and records. "I don't know that I've ever seen what I considered
to be an ideal trailer for a picture one has made," he says,
"but then your interests are so much more separate than
the sales function of that piece."

    Schaffner will make editorial changes after previews,
sometimes, as was the case for Sphinx, after the film is
released, but his chores on a film have still not ended.
For such an intensely private man, Schaffner will unhesi-
tatingly make appearances or give interviews--do whatever
the situation demands to promote the film.

Summary

Schaffner is intimately involved in all facets of the filmmaking process. His skills, now so well-polished, were first
honed when he was directing live television. In the golden
age of cinema, a writer wrote, a director directed, and an
editor edited; but in the golden age of television, the director had to interact with all the artists and craftsmen on
the show--from the moment he picked up the script until
the telecast was over. At times chaotic, the live television
experience made the director conscious of the value of a
smoothly functioning machine.

Opposite, a distinguished group of American directors wel-
comes an honored guest, Akira Kurosawa, 1981: (front)
Schaffner, Martin Ritt, William Wyler, Kurosawa, King
Vidor, Arthur Hiller, Samuel Fuller; (rear) Herbert Ross,
George Schaefer, Rouben Mamoulian, unidentifiable, Irvin
Kirschner.

Schaffner applied his television habits to cinema: he
works with the film writer in much the same way as he did
in television, except that he has more time; he works with
the actors in a similar way, albeit with little or no time for
rehearsal; he studies the art director's floor plans with
equal diligence; rather than talking to three cameramen and
giving them instructions via headphones, he discusses the
look of a film, lighting, and camera moves in detail with his
cinematographer; instead of editing himself on the spot, he
holes up in the cutting room with the editor. "He's calm,
quiet, orderly, business-like, rather than passionate and
spontaneous," Reginald Rose states. "This observation is
no way critical of Frank as a human being or as a director.
He couldn't be better as both. It's simply his style."

Just as he knew that no one man ever made a television show by himself, Schaffner realizes no one man can
make a film by himself. Film is a collaborative business that
sometimes becomes a collaborative art; to guide his film into
the latter category, a director employs the best people in
their respective fields. Schaffner has a command of the
medium that enables him to choose the right people--
professionals, like himself.

In discussing the necessary attributes of a good director, Charlton Heston mentions talent, intelligence, self-
discipline, and endurance, but concludes that, first and
foremost, the director must be a good captain: "His prime
virtue on a set is that he's a good captain," Heston says of
Schaffner, "the best I've ever seen."[40] The captain's job
is to get the best out of his cast and crew--both as indi-
viduals and as a unit--for the good of the film. "Franklin
Schaffner has the ability," Jerry Goldsmith has observed,
best describing what this director can do, "to bring everyone's interest out and to know what their contribution is--
what he wants them to contribute to a film, what they want
to contribute to the film."[41] The importance of interpersonal relationships in filmmaking cannot be stressed too
strongly. Most revealing in Heston's remark is the rank
he assigns Schaffner--a captain, rather than the cigar-
chomping general Bruce Cook suggests he resembles. A
general is too far removed from the action: albeit its leader, a captain is part of the team, at the center of the action; teamwork is essential in keeping the unit moving to
accomplish its goal. The testimony of his colleagues offers

proof that Schaffner can be surprisingly patient and encouraging in the matter of creative give and take. He will
go to great lengths in allowing his collaborators freedom:
if a new approach doesn't work, it's all right; if it does
work, he will use it--which, in view of what his collaborators know about his preparation, is indeed some kind of an
achievement.

As the overseer of a film, the director must have
authority: in this, Schaffner is abetted by his appearance
--his mere presence commands respect. His presence also
lends itself to a gentler side of the overseer's duty--as the
father figure on the set. First of all, Schaffner is a fine
man, something people working with him can immediately
sense; his set is filled with some of the nicest people in
the business. Fred Koenekamp is not alone when he says,
"Not only do I admire the man, I love the man. I'd do
anything in the world for him." When a talented group of
artists shares that attitude and is willing to move mountains, a director's life becomes easier and, personally, more
enriching. ("I'm not sure this should be quoted, but,")
Philip Barry, Jr. has said, "for years I've said, 'When I
grow up I want to be Frank Schaffner.' "

In the end, filmmaking is people working with other
people. It's no great secret--the great film directors have
always known this--but putting it effectively into action is
another story. "I have unlimited admiration for him as a
director," says Frank McCarthy. "I've never seen anybody
handle people the way he does."

Evaluation

I think he's a great American director beyond any
doubt at all. His style is clear and established.
There is a grandeur that he brings to pictures.
                                        --Peter Bart

At the beginning of his film career, Schaffner was a cult
director, known as a cool intellectual who made theatrical
and high-minded films with serious statements, arcane and
exotic details. The cult disbanded after the overwhelming
success of Planet of the Apes; its remnants were shattered
when he won an Academy Award for his direction of Patton.

Schaffner had reached a level of success far removed from
the critical plateau of succès d'estime; he had become a
major American director of international renown.

    Reaching the top of one's profession is quite satisfy-
ing in itself, but one's personal ambitions are always elusive. As a perfectionist, Schaffner can never be totally
content with what he has done--this is part of the directorial personality. There is always something more he
could have done, always untold worlds left to explore in
film. Schaffner thrived in the days of live television
drama, directing the steady flow of scripts that were assigned to him every other week: if a particular script was
bad, he would soon, at the pace he worked, come up with
a good one. Weaned on such a routine, Schaffner would
have fit in nicely during the golden age of Hollywood, when
the studio acquired and developed properties before hand-
ing them over to the director. Such a system is a thing of
the past; today's director must find his own material, and
even if a director has specific ideas and themes in mind,
he may not find the right script--Steve McQueen and Franklin J. Schaffner, for example, never found the western they
wanted to do together.

    In a 1963 interview, Schaffner outlined the types of
scripts he was seeking for DuPont Show of the Week:
(1) a love story with a strong heroine; (2) a drama about
the infinite world of a young child; (3) an allegory along
the lines of The Man Without a Country; (4) a modern St.
Joan allegory; (5) a Rififi or Diabolique type of show.[42]
The list demonstrates that a director's taste and interests
won't change too dramatically with the passage of time: a
dozen years later, he would realize number three and hint
at number two in Islands in the Stream. As early as a
decade before that 1963 interview, Schaffner had already
been typed as an action director, a man's director, so, to
work against that stereotype, he sought categories with
women: within the parameters of an action film, Sphinx
comes close to fulfilling numbers one and five; unhappily,
the film did little to change his image.

    Speaking both as friend and colleague, George Roy
Hill comments:

    I sometimes wish he weren't so conservative in his

choice of subjects. In fact, he's a classic film director and I wish he had experimented a bit more
because I think he tends to do material that's classic in form. That doesn't mean they're not magnificent, but I just wish--and this is just a minor point
--I just would've been interested to see what he
would've done with more experimental material.
What he does he does marvelously well.

Lately, in selecting material, Schaffner has gone away from
his strengths, moving to areas he admits he is not the most
proficient in--which uneven results. Sphinx and Yes, Giorgio are hardly experimental, but they are new additions to
the Schaffner canon; a critic can surely find the outsized
and obsessive hero out of his time and element in Ahmed
Khazzan and Giorgio Fini, even if they are light years away
from Schaffner's prototypical heroes, Papillon and Patton.
Schaffner's comedic gifts, however, lie in the realm of high,
light, and sophisticated comedies--a type of film no longer
made today; a George Roy Hill undoubtedly could have done
more with what Sphinx and Yes, Giorgio had to offer, but
then, a tit for a tat, Schaffner would have been the better
choice to have directed James Michener's Hawaii. It's not
difficult to understand why Schaffner would want to branch
out in new directions, but, realistically, a director runs a
professional risk in doing so. The motion picture industry
is very much a business, and no one who makes films that
don't show a profit can long remain a working director or
producer. Therein lies the filmmaker's dilemma: a director
who remains true to his strengths risks unemployment and
artistic stagnation.

    It is entirely possible that Schaffner was profoundly
disappointed by the fate of Islands in the Stream, a work
of depth and poignance, whose power increases each time it
is seen. As opposed to a case of a filmmaker summing up
his entire career (e.g., Frank Capra's 1946 production of
It's a Wonderful Life), and, having said it all, being left
with nowhere else to go but down, never to hit such heights
again, Islands in the Stream was more of a signal that a
gifted filmmaker had hit his stride and was embarking on a
new period of maturity and excellence. To have such a
work be ignored by both critics and audiences must surely
be an unsettling experience; it seems to have marked a
turning point in the direction of Schaffner's career. For a

man regarded as a director of highly literate work, Schaffner has since selected seemingly safer material; certainly
none of the films he has made since approaches the ambition
of Islands in the Stream.

    Schaffner, as George Roy Hill has noted, is a classic
filmmaker. Recently, his films have been subject to criticism not only for their content but their style. "As soon
as he became successful enough to command large budgets,"
Pauline Kael, an early Schaffner supporter, wrote, "his
camera began to linger on broad avenues, palatial rooms,
entrance ways and exits, big men standing against the
horizon."[43] As his subjects grew larger, Schaffner's style
became more majestic. By way of contrast, consider the
roundup of the astronauts scene in an earlier film, Planet
of the Apes: when an ape roar is heard, human beings
run frantically through a corn field; in long or close shot,
Schaffner's camera is always on the move; broken up by
rapid zooms, the diverse shots constitute a superb action
montage. Later in the film, when he learns he's to be
gelded, Taylor escapes through the institute's corridors
to the compound and into the village; stationary action shots
are intercut with moving action shots, an upside down shot
is followed by ground-level shots; chased by apes, Taylor
runs inside a temple, in and out of a museum, up and down
steps, before he is surrounded by the village apes who
look upon him as a mad animal; the tempo momentarily sub-
sides in a long pan of frightened ape faces as they prepare
to stone him; finally, three apes perched on an arch drop
a net over him and jump down, hoisting Taylor in the air.

    These two sequences are truly exhilarating to behold,
but, since Planet of the Apes, Schaffner has elected not
to display that kind of bravura filmmaking; none of his
later films contain moments with such cinematic razzle-dazzle.
These sequences exist as proof that Schaffner can be an
incomparable director of viscerally exciting scenes; he's
neither incapable nor has forgotten how. Rather, Schaffner
has consciously chosen a style that relies more on composition and long takes than camera movement or cutting: it
aspires to be the cinematic equivalent of Leo Tolstoy's noble
simplicity, a style more appreciated in Europe (much as
an identical style would be more appreciated in America
if the director were European). Fitting the demands of
epic subjects, its austerity also works well with simple but

deep dramas, adding significance to basic truths in the
drama of life. When applied to melodramatic material that
cries out for the cinematic bounce Schaffner is fully capable of delivering, it can seem inappropriate, even heavy-
handed. Yet, he has opted for this stately directorial
style; perhaps that's what his mentor Felix Jackson refers
to when he says, "He has a basic integrity in every picture he's made." It is his style, and he will continue to
use it. Visually a sumptuous sight, Schaffner's epic style
is unique in American cinema.

Franklin J. Schaffner has come to a crossroad in the
1980s. The motion picture industry itself, as Schaffner
has observed, has simultaneously come to a crossroad:

> We're facing an economic emergency in which those
> who finance and distribute movies don't know how
> to gross the $45 million they need to break even on
> an average film. We no longer know where the au-
> dience is, who the audience is, or what the audi-
> ence wants.[44]

Thus far, the decade has not been too kind to the
brilliant young directors who came out of live television in
the 1950s: Arthur Penn's Four Friends (1981) was not successful, neither was Robert Mulligan's Kiss Me Goodbye
(1982); John Frankenheimer's The Challenge (1982) did not
enjoy a full theatrical release; unlike the John Irving novel,
George Roy Hill's production of The World According to
Garp (1982) fell short of capturing the fancy of critics or
audiences. The ubiquitous Sidney Lumet--who has more
flops to his credit than the rest of the group--has managed
to fare the best, only because he works with the speed and
regularity of a live television director, and, when one of
his films bombs, he already has another in the can and is
working on a new project.

"He's still out there," Herbert Brodkin says of
Schaffner, speaking as one professional about another,
"sometimes doing good work in a medium that makes pictures for children." If comic book movies are popular
these days and easily financed, neither Schaffner nor his
contemporaries can easily commit to doing them. Peter
Bart comments:

> These are very serious, literate men--far more in-
> telligent, far more astute intellectually, than the
> present generation of young directors on the way
> up. I still think they can deal with subjects that
> will get a big audience, provided they deal with it
> on a light basis. In other words, I think [they
> have] fallen into a trap with their budgets--they're
> all gigantic, overblown pictures.... I really think
> there's a self-defeating spiral. If you make $20-25
> million pictures, unless you make comic strip pic-
> tures, you're going to die with those pictures.

It is a quandary younger directors face as well: fewer
films are produced each year; subjects are softened and
made escapist to attract the widest possible audience,
justifying the enormous and ever-increasing sums of money
spent on production; small films are economically impractical
--the cost of exploitation is so prohibitively expensive that
it is almost safer to produce a $40 million movie aimed at the
heart of the American middle class than a $400,000 issue-
oriented film aimed at a selected audience.

Schaffner and his contemporaries are firm believers
in the value of a good script. They know that the root of
many motion picture problems can be traced back to the
screenplay: if they are not on paper, the ideas and themes
won't be apparent on the screen. But, for all their work
in close quarters on a script, perhaps the directors of the
live television generation have become less flexible in their
dealings with the writer; possibly this fundamentally intimate collaboration has become less of a two-way street as
the directors' salaries and control over their films escalate.

Franklin J. Schaffner is a highly civilized man with
refined tastes: the values he embodies may no longer be
fashionable in the contemporary scene. If so, Schaffner is
becoming as one of his heroes in real life--a sobering statement about the times. It was earlier noted how Sam Spiegel's taste and literary standards had seemed to go out of
style; now, over a dozen years after Nicholas and Alexandra,
many of those traits attributed to Spiegel can be applied to
Schaffner. Spiegel, however, has since responded by producing Betrayal (1983), perhaps the smallest film of his career; by making a small but literate picture, Spiegel returned to his origins as a producer.

Delbert Mann, the first television director to make good in Hollywood, recently directed "All the Way Home" (1981) and "The Member of the Wedding" (1982) for NBC Live Theatre; he has come full circle, returned to his roots. Perhaps the audience most receptive to the taste, style, and work of this generation of directors doesn't go to the movies anymore and watches television instead. Indeed, during the absence of these directors, a significant development beyond the television movie was legitimatized in 1976, in the wake of ABC's Rich Man, Poor Man--the miniseries. It once would have been inconceivable for a best-selling novel by a major author to be sold directly to television; those old notions were demolished with the spectacular success of the same network's presentation of Alex Haley's Roots in 1977. Television companies can outbid film companies for a major book; some authors prefer to sell their books to television, where a more extensive treatment of their work is possible; big names on either side of the film camera have made the leap to television. In 1983, hundreds of millions watched The Winds of War and The Thorn Birds on ABC, the network leader of the long form; the miniseries remains no less a major force in the entertainment picture.

Schaffner has not ruled out television--quite the contrary. Television brought its own kind of rewards, and Schaffner has wanted to do more work in that medium ever since he left it. There is, as he says, a slight problem:

> I am so far removed from it now, as I am from the theatre, that nobody ever thinks of me. That's what it amounts to. I guess if I took an ad in Variety and said, "Hey, I'm available for television or theatre," somebody would think of me.

Nobody has ever asked him to cover a global event via satellite, nor a live news, sports, or entertainment show, nor a special or a weekly series. What he is instead asked to do always resembles some film he's made; if he refuses to repeat himself on film, he will refuse to repeat himself on television.

For years, cable/pay TV was discussed in almost utopian terms as the entertainment media's savior--all kinds of programs for all kinds of audiences; now that the future

is here, all kinds of audiences are still awaiting their programs. Another staging of a Neil Simon play scarcely constitutes a major breakthrough; furthermore, it won't look
any better than or different from what already exists on
network television. Television was unlike any other medium when Schaffner began his career--unique, as were its
production methods, which he helped pioneer and develop.
Production innovations commensurate to the other differences
between network television and cable/pay TV would tend to
present more of a challenge to a man who has directed over
400 network television shows.

James Clavell's Shogun, another widely heralded and
successful miniseries, would not have been out of place in
Schaffner's body of work: it is the stuff of a sprawling
epic; it has the ironic distance of time and place; Black-
thorne is of the same clay as a Schaffner hero (and that
Schaffner spent the first six years of his life in Japan
would have been no particular disadvantage). The point
is not that Schaffner should have directed it, but that
such large-scale historical adventures as Shogun should be
made as theatrical films: these types of stories are seen
to their best advantage in wide screen 70mm.

Given the limitations of the television screen, no
wonder a staple of live television was intimate human drama,
the kitchen sink school of drama; the common man has always fared best in the history of the television medium. A
Schaffner hero is larger than life, as are his exploits; physically, a Schaffner film should be larger than life as well.
Considering the thematic content of his films, it is not surprising that he is so adept with the wide screen--it is as
large as moving pictures get. A Schaffner character is not
meant for the television screen, where he will be physically
smaller than life. It is truly doubtful if the image of General George S. Patton, Jr. standing in front of a mammoth
American flag would have worked its way into the American
culture had it been shot for a television movie.

"It's like reading a lavish edition of Shakespeare on
microfilm," Schaffner says about films on television. "You
can't drink in the folio or get a sense of the craft that went
into it." He is at his best practicing what seems to be a
dying art form: transforming a 500-plus-page book into a
two-hour film. Schaffner's greatest strength is the big

picture, featuring an outsized hero set against a magnificent background. Whatever the setting, the film is a realistic drama with moral concerns, scope, and action: the Schaffner hero embarks on some monumental journey, be it physical or spiritual, in which his very existence as a man is at stake.

Securing financing for such a film is not the easiest of tasks in the 1980s. The fact is there never was a time in Hollywood when it was easy to make movies with messages, yet, throughout the history of American cinema, certain producers and directors have always fought the uphill battle to film a serious subject, sometimes with results pleasing to the studio, critics, and general public alike. If today's filmgoer is overwhelmingly young, and the majority of product is aimed at that market, a sizeable market still remains for a Schaffner film. The success of the recent "adult weepies" trend (Kramer versus Kramer, 1979; Ordinary People, 1980; On Golden Pond, 1981; and Terms of Endearment, 1983--all films that could have been made directly for the television screen) indicates that there is a large adult audience just waiting to be tapped--if studios and distributors will only provide the proper product. The old Hollywood adage, a good picture makes money, still applies; a good wide-screen picture can make money. Schaffner's themes are universal; released on a natural course, his films will find their audience.

Franklin J. Schaffner has been a proven success in three media: although versatile enough to move with complete ease from film to television or stage, Schaffner, given his thematic concerns and technical expertise, is best suited to the cinema and the big picture. Schaffner's all-encompassing wide screen brackets a film founded on character, a personal and intimate story melded with the action and events of history to create a picture of epic proportions; like a detailed mosaic or a richly woven tapestry, it is a work in which extraordinary efforts have been made to hide the craft. This is his mark of excellence: a film made by a director with a historian's touch.

It is appropriate to conclude with a statement by Worthington Miner, the late mentor of Franklin J. Schaffner:

I do not think in spite of his Oscar, I don't think

he's had the recognition he should have had....
There's a validity to most of what he does that I
often find lacking in people that are being acclaimed
.... It's partly because his material hasn't been as
good as his talent.... I think that Frank has an
elegant chance of getting to the place where he will
go--very high.... He has to his credit a couple of as
good pictures as there are around already, and I
think that any day he may have the one that gets
the proper recognition.

NOTES

Chapter 1: Introduction

1. Fred Robbins, "Nicholas and Alexandra," Show, January 1972,
   p. 31.

2. Andrew Sarris, "Director of the Month--Franklin Schaffner:
   The Panoply of Power," Show, April 1970, p. 23.

3. Kevin Thomas, "Balancing Act Pays off for 'Patton' Director,"
   Los Angeles Times, Part IV, May 7, 1970, p. 1.

4. Jack Hofferkamp, "Schaffner Has His Fingers Crossed,"
   Los Angeles Times, Part IV, January 4, 1974, p. 18.

5. Bruce Cook, Dalton Trumbo (New York: Charles Scribner's
   Sons, 1977), p. 7.

6. Herb A. Lightman, "On Location with 'ISLANDS IN THE
   STREAM,'" American Cinematographer, November 1976,
   p. 1259.

7. Malcolm Cowley, "Third Act and Epilogue," F. Scott Fitzgerald, edited by Arthur Mizener (Englewood Cliffs, NJ:
   Prentice-Hall, Inc., 1963), p. 66.

8. John Brady, The Craft of the Screenwriter (New York:
   Simon and Schuster, 1981), p. 168.
   "Wide screen" actually refers to a camera mask with a
   1.65:1 or 1.85:1 aspect ratio (as opposed to the former
   1.33:1 standard)--not, as it is commonly used (or misused),
   to denote the 2.3:1 or 2.5:1 aspect ratio. In this text, however, the term "wide screen" is employed as a synonym for
   the image projected by the anamorphic lens--thereby perpetu-
   ating the popular misconception of the term.
   Finally, one last critical hurdle: the comparison with David
   Lean is inevitable, so inevitable that it has been made ad
   nauseam. Lean directed Bridge on the River Kwai, Lawrence
   of Arabia, and Doctor Zhivago; Schaffner directed Patton,
   Papillon, and Nicholas and Alexandra. Indeed, both directors
   know how to use the wide screen, both have a way with epic
   films, but further discussion can only lead to invidious com-
   parisons; in making such a comparison, one critic crowned

Schaffner "atop the throne of epicdom." (James Delson, "Papillon: An Intraview," Take One, Vol. 4, No. 1, 1974, p. 29.) The reality is that these kinds of screen epics are seldom made nowadays. If the comparison of these two distinguished directors signifies a standard for cinematic quality, fine; otherwise, this is the first and last time this particular topic will be mentioned in the text.

9. Joseph Wershba, "Close Up: TV Producer," New York Post, November 26, 1962, p. 29.

10. It is quite impossible to give an exact figure of the number of shows Schaffner directed or the number of hours he directed because of his days in News and Public Affairs, when he directed almost everything every day.

11. Christopher Wicking and Tise Vahimagi, The American Vein (New York: E. P. Dutton, 1971), pp. 111-112.

12. Sidney Wise, Presentation of a honorary Doctor of Humane Letters degree to Franklin J. Schaffner, Franklin and Marshall College, Lancaster, PA, December 4, 1977.

13. Donald Chase, Filmmaking: The Collaborative Art (Boston: Little, Brown and Company, 1975), p. 23.

Chapter 2: The Television Career of Franklin Schaffner

1. "Life Goes on a Bicycle Weekend," Life, May 25, 1942, p. 103.

2. Margaret Clark, Letter, Look, December 28, 1943, p. 8.

3. Richard Gehman, "Punch One, Cue the Dolly and Kill the Baby!" TV Guide, July 13, 1963, p. 26.

4. The March of Time directors themselves were paid the grand sum of $150 a week.

5. Raymond Fielding, The March of Time, 1935-1951 (New York: Oxford University Press, 1978), p. 290.

6. Christopher H. Sterling and John M. Kittross, Stay Tuned (Belmont, CA: Wadsworth Publishing Company, 1978), p. 208.

7. William S. Paley, As It Happened (Garden City, NY: Doubleday & Company, Inc., 1979), p. 215.

8. Paley, pp. 216-217.

9. Worthington Miner, "Radio and Television Drama in the United

States," The Reader's Encyclopedia of World Drama, edited by John Gassner and Edward Quinn (New York: Thomas Y. Crowell Company, 1969), p. 699.

10. Miner, p. 697.

11. Paley, p. 217.

12. Miner, p. 696.

13. Harriet Van Horne, "The Living Theatre of Television," Theatre Arts, September 1951, p. 53.

14. Charles Adams, "The Stage Director in Television," Theatre Arts, October 1951, p. 47.

15. Fielder Cook and Franklin Schaffner, "The TV Director: A Dialogue," The Progress in Television, edited by A. William Bluem and Roger Manvell (New York: The Focal Press Ltd., 1967), p. 41.

16. Erik Barnouw, The Image Empire: A History of Broadcasting in the United States, Vol. III (New York: Oxford University Press, 1970), p. 32.

17. The best analysis of this period and film style can be found in Mario Beguiristain's unpublished Ph.D. dissertation, "Theatrical Realism: An American Film Style of the Fifties," Department of Cinema, University of Southern California, 1978.

18. Barnouw, The Image Empire, p. 31.

19. Paddy Chayefsky, Television Plays (New York: Touchstone/Simon and Schuster, 1955), pp. 81 and 129.

20. Adams, p. 78.

21. "He's very handsome," Robert Fryer says of Schaffner. "Always teased him, sure, and tried to get him to do something." For the record, Schaffner did make one appearance before the television cameras, as an actor in Mama. When asked if he did it as a favor to Ralph Nelson, Schaffner answers tersely, "More as a favor to me." The favor was never repeated.

22. Paley, p. 277.

23. Harriet Van Horne, "Don't Look Now," Theatre Arts, October 1952, p. 88.

24. Paley, p. 219.

25. Gore Vidal, Visit to a Small Planet and Other Television Plays
    (Boston: Little, Brown and Company, 1956), p. 39.

26. Vidal, p. 38.

27. Vidal, pp. xiv-xv.

28. Reginald Rose, Six Television Plays (New York: Simon and
    Schuster, 1956), p. 104.

29. Rex Polier, "Reflections on TV's Golden Age," Los Angeles
    Times, Part VI, January 1, 1982, p. 9.

30. Rod Serling, "The Strike," Best Television Plays, edited by
    Gore Vidal (New York: Ballantine Books, Inc., 1956), p.
    180.

31. Alexander Kendrick, Prime Time: The Life of Edward R.
    Murrow (Boston: Little, Brown and Company, 1969), p. 360.

32. Fred W. Friendly, Due to Circumstances Beyond Our Control
    (New York: Random House, 1967), p. 45.

33. Pete Martin, "I Call on Edward R. Murrow," Saturday Evening
    Post, January 18, 1958, p. 79.

34. Kendrick, p. 364.

35. John Frankenheimer was an A.D. on this show, but, as his
    duties were out in the field, he did not meet Schaffner until
    a few years later.

36. This is a very rare occasion of Edward R. Murrow losing his
    composure on the air: Groucho Marx only has to say, "Hello,
    Eddie," and Murrow is reduced to helpless laughter and heard
    to mutter, not once but twice, "I knew this was a mistake."
    Also appearing, singing "I Hear Music (and there's no one
    there)" with her father, is Melinda, Marx's then seven-and-a-
    half-year-old daughter, for whom Murrow, on behalf of his
    son, tries to arrange a match.

37. Rose, p. 158.

38. Rose, p. 302.

39. "Sunday Is a Big Day for Tuesday," Milwaukee Journal, May
    19, 1963, p. 7.

40. Martin Ritt is a subject deserving of further study. Although
    well-regarded for his work in the medium, he is not usually

associated with that group of men who were considered the most prominent directors of live television; yet, his first film, <u>Edge of the City</u> (1957), was made six years before Schaffner's first film. This is all the more remarkable inasmuch as Ritt was also blacklisted in the days of his television career.

41. The basis of a long-standing gag between Fred Coe and Martin Manulis was that Coe produced the film version of <u>The Miracle Worker</u>, which Manulis had produced for <u>Playhouse 90</u>, and Manulis produced the film version of <u>The Days of Wine and Roses</u>, which Coe had produced for <u>Playhouse 90</u>.

42. Coe would later produce and/or direct such Broadway shows and films as <u>The Miracle Worker</u>, <u>Two for the Seesaw</u>, <u>Wait Until Dark</u>, and <u>A Thousand Clowns</u>. In 1979, he would die, somewhat ironically, supervising another television production of <u>The Miracle Worker</u>.

43. Eric Sevareid, Letter to Franklin Schaffner, December 16, 1958. Franklin J. Schaffner's Personal Files.

44. Cecil Smith, "Rod Serling's Scripts Hit Like Heavyweight," <u>Los Angeles Times</u>, Part V, October 14, 1956, p. 5.

45. Rod Serling, "The Velvet Alley," <u>Playhouse 90</u>, final revision, January 7, 1959, p. 61. Rod Serling Collection, Special Collections, University Research Library, University of California at Los Angeles.

46. Serling, "The Velvet Alley," p. 104.

47. Elliott Jay Novak, "Requiem for a Screenwriter," <u>The Hollywood Reporter 45th Anniversary Issue</u>, 1975, p. 178.

48. "Rose." [George Rosen], "The Wicked Scheme of Jebal Deeks," <u>Variety</u>, November 18, 1959, p. 33.

49. Alec Guinness, Letter to Franklin Schaffner, November 3, 1959. Franklin J. Schaffner's Personal Files.

50. Miner, p. 699.

51. Rose, p. 249.

52. Friendly, p. 99.

53. Barnouw, <u>The Image Empire</u>, p. 37.

54. Kenneth Geist, "Chronicler of Power, an interview with Franklin Schaffner," <u>Film Comment</u>, September–October 1972, p. 30.

55. Kay Gardella, "Producer Manulis Excited Over Return of TV Drama," New York Daily News, August 10, 1966, p. 93.

56. Miner, p. 700.

57. Geist, p. 30.

58. Terry Curtis Fox, "Franklin Schaffner's Films: Where Worlds Collide," New York Daily News, Leisure, March 13, 1977, p. 5.

59. Cook and Schaffner, p. 41.

60. Cook and Schaffner, p. 42.

61. Franklin Schaffner, "The Best and the Worst of It," Films and Filming, October 1964, p. 9.

62. Gehman, p. 27.

63. Gehman, p. 28.

Chapter 3: The Film Career of Franklin J. Schaffner

1. Ralph Appelbaum, "Flying High," Films and Filming, August 1979, pp. 16-17.

2. Kenneth Geist, "Chronicler of Power, an interview with Franklin J. Schaffner," Film Comment, September-October 1972, p. 30.

3. Rachel Coffin, ed., New York Theatre Critics' Reviews, Vol. XXI, Number 24, 1961, pp. 168-171.

4. Today, Robert Fryer, despite his success in the film arena, concentrates on his first love, as artistic director of the Center Theatre Group/Music Center/Ahmanson Theatre in Los Angeles, where, thus far, he has unsuccessfully tried to coax a member of the play selection committee, the man who directed the film version of The Boys from Brazil for him, into directing a stage production.

5. Kevin Thomas, "Schaffner: TV to Big Screen," Los Angeles Times, Part IV, March 17, 1966, p. 14.

6. Stephen Gethers, A Summer World, Revised, Twentieth Century-Fox, June 19, 1961, p. 126. Franklin J. Schaffner Film Library, Franklin and Marshall College.

7. Franklin J. Schaffner, Letter to Jerome Hellman, July 7, 1961. Franklin J. Schaffner's Personal Files.

8. Paul Gardner, "Boy Scout with the Midas Touch," New York Times, Section 2, January 31, 1965, p. 13.

9. "Rose." [George Rosen], "The Good Years," Variety, January 17, 1962, p. 37.

10. Perry Wolff, A Tour of the White House with Mrs. John F. Kennedy (Garden City, NY: Doubleday & Company, Inc., 1962), p. 240.

11. Wolff, p. 1.

12. Although Schaffner had directed their appearance on Person to Person, he was in the studio and not on location; he finally met the Kennedys on this tour of the White House.

13. Harriet Van Horne, "A First Lady of Taste," New York World-Telegram, February 15, 1962, p. 19.

14. Pierre Salinger, Letter to Franklin Schaffner, May 4, 1963. Franklin J. Schaffner's Personal Files.

15. Jack Mathews, "Shrinking Screens Are a Big Problem for This Director," Detroit Free Press, April 7, 1981, p. 80.

16. Mel Gussow, Don't Say Yes Until I Finish Talking: A Biography of Darryl F. Zanuck (Garden City, NY: Doubleday & Company, Inc., 1971), p. 237.

17. Rowland Barber, "The Mighty Sound Track in Bungalow Ten," Show, March 1962, p. 86.

18. Budd Schulberg, Moving Pictures: Memories of a Hollywood Prince (New York: Stein and Day, 1981), pp. 301-302.

19. Jerry Wald, Letter to Franklin Schaffner, May 28, 1962. Franklin J. Schaffner's Personal Files.

20. Cecil Smith, "No Real Need to Defend this One," Los Angeles Times, Part IV, May 1, 1962, p. 14.

21. James Power, "The Stripper," The Hollywood Reporter, April 24, 1963, p. 3.

22. William Inge, A Loss of Roses (New York: Random House, 1960), p. 126.

23. Dean Gautschy, "Any Resemblance Isn't Coincidental," Los Angeles Herald-Examiner, June 24, 1962, p. 4.

24. Bosley Crowther, "The Stripper," The New York Times Film

Reviews 1913-1968, Vol. 5 (New York: The New York Times and Arno Press, 1970), pp. 3394-3395.

25. "Tube." [Larry Tubell], "The Stripper," *Daily Variety*, April 24, 1963, p. 3.

26. Darryl F. Zanuck, Letter to Franklin Schaffner, December 20, 1962. Franklin J. Schaffner's Personal Files.

27. Power, p. 3.

28. Robin Bean, "Woman of Summer," *Films and Filming*, June 1963, p. 42.

29. Fielder Cook and Franklin Schaffner, "The TV Director: A Dialogue," *The Progress in Television*, edited by A. William Bluem and Roger Manvell (New York: The Focal Press Ltd., 1967), pp. 38-39.

30. Brendan Gill, "Another Writer," *The New Yorker*, April 18, 1964, p. 120.

31. Gore Vidal, *The Best Man* (Boston: Little, Brown and Company, 1960), p. xi.

32. Vidal, p. 88.

33. For the record, both producers would eventually direct films: in addition to producing *Little Big Man* (1971) and *Shoot the Moon* (1982), Stuart Millar has directed *When the Legends Die* (1973) and *Rooster Cogburn* (1975); in addition to producing *The Graduate* (1967) and *The Great White Hope* (1971), Lawrence Turman has directed *Marriage of a Young Stockbroker* (1971) and *Second Thoughts* (1983).

34. Sidney Wise, "Politicians: A Film Perspective," *NEWS for Teachers of Political Science*, Winter 1982, p. 2.

35. "Dialogue on Film: Gore Vidal," *American Film*, April 1977, p. 42.

36. Arthur Schlesinger, Jr., "Decline and Fall," *Show*, June 1964, p. 11.

37. "Dialogue on Film: Gore Vidal," p. 40.

38. Cook would be involved in another interesting mixed media project: *Too Far to Go*, a 1979 television movie based on John Updike stories directed by Cook, was released to motion picture theatres in 1982.

39. Bill Shea, "TV as Passe as Nickelodeon," Film Daily, January 14, 1965, p. 1.

40. "Horo." [Murray Horowitz], "John F. Kennedy, May 29, 1964," Variety, June 3, 1964, p. 54.

41. The New York Times Film Reviews, p. 3578.

42. Leslie Stevens, The Lovers (New York: Samuel French, Inc., 1956), p. 272.

43. Charlton Heston, The Actor's Life, edited by Hollis Alpert (New York: E. P. Dutton, 1978), pp. 160-161.

44. Heston, p. 137.

45. In the credits, Alexander Golitzen is listed in first position as art director. This is a remnant of the Universal studio system, Golitzen being head of the art department: should any Universal studio film win an Academy Award for art direction, he, despite having made no contribution to its design, would win an Oscar.

46. Heston, p. 21. The name of Eliot Elisofon, a well-known Life photographer who wanted to be involved in motion pictures, can be found in the credits. His contribution to the visual look of the film was minimal: having found out the hard way that nobody told Russell Metty what to do with a motion picture camera, Elisofon returned to shooting magazine stills.

47. The credits, by Pacific Titles, are in bright red letters, making them hard to read. This was yet another grievance the creative team had against the studio.

48. Heston, p. 214.

49. Folmar Blangsted, "The War Lord," The Cinemaeditor, Fall 1965, p. 7.

50. "Neurotic Knight," Newsweek, December 6, 1965, p. 106.

51. David Wilson, "The War Lord," Sight and Sound, Spring 1966, p. 75.

52. James Powers, "'War Lord' Exotic Epic with Formidable Cast," The Hollywood Reporter, October 4, 1965, p. 3.

53. Heston, p. 199.

54. Frank Tarloff would later sue Chester to collect the $71,279 the producer had neglected to pay him for his services on Father Goose.

55. Robert Solo, Memo, August 17, 1965. The Double Man Files, Warner Bros. Collection, Archives of the Performing Arts, University Library, University of Southern California.

56. Geoffrey M. Shurlock, Letter to Jack L. Warner, April 13, 1966. The Double Man Files, Warner Bros. Collection, USC.

57. Jack L. Warner, Memo to Walter MacEwen, October 19, 1966. The Double Man Files, Warner Bros. Collection, USC.

58. "Rich." [Richard Alberino], "The Double Man," Variety, April 26, 1967, p. 6.

59. The New York Times Film Reviews, p. 3754.

60. Kevin Thomas, "The Double Man," Los Angeles Times, Part IV, May 22, 1968, p. 16.

61. Dale Munroe, "Director Franklin Schaffner from PLANET OF THE APES to PATTON," Show, August 6, 1970, p. 16.

62. Kevin Thomas, "'Planet of the Apes' Out of this World," Los Angeles Times, Calendar, March 24, 1968, p. 18.

63. Pierre Boulle, Planet of the Apes, translated by Xan Fielding (New York: The Vanguard Press, Inc., 1963), p. 194.

64. Charles F. Greenlaw, Memo, January 25, 1965. Planet of the Apes Files, Warner Bros. Collection, USC.

65. It is interesting to speculate what Blake Edwards would have done with the night on the town sequence in which Thomas gets rip-roaring drunk at an ape night club.

66. Walter MacEwen, Memo to Charles Greenlaw, March 30, 1965. Planet of the Apes Files, Warner Bros. Collection, USC.

67. Heston, p. 248.

68. Planet of the Apes Test, [1966]. Franklin J. Schaffner Film Library, Franklin and Marshall College.
    This short film actually consists of two separate tests: the first part, narrated by Paul Frees, is an animated storyboard that Abrahams put together of the water colors Jacobs had prepared for Warner Bros.; the second part is the scene Schaffner shot.

69. Wilson, p. 24.

70. Dale Winogura, "Dialogues on Apes, Apes, and More Apes," Cinefantastique, Summer 1972, p. 26.

71. Heston, p. 203.

72. Herb A. Lightman, "Filming 'PLANET OF THE APES,'" American Cinematographer, April 1968, p. 278.

73. Lightman, p. 258.

74. John Gregory Dunne, The Studio (New York: Farrar, Straus & Giroux, 1969), pp. 94-95.

75. Winogura, p. 34.

76. Stewart, the fourth astronaut, is a woman with whom Taylor seems to have some sort of romantic attachment; she dies in the crash. According to Charlton Heston, an octogenarian woman was hired to portray, under make-up, the dead Stewart. (Heston, p. 276.)

77. Earle Hagen, Scoring for Films (New York: E. D. J. Music, Inc., 1971), p. 165.

78. Dunne, p. 112.

79. Joseph Morgenstern, "Monkey Lands," Newsweek, February 26, 1968, p. 84.

80. Pauline Kael, "Apes Must Be Remembered, Charlie," The New Yorker, February 17, 1968, p. 108.

81. Kael, p. 108.

82. Richard Schickel, "Second Thoughts on Ape-Men," Life, May 10, 1968, p. 20.

83. Lightman, p. 278.

84. Winogura, p. 26.

85. Beneath the Planet of the Apes was directed by Ted Post, 1969; Escape from the Planet of the Apes, Don Taylor, 1970; Conquest of the Planet of the Apes, J. Lee Thompson, 1972; Battle for the Planet of the Apes, J. Lee Thompson, 1973. For the record, there were also two television series: Planet of the Apes, CBS, which lasted half a season in 1974, and Return to the Planet of the Apes, a cartoon show on NBC, 1975-1976.

86. Gerald Pratley, "Patton: Lust for Glory," Focus on Film, May-August 1970, p. 14.

87. Ladislas Farago, Patton: Ordeal and Triumph (New York: Ivan Obolensky, Inc., 1964), p. 201.

Notes   443

88. Omar N. Bradley, A Soldier's Story (New York: Henry Holt and Company, 1951), p. 177.

89. Charles Champlin, "'Patton' Features George C. Scott as 'Old Blood and Guts,'" Los Angeles Times, Calendar, February 15, 1970, p. 18.

90. A comprehensive account of McCarthy's struggle, which this study unavoidably overlaps, is included in Lawrence H. Suid's Guts and Glory (Reading, MA: Addison-Wesley Publishing Company, 1978), pp. 244-254.

91. Darryl Zanuck, Memo to Richard Zanuck, February 11, 1966. Edmund H. North Collection, Special Collections, University Research Library, UCLA.

92. William L. Guthrie, Memo to Steve Trilling, October 6, 1953. Patton Files, Warner Bros. Collection, USC.
    The memo reveals that McCarthy was far from the only one who thought the Patton story was a good idea for a film. In addition to Fox and Warners, Universal, M-G-M, Columbia, Paramount, and William Goetz Productions were all interested in making a film about Patton.

93. Farago, p. 41.

94. Darryl Zanuck, Memo to Richard Zanuck, January 7, 1966. Edmund H. North Collection.

95. Patton's orderly, Sgt. William George Meeks, is portrayed by James Edwards, whose presence evokes strong memories of another Second World War film in which he starred, Home of the Brave (1949).

96. Betty Spence, "Jerry Goldsmith: The Man and His Movie Music," Los Angeles Times, Calendar, February 7, 1982, p. 30.

97. Stanley Kauffmann, Figures of Light (New York: Harper & Row, Publishers, 1971), p. 236.

98. It is fair to say that in George S. Patton, Jr., George C. Scott found the role of his career. Similarly sharing a fascination for the general, albeit to a different degree, Ladislas Farago wrote another book about him, The Last Days of Patton, published in 1981. To no one's great surprise, George C. Scott would like to make the film version of this book-- his own way, without interference from anybody else. If the film is ever made, it will be interesting to see how Scott fares without Schaffner.

99. Ivan Butler, The War Film (New York: A. S. Barnes and Company, 1974), p. 141.

100. By coincidence, in order to protect Hello, Dolly, Fox also delayed the release of another military related film, M*A*S*H, until February.

101. Some distributors on the international market have the right to sell a film as they see fit. In Great Britain, for example, the title of the film became Patton: Lust for Glory, a subtitle once considered but rejected for America; Lust for Glory, however, does sound more fitting for the country of Bernard Law Montgomery, clearly depicted in the film as the war's second greatest prima donna, if not the greatest.

102. Vincent Canby, "Patton: He Loved War," The New York Times, Arts and Leisure, February 18, 1970, p. 1.

103. Pauline Kael, "The Man Who Loved War," The New Yorker, January 31, 1970, p. 73.

104. Ronald Reagan, Letter to Frank McCarthy, March 10, 1970. Franklin J. Schaffner's Personal Files.

105. Kael, "The Man Who Loved War," p. 73.

106. Andrew Sarris, "Director of the Month--Franklin Schaffner: The Panoply of Power," Show, April 1970, p. 23.

107. Darryl Zanuck, Cable to Elmo Williams, January 15, 1970. Franklin J. Schaffner's Personal Files.

108. Ruth Ellen Patton Totten, Letter to Frank McCarthy, March 5, 1970. Franklin J. Schaffner's Personal Files.

109. Ruth Ellen Totten, "'Patton' Saluted by His Daughter," Hamilton Wenham Chronicle, March 11, 1970, p. 1.

110. The 43rd Annual Academy Awards Program, NBC, April 15, 1971. Franklin J. Schaffner's Personal Collection.

111. Ladislas Farago, Letter to Franklin J. Schaffner, May 20, 1970. Franklin J. Schaffner's Personal Files.

112. Robert K. Massie, Nicholas and Alexandra (New York: Dell Publishing Company, Inc., 1967), p. 530.
     Apparently, Massie's research inspired him enough to write another biography with a Russian backdrop, Peter the Great, 1980.

113. Peter Viertel, White Hunter, Black Heart (Garden City, NY: Doubleday & Company, Inc., 1953), pp. 15 and 299.

114. "George Stevens Joins Sam Spiegel on Col's 'Nicholas,'"
   Daily Variety, February 19, 1968, p. 11.

115. "George Stevens Joins Sam Spiegel," p. 11.

116. Geist, p. 35.

117. John Box, Memo to Antonio Castillo, November 12, 1970.
   Franklin J. Schaffner's Personal Files.

118. Massie, p. 43.

119. Schaffner immediately heard from an outraged James Goldman
   who had learned Spiegel was considering breaking the non-
   star policy by hiring Julie Christie to play Alexandra. While
   granting that she might be fine playing the household nanny
   Tegleva, he insisted the actress would be miscast in a regal
   role. (James Goldman, Letter to Franklin J. Schaffner, October 14, 1970. Franklin J. Schaffner's Personal Files.)

120. Fred Robbins, "Nicholas and Alexandra," Show, January
   1972, p. 35.

121. Richard Schickel, "Lesé Majesté in Panavision," Life, January 14, 1972, p. 14.

122. Craig Fisher, "'Nicholas and Alexandra' is a Literate, Grand
   Spectacle," The Hollywood Reporter, December 13, 1971, p. 3.

123. Robert K. Massie, Letter to Franklin J. Schaffner, October
   30, 1971. Franklin J. Schaffner's Personal Files.

124. Roderick Mann, "Spiegel: Back Into the Movie-Making
   Maelstrom," Los Angeles Times, Calendar, June 20, 1982,
   p. 35.

125. Arthur Knight, "Uneasy Lies the Head," Saturday Review,
   January 15, 1972, p. 17.

126. James Goldman, Letter to Franklin J. Schaffner, November 2,
   1971. Franklin J. Schaffner's Personal Files.

127. Fisher, p. 35.

128. As Goldman had recently written the book for Hal Prince's
   production of the Stephen Sondheim musical Follies and was
   now working on the Fowles assignment, there was industry
   speculation that it meant Schaffner would also direct the
   film version of Follies.

129. Franklin J. Schaffner, Letter to Sidney Wise, July 16, 1974.

Franklin J. Schaffner Film Library, Franklin and Marshall
College.

130. "The Fabulous Escapes of Papillon," Life, November 13, 1970,
p. 50.

131. Henri Charrière, Papillon, translated by June P. Wilson and
Walter B. Michaels (New York: Pocket Books, 1971), pp.
7-8.

132. Charrière, p. 153.

133. "The American Film Institute Seminar with Franklin Schaffner,"
February 21, 1974, pp. 33-34. Transcript 192, Louis B.
Mayer Library, American Film Institute.

134. Frank Capra, The Name Above the Title (New York: The
Macmillan Company, 1971), p. 471.

135. Howard Koch, "Power Drive," Close-Ups, edited by Danny
Peary (New York: Workman Publishers, 1978). p. 279.
    Eleanor Coppola's Notes begins with Francis Coppola of-
fering the Willard role in Apocalypse Now to Steve McQueen
(who would have undoubtedly been the best actor for the
role--the film suffers from his absence). McQueen eventually
turned down the part, but, in order to hold on to him, Coppola offered him the Kurtz role, the three-week part.
"McQueen's agent says that Steve will do it, but that he
wants the same money as the seventeen-week part, $3 mil-
lion," Mrs. Coppola writes, "because the film will earn it
back in foreign sales anyway." (Eleanor Coppola, Notes
[New York: Simon and Schuster, 1979], p. 12.) When
offered the $3 million for the Kurtz role, McQueen turned it
down anyway.

136. John Brady, The Craft of the Screenwriter (New York:
Simon and Schuster, 1981), p. 119.

137. Brady, p. 120. In his script Goldman describes Louis Dega
as "a Peter Finch type." (William Goldman, Papillon, Third
Draft, April 5, 1972, p. 7. Theatre Arts Library, UCLA.)

138. Schaffner, Letter to Sidney Wise.

139. Paul D. Zimmerman, "Stuck on an Island," Newsweek,
December 17, 1973.

140. Papillon originally received an "R" rating, but, due to its
considerable investment in the film, Allied Artists successfully appealed and won a "PG" rating, which would attract
a wider audience. Paul Bernstein of Chicago, taking his

three daughters to Papillon expecting a family film, was so upset by what he saw, he sued Allied Artists, the Motion Picture Association of America, and the General Cinema theatre chain for $250,000. Bernstein had a point: compared with other films of its time, Papillon, with its violence, male and female nudity, should have been rightfully rated "R."

141. "Murf." [Art Murphy], Daily Variety, December 11, 1973, p. 3.

142. Such were the behind-the-scenes financial machinations that the director isn't quite certain but suspects Papillon's final budget was closer to $15 million than the reported $13 million. For all the wheeling and the dealing, after the film was released and had become a worldwide success, Schaffner, McQueen, and Hoffman had the books audited to see what had happened to their profit participation, eventually leading to an outside settlement with Dorfmann. (Time/Life Inc., being associated with Laffont, was somehow mysteriously involved in all of this as well.) None of this is that uncommon in the entertainment world, but the television sale was decidedly unusual: ABC bought the rights from Allied Artists while CBS bought the rights from Dorfmann and Richmond. After years of litigation, in only one of the many court cases the film engendered, CBS finally won the rights to televise Papillon.

143. Schaffner, Letter to Sidney Wise.

144. Bruce Cook, Dalton Trumbo (New York: Charles Scribner's Sons, 1977), p. 7.

145. Andrew Sarris, "The Perils of Papillon," Village Voice, January 10, 1974, p. 57.

146. Stuart Byron, "Papillon," The Real Paper [Boston], December 19, 1973, p. 34.

147. "AFI Seminar," Feb. 21, 1974, p. 24.

148. "The Fabulous Escapes of Papillon," p. 50.

149. Byron, p. 34.

150. Sarris, "The Perils of Papillon," p. 57.

151. Alan R. Howard, "Papillon," The Hollywood Reporter, December 11, 1973, p. 3.

152. Interestingly enough, veteran director William ("Wild Bill") Wellman was also considered for the role of the coach.

153. Ernest Hemingway, Islands in the Stream (New York: Charles Scribner's Sons, 1970), p. 326.

154. Peter Bart was indirectly responsible for the situation, having originally packaged The Getaway for McQueen, Peter Bogdanovich, and Cybill Shepherd; Robert Evans, however, looking for a property in which to star his wife, Ali MacGraw, requested a synopsis of the script. "Ali and Steve met at Bob's house some weeks earlier," Bart recalls, "and there was something going on. You could see that there was a real chemistry between them, and so, like a schmuck, I totally forgot this whole thing.... So Ali comes to me and says, 'I want to do this picture.' Well, the chronology was she arrived on the set at 5:00 Saturday and by 6:15 was bedded down by McQueen."

155. The actor seems to have sold himself short. After The Towering Inferno in 1974, when he received billing over Paul Newman, the nearest rival of his generation, Steve McQueen, having accomplished as much as any movie star can expect out of his career, dropped out of sight for several years. When he re-emerged it was in a most unlikely but courageous project, The Enemy of the People (1976); Ibsen being box-office poison even in the theatre, there was no way the film could make money. McQueen further sabotaged the project by being totally unrecognizable: long hair and a beard cover his features; the final touch is the pair of spectacles that hides his blue eyes. Out of this new incarnation comes a different voice quality, the sound and tone of which is reminiscent of a Henry Fonda. From Bogart to Cagney to Tracy to Wayne and now to Fonda--Steve McQueen had more range than was given credit to him. The film is proof that his untimely death cut short what would have turned out to be more than an uncommonly interesting career.
How much of George C. Scott's performance as Hudson in Islands in the Stream is due to his acceptance of the McQueen script cannot be determined; certainly, in that his style was not so much to act but to be, McQueen would have been at least as leisurely as Hudson.

156. Peter Bart, "'Islands': A Film with Hemingway in Mind," Los Angeles Times, Calendar, March 13, 1977, p. 22.

157. Princess Grace, Letter to Franklin J. Schaffner, June 26, 1975. Franklin J. Schaffner's Personal Files.

158. Herb A. Lightman, "On Location with 'ISLANDS IN THE STREAM,'" American Cinematographer, November 1976, p. 1222.

159. Evidently Peter Bart and Denne Bart Petticlerc found it so

stimulating working together on the Hemingway project, they began collaborating on a novel entitled Gulf Stream, a saga about Cuba that was published in 1979 as Destinies.

160. William Creber, "Re-creating on Film the World of Ernest Hemingway," American Cinematographer, November 1976, p. 1276.

161. Ken Wales, "The Impossible Takes a Little Longer," American Cinematographer, November 1976, p. 1233.

162. "The American Film Institute Seminar with Franklin Schaffner," November 1, 1978, p. 40. Transcript 527, Louis B. Mayer Library, American Film Institute.

163. Vincent Canby, "'Islands in the Stream' Meanders Out of Control," The New York Times, March 10, 1977, p. 46.

164. Ernest Hemingway, To Have and Have Not (New York: Charles Scribner's Sons, 1937), p. 225.

165. "Murf." [Art Murphy], "Islands in the Stream," Daily Variety, March 4, 1977, p. 6.

166. David Picker, Letter to Franklin J. Schaffner, May 21, 1976. Franklin J. Schaffner's Personal Files.

167. Arthur Knight, "Islands in the Stream," The Hollywood Reporter, March 4, 1977, p. 3.

168. Jack Kroll, "Poor Papa," Newsweek, March 14, 1977, p. 94.

169. Judith Crist, "A Precious Burst of Hemingway," Saturday Review, March 19, 1977, p. 40.

170. John Huston, An Open Book (New York: Alfred A. Knopf, 1980), p. 328.

171. Dale Winogura, "Silver Screen," Cinemaphile, March 1977, p. 10.

172. Andrew Sarris, "Has the Hemingway Hero Had It?" Village Voice, March 28, 1977, p. 41.

173. "Agreement between the Government of Israel and Warner Brothers, Inc.," August 19, 1976. Franklin J. Schaffner's Personal Files.

174. In the "official" version sanctioned by the Israeli government, Operation Thunderbolt (1977), directed by Menahem Golan, the interior of a 747 was used instead of an airbus; so much for accuracy.

175. Franklin J. Schaffner, Memo to Ted Ashley, October 8, 1976. Franklin J. Schaffner's Personal Files.

176. "The Unmaking of Entebbe," Newsweek, November 8, 1976, p. 42.

177. Rob Edelman, "The Boys from Brazil," Films in Review, November 1978, p. 569.

178. Ira Levin, The Boys from Brazil (New York: Random House, 1976), p. 14.

179. Ralph Appelbaum, "Master Plans," Films and Filming, February 1977, p. 17.

180. Bernard Drew, "Lord Laurence Olivier as Nazi Hunter," American Film, July-August 1978, p. 12.

181. "AFI Seminar," Nov. 1, 1978, p. 19. Heywood Gould's script plays heavily on motion picture imagery for the scene: "Action" is the command to attack; "cut" the command to stop; and "print" the command to go for the throat. Bobby effectively directs Mengele's death scene.

182. Jack Kroll, "Little Hitlers," Newsweek, October 9, 1978, p. 92.

183. Levin, p. 271.

184. Edelman, p. 570. The mustache instantly reminds film buffs of the role Gregory Peck played in The Gunfighter (1950), which was unsuccessful at the box office, thereby prompting Darryl Zanuck's edict forbiding Peck to wear a mustache in any Twentieth Century-Fox picture.

185. Robert Osborne, "The Boys from Brazil," The Hollywood Reporter, September 25, 1978, p. 3.

186. Robin Cook, Sphinx (New York: New American Library, 1979), p. 137.

187. Billy Kocian, "In Budapest the Sound Is 'Doodah' as Crew Shoots a 'Sphinx' Scene," Daily Variety, February 12, 1980, p. 14.

188. Todd McCarthy, "Schaffner Is Still High on O'seas Lensing After 12 Years," Daily Variety, January 29, 1981, p. 6.

189. Robin Cook, p. 198.

190. William Hall, "Film Making in Pharaoh Land: Tut Tut," Los Angeles Times, Calendar, May 11, 1980, p. 6.

191. Henry Rogers, Letter to Lloyd Leipzig, August 22, 1980. Franklin J. Schaffner's Personal Files. Rogers and Cowan handled some of the public relations chores on Sphinx; that Rogers is Orion's Mike Medavoy's father-in-law is mere coincidence.

192. "Cart." [Todd McCarthy], "Sphinx," Daily Variety, February 11, 1981, p. 3.

193. Merrill Shindler, "Sphinx," Los Angeles, March 1981, p. 238.

194. Arthur Knight, "Sphinx," The Hollywood Reporter, February 11, 1981, p. 14.

195. Barry Brennan, "Preposterous and Delightful," Evening Outlook [Santa Monica, CA], February 12, 1981, p. B-6.

196. "Sphinx," Season Ticket, January 1981, p. 10. Sphinx, for some reason, as mysterious as the eponymous creature of its title, seems to play better on a television screen. Not only is it more dramatically effective, Sphinx, which was shot in Panavision, looks as if it could have been visually composed for the television screen.

197. Martin Bernheimer, "Luciano, the Lyric Muse and the Silver Screen," Los Angeles Times, Calendar, September 26, 1982, p. 52.

198. Donna Perlmutter, "Luciano Pavarotti's Gone Hollywood," Los Angeles Herald-Examiner, August 18, 1981, p. B-1.

199. Anne Piper, Yes, Giorgio (London: Heinemann, 1961), p. 181.

200. Alain Bernheim, Letter to Adolph Green, May 1, 1980. Franklin J. Schaffner's Personal Files.

201. In the opening credits of Schaffner's cut of the film, shown at M-G-M's screening room #1 on March 3, 1982, a title card reading "A Peter Fetterman-Alain Bernheim Production" appeared directly after the "A Franklin J. Schaffner Film" title card. Apparently, the producers were willing enough to follow Schaffner in the credits, but quarreled over their own billing; the situation worsened when Herbert H. Breslin inquired about billing for himself. No satisfactory arrangement could be made among the three men; M-G-M finally decided to drop that particular title card entirely.

202. Kevin Thomas, "Pavarotti Is Singing in the Frame," Los Angeles Times, Part V, September 25, 1982, p. 7.

203. "Yes, Giorgio Sneak Preview Results," National Research

Group, Inc., May 4, 1982. Franklin J. Schaffner's Personal Files.

204. Stanley Kauffmann, "A Handful of Stars," New Republic, October 25, 1982, p. 22.

205. David Linck, "Yes, Giorgio," Boxoffice, November 1982, p. 56.

206. Norman Steinberg, Yes, Giorgio, Revised Final Draft, April 10, 1981, p. 17. Franklin J. Schaffner's Personal Files.

207. The Turandot rehearsal of the October 17, 1980 script was written as a comedy sequence in which everything goes wrong, not unlike the Met disaster Giorgio describes in the film or, for that matter, the finale of Everybody Does It (1949), a rather tame film adaptation of James M. Cain's Career in C Major. Figuring two scenes of mishaps at the Met would be redundant, Schaffner elected not to film a flashback. Since the dragon scene is not played for laughs, the inclusion of the comedy scene would not have had an adverse effect on the rest of the film; Yes, Giorgio could have used another comic "mishap," and it would have served the comedy more appropriately than the film's food fight.

208. Ginger Varney, "Yes, Giorgio," L. A. Weekly, October 8, 1982, p. 58.
      Like Jolson, Giorgio in the 1980 script is so absorbed in his singing that he doesn't realize the woman walks out on him. The film, of course, works better with the recognition of his loss; Schaffner had to persuade studio president Freddie Fields that it should end not on Pamela but on Giorgio, as planned.

209. Jeff Silverman, "Page 2," Los Angeles Herald-Examiner, May 13, 1981, p. A-2.

210. Ralph Kaminsky, "'Giorgio's Schaffner Forecasting Big Response to Pop Opera Pic," Film Journal, September 24, 1982, p. 5.

211. Robert Osborne, "Yes, Giorgio," The Hollywood Reporter, September 15, 1982, pp. 3 and 13.

212. Alan Rich, "The Wasting of Pavarotti," New York, May 18, 1981, pp. 31 and 32.

Chapter 4: Conclusion

1. Andrew Sarris, "Director of the Month--Franklin Schaffner:

The Panoply of Power," Show, April 1970, p. 23. Kenneth
Geist, "Chronicler of Power, an interview with Franklin
Schaffner," Film Comment, September–October 1972, p. 30.
Sharon Russell, "Franklin J. Schaffner," Film Reader, No. 1,
1975, p. 108.

2. Vincent Canby, "'Nicholas and Alexandra' Depicts Fall of
   Romanovs," The New York Times, December 14, 1971, p. 54.

3. James Delson, "Papillon: An Interview," Take One, Vol. 4,
   No. 1, 1974, p. 29.

4. Delson, p. 29.

5. Ralph Appelbaum, "Master Plans," Films and Filming, February
   1979, p. 15.

6. Eric Sherman, Directing the Film (Boston: Little, Brown and
   Company, 1976), p. 57.

7. "Should Directors Produce?" Action, July–August 1968, p. 11.

8. John Brady, The Craft of the Screenwriter (New York: Simon
   and Schuster, 1981), pp. 203-204.

9. Bruce Cook, "War Between the Writers and Directors, Part II:
   The Directors," American Film, June 1976, p. 53.

10. "Franklin J. Schaffner" (Feature Story), Papillon Publicity
    Release, Allied Artists, 1973, p. 1.

11. Sherman, p. 104.

12. Sherman, p. 58.

13. Sherman, p. 100.

14. Appelbaum, p. 15.

15. "The American Film Institute Seminar with Franklin Schaffner,"
    March 16, 1977, p. 26. Transcript 397, Louis B. Mayer Li-
    brary, American Film Institute.

16. Sherman, p. 213.

17. Franklin J. Schaffner, Interview by Arthur Knight, January 8,
    1981. Tape 738, Archives of Performing Arts, University Li-
    brary, University of Southern California.

18. Stanley Lloyd Kaufman, Jr., "The Early Franklin J. Schaffner,"
    Films in Review, August–September 1969, p. 418.

454 Franklin J. Schaffner

19. Charlton Heston, Dialogue on Film, No. 1, 1972, p. 9.

20. "The American Film Institute Seminar with Franklin Schaffner," February 21, 1974. p. 7. Transcript 192, Louis B. Mayer Library, American Film Institute.

21. "The American Film Institute Seminar with Franklin Schaffner," November 1, 1978, p. 114. Transcript 527, Louis B. Mayer Library, American Film Institute.

22. "AFI Seminar," Feb. 21, 1974, p. 36.

23. Russell, p. 106.

24. Jose Lopez Rodero, Letter to Franklin J. Schaffner, October 13, 1973. Franklin J. Schaffner's Personal Files.

25. "Sphinx Call Sheet," January 8, 1980. Franklin J. Schaffner's Personal Files.

26. "AFI Seminar," Feb. 21, 1974, p. 13.

27. Dialogue on Film, p. 9.

28. Sherman, p. 143.

29. Barry Brennan, "Preposterous and Delightful," Evening Outlook [Santa Monica, CA], February 12, 1981, p. B-6.

30. "AFI Seminar," Nov. 1, 1978, p. 14.

31. "AFI Seminar," March 16, 1977, p. 27.

32. "AFI Seminar," March 16, 1977, p. 12.

33. Sherman, p. 244.

34. Franklin J. Schaffner, Notes to Paul Barry, February 12, 1970. Franklin J. Schaffner's Personal Files.

35. Betty Spence, "Jerry Goldsmith: The Man and His Movie Music," Los Angeles Times, Calendar, February 7, 1982, p. 30.

36. Donald Chase, Filmmaking: The Collaborative Art (Boston: Little, Brown and Company, 1975), p. 278.

37. Derek Elley, "Jerry Goldsmith," Films and Filming, June 1979, p. 21.

38. Chase, p. 283.

39. For all his efforts on a soundtrack, Schaffner likes to tell the
     story about The Boys from Brazil's preview at the finest and
     fanciest 70mm, 6-track Dolby stereo theatre in Boston: the
     house owner was miffed to learn that the director had brought
     a 35mm monaural print, but when the Twentieth Century-Fox
     representative accompanying Schaffner took a look backstage,
     he discovered that this state of the art theatre only had one
     instead of five speakers--meaning that anytime a speaker blew
     in one of the exhibitor's other theatres, somebody would come
     along to "borrow" a speaker from the deluxe house.
         His point is evident: a lot of hard work can and often
     does go for naught if the theatre is ill-equipped. The same
     applies for projectors, projectionists, and projection: all too
     many theatres never show a wide-screen film in its true as-
     pect ratio.

40. Dialogue on Film, No. 1, 1972, p. 9.

41. Chase, p. 282.

42. Walter Hawver, "A Long Hunt for Originality," Knickerbocker
     News [Albany, NY], June 4, 1963, p. 9A.

43. Pauline Kael, "Furry Freaks," The New Yorker, October 9,
     1978, p. 167.

44. Stephen Sinclair, "From the Council," The Cultural Post,
     March-April 1982, p. 19.

VIDEOGRAPHY

The television shows directed by Franklin Schaffner are listed in chronological order. The key to abbreviations is as follows:

p	producer
ep	executive producer
a	original author
s	scriptwriter
	(adaptation or original)
h	host or moderator
c	cast

Parenthetically following the credits of certain programs are abbreviations, denoting the institutions whose copies were viewed for the purposes of this study:

MB	Museum of Broadcasting
UCLA	ATAS-UCLA Television Archives
W	Wisconsin Center for Film and Theatre Research
F&M	Franklin J. Schaffner Film Library, Franklin and Marshall College
FJS	Franklin J. Schaffner's Personal Collection

The credits for Person to Person, beginning in 1953, are recorded in one continuous section, breaking the chronological order. Its list only represents the shows viewed for this study and by no means constitutes his entire output--he directed every installment from the program's debut until the end of the 1956-1957 season, thereafter directing occasional segments for two more years. Therefore, this videography cannot claim to be a complete inventory of every Franklin Schaffner television show. Furthermore, in addition to the titles listed below, Schaffner also directed, when he was with CBS News and Public Affairs in 1948-1949, a wide range of subjects including: Basketball, Boxing, Horse Races, Beauty Contests, Parades, and News.

Brooklyn Dodgers Baseball, CBS, 1948
    h: Red Barber

The United Nations in Action, CBS, 1948-1949
    p: Robert Bendick; h: Larry LeSueur, Ned Calmer

U.N. Casebook, CBS, 1948-1949
     p: Robert Bendick; h: Lyman Bryson, Quincy Howe

The People's Platform, CBS, 1948-1949
     "Must We Have a Fourth Round of Wage Increases?" December
7, 1948
     p: Leon Levine; h: Dwight Cook, with J. Raymond Walsh,
Lawrence Fertig (MB)

     "Have We Appropriated Too Much or Too Little for Our Armed
Forces?"/"Is Social Welfare Being Crowded Into a Corner by Mili-
tary Preparations?" January 24, 1949
     p: Leon Levine; h: Quincy Howe, with Norman Thomas,
Major George Fielding Eliot (MB)

Presidential Straws in the Wind, CBS, 1948
     p: Robert Bendick; h: Elmo Roger, Lyman Bryson

The 1948 Political Conventions, CBS, 1948
     p: Robert Bendick; h: Edward R. Murrow, Douglas Edwards

Lamp Unto My Feet, CBS, 1948-1949
     p: Ruth Ashton

Blues by Bargy, CBS, 1948-1949
     h: Jeane Bargy

Preview, CBS, March 7, 1949-September 5, 1949
     p: David Sherman; h: Tex McCrary and Jinx Falkenburg

Wesley, CBS, May 8, 1949-August 30, 1949
     p: Worthington Miner; a & s: Samuel Taylor; c: Frank
Thomas, Mona Thomas, Donald Devlin, Johnny Stewart

Studio One, CBS, 1949
     "The Rival Dummy," September 19, 1949
     p: Worthington Miner; a: Ben Hecht; s: Worthington Miner
and David Opotashu; c: Paul Lukas, Anne Francis

     "Mrs. Moonlight," October 3, 1949
     p: Worthington Miner; a: Ben Levy; s: William Jayne;
c: Katherine Bard, James MacCall, Una O'Connor

     "Two Sharp Knives," November 14, 1949
     p: Worthington Miner; a: Dashiell Hammett; s: Carl Bixby;
c: Hildy Parks, Stanley Ridges

     "At Mrs. Beam's," November 28, 1949
     p: Worthington Miner; a: C. K. Munro; s: Charles Monroe;
c: Eva Gabor, John Baragrey, Mildred Natwick, Cathleen Cordell

"Jane Eyre," December 12, 1949
    p: Worthington Miner; a: Charlotte Bronte; s: Sumner
Locke Elliott; c: Charlton Heston, Mary Sinclair, Mary Malone (F&M)

"The Inner Light," December 26, 1949
    p: Worthington Miner; a: Dr. Hugo Csergo; s: Joseph Liss;
c: Margaret Phillips, Richard Purdy

Young and Gay, Premiere, CBS, January 1, 1950
    p: Carol Irwin; a: Cornelia Otis Skinner and Emily Kim-
brough; c: Bethel Leslie, Mary Malone

Studio One, CBS, 1950
    "Beyond Reason," January 9, 1950
    p: Worthington Miner; a: Devery Freeman; s: Worthington
Miner; c: Mary Sinclair, Haila Stoddard, Stanley Ridges, Richard
Derr

    "The Rockingham Tea Set," January 23, 1950
    p: Worthington Miner; a: Virginia D. Dawson; s: Worthing-
ton Miner and Matthew Harlib; c: Louise Albritton, Grace Kelly,
Judson Laire, Katherine Emmett, Katherine Willard

    "The Loud Red Patrick," February 6, 1950
    p: Worthington Miner; a: John Boruff and Ruth McKenney;
s: Worthington Miner; c: Dick Foran, Peg Hillias, Joy Geffen

    "The Wisdom Tooth," February 20, 1950
    p: Worthington Miner; a: Marc Connelly; s: Worthington
Miner; c: Jack Lemmon, Barbara Bolton

    "The Dreams of Jasper Hornby," March 6, 1950
    p: Worthington Miner; a: Kevin Mullin; s: Kevin Mullin and
Worthington Miner; c: David Wayne, Doris Rich, Tom Carney, Alan
Stevenson

    "The Survivors," March 20, 1950
    p: Worthington Miner; a: Irwin Shaw and Peter Viertel;
s: Worthington Miner and Milton Wayne; c: Donald Curtis, Leslie
Nielsen, Stanley Ridges

    "The Scarlet Letter," April 13, 1950
    p: Worthington Miner; a: Nathaniel Hawthorne; s: Joseph
Liss; c: Mary Sinclair, John Baragrey, Richard Purdy

    "Torrents of Spring," April 17, 1950
    p: Worthington Miner; a: Ivan Turgenev; s: Joseph Liss;
c: John Baragrey, Louise Albritton

    "Miracle in the Rain," May 1, 1950
    p: Worthington Miner; a: Ben Hecht; s: David Shaw;
c: Jeffrey Lynn, Joy Geffen, Eleanor Wilson

"The Ambassadors," May 15, 1950
p: Worthington Miner; a: Henry James; s: Worthington
Miner; c: Ilona Massey, Judson Laire, Robert Sterling, Katherine
Willard [Restaged for Studio One, February 26, 1951] (FJS)

"The Man Who Had Influence," May 29, 1950
p: Worthington Miner; a: Don Mankiewicz; s: Nancy Moore
and Worthington Miner; c: Robert Sterling, Stanley Ridges, King
Calder, Anne Marno

"My Granny Van," June 26, 1950
p: Worthington Miner; a: George S. Perry; s: Loren Disney; c: Sally Chamberlin, E. G. Marshall, Mildred Natwick, Dean
Harens

Ford Theater, CBS, 1950-1951
    "The Traitor," September 8, 1950
    p: Garth Montgomery; a: Herman Wouk; s: Jack Kirland;
c: Lee Tracy, Barbara Ames, Walter Hampden

    "The Married Look," September 22, 1950
    p: Garth Montgomery; a: Robert Nathan; s: Howard
Rodman; c: Paul Kelly, Lois Wilson, Betsy Blair

    "The Marble Faun," October 6, 1950
    p: Garth Montgomery; a: Nathaniel Hawthorne; s: David
Davidson; c: Anna Lee, Alan Shayne, Sally Chamberlin, Wesley
Addy

    "Angel Street," October 20, 1950
    p: Garth Montgomery; a: Patrick Hamilton; c: Judith
Evelyn, Ferdi Hoffman, Ernest Cossart

    "Heart of Darkness," November 3, 1950
    p: Garth Montgomery; a: Joseph Conrad; s: Joseph Liss;
c: Richard Carlson, Richard Purdy, Murvyn Vye, Faith Brook
[Repeated on Ford Theater, March 23, 1951] (FJS)

    "The Whiteheaded Boy," November 17, 1950
    p: Garth Montgomery; a: Lennox Robinson; s: Willard
Keefe; c: Barry Fitzgerald, Mildred Natwick, Biff McGuire,
Elmer Rande

    "Another Darling," December 1, 1950
    p: Garth Montgomery; a: Zoë Akins; s: Nancy Moore;
c: Patricia Crowley, Jack Ewing

    "Alice in Wonderland," December 15, 1950
    p: Garth Montgomery; a: Lewis Carroll; s: Lois Jacoby;
c: Iris Mann, Richard Waring, Dorothy Jarnac, Rex O'Malley, Jack
Albertson, Biff McGuire, Jack Lemmon

"Cause for Suspicion," December 29, 1950
    p: Garth Montgomery; a: Peggy Lamson; s: Joseph Liss;
c: Glenn Langan, Louisa Horton, Dean Harens

The Presentation of the Look Magazine TV Awards, CBS, January 12,
1951
    p: Marlo Lewis; h: Ed Sullivan

Ford Theater, CBS, 1951
    "Final Copy," January 26, 1951
    p: Garth Montgomery; s: Jay Barbette; c: Robert Sterling,
Hugh Franklin, Anna Minot, Wally Cox

    "Spring Again," February 9, 1951
    p: Garth Montgomery; a: Isabel Leighton and Bertram
Bloch; s: Lois Jacoby; c: Dorothy Gish, Walter Hampden

    "The Golden Mouth," February 23, 1951
    p: Garth Montgomery; a: Charles S. Belden and Frederic
Stephani; s: Joseph Liss; c: Henry Hull, John Forsythe, Virginia
Gilmore, Gerald Mohr, Anne Marno

    "The Ghost Patrol," March 9, 1951
    p: Garth Montgomery; a: Sinclair Lewis; s: William Kendall
Clarke; c: Ernest Truex, Jane Seymour, Dennis Harrison

    "Ticket to Oblivion," April 6, 1951
    p: Werner Michel; a: Robert Parker; s: George Oppen-
heimer; c: Signe Hasso, Anthony Quinn

    "The Touchstone," April 20, 1951
    p: Werner Michel; a: Edith Wharton; s: Jerome David Riss
and Lois Jacoby; c: Margaret Sullavan, Paul McGrath, Jerome
Cowan (UCLA)

    "Dead on the Vine" (aka: "Laurel"), May 4, 1951
    p: Werner Michel; a: Alice Fellows; s: Joseph Liss; c:
Margaret Phillips, William Prince, John Alexander, Faith Brook

    "Peter Ibbetson," May 18, 1951
    p: Werner Michel; a: George du Maurier; s: Lois Jacoby;
c: Richard Greene, Stella Andrew, Iris Mann, Anna Lee, Ivan
Simpson

    "Three in a Room," June 1, 1951
    p: Werner Michel; a: Walter Karig; s: George Oppenheimer;
c: Judith Evelyn, Louisa Horton, Pat Kirkland

    "Night Over London," June 15, 1951
    p: Werner Michel; a: Kay Boyle; s: David Davidson; c:
Stella Andrew, Hugh Reilly

The Victor Borge Show, NBC, February 3, 1951–June 30, 1951
     p: Bruce Dodge; featuring Art Carney

Studio One, CBS, 1951–1953
     "The Little Black Bag," September 24, 1951
     p: Worthington Miner; a: Samuel R. Golding; s: Lois
Jacoby; c: Harry Townes, Eli Mintz, Howard St. John

     "Mighty Like a Rogue," October 8, 1951
     p: Worthington Miner; a: Day Keene; s: Lewis Meltzer;
c: Tom Ewell, Nita Talbot, Joshua Shelley

     "Macbeth," October 22, 1951
     p: Worthington Miner; a: William Shakespeare; s: Worthing-
ton Miner; c: Charlton Heston, Judith Evelyn, Darren McGavin (MB)

     "The Hero," November 5, 1951
     p: Worthington Miner; s: Irwin Lewis; c: Patricia Collinge,
Paul Hartman

     "The King in Yellow," November 19, 1951
     p: Worthington Miner; a: Raymond Chandler; s: Worthing-
ton Miner; c: Carol Bruce, Walter (Jack) Palance

     "Mutiny on the Nicolette," December 3, 1951
     p: Worthington Miner; a: James Norman; s: Joseph Liss;
c: Boris Karloff, Anthony Ross, Ralph Nelson, James Westerfield

     "The Innocence of Pastor Muller," December 17, 1951
     p: Worthington Miner; a: Carlo Beuf; s: Worthington
Miner; c: Maria Riva, Walter Slezak, John Baragrey

     "The Paris Feeling," December 31, 1951
     p: Worthington Miner; a: Paul Horgan; s: Patricia Collinge;
c: Wright King, Ann Gillis, George Voskovec

     "Waterfront Boss," January 14, 1952
     p: Worthington Miner; a: Edward D. Radin; s: Joseph Liss;
c: Roy Hargrave, Kent Smith; narrator: Don Hollenbeck

     "Burden of Guilt," January 28, 1952
     p: Worthington Miner; a: John and Ward Hawkins; s:
Worthington Miner; c: Frank Albertson, Anthony Ross, Ralph Nelson, Robert Stanton

     "Rangoon Run" (aka: "Pagoda"), February 11, 1952
     p: Worthington Miner; a: James Atlee Phillips; s: Joseph
Liss; c: John Forsythe, Sono Asato

     "Letter from a Unknown Woman," February 25, 1952
     p: Worthington Miner; a: Stefan Zweig; s: Worthington
Miner; c: Viveca Lindfors, Melvyn Douglas, Jean-Pierre Aumont

"Wings of the Dove," March 10, 1952
p: Worthington Miner; a: Henry James; s: Howard Merrill;
c: Charlton Heston, Stella Andrew, Felicia Montealegre

"Miss Hargreaves," March 24, 1952
p: Worthington Miner; a: Frank Baker; s: Sumner Locke
Elliott; c: Mary Wickes, Tony Randall

"Pontius Pilate," April 7, 1952
p: Worthington Miner; a: Michael Dyne; s: Worthington
Miner; c: Cyril Ritchard, Geraldine Fitzgerald, Alan Shayne,
Francis L. Sullivan

"Lily, the Queen of the Movies," April 21, 1952
p: Donald Davis with Dorothy Matthews; a: Paul Gallico;
s: Alvin Sapinsley; c: Glynis Johns, Richard Ney, David B.
Greene

"Treasure Island," May 5, 1952
p: Donald Davis with Dorothy Matthews; a: Robert Louis
Stevenson; s: Donald Davis; c: Francis L. Sullivan, Albert
Dekker, Peter Avrano

"A Connecticut Yankee In King Arthur's Court," May 19,
1952
p: Donald Davis with Dorothy Matthews; a: Mark Twain;
s: Alvin Sapinsley; c: Thomas Mitchell, Boris Karloff, Loretta
Daye (MB)

"Captain-General of the Armies," June 2, 1952
p: Donald Davis with Dorothy Matthews; a: Robert Sherman
Townes; s: James Costigan; c: Richard Carlson, Victor Jory,
Lydia Clarke

"International Incident," June 16, 1952
p: Donald Davis with Dorothy Matthews; a: S. B. Hough;
s: Whitfield Cook; c: Lloyd Bridges, Victor Jory, Hildy Parks,
Patricia Wheel

"The Kill," September 22, 1952
p: Donald Davis with Dorothy Matthews; a: Owen Cameron;
s: Reginald Rose; c: Dick Foran, Nina Foch, Grace Kelly, Lynn
Loring

"The Doctor's Wife," October 6, 1952
p: Donald Davis with Dorothy Matthews; a: Nelia Gardner
White; s: David Shaw; c: John Dall, June Lockhart

"The Great Conspiracy," October 20, 1952
p: Donald Davis with Dorothy Matthews; c: Priscilla Gillette,
Scott Forbes

"The Astonishing Mr. Glencannon," November 10, 1952
p: John Haggott; a: Guy Gilpatric; s: Alvin Sapinsley;
c: Rhys Williams, John McQuade

"The Formula," November 24, 1954
p: John Haggott; a: Gordon Sager; s: Reginald Rose;
c: Frances Starr, Gene Lyons, Patricia Wheel, Charles Andre

"The Hospital," December 8, 1952
p: Fletcher Markle; a: Kenneth Fearing; s: A. J. Russell;
c: Leslie Nielsen, Victor Jory, Nancy Marchand

"The Nativity," December 22, 1952
p: Fletcher Markle; s: Andrew Allan; c: Marian Wolfe,
Paul Tripp, Thomas Chalmers

"Black Rain," January 5, 1953
p: Fletcher Markle; a: Georges Simenon; s: Gerald Savory;
c: Fay Bainter, Harry Townes, Nan McFarland, Susan Halloran

"Signal Thirty-Two," January 19, 1953
p: Fletcher Markle; a: Mackinlay Kantor; s: Stanley Niss;
c: Joe Maross, Roy Roberts, Gene Lyons, Jacqueline Susann

"Mark of Cain," February 2, 1953
p: Fletcher Markle; s: Stanley Niss; c: Warren Stevens,
Everett Sloane, Mildred Dunnock

"The Walsh Girls," February 16, 1953
p: Fletcher Markle; a: Elizabeth Janeway; s: A. J. Russell; c: Jane Wyatt, Mary Orr

"My Beloved Husband," March 2, 1953
p: Fletcher Markle; a: Philip Loraine; s: Robert Wallsten;
c: Fletcher Markle, Mary Alice Moore, Ruth Warrick, Anthony Ross
(UCLA)

"A Breath of Air," March 16, 1953
p: Fletcher Markle; a: Rumer Godden; s: Brainerd Duffield;
c: Margaret O'Brien, Everett Sloane

"At Midnight on the 31st of March," March 30, 1953
p: Fletcher Markle; a: Josephine Young Case; s: Robert
Anderson; c: Lamont Johnson, Anthony Ross, June Lockhart, Joe
Maross, Paul Tripp (UCLA)

"The Magic Lantern," April 13, 1953
p: Fletcher Markle; a: Robert Carson; s: Brainerd Duffield;
c: James Dunn, Pat O'Malley, Leatrice Joy, Nils Asther, Carmel
Myers

"Along Came a Spider," April 27, 1953
    p: Fletcher Markle, s: Stanley Niss; c: Felicia Montealegre,
James Daly, Patricia Wheel

"King Coffin," May 11, 1953
    p: Fletcher Markle; a: Conrad Aiken; c: Zachary Scott,
Ruth Ford, Joe Maross

"Fly with the Hawk," May 25, 1953
    p: Fletcher Markle; s: Stanley Niss; c: Mercedes McCam-
bridge, James Daly, Jack Klugman

"Conflict," June 8, 1953
    p: Fletcher Markle; s: A. J. Russell; c: John Forsythe,
Nancy Kelly

Person to Person, CBS, 1953-1959
    p: John Aaron, Jesse Zosmer; field directors: Charles N.
Hill, Robert M. Sammon; researcher/writers: John Horn, David
Moore, Aaron Ehrlich, Liz Schofield

"John F. Kennedy/William Dean," October 30, 1953 (MB)
"George Meany/Ethel Waters," January 8, 1954 (UCLA)
"Eleanor Roosevelt," January 22, 1954 (UCLA)
"David Sarnoff," March 12, 1954 (MB)
"Groucho Marx/James P. Mitchell," April 9, 1954 (MB)
"Clarence Pickett/Marlon Brando," April 16, 1954 (UCLA)
"Humphrey Bogart and Lauren Bacall," September 3, 1954
(UCLA)
"Milton Greene (Marilyn Monroe)/Thomas Beecham," April 8,
1955 (UCLA)
"Amy Vanderbilt/Ernie Kovacs," June 24, 1955 (MB)
"Noel Coward," April 27, 1956 (UCLA)
"Phil Silvers," November 18, 1955 (UCLA)
"Frank Sinatra," September 14, 1956 (MB)
"Harpo Marx," January 3, 1958 (MB)
"Agnes De Mille/Russel Crouse," November 1958 (UCLA)
"Fidel Castro," February 6, 1959 (UCLA)

Studio One, CBS, 1953-1955
    "Hound-Dog Man," September 28, 1953
    p: Felix Jackson; a: Fred Gipson; s: Mel Goldberg;
c: Jackie Cooper, E. G. Marshall, Betsy Palmer, Bruce Gordon,
Sylvia Wald, Charles Taylor

"Music and Mrs. Pratt," October 12, 1953
    p: Felix Jackson; s: Harry W. Junkin; c: Elsa Lanchester,
Philip Abbott

"Another Caesar," October 26, 1953
    p: Felix Jackson, a: Rudolpho Usigli; s: Michael Dyne;
c: Robert Keith, Frances Fuller, Arnold Moss

"Camille," November 9, 1953
    p: Felix Jackson; a: Alexandre Dumas, fils; s: Thomas W.
Phipps; c: Michele Morgan, Romney Brent, Arthur Franz,
Frederic Worlock

"Buffalo Bill Is Dead," November 23, 1953
    p: Felix Jackson; s: Rod Serling; c: Anthony Ross, William Harrigan, Florenz Ames

"Dry Run," December 7, 1953
    p: Felix Jackson; a: Capt. Robert I. Olsen; s: David
Shaw; c: Walter Matthau, Perry Fiske, Arthur Franz, John Conwell

"Cinderella '53," December 21, 1953
    p: Felix Jackson; s: Arnold Schulman; music: Arthur
Schwartz; lyrics: Howard Dietz, Dorothy Fields, Ira Gershwin,
Frank Loesser, Leo Robin; c: Ann Crowley, Conrad Janis, Nydia
Westman

"Runaway," January 4, 1954
    p: Felix Jackson; s: A. J. Russell; c: Jack Carter,
Charlie Ruggles, Mary Wickes, Wallace Ford

"A Criminal Design," January 18, 1954
    p: Felix Jackson; a: William Fay; s: A. J. Russell;
c: Richard Kiley, Geraldine Brooks, Luther Adler, Haila Stoddard

"Herman Came By Bomber," February 1, 1954
    p: Felix Jackson; s: Rod Serling; c: Paul Langton, Steven
Meininger, Gwen Anderson

"Dark Possession," February 15, 1954
    p: Felix Jackson; s: Gore Vidal; c: Geraldine Fitzgerald,
Leora Thatcher, Barbara O'Neil, Leslie Nielsen, Helen Auerbach,
Bramwell Fletcher (MB)

"Side Street," March 1, 1954
    p: Felix Jackson; a: Nathaniel Benchley; s: Norman
Lessing; c: Peter Lind Hayes, Mary Healy, David Opatoshu, Biff
McGuire, Joanne Linville

"Thunder on Sycamore Street," March 15, 1954
    p: Felix Jackson; s: Reginald Rose; c: Whitfield Connor,
Neil O'Day, Robert Bussard, Dickie Olsen, Lee Begere, Anna
Cameron, Harry Sheppard, Kenneth Utt

"Paul's Apartment," March 29, 1954
    p: Felix Jackson; a: Van Siller; s: Robert Wallsten; c:
Eva Gabor, Richard Kiley, David White

"Jack Sparling, Forty-Six," April 12, 1954

p: Felix Jackson; s: Harry W. Junkin; c: Chester Morris, Mary Astor, Lois Smith

"Romney," April 26, 1954
p: Felix Jackson; a: A. L. Barker; s: Lois Landaver; c: Laurence Hugo, Barbara O'Neil, Oliver Andes, Howard St. John

"Fear Is No Stranger," May 10, 1954
p: Felix Jackson; s: Henry Misrock; c: Patricia Breslin, Madge Evans, Jerome Cowan, Peggy Allenby

"A Man and Two Gods," May 24, 1954
p: Felix Jackson; a: Jean Morris; s: Gore Vidal; c: John Baragrey, Charles Korvin, Patricia Wheel, Paul Stevens, John Cassavettes

"The Strike," June 7, 1954
p: Felix Jackson; s: Rod Serling; c: James Daly, Frank Marth, Bert Freed, Roy Roberts

"Twelve Angry Men," September 20, 1954
p: Felix Jackson; s: Reginald Rose; c: Robert Cummings, Franchot Tone, Edward Arnold, John Beal, Walter Abel, Bart Burns, Lee Phillips, Paul Hartman, Joseph Sweeney, George Voskovec, Norman Fell, Will West (MB)

"Prelude to Murder," October 4, 1954
p: Felix Jackson; a: Walter C. Brown; s: William Templeton; c: Otto Kruger, Phyllis Kirk, James Daly

"The Boy Who Changed the World," October 18, 1954
p: Felix Jackson; s: Joseph Schrank; c: John Beal, Ruth Hussey, Frank Overton, Edward Andrews, Michael Allen; guest: Charles Edison

"The Man Who Owned the Town," November 1, 1954
p: Felix Jackson; s: David P. Harmon; c: Paul Stevens, Leslie Nielsen, John Kellogg, Johnny Devlin

"Let Me Go, Lover," November 15, 1954
p: Felix Jackson; a: Charlotte Armstrong; s: Henry Misrock; c: Joe Maross, Connie Sawyer, Anthony Ross, Cliff Norton

"The Deserter," November 29, 1954
p: Felix Jackson; a: Lowell Barrington; s: S. Lee Pogostin; c: June Lockhart, James Gregory. Logan Ramsay, Harry Townes, Margaret Wycherly

"12:30 A.M.," December 13, 1954
p: Felix Jackson; s: Reginald Rose; c: Van Dyke Parks, Katherine Bard, Don Gibson

"The Cuckoo in Spring," December 27, 1954
    p: Felix Jackson; a: Elizabeth Cadell; s: Sam Hall;
c: Charles Coburn, Richard Kiley, Louise King, Leatrice Joy,
David White

"Grandma Rolled Her Own," January 10, 1955
    p: Felix Jackson; s: Harry W. Junkin; c: Cathleen Nes-
bitt, Oliver Andes, Kay Medford

"It Might Happen Tomorrow," January 14, 1955
    p: Felix Jackson; s: Carey Wilber; c: Barry Sullivan,
Anthony Franciosa, Bert Freed, Dana Wynter

"A Stranger May Die," February 7, 1955
    p: Felix Jackson; c: Jack Warden, Jack Mullaney, Frank
Campanella, Mark Richman, Don Gibson, Martin Rudy, Carroll
Baker

"The Eddie Chapman Story," February 21, 1955
    p: Felix Jackson; a: Frank Owen; s: William Templeton;
c: Ropy Deane, John Mackwood, David Lewis

"Millions of Georges," March 7, 1955
    p: Felix Jackson; s: Joe Masteroff; c: Joan Lorring, Scott
Brady, Hope Emerson, Barry McGuire

"Dominique," March 28, 1955
    p: Felix Jackson; a: Daniel Hollywood; s: Ernest Kinoy;
c: Ralph Meeker, Marisa Pavan, John McGiver, Phyllis Hill

"Passage at Arms," April 11, 1955
    p: Felix Jackson; s: Irving Elman; c: Robert Sterling,
Maria Riva, Theodore Bikel

The Best of Broadway, CBS, 1955
    "Broadway," May 4, 1955
    p: Felix Jackson; a: Philip Dunning and George Abbott;
c: Joseph Cotten, Piper Laurie, Keenan Wynn, Gene Nelson, Akim
Tamiroff

Studio One, CBS, 1955
    "Strange Companion," May 16, 1955
    p: Felix Jackson; a: John van Druten and Christopher
Isherwood; s: Don Ettlinger; c: Peggy Ann Garner, Cathleen
Nesbitt, Laurence Hugo

"Operation Home," May 30, 1955
    p: Felix Jackson; s: William M. Altman; c: John Forsythe,
John Gibson, Don Hanmer, P. J. Kelly, Nita Talbot

"The Incredible World of Horace Ford," June 13, 1955

p: Felix Jackson; s: Reginald Rose; c: Art Carney, Leora
Dana, Jane Seymour, Jason Robards, Jr.

"Three Empty Rooms," September 26, 1955
p: Felix Jackson; s: Reginald Rose; c: Steve Brodie,
Barbara Baxley, Eli Mintz, Joseph Sweeney

"A Most Contagious Game," October 17, 1955
p: Felix Jackson; a: Samuel Grafton; s: Don Ettlinger;
c: Steve Cochran, Kenny Delmar, Edward Andrews, Bert Freed

"Shakedown Cruise," November 7, 1955
p: Felix Jackson; s: Loring Mandel; c: Richard Kiley, Lee
Marvin, George Matthews, Don Gordon, Clint Young

Ford Star Jubilee, CBS, 1955
    "The Caine Mutiny Court Martial," November 19, 1955
p: Paul Gregory; CBS supervisor: Harry Ackerman; a:
Herman Wouk; s: Paul Gregory and Franklin Schaffner; c: Lloyd
Nolan, Barry Sullivan, Frank Lovejoy, Ainslie Pryor, Charles
Nolte (FJS)

Studio One, CBS, 1955-1956
    "The Man Who Caught the Ball at Coogan's Bluff," November
28, 1955
p: Felix Jackson; s: Rod Serling; c: Alan Young, Giselle
MacKenzie, Henry Jones, Benny Baker

"Miracle at Potter's Farm," December 19, 1955
p: Felix Jackson; s: Kathleen and Robert Howard Lindsay;
c: Natalie Wood, Frank McHugh, Luke Halpin

"The Talented Mr. Ripley," January 9, 1956
p: Felix Jackson; a: Patricia Highsmith; s: Marc Brandel;
c: Keefe Brasselle, Patricia Smith, Vaughan Taylor, William Redfield

"My Son, Johnny," January 30, 1956
p: Felix Jackson; a: John McNulty; s: Kathleen and
Robert Howard Lindsay; c: Wendell Corey, Paul Hartman, Neva
Patterson, Larry Gates, Luke Halpin, Cliff Norton

"Circle of Guilt," February 20, 1956
p: Felix Jackson; s: Mel Goldberg; c: Keenan Wynn, Julie
Adams, Fred Clark, Peter Graves

"Flower of Pride," March 12, 1956
p: Felix Jackson; s: Michael Dyne; c: Trevor Howard,
Geraldine Fitzgerald, Felicia Montealegre, Halliwell Hobbes

"A Tale of St. Emergency," March 26, 1956

p: Felix Jackson; a: Jackie Gleason; s: Howard Rodman;
c: Red Buttons, Henry Jones, Cecil Kellaway, Russell Collins,
James Barton, Paul Ford

"The Arena," April 9, 1956
p: Felix Jackson; s: Rod Serling; c: Wendell Corey,
Chester Morris, John Cromwell, Leora Dana (MB)

"The Drop of a Hat," May 7, 1956
p: Felix Jackson; s: Dick Berg; c: Nina Foch, Elizabeth
Montgomery, Jayne Meadows, Valerie Bettis, George Voskovec

"Family Protection," May 28, 1956
p: Felix Jackson; s: Palmer Thompson; c: Everett Sloane,
Joanne Woodward, Corey Allen

The Kaiser Aluminum Hour, NBC, 1956-1957
"The Army Game," July 3, 1956
ep: Worthington Miner; p: Franklin Schaffner; s: Loring
Mandel and Mayo Simon; c: Paul Newman, Philip Abbott, George
Grizzard, Edward Andrews, Jan Miner

"Roar of the Lion," July 31, 1956
ep: Worthington Miner; p: Franklin Schaffner; s: M. A.
Ellis; c: Nancy Kelly, Ann Shoemaker

"Antigone," September 11, 1956
ep: Worthington Miner; p: Franklin Schaffner; a: Jean
Anouilh; s: Lewis Galantiere; c: Claude Rains, Marisa Pavan,
Mildred Natwick, Felicia Montealegre (FJS)

"Angel's Ransom," October 23, 1956
ep: Worthington Miner; p: Franklin Schaffner; a: David
Dodge; s: Evan Hunter; c: Hume Cronyn, Robert Sterling,
Geraldine Brooks, Paul Langton, Pernell Roberts (FJS)

"The Rag Jungle," November 20, 1956
ep: Worthington Miner; p: Franklin Schaffner; s: Steven
Gethers; c: Paul Newman, Nehemiah Persoff, Don Gordon (FJS)

"So Short a Season," February 12, 1957
p: Franklin Schaffner; s: Gene Roddenberry; c: Albert
Salmi, John Litel, Hope Emerson, Rip Torn, John Baer, Susan
Oliver

Producers' Showcase, NBC, 1957
"The Great Sebastians," April 1, 1957
ep: Mort Abrahams; associate producer: Leo Davis; s:
Howard Lindsay and Russell Crouse; c: Alfred Lunt, Lynn Fontanne, Akim Tamiroff, Simon Oakland (MB)

470   Franklin J. Schaffner

Playhouse 90, CBS, 1957-1959
    "The Playroom," October 10, 1957
    p: Martin Manulis; s: Tad Mosel; c: Nina Foch, Tony Ran-
dall, Patricia Neal, Mildred Dunnock

    "The Clouded Image," November 7, 1957
    p: Martin Manulis; a: Josephine Tey; s: James P. Cavanagh;
c: Farley Granger, Vincent Price, Judith Anderson, Terry Moore,
Patty McCormack, John Williams

    "The Panic Button," November 28, 1957
    p: Martin Manulis; s: Rod Serling; c: Robert Stack, Vera
Miles, Lee J. Cobb

    "For I Have Loved Strangers," December 19, 1957
    p: Martin Manulis; a: Don Murray and Fred Clasel; s:
Elick Moll; c: Don Murray, Hope Lange, Vladimir Sokoloff

    "The Eighty-Yard Run," January 16, 1958
    p: Martin Manulis; a: Irwin Shaw; s: David Shaw; c:
Paul Newman, Joanne Woodward, Richard Anderson, Red Sanders
(MB)

    "Point of No Return," February 20, 1958
    p: Martin Manulis; a: John P. Marquand (and a play by
Paul Osborn); s: Frank D. Gilroy; c: Charlton Heston, Hope
Lange, Katherine Bard

    "The Right Hand Man," March 29, 1958
    p: Martin Manulis; a: Garson Kanin; s: Dick Berg; c:
Dana Andrews, Anne Baxter

    "Nightmare at Ground Zero," May 15, 1958
    p: Martin Manulis; a: Dr. John C. Clark and Robert Cahn;
s: Paul Monash; c: Barry Sullivan, Jack Warden, Carl Benton
Reid

    "The Innocent Sleep," June 5, 1958
    p: Martin Manulis; s: Tad Mosel; c: Hope Lange, Dennis
King, Buster Keaton, John Ericson, Hope Emerson

    "The Great Gatsby," June 26, 1958
    p: Martin Manulis; a: F. Scott Fitzgerald; s: David Shaw;
c: Robert Ryan, Jeanne Crain, Rod Taylor, Patricia Barry, Philip
Reed, Virginia Grey

    "Word From a Sealed-Off Box," October 30, 1958
    p: Fred Coe; a: Henriette Rosenburg; s: Mayo Simon;
c: Maria Schell, Jean-Pierre Aumont, Theodore Bikel, Betsy Von
Furstenberg, Vivian Nathan

"Seven Against the Wall," December 11, 1958
    p: John Houseman; s: Howard Browne; c: Paul Lambert,
Dennis Patrick, Tige Andrews, Warren Oates; narrator: Eric
Sevareid

"The Velvet Alley," January 22, 1959
    p: Herbert Brodkin; s: Rod Serling; c: Art Carney, Jack
Klugman, Katherine Bard, Leslie Nielsen, Bonita Granville, Alexander Scourby, George Voskovec

"The Raider," February 19, 1959
    p: Herbert Brodkin; s: Loring Mandel; c: Paul Douglas,
Frank Lovejoy, Rod Taylor, Donald Crisp, Leif Erickson, Leon
Ames

"In Lonely Expectation," April 2, 1959
    p: Herbert Brodkin; s: Mayo Simon; c: Diane Baker,
Susan Harrison, Philip Abbott

"Dark December," April 30, 1959
    p: Peter Kortner; s: Merle Miller; c: Barry Sullivan,
James Whitmore, Paul Burke, Warren Beatty, Lili Darvas, Richard
Beymer, Michael Landon, Ronny Howard

"The Rank and File," May 28, 1959
    p: Herbert Brodkin; s: Rod Serling; c: Van Heflin,
Charles Bronson, Luther Adler, Harry Townes, Carl Benton Reid

Ford Startime, NBC, 1959
    "The Wicked Scheme of Jebal Deeks," November 10, 1959
    ep: Hubbell Robinson; p: Franklin Schaffner; s: John D.
Hess; c: Alec Guinness, Henry Jones, Patricia Barry, Roland
Winters, William Redfield

Playhouse 90, CBS, 1959-1960
    "The Silver Whistle," December 24, 1959
    p: Herbert Brodkin; s: Robert McEnroe; c: Eddie Albert,
Henry Jones, Bethel Leslie, Harry Townes, Margaret Hamilton

    "The Cruel Day," February 24, 1960
    p: Herbert Brodkin; s: Reginald Rose; c: Van Heflin,
Cliff Robertson, Raymond Massey, Phyllis Thaxter, Nehemiah
Persoff, Charles Bronson

The Defenders, CBS, 1961-1962
    "Killer Instinct," September 23, 1961
    p: Herbert Brodkin; s: John Vlahos; c: E. G. Marshall,
Robert Reed, William Shatner, Joanne Linville, Mitch Ryan, Lester
Rawlins (W)

    "The Boy Between," October 21, 1961

p: Herbert Brodkin; s: Robert Thom; c: E. G. Marshall, Robert Reed, Norma Crane, Ilka Chase, Arthur Hill, Joan Hackett, Richard Thomas, Polly Rowles, Anne Seymour, Barnard Hughes (W)

"The Attack," December 9, 1961
p: Herbert Brodkin; s: John Bloch; c: E. G. Marshall, Robert Reed, Richard Kiley, Barbara Barrie, Nancy Marchand, J. D. Cannon, Martin Sheen (W)

"Gideon's Follies," December 23, 1961
p: Herbert Brodkin; s: Robert Crean; c: E. G. Marshall, Robert Reed, Shirl Conway, Gloria De Haven, Eva Gabor, Zohra Lampert, Julie Newmar, Tsai Chin, Arthur Hughes, Conrad Bain (W)

"The Tarnished Cross," March 17, 1962
p: Herbert Brodkin; s: Reginald Rose; c: E. G. Marshall, Robert Reed, Biff McGuire, Martin Sheen, Bill Gunn (W)

"Reunion With Death," April 21, 1962
p: Herbert Brodkin; s: David Shaw; c: E. G. Marshall, Robert Reed, H. M. Wynant, Leonard Stone, Robert Webber, Lee Phillips, Woodrow Parfrey, Michael Conrad, Gene Wilder (W)

The Good Years, CBS, January 12, 1962
p: Leland Hayward and Marshall Jamison; a: Walter Lord; s: A. J. Russell; c: Henry Fonda, Lucille Ball, Mort Sahl

A Tour of the White House with Mrs. John F. Kennedy, CBS, February 14, 1962
p & s: Perry Wolff; h: Jacqueline Kennedy, Charles Collingwood

DuPont Show of the Week, NBC, 1962-1964
"The World's Greatest Robbery," Part I, April 29, 1962; Part II, May 6, 1962
p: Franklin Schaffner; s: Loring Mandel; c: R. G. Armstrong, Paul Mazursky, Cliff Osmond; narrator: Barry Sullivan

"Windfall," January 13, 1963
ep: Franklin Schaffner; p: Jacqueline Babbin; s: Roger O. Hirson; c: Eddie Albert, Glynis Johns (FJS)

"Two Faces of Treason," February 10, 1963
ep: Franklin Schaffner; p: Jacqueline Babbin; s: Phil Reisman, Jr.; c: Larry Blyden, Lloyd Nolan (FJS)

"The Shark," April 7, 1963
ep: Franklin Schaffner; p: Jacqueline Babbin; s: Larry Marcus; c: Anthony Franciosa, Skip Homier, Diana Hyland, Fred Stewart

"The Legend of Lylah Clare," May 15, 1963
   ep: Franklin Schaffner; p: Jacqueline Babbin; s: Robert
Thom; c: Alfred Drake, Tuesday Weld, Michael Tolan, Sorrell
Booke (FJS)

"Jeremy Rabbitt, the Secret Avenger," April 5, 1964
   ep: Franklin Schaffner; p: Philip Barry, Jr.; s: Robert
Thom; c: Frank Gorshin, Franchot Tone, Jim Backus, Brian Donlevy, Walter Matthau, Carolyn Jones, Jennifer West (FJS)

"Don't Go Upstairs," May 17, 1964
   ep: Franklin Schaffner; p: Philip Barry, Jr.; s: Roger O.
Hirson; c: James Daly, Charles Aidman, Mary Fickett

"More, More, More, More," May 31, 1964
   ep: Franklin Schaffner; p: Philip Barry, Jr.; s: John D.
Hess; c: Fred Clark, Patricia Barry, Martin Milner, Corinne Calvet

"Ambassador at Large," June 14, 1964
   ep: Franklin Schaffner; p: Philip Barry, Jr.; s: Loring
Mandel; c: Arthur Kennedy, Peter Falk, Diana Muldaur, Larry
Hagman, Andrew Duggan

John F. Kennedy, May 29, 1964, CBS, May 29, 1964
   ep: Perry Wolff; p: Franklin Schaffner (Hyannisport), Neil
Cunningham (New York), Harry Morgan (Europe)

ABC Stage '67, ABC, 1967
   "The Wide Open Door," April 20, 1967
   ep: Hubbell Robinson; p: Franklin Schaffner; a: T. E. B.
Clarke; s: T. E. B. Clarke, Tom Waldman and Frank Waldman;
c: Tony Randall, Honor Blackman, Reginald Gardiner, Bernard
Fox, Richard Haydn, Leon Ames (FJS)

FILMOGRAPHY

The Stripper, Twentieth Century-Fox, 1963

Black and white; CinemaScope; 95 minutes

Producer: Jerry Wald; associate producer: Curtis Harrington; screenplay: Meade Roberts (based on A Loss of Roses, a play by William Inge); director of photography: Ellsworth Fredericks; art direction: Jack Martin Smith, Walter M. Simonds; editor: Robert Simpson; music: Jerry Goldsmith; sound: W. D. Flick, Warren B. Delaplain; assistant director: Eli Dunn

Cast: Joanne Woodward (Lila); Richard Beymer (Kenny); Claire Trevor (Helen); Carol Lynley (Miriam); Robert Webber (Ricky); Louis Nye (Ronnie); Gypsy Rose Lee (Madame Olga); Michael J. Pollard (Jelly); Sondra Kerr (Edwina)

The Best Man, United Artists, 1964

Black and white; 1:33; 102 minutes

Producers: Stuart Millar and Lawrence Turman; screenplay: Gore Vidal (based on his play); director of photography: Haskell Wexler; art direction: Lyle R. Wheeler; editor: Robert E. Swink; music: Mort Lindsay; costumes: Dorothy Jenkins; sound: Jack Solomon, Richard Mansfield; assistant director: Richard Moder

Cast: Henry Fonda (William Russell); Cliff Robertson (Joe Cantwell); Edie Adams (Mabel Cantwell); Margaret Leighton (Alice Russell); Shelley Berman (Sheldon Bascomb); Lee Tracy (Art Hockstader); Ann Sothern (Mrs. Gammadge); Gene Raymond (Don Cantwell); Kevin McCarthy (Dick Jensen); Mahalia Jackson (herself); Howard K. Smith (himself); John Henry Faulk (T. T. Claypoole); Richard Arlen (Oscar Anderson); William R. Ebersol (Governor Merwin)

The War Lord, Universal, 1965

Technicolor; Panavision; 123 minutes

Producer: Walter Seltzer; screenplay: John Collier, Millard Kaufman (based on The Lovers, a play by Leslie Stevens); director of photography: Russell Metty; art direction: Alexander Golitzen, Henry Bumstead; editor: Folmar Blangsted; costumes and technical adviser: Vittorio Nino Novarese; music: Jerome Moross; matte supervisor: Albert Whitlock; sound: John McCarthy, Oliver Emert; unit production manager: Norman Deming; assistant director: Douglas Green

Cast: Charlton Heston (Chrysagon); Richard Boone (Bors); Rosemary Forsythe (Bronwyn); Maurice Evans (Priest); Guy Stockwell (Draco); Niall MacGinnis (Odins); Henry Wilcoxon (Frisian Prince); James Farentino (Marc); Sammy Ross (Volc); Woodrow Parfrey (Piet)

The Double Man, Albion/Warner Bros.-Seven Arts, 1968

Technicolor; 1:85; 110 minutes

Producer: Hal E. Chester; screenplay: Frank Tarloff, Alfred Hayes (based on Legacy of a Spy by Henry S. Maxfield); director of photography: Denys Coop; art direction: Arthur Lawson; editor: Richard Best; music: Ernie Freeman; sound: Tony Wolf, Len Shilton; assistant directors: Ron Jackson, William Cartlidge

Cast: Yul Brynner (Dan Slater/Kalmar); Britt Ekland (Gina); Anton Diffring (Berthold); Clive Revill (Frank Wheatly); Moira Lister (Mrs. Carrington); Lloyd Nolan (Edwards)

Planet of the Apes, Twentieth Century-Fox, 1968

Color by Deluxe; Panavision; 112 minutes

Producer: Arthur P. Jacobs; associate producer: Mort Abrahams; screenplay: Rod Serling, Michael Wilson (based on the book by Pierre Boulle); director of photography: Leon Shamroy; art direction: Jack Martin Smith, William J. Creber; creative make-up: John Chambers; make-up: Ben Nye, Don Striepeke, Paul Malcolm; costumes: Morton Haack; special photographic effects: L. B. Abbott, Art Cruickshank, Emil Kosa, Jr.; editor: Hugh S. Fowler; music: Jerry Goldsmith; sound: Herman Lewis, David Dockendorf; unit production manager: William Eckhardt; assistant director: William Kissel

Cast: Charlton Heston (George Taylor); Roddy McDowall (Cornelius); Kim Hunter (Zira); Maurice Evans (Dr. Zaius); James Whitmore (President of the Assembly); James Daly (Honorius); Linda Harrison (Nova); Robert Gunner (Landon); Lou Wagner (Lucius); Woodrow Parfrey (Maximus); Jeff Burton (Dodge)

Patton, Twentieth Century-Fox, 1970

Color by Deluxe; Dimension 150; 173 minutes

Producer: Frank McCarthy; associate producer: Frank Caffey;
screenplay: Francis Ford Coppola, Edmund H. North (based on
Patton: Ordeal and Triumph by Ladislas Farago and A Soldier's
Story by Omar N. Bradley); director of photography: Fred Koenekamp; art direction: Urie McCleary and Gil Parrondo; special
photographic effects: L. B. Abbott, Art Cruickshank; senior military advisor: General of the Army, Omar N. Bradley; technical
advisors: General Paul D. Harkins, Colonel Glover S. Johns, Jr.;
editor: Hugh S. Fowler; music: Jerry Goldsmith; sound: James
Corcoran, Douglas Williams, Murray Spivack, Don Bassman, Ted
Soderberg; unit production managers: Francisco Day, Eduardo G.
Maroto, Tadeo Villalba; assistant directors: Eli Dunn, Jose Lopez
Rodero

Cast: George C. Scott (Patton); Karl Malden (Bradley); Stephen
Young (Col. Chet Hansen); Michael Strong (Gen. Hobart Carver);
Morgan Paull (Capt. Dick Jensen); Michael Bates (Field Marshal
Montgomery); Karl Michael Vogler (Field Marshal Rommel); Edward
Binns (Gen. Bedell Smith); Lawrence Dobkin (Col. Bell); John
Doucette (Gen. Lucien Truscott); Richard Muench (Gen. Alfred
Jodl); Siegfried Rauch (Capt. Steiger); Paul Stevens (Col. Charles
Codman); Tim Considine (solider who gets slapped); James Edwards
(Sgt. George Meeks)

Nicholas and Alexandra, Horizon/Columbia, 1971

Technicolor; Panavision; 185 minutes

Producer: Sam Spiegel; associate producer: Andrew Donally;
screenplay: James Goldman (based on the book by Robert K. Massie); additional dialogue: Edward Bond; director of photography:
Freddie Young; production design and second unit director: John
Box; art direction: Jack Maxted, Ernest Archer, Gil Parrondo;
costumes: Yvonne Blake, Antonio Castillo; casting: Maude Spector; editor: Ernest Walter; music: Richard Rodney Bennett;
sound: George Stephenson, Garry Humphreys; production supervisor: Luis Roberts; assistant director: Jose Lopez Rodero

Cast: Michael Jayston (Nicholas); Janet Suzman (Alexandra);
Roderic Noble (Alexis); Ania Marson (Olga); Lynne Frederick
(Tatiana); Candace Glendenning (Marie); Fiona Fullerton (Anastasia);
Harry Andrews (Grand Duke Nicholas); Irene Worth (Queen Mother
Marie Fedorovna); Tom Baker (Rasputin); Jack Hawkins (Count
Fredericks); Timothy West (Dr. Botkin); Guy Rolfe (Dr. Fedorov);
John Wood (Col. Kobylinsky); Laurence Olivier (Count Witte); Eric
Porter (Stolypin); Michael Redgrave (Sazonov); John McEnery

(Kerensky); Michael Bryant (Lenin); Vivian Pickles (Madame Krup-
skaya); Ian Holm (Yakovlev); Alan Webb (Yurovsky); Leon Lissek
(Avadeyev); Roy Dotrice (Gen. Alexeiev); Martin Potter (Prince
Yussoupov); Richard Warwick (Grand Duke Dimitri); Alexander
Knox (Ambassador Root); Curt Jurgens (Sklarz)

Papillon, Allied Artists, 1973

Technicolor; Panavision; 150 minutes

Producers: Robert Dorfmann, Franklin J. Schaffner; executive
producer: Ted Richmond; screenplay: Dalton Trumbo, Lorenzo
Semple, Jr. (based on the book by Henri Charrière); director of
photography: Fred Koenekamp; production design: Anthony Masters; art director: Jack Maxsted; make-up: Charles H. Schram;
editor: Robert E. Swink; music: Jerry Goldsmith; sound: Richard
Portman, Derek Ball; assistant directors: Jose Lopez Rodero, Juan
Lopez Rodero

Cast: Steve McQueen (Papillon); Dustin Hoffman (Dega); Victor
Jory (Indian Chief); Don Gordon (Julot); Anthony Zerbe (Leper
Colony Chief); Robert Deman (Maturette); Woodrow Parfrey (Clusiot);
Bill Mumy (Lariot); George Couloucis (Dr. Chatal); Ratna Assan
(Zoraima); William Smithers (Warden Barrot); Gregory Sierra (An-
tonio); Barbara Morrison (Mother Superior); Ellen Moss (Nun); Don
Hanmer (Butterfly Trader); Dalton Trumbo (Commandant)

Islands in the Stream, Paramount, 1977

Metrocolor; Panavision; 105 minutes

Producers: Peter Bart, Max Palevsky; screenplay: Denne Bart
Petticlerc (based on the book by Ernest Hemingway); director of
photography: Fred Koenekamp; production design: William J.
Creber; editor: Robert E. Swink; music: Jerry Goldsmith; sound:
John K. Wilkinson, Darin Knight; assistant director: Kurt Neumann

Cast: George C. Scott (Thomas Hudson); David Hemmings (Eddy);
Gilbert Roland (Captain Ralph); Susan Tyrrell (Lil); Richard Evans
(Willy); Claire Bloom (Audrey); Julius Harris (Joseph); Hart Boch-
ner (Tom); Brad Savage (Andrew); Michael-James Wixted (David)

The Boys from Brazil, ITC/Twentieth Century-Fox, 1978

Color by Deluxe; 1:85; 123 minutes

Executive producer: Robert Fryer; producers: Martin Richards,
Stanley O'Toole; screenplay: Heywood Gould (based on the book

by Ira Levin); director of photography: Henri Decae; production
design: Gil Parrondo; art direction: Peter Lamont; costumes:
Anthony Mendleson; technical advisor: Dr. Derek Bromhall; editor:
Robert E. Swink; music: Jerry Goldsmith; sound: Derek Ball;
assistant director: Jose Lopez Rodero

Cast: Gregory Peck (Josef Mengele); Laurence Olivier (Ezra Lieber-
man); James Mason (Eduard Seibert); Lilli Palmer (Esther Lieber-
man); Uta Hagen (Frieda Maloney); Steven Guttenberg (Barry
Kohler); Denholm Elliott (Sidney Beynon); Rosemary Harris (Frau
Doring); John Dehner (Henry Wheelock); Anne Meara (Mrs. Curry);
Jeremy Black (Erich, Jack, Simon, Bobby); David Hurst (Strasser);
Walter Gotell (Mundt), Bruno Ganz (Bruckner)

Sphinx, Orion/Warner Bros., 1981

Technicolor; Panavision; 117 minutes

Executive producer: Franklin J. Schaffner; producer: Stanley
O'Toole; screenplay: John Byrum (based on the book by Robin
Cook); director of photography: Ernest Day; production design:
Terence Marsh; supervising art director: Peter Lamont; art di-
rector: Gil Parrondo; costumes: Judy Moorcroft; editors: Robert
E. Swink, Michael F. Anderson; music: Michael J. Lewis; sound
(Dolby): Cyril Swern; assistant director: Jose Lopez Rodero

Cast: Lesley-Anne Down (Erica Baron); Frank Langella (Ahmed
Khazzan); Maurice Ronet (Yvon); Sir John Gielgud (Abdul Hamdi);
Vic Tablian (Khalifa); Martin Bensom (Muhammed); John Rhys-
Davies (Stephanos Markoulis); Nadim Sawalha (Gamal); Tutte Lem-
kov (Tewfik); Saeed Jaffrey (Selim); Eileen Way (Aida)

Yes, Giorgio, M-G-M, 1982

Metrocolor; Panaflex 1:85; 110 minutes

Producer: Peter Fetterman; executive producers: Alain Bernheim,
Herbert H. Breslin; associate producer: Terry Carr; screenplay;
Norman Steinberg (based on the book by Anne Piper); director of
photography: Fred Koenekamp; production design: William J.
Creber; costumes: Rita Riggs; editor: Michael F. Anderson;
music: Michael J. Lewis; "If We Were in Love," music by John
Williams, lyrics by Alan and Marilyn Bergman; opera consultant:
Lofti Mansouri; sound (Dolby): Charles M. Wilborn, Michael J.
Kohut, Carlos De Larios, Jay M. Harding, Gregory H. Watkins;
unit production manager: Joan Bradshaw; location consultant:
Ken Wales; assistant director: Gary Daigler

Cast: Luciano Pavarotti (Giorgio Fini); Kathryn Harrold (Pamela

Taylor); Eddie Albert (Henry Pollack); Paola Borboni (Sister
Theresa); James Hong (Kwan); Beulah Quo (Mei Ling); Norman
Steinberg (Dr. Barmen); Rod Corbin (Ted Mullane); Kathryn Fuller
(Faye Kennedy); Joseph Mascolo (Dominic Giordano), Karen Konda-
zian (Francesca Giordano); Leona Mitchell (herself); Kurt Adler
(himself); Emerson Buckley (himself); Alexander Courage (conduc-
tor, Turandot); Paul Marin (Nello Jori)

BIBLIOGRAPHY

Books

Aaronson, Charles S., ed. International Television Almanac, 1956. New York: Quigley Publications, 1955.

Barnouw, Erik. The Image Empire, A History of Broadcasting in the United States, Volume III--from 1953. New York: Oxford University Press, 1970.

_____. Tube of Plenty. New York: Oxford University Press, 1975.

Behlmer, Rudy, ed. The Adventures of Robin Hood. Madison, WI: University of Wisconsin Press, 1979.

Bluem, A. William, and Roger Manvell, eds. The Progress in Television. New York: The Focal Press, Ltd., 1967.

Bowles, Stephen E. Sidney Lumet: A Guide to References and Resources. Boston: G. K. Hall & Co., 1979.

Brady, John. The Craft of the Screenwriter. New York: Simon and Schuster, 1981.

Brooks, Tim, and Earle Marsh. The Complete Directory to Prime Time Network TV Shows 1946-Present. New York: Ballantine Books, 1979.

Brown, Les, ed. The New York Times Encyclopedia of Television. New York: New York Times Books, 1977.

Butler, Ivan. The War Film. New York: A. S. Barnes and Company, 1974.

Capra, Frank. The Name Above the Title. New York: The Macmillan Company, 1971.

Chase, Donald. Filmmaking: The Collaborative Art. Boston: Little, Brown and Company, 1975.

Chayefsky, Paddy. Television Plays. New York: Touchstone/ Simon and Schuster, 1955.

Close-Up. New York: CBS, Inc., 1949.

Coffin, Rachel W., ed. New York Theatre Critics' Reviews. Vol. XXI, Number 24, 1961.

Cook, Bruce. Dalton Trumbo. New York: Charles Scribner's Sons, 1979.

Coppola, Eleanor. Notes. New York: Simon and Schuster, 1979.

Dunne, John Gregory. The Studio. New York: Farrar, Straus & Giroux, 1969.

Fielding, Raymond. The March of Time, 1935-1951. New York: Oxford University Press, 1978.

Fonda, Henry, and Howard Teichmann. Fonda: My Life. New York: New American Library, 1981.

Friendly, Fred W. Due to Circumstances Beyond Our Control. New York: Random House, 1967.

Gassner, John, and Edward Quinn, eds. The Reader's Encyclopedia of World Drama. New York: Thomas Y. Crowell Company, 1969.

Gianakos, Larry James. Television Drama Series Programming: A Comprehensive Chronicle, 1959-1975. Metuchen, NJ: Scarecrow Press, 1978.

_____. Television Drama Series Programming: A Comprehensive Chronicle, 1947-1959. Metuchen, NJ: Scarecrow Press, 1981.

Gussow, Mel Don't Say Yes Until I Finish Talking: A Biography of Darryl F. Zanuck. Garden City, NY: Doubleday and Company, Inc., 1971.

Hagen, Earle. Scoring for Film. New York: E. D. J. Music, Inc., 1971.

Hemingway, Ernest. To Have and Have Not. New York: Charles Scribner's Sons, 1937.

Heston, Charlton. The Actor's Life: Journals 1956-1976. Edited by Hollis Alpert. New York: E. P. Dutton, 1978.

Huston, John. An Open Book. New York: Alfred A. Knopf, 1980.

Kael, Pauline. When the Lights Go Down. New York: Holt, Rinehart and Winston, 1980.

Kauffmann, Stanley. Figures of Light. New York: Harper & Row, Publishers, 1971.

Kendrick, Alexander. Prime Time: The Life of Edward R. Murrow. Boston: Little, Brown and Company, 1969.

Knight, Arthur. The Liveliest Art: A Panoramic History of the Movies. Revised edition. New York: New American Library, 1979.

McCabe, John. The Comedy World of Stan Laurel. Garden City, NY: Doubleday & Company, Inc., 1974.

McNeil, Alex. Total Television: A Comprehensive Guide to Programming from 1948 to 1980. New York: Penguin Books, 1980.

Mandel, Loring. Advise and Consent. Garden City, NY: Doubleday & Company, Inc., 1961.

Mizener, Arthur, ed. F. Scott Fitzgerald. Englewood Cliffs, NJ: Prentice-Hall, Inc., 1963.

Paley, William S. As It Happened. Garden City, NY: Doubleday & Company, Inc., 1979.

Parish, James Robert. Actors' Television Credits 1950-1972. Metuchen, NJ: Scarecrow Press, Inc., 1973.

Parish, James Robert, with Mark Trost. Actors' Television Credits: Supplement I. Metuchen, NJ: Scarecrow Press, 1978.

Peary, Danny, ed. Close-Ups. New York: Workman Publishers, 1978.

Pratley, Gerald. The Cinema of John Frankenheimer. New York: A. S. Barnes and Company, 1969.

Rose, Reginald. Six Television Plays. New York: Simon and Schuster, 1956.

Schulberg, Budd. Moving Pictures: Memories of a Hollywood Prince. New York: Stein and Day, 1981.

Sherman, Eric. Directing the Film. Boston: Little, Brown and Company, 1976.

Shulman, Arthur and Roger Youman. How Sweet It Was. New York: Bonanza Books, 1966.

Sterling, Christopher H., and John M. Kittross. Stay Tuned. Belmont, CA: Wadsworth Publishing Company, 1978.

Suid, Lawrence H. Guts and Glory. Reading, MA: Addison-
    Wesley Publishing Company, 1978.

Terrace, Vincent. The Complete Encyclopedia of Television Pro-
    grams. Revised edition. New York: A. S. Barnes and
    Company, 1979.

Vidal, Gore. Rocking the Boat. Boston: Little, Brown and
    Company, 1962.

_____. Visit to a Small Planet and Other Television Plays.
    Boston: Little, Brown and Company, 1956.

Viertel, Peter. White Hunter, Black Heart. Garden City, NY:
    Doubleday & Company, 1953.

Wicking, Christopher, and Tise Vahimagi. The American Vein.
    New York: E. P. Dutton, 1979.

Wilk, Max. The Golden Age of Television. New York: Delacorte
    Press, 1976.

Wilson, Robert, ed. The Film Criticism of Otis Ferguson.
    Philadelphia: Temple University Press, 1971.

Wolff, Perry. A Tour of the White House with Mrs. John F. Ken-
    nedy. Garden City, NY: Doubleday & Company, 1962.

Wood, Robin. Arthur Penn. New York: Praeger, 1969.

Zuker, Joel S. Arthur Penn: A Guide to References and Re-
    sources. Boston: G. K. Hall & Co., 1980.

Articles and Periodicals

Adams, Charles. "The Stage Director in Television." Theatre
    Arts, October 1951.

Appelbaum, Ralph. "Flying High." Films and Filming, August
    1979.

_____. "Master Plans." Films and Filming, February 1979.

Arlen, M. J. "At Last! The Mighty Marvelous Waldmachine."
    Esquire, May 1962.

Aurthur, Robert Alan. "Hanging Out." Esquire, May 1973.

"Award Winner: Franklin Schaffner." Action, May-June 1971.

Barber, Rowland. "The Mighty Sound Track in Bungalow Ten."
    Show, March 1962.

Bart, Peter. "'Islands': A Film with Hemingway in Mind."
    Los Angeles Times, Calendar, March 13, 1977.

Bernheimer, Martin. "Luciano, the Lyric Muse and the Silver
    Screen." Los Angeles Times, Calendar, September 26, 1982.

Blangsted, Folmar. "The War Lord." The Cinemaeditor, Fall 1965.

Clark, Margaret. Letter. Look, December 28, 1943.

Cook, Bruce. "War Between the Writers and Directors, Part II:
    The Directors." American Film, June 1976.

Creber, William. "Recreating on Film the World of Ernest Heming-
    way." American Cinematographer, November 1976.

Delson, James. "PAPILLON: An Intraview." Take One, Vol. 4,
    No. 1, 1974.

"Dialogue on Film: Gore Vidal," American Film, April 1977.

Drew, Bernard. "Lord Laurence Olivier as Nazi Hunter." American
    Film, July-August 1978.

Elley, Derek. "Jerry Goldsmith." Films and Filming, June 1979.

"The Fabulous Escapes of Papillon." Life, November 13, 1970.

Fadiman, William. "But Compared to the Original." Films and Film-
    ing, February 1965.

Fox, Terry Curtis. "Franklin Schaffner's Films: Where Worlds
    Collide." New York Daily News, Leisure, March 13, 1977.

Gardella, Kay. "Producer Manulis Excited Over Return of TV Dra-
    ma." New York Daily News, August 10, 1966.

Gardner, Paul. "Boy Scout with the Midas Touch." The New York
    Times, Section 2, January 31, 1965.

Gautschy, Dean. "Any Resemblance Isn't Coincidental." Los An-
    geles Herald-Examiner, June 24, 1962.

Gehman, Richard. "Punch One, Cue the Dolly and Kill the Baby!"
    TV Guide, July 13, 1963.

Geist, Kenneth. "Chronicler of Power, an Interview with Franklin
    Schaffner." Film Comment, September-October 1972.

"George Stevens Joins Sam Spiegel on Col's 'Nicholas.'" Daily
        Variety, February 19, 1968.

Hall, William. "Film Making in Pharaoh Land." Los Angeles Times,
        Calendar, May 11, 1980.

Hawver, Walter. "A Long Hunt for Originality." Knickerbocker
        News [Albany, NY], June 4, 1963.

Heston, Charlton. Dialogue on Film, No. 1, 1972.

Hofferkamp, Jack. "Schaffner Has His Fingers Crossed." Los
        Angeles Times, Part IV, January 4, 1974.

Kaminsky, Ralph. "'Giorgio's' Schaffner Forecasting Big Response
        to Pop Opera Pic." Film Journal, September 24, 1982.

Kaufman, Stanley Lloyd, Jr. "The Early Franklin J. Schaffner."
        Films in Review, August-September 1969.

Knickerbocker, Paine. "Producer Discusses New Low-Budget Film."
        San Francisco Chronicle, March 3, 1965.

Knight, Arthur. "The Man from WHO." Saturday Review, August
        11, 1962.

Kocian, Billy. "In Budapest the Sound Is 'Doodah' as Crew Shoots
        a 'Sphinx' Scene." Daily Variety, February 12, 1980.

Koenekamp, Fred. "A Cameraman's Diary of Photographing 'ISLANDS
        IN THE STREAM.'" American Cinematographer, November
        1976.

"Life Goes on a Bicycle Weekend." Life, May 25, 1942.

Lightman, Herb A. "Filming 'PLANET OF THE APES.'" American
        Cinematographer, April 1968.

_____. "On Location with 'ISLANDS IN THE STREAM.'"
        American Cinematographer, November 1976.

McCarthy, Todd. "Schaffner Is Still High on O'seas Lensing After
        12 Years." Daily Variety, January 29, 1981.

Mann, Roderick. "Spiegel: Back Into the Movie-Making Maelstrom."
        Los Angeles Times, Calendar, June 20, 1982.

Martin, Pete. "I Call on Edward R. Murrow." Saturday Evening
        Post, January 18, 1958.

Mathews, Jack. "Shrinking Screens Are a Big Problem for This
        Director." Detroit Free Press, April 7, 1981.

Mitchell, George J. "The Photography of 'PATTON.'" American
    Cinematographer, August 1970.

Munroe, Dale. "Director Franklin Schaffner: From PLANET OF
    THE APES to PATTON." Show, August 6, 1970.

Novak, Elliott Jay. "Requiem for a Screenwriter." The Hollywood
    Reporter 45th Anniversary Issue, 1975.

Perlmutter, Donna. "Luciano Pavarotti's Gone Hollywood." Los
    Angeles Herald-Examiner, Section B, August 18, 1981.

Polier, Rex. "Reflecting on TV's Golden Age." Los Angeles Times,
    Part VI, January 1, 1982.

Pratley, Gerald. "An Interview with Franklin Schaffner." Cineaste,
    Summer 1969.

_____. "PATTON: Lust for Glory." Focus on Film, May-
    August, 1970.

Rich, Alan. "The Wasting of Pavarotti." New York, May 18, 1981.

Robbins, Fred. "Nicholas and Alexandra." Show, January 1972.

Russell, Sharon. "Franklin J. Schaffner." Film Reader, #1, 1975.

Sarris, Andrew. "Director of the Month--Franklin Schaffner: The
    Panoply of Power." Show, April 1970.

Schaffner, Franklin. "The Best and the Worst of It." Films and
    Filming, October 1964.

Schaffner, Franklin J., as told to James Link. "Direct It: Patton's
    Franklin J. Schaffner Tells You How...." Video Review, July
    1981.

Shea, Bill. "TV as Passe as Nickelodeon." Film Daily, January
    14, 1965.

"Should Directors Produce?" Action, July-August 1968.

Silverman, Jeff. "Page 2." Los Angeles Herald-Examiner, Section
    B, May 13, 1981.

Sinclair, Stephen. "From the Council." The Cultural Post, March-
    April 1982.

Smith, Cecil. "Rod Serling's Scripts Hit Like Heavyweight." Los
    Angeles Times, Part V, October 14, 1956.

Spence, Betty. "Jerry Goldsmith: The Man and His Movie Music."
Los Angeles Times, Calendar, February 7, 1982.

Steele, Robert. "Patton." Film Heritage, Summer 1970.

"Sunday Is a Big Day for Tuesday." Milwaukee Journal, May 19,
1963.

Thomas, Kevin. "Balancing Act Pays Off for 'Patton' Director."
Los Angeles Times, Part IV, May 7, 1970.

_____. "Schaffner: TV to Big Screen." Los Angeles Times,
Part IV, March 17, 1966.

"U in Pre-Sell High Via 'Lord,': Seltzer." Film Daily, September
3, 1965.

"The Unmaking of Entebbe." Newsweek, November 8, 1976.

Van Horne, Harriet. "Don't Look Now." Theatre Arts, October
1952.

_____. "The Living Theatre of Television." Theatre Arts,
September 1951.

Wales, Ken. "The Impossible Takes a Little Longer." American
Cinematographer, November 1976.

Wershba, Joseph. "Close Up: TV Producer." New York Post,
November 26, 1962.

Wilson, David. "Franklin Schaffner." Sight and Sound, Spring
1966.

Winogura, Dale. "Dialogues on Apes, Apes, and More Apes,"
Cinefantastique, Summer 1972.

Wise, Sidney. "Politicians: A Film Perspective." NEWS for
Teachers of Political Science, Winter 1982.

Source Material

Boulle, Pierre. Planet of the Apes. Translated by Xan Fielding.
New York: Vanguard Press, 1963.

Bradley, Omar N. A Soldier's Story. New York: Henry Holt and
Company, 1951.

Charrière, Henri. Papillon. Translated by June P. Wilson and

Walter B. Michaels. New York: William Morrow and Company, Inc., 1970.

Cook, Robin. Sphinx. New York: G. P. Putnam's Sons, 1979.

Drury, Allen. Advise and Consent. Garden City, NY: Doubleday & Company, Inc., 1959.

Farago, Ladislas. Patton: Ordeal and Triumph. New York: Ivan Obolensky, Inc., 1964.

Inge, William. A Loss of Roses. New York: Random House, 1960.

Hemingway, Ernest. Islands in the Stream. New York: Charles Scribner's Sons, 1970.

Levin, Ira. The Boys from Brazil. New York: Random House, 1976.

Lindsay, Howard, and Russel Crouse. The Great Sebastians. New York: Random House, 1956.

Massie, Robert K. Nicholas and Alexandra. New York: Atheneum, 1967.

Maxfield, Henry S. Legacy of a Spy. New York: Harper and Brothers, 1958.

Piper, Anne. Yes, Giorgio. London: Heinemann, 1961.

Stevens, Leslie. The War Lord. New York: Samuel French, Inc., 1956.

Vidal, Gore. The Best Man. Boston: Little, Brown and Company, 1960.

Screenplays

Byrum, John. Sphinx, October 21, 1980. Louis B. Mayer Library, American Film Institute.

Collier, John, and Millard Kaufman. The War Lord, Final Screenplay, September 21, 1964. Walter Seltzer Collection, Archives of Performing Arts, University Library, University of Southern California.

Coppola, Francis Ford. Patton, December 27, 1965. Edmund H. North Collection, Special Collections, University Research Library, University of California at Los Angeles.

Coppola, Francis Ford, and Edmund H. North. Patton, January 31, 1969. Franklin J. Schaffner Film Library, Franklin and Marshall College.

Gethers, Steven. A Summer World, Revised, June 19, 1961. Franklin J. Schaffner Film Library, Franklin and Marshall College.

Goldman, James. Nicholas and Alexandra, Final Script, November 13, 1970. Franklin J. Schaffner's Personal Files.

Goldman, William. Papillon, Third Draft, April 5, 1972. Theatre Arts Library, University Research Library, UCLA.

Gould, Heywood. The Boys from Brazil, Final Draft, October 1, 1977. Franklin J. Schaffner Film Library, Franklin and Marshall College.

Hayes, Alfred. Celebration [The Stripper], First Draft Screenplay, December 15, 1960. Twentieth Century-Fox Screenplay Collection, Archives of Performing Arts, USC.

Hayes, Alfred, and Frank Tarloff. The Double Man, June 1966. Warner Bros. Collection, Archives of Performing Arts, USC.

Petticlerc, Denne Bart. Islands in the Stream, First Draft, n.d. [1974]. Franklin J. Schaffner's Personal Files.

_____. Islands in the Stream, Final shooting script, n.d. [1975]. Franklin J. Schaffner Film Library, Franklin and Marshall College.

Randle, I. V., and Brian Clemens. Legacy of a Spy [The Double Man], July 1962. Warner Bros. Collection, Archives of Performing Arts, USC.

Roberts, Meade. Celebration [The Stripper], Revised Final, May 11, 1962. Twentieth Century-Fox Screenplay Collection, Archives of Performing Arts, USC.

Ross, Kenneth. The Boys from Brazil, 2nd Draft, March 18, 1977. Theatre Arts Library, UCLA.

_____. The Entebbe Project, unfinished, n.d. [1976]. Franklin J. Schaffner's Personal Files.

Serling, Rod. Planet of the Apes, March 1, 1965. Franklin J. Schaffner Film Library, Franklin and Marshall College.

_____. "The Velvet Alley," Playhouse 90, final revision,

January 7, 1959. Rod Serling Collection, Special Collections, UCLA.

Steinberg, Norman. Yes, Giorgio, October 17, 1980. Franklin J. Schaffner's Personal Files.

_____. Yes, Giorgio, Revised Final Draft, April 10, 1981. Franklin J. Schaffner's Personal Files.

Tarloff, Frank. Legacy of a Spy [The Double Man], 1965. Warner Bros. Collection, Archives of Performing Arts, USC.

Tarloff, Frank, and Clive Exton. Legacy of a Spy [The Double Man], March 1966. Warner Bros. Collection, Archives of Performing Arts, USC.

Trumbo, Dalton. Papillon, Final, February 1, 1973. Franklin J. Schaffner Film Library, Franklin and Marshall College.

Vidal, Gore. The Best Man, November 28, 1961. Franklin J. Schaffner Film Library, Franklin and Marshall College.

_____. The Best Man, Final Revised, August 28, 1963. Lawrence Turman Collection, Special Collections, UCLA.

_____. The Best Man, Continuity Script, March 27, 1964. Lawrence Turman Collection, Special Collections, UCLA.

Wilson, Michael. Planet of the Apes, May 5, 1967. Archives of Performing Arts, USC.

Reviews

Adler, Renata. "The Double Man." New York Times Film Reviews 1913-1968. Vol. 5. New York: The New York Times and Arno Press, 1970.

Bean, Robin. "Woman of Summer." Films and Filming, June 1963.

Brennan, Barry. "Preposterous and Delightful." Evening Outlook [Santa Monica, CA], Section B, February 12, 1981.

Byron, Stuart. "Papillon." The Real Paper [Boston], December 19, 1973.

Canby, Vincent. "'Islands in the Stream' Meanders Out of Control." The New York Times, March 10, 1977.

_____. "'Nicholas and Alexandra' Depicts Fall of Romanovs." The New York Times, December 14, 1971.

_____. "Patton: He Loved War." The New York Times, Arts & Leisure, February 18, 1970.

"Cart." [Todd McCarthy]. "Sphinx." Daily Variety, February 11, 1981.

Champlin, Charles. "'Patton' Features George C. Scott as 'Old Blood and Guts.'" Los Angeles Times, Calendar, February 15, 1970.

Crist, Judith. "A Precious Burst of Hemingway." Saturday Review, March 19, 1977.

Crowther, Bosley. "The Stripper." The New York Times Film Reviews 1913-1968. Vol. 5. New York: The New York Times and Arno Press, 1970.

_____. "The War Lord." The New York Times Film Reviews 1913-1968. Vol. 5. New York: The New York Times and Arno Press, 1970.

Edelman, Rob. "The Boys from Brazil." Films in Review, November 1978.

Fisher, Craig. "'Nicholas and Alexandra' is a Literate, Grand Spectacle." The Hollywood Reporter, December 13, 1971.

Gill, Brendan. "Another Writer." The New Yorker, April 18, 1964.

"Horo." [Murray Horowitz]. "John F. Kennedy, May 29, 1964." Variety, June 3, 1964.

Howard, Alan R. "Papillon." The Hollywood Reporter, December 11, 1973.

Kael, Pauline. "Apes Must Be Remembered, Charlie." The New Yorker, February 17, 1966.

_____. "Furry Freaks." The New Yorker, October 9, 1978.

_____. "Labyrinths." The New Yorker, December 24, 1973.

_____. "The Man Who Loved War." The New Yorker, January 31, 1970.

Kauffmann, Stanley. "A Handful of Stars." New Republic, October 25, 1982.

Knight, Arthur. "Islands in the Stream." The Hollywood Reporter, March 4, 1977.

_____. "Sphinx." The Hollywood Reporter, February 11, 1981.

_____. "Uneasy Lies the Head." Saturday Review, January 15, 1972.

Kroll, Jack. "Little Hitlers." Newsweek, October 9, 1978.

_____. "Poor Papa." Newsweek, March 14, 1977.

Linck, David. "Yes, Giorgio." Boxoffice, November 1982.

Morgenstern, Joseph. "Monkey Lands." Newsweek, February 17, 1968.

"Murf." [Art Murphy]. "Islands in the Stream." Daily Variety. March 4, 1977.

_____. "Papillon." Daily Variety, December 11, 1973.

"Neurotic Knight." Newsweek, December 6, 1965.

Osborne, Robert. "The Boys from Brazil." The Hollywood Reporter, September 25, 1978.

_____. "Yes, Giorgio." The Hollywood Reporter, September 15, 1982.

Powers, James. "The Stripper." The Hollywood Reporter, April 24, 1963.

_____. "'War Lord' Exotic Epic with Formidable Cast." The Hollywood Reporter, October 4, 1965.

"Rich." [Richard Alberino]. "The Double Man." Variety, April 26, 1967.

"Rose." [George Rosen]. "The Good Years." Variety, January 17, 1962.

_____. "The Wicked Scheme of Jebal Deeks." Variety, November 18, 1959.

Sarris, Andrew. "Has the Hemingway Hero Had It?" Village Voice, March 28, 1977.

_____. "The Perils of Papillon." Village Voice, January 10, 1974.

Schickel, Richard. "Lesé Majesté in Panavision." Life, January 14, 1972.

_____. "Second Thoughts on Ape-Men." Life, May 10, 1968.

Schlesinger, Arthur, Jr. "Decline and Fall." Show, June 1964.

Shindler, Merrill. "Sphinx." Los Angeles Times, March 1981.

Smith, Cecil. "No Real Need to Defend This One." Los Angeles Times, Part IV, May 1, 1962.

"Sphinx." Season Ticket, January 1982.

Thomas, Kevin. "The Double Man." Los Angeles Times, Part VI, May 22, 1968.

_____. "Pavarotti Is Singing in the Frame." Los Angeles Times, Part V, September 25, 1982.

_____. "'Planet of the Apes' Out of This World." Los Angeles Times, Calendar, March 24, 1968.

Totten, Ruth Patton. "'Patton' Saluted by His Daughter." Hamilton Wenham Chronicle, March 11, 1970.

"Tube." [Larry Tubell]. "The Stripper." Daily Variety, April 24, 1963.

Van Horne, Harriet. "A First Lady of Taste." New York World-Telegram, January 15, 1962.

Varney, Ginger. "Yes, Giorgio." L. A. Weekly, October 8, 1982.

Wilson, David. "The War Lord." Sight and Sound, Spring 1966.

Zimmerman, Paul. "Stuck on an Island." Newsweek, December 17, 1973.

Interviews

Abrahams, Mort. Telephone Interview, June 22, 1981.

_____. Personal Interview, June 18, 1982.

Anderson, Michael F. Personal Interview, July 20, 1983.

Babbin, Jacqueline. Personal Interview, June 22, 1981.

Barr, Shober. Telephone Interview, July 24, 1981.

Barry, Philip, Jr. Personal Interview, June 29, 1981.

Bart, Peter. Personal Interview, January 28, 1983.

Brodkin, Herbert. Personal Interview, July 13, 1981.

Cook, Fielder. Personal Interview, September 21, 1981.

Creber, William J. Personal Interview, December 21, 1982.

Darlington, James. Personal Interview, July 22, 1981.

Fryer, Robert. Personal Interview, February 8, 1982.

Goldsmith, Jerry. Personal Interview, January 31, 1983.

Harrington, Curtis. Telephone Interview, December 2, 1981.

Heston, Charlton. Personal Interview, August 9, 1982.

Hill, George Roy. Personal Interview, February 9, 1982.

Houseman, John. Telephone Interview, June 27, 1981.

Jackson, Felix. Personal Interview, April 4, 1981.

Koenekamp, Fred J. Personal Interview, January 4, 1983.

McCarthy, Frank. Personal Interview, June 14, 1982.

Mandel, Loring, and Mayo Simon. Personal Interview, November 8, 1981.

Manulis, Martin. Personal Interview, July 1, 1981.

Markle, Fletcher. Telephone Interview, June 9, 1981.

Miner, Worthington. Personal Interview, July 7, 1981.

Schaffner, Franklin J. Personal Interview, January 28, 1981.

_____. Personal Interview, February 25, 1981.

_____. Personal Interview, November 29, 1981.

_____. Personal Interview, December 13, 1981.

_____. Personal Interview, March 13, 1982.

_____. Personal Interview, May 15, 1982.

_____. Personal Interview, May 22, 1982.

_____. Personal Interview, May 29, 1982.

_____. Personal Interview, June 5, 1982.

_____. Personal Interview, June 12, 1982.

_____. Personal Interview, June 19, 1982.

_____. Personal Interview, August 14, 1982.

_____. Personal Interview, August 21, 1982.

_____. Personal Interview, September 25, 1982.

_____. Personal Interview, October 2, 1982.

_____. Personal Interview, December 9, 1982.

_____. Interview by Edward Anhalt, University of Southern
California, Cinema 599 Screenwriting Seminar, October 22,
1980.

_____. Interview by Arthur Knight, USC, Cinema 466 Seminar,
screening of Islands in the Stream, March 10, 1977. Tape
738, Archives of Performing Arts, USC.

_____. Interview by Arthur Knight, USC, Cinema 466 Seminar,
screening of Sphinx, January 8, 1981. Tape 397, Archives
of Performing Arts, USC.

_____. Interview by Frank McCarthy, Directors Guild of Amer-
ica, June 9, 1982.

Seltzer, Walter. Personal Interview, May 24, 1982.

Taylor, Ruth Ashton. Telephone Interview, April 7, 1981.

Turman, Lawrence. Telephone Interview, March 25, 1982.

Letters

Bendick, Robert. Letter to author, June 8, 1981.

Bernheim, Alain. Letter to Adolph Green, May 1, 1980. Franklin
J. Schaffner's Personal Files.

Boretz, Alvin. Letter to author, February 8, 1982.

Brodkin, Herbert. Letter to author, March 3, 1981.

Farago, Ladislas. Letter to Franklin J. Schaffner, May 20, 1970.
Franklin J. Schaffner's Personal Files.

Goldman, James. Letter to Franklin J. Schaffner, October 14, 1970.
Franklin J. Schaffner's Personal Files.

Guinness, Alec. Letter to Franklin J. Schaffner, November 3,
1959. Franklin J. Schaffner's Personal Files.

Houseman, John. Letter to author, June 22, 1981.

Mandel, Loring. Letter to author, February 12, 1982.

Massie, Robert K. Letter to Franklin J. Schaffner, October 30,
1971. Franklin J. Schaffner's Personal Files.

Picker, David. Letter to Franklin J. Schaffner, May 21, 1976.
Franklin J. Schaffner's Personal Files.

Princess Grace. Letter to Franklin J. Schaffner, June 26, 1975.
Franklin J. Schaffner's Personal Files.

Reagan, Ronald. Letter to Frank McCarthy, March 10, 1970.
Franklin J. Schaffner's Personal Files.

Rodero, Jose Lopez. Letter to Franklin J. Schaffner, October 13,
1973. Franklin J. Schaffner's Personal Files.

Rose, Reginald. Letter to author, March 2, 1982.

Salinger, Pierre. Letter to Franklin J. Schaffner, May 4, 1963.
Franklin J. Schaffner's Personal Files.

Saudek, Robert. Letter to author, September 14, 1981.

Schaffner, Franklin. Letter to Jerome Hellman, July 7, 1961.
Franklin J. Schaffner's Personal Files.

Schaffner, Franklin J. Letter to Sidney Wise, July 16, 1974.
Franklin J. Schaffner Film Library, Franklin and Marshall
College.

Swink, Robert. Letter to author, December 15, 1982.

Totten, Ruth Ellen Patton. Letter to Frank McCarthy, March 5,
1970. Franklin J. Schaffner's Personal Files.

Wald, Jerry. Letter to Franklin J. Schaffner, May 28, 1962.
Franklin J. Schaffner's Personal Files.

Zanuck, Darryl. Letter to Franklin J. Schaffner, December 20,
1962. Franklin J. Schaffner's Personal Files.

Unpublished Material

"The American Film Institute Seminar with Franklin Schaffner,"
February 21, 1974. Transcript 192, Louis B. Mayer Library,
American Film Institute.

"The American Film Institute Seminar with Franklin Schaffner,"
October 16, 1974. Transcript 214, Louis B. Mayer Library,
American Film Institute.

"The American Film Institute Seminar with Franklin Schaffner,"
March 16, 1977. Transcript 397, Louis B. Mayer Library,
American Film Institute.

"The American Film Institute Seminar with Franklin Schaffner,"
November 1, 1978. Transcript 527, Louis B. Mayer Library,
American Film Institute.

Beguiristain, Mario. "Theatrical Realism: An American Film Style
of the Fifties." Unpublished Ph.D. dissertation, Department
of Cinema, University of Southern California, 1978.

"Franklin J. Schaffner (Feature Story)." Papillon Publicity Release,
Allied Artists, 1973.

Shores, Edward Francis. "Popular Art: The Films of George Roy
Hill." Unpublished Ph.D. dissertation, Graduate Council of
the University of Florida, 1977.

Wise, Sidney. Presentation of honorary Doctor of Humane Letters
degree to Franklin J. Schaffner, Franklin and Marshall College, December 4, 1977.

Other Sources

"Agreement between the Government of Israel and Warner Brothers,
Inc.," August 19, 1976. Franklin J. Schaffner's Personal
Files.

"The Cave," World Security Workshop, ABC Radio, May 8, 1947,
written by Franklin Schaffner, produced by Robert Saudek,
directed by Clark Andrews, with Joe de Santis, Joseph Conway. Museum of Broadcasting.

The Double Man Files. Warner Bros. Collection, Archives of Performing Arts, University Library, University of Southern
California.

Patton Files. Edmund H. North Collection, Special Collections,
University Research Library, University of California at Los
Angeles.

Patton Files.   Warner Bros. Collection, Archives of Performing Arts,
    USC.

Planet of the Apes Files.   Warner Bros. Collection, Archives of
    Performing Arts, USC.

Planet of the Apes Test, [1966].   Franklin J. Schaffner Film Li-
    brary, Franklin and Marshall College.

Production and Biography Files.   Margaret Herrick Library, Acad-
    emy of Motion Picture Arts and Sciences.

INDEX